Flying Fifteen

Ck
Celebrity

Yngling

Albacore

Pelican

Wayfarer

Inland Cat

Maverick

Force 5

Tornado

P
Pioneer

W
32
Westsail 32

GP 14

Explorer

Mercury (cb)

Z
Zephyr

2t6
Excalibur

Beetle Cat

Samuri

E
Ensign

Ariel

Seminole

A 35
Alberg 35

'Manui Kai'
20' cat

E22
Etchells 22

Ac/25
Amphibicon

NA-3
Naval Academy

M
33T
Morgan 33

S0-AWH-757

Catalina 22

 Windrose series

 Tanzier 22

 Venture

 Cape Cod Cat

 Matilda

Newport 16

 Balboa 23

This page includes portable cabin sailboat insignias.

 Ensenada 20

 Balboa 21

 Balboa 26

 WW Potter

 San Juan 21

 South Coast 22

Mariner

O'Day 22

Santana 21

 Ranger 23

Montgomery 17

Cal 21

 24' Yankee Seahorse

Irwin

Columbia 23

 Helsen 22

Newport 21'

Midship 25

American 25

 Guppy 13

Some dinghy letters represent yacht clubs.

MYC
Miami
Yacht Club

SYC
Seawanhaka
Yacht Club

EYC
Edgartown
Yacht Club

DYC
Darien
Yacht Club

Naples Sabot	Penguin	International 14	Finn
Down East 38	Grampian	Seafarer	Westsail 32
Lightning	Flying Dutchman	Tech Dinghy, Tempest	Snipe
One Ten	5.5 meter	Soling	Pacific Cat
M 20 Scow	Columbia Challenger	Newporter	CSK catamaran
Hobie Cat	Thistle	Star	Comet
Coronado 15			Flattie, Geary 18
Windmill	Aqua Cat	Kite	El Toro

name _____
address _____
phone _____

The first copies of our sailing book were delivered to us June 15, 1956...an anniversary we celebrated in 1981 25 years later with sailing friends of many years. It brought back many memories.

The New York art mills were very challenging and time consuming for an artist from Wyoming. My wife demanded I choose a hobby. The answer a few seconds later.....
"sailing".... after which I returned to the drawing board.

A week later we had a downpayment on our first sailboat which was cunning and conniving, it hated me.

The first mate quietly enjoying my endless mistakes asked-
"Why don't you draw the book on sailing you were trying to find in bookstores and libraries?" We had 11 sailing books, each written in its "foreign" language I couldn't understand.

Seven years later after moving to California we published the book ourselves ... the wrong (pocketbook) size, the first soft cover book to sell in book stores. It had open end type columns, the first non-religious "bible", and the ample collection of my mistakes to help future sailors.

Our first edition started in 1950, printed in 1956, covered the traditional world of wooden boats, manila rope, and canvas sails...with minimum standardization.

Fiberglass outboard boats were common by 1955, with fiberglass sailboat dinghies and Dacron sails reaching the market around 1960. Dacron and nylon rope were becoming standard along with stainless rigging.

Olympic competition for a two man keel boat introduced the Tempest with 8 wins in 9 races, losing its rudder in one race. After an outstanding start ... its major and only contribution was to stimulate manufacturers to produce better stainless hardware in volume.

Sailing Illustrated

We had to return to the drawing board to detail and update the new plateau of the specialized hardware of competitive class sailboats rapidly coming into prominence.

We also needed to detail the other accompanying sailboat industry revolutions rapidly taking place. These were the new sail cloth standards, following the stabilizing of Dacron sail cloth, plus the new education sailors faced with the controlled flexing of new aluminum masts.

Fiberglass cabin sailboats began to slowly emerge in small sizes around 1962, with builders adding larger sailboats as their lines expanded. Our Columbia Challenger for example was the first sailboat produced in sufficient volume to become a recognized racing class in one year.

Columbia was the first leader on the west coast, followed rapidly by its neighbor the Jensen Cal line. Both grew in volume to eventually produce sailboats 40 foot long and larger . . . followed by other builders nationwide.

●

The 1970 big sailboat era started with big dinghy racers such as "Windward Passage" with the latest hardware designs operated by seasoned ("professional?") crews.

After builders found in a survey that less than 10% of cabin boat owners wanted to actively race, the cruising boat had a shaky start with questionable hulls available, and underpowered sail rigs. New builders moved in to specialize in a wide variety of cruising sailboats.

●

The new trailerable cabin sailboat mushroomed around 1970 adding to the mobility of sailboats to 24' long, with sailors no longer restricted to sailing in one area.

●

Our book has provided more surprises than this sailboat artist ever dreamed of in 1949 . . . covering wooden sailboats designed in 1909 and 1954, plus a variety of class sailboats between . . . then to the latest Optimist, Force 5, Windsurfer, and Catalina 38 IOR designs. What tomorrow's favorite sailboats will be is anyone's guess!

Happy Sailing,
Patrick M. Royce

May, 1982
Newport Beach, California

There are a wide variety of racing classes and handicapping (formula) methods to be analyzed.

- ONE-DESIGN sailboats are made to same design spec's with owners joining class association for racing and comradeship. STRICT*one-design classes (Laser) allow no modification of sail, rigging, hull shape. OPEN**one-design classes provide self improvement standards varying class to class.

- DEVELOPMENT CLASSES***similar to one-design classes with wider rule latitude. Flying Dutchman has elastic deck and equipment rules, strict hull, mast spec's. Int'l 14 is closer to meter rules as hull design changes may also be involved.

- OLYMPIC CLASSES for 1984 are Flying Dutchman, Star, Finn, Tornado Cat, 470, and Soling. These are the classes chosen for the next International Olympic use by the International Yacht Racing Union (IYRU) presiding over international sailboat racing. Letters on sail numbers will refer to owners country such as US–United States, MX–Mexico, K–United Kingdom. It is wonderful to see a 1911 design back in the Olympics . . . the Star

- METER craft have various sizes (see page 259) designed to a mathematical formula, juggled within the rules to try to make each new meter boat a better performer.

- HANDICAP RATING (pgs. 258-9) is a theoretical mathematical rated length/seconds per mile of given rating, to help provide a method for various kinds, sizes, and lengths of sailboats to compete on an equal basis.

- OOAK SERIES refer to YACHTING "One-of-a-Kind-Races" so one-design and other classes are able to compete against each other every three years in five divisions.

- PORTSMOUTH HANDICAP (pg. 258) is a yardstick used for competition between one-design classes, parallel to OOAK one-design handicapping methods.

- LEVEL RATING (pgs. 258-9) cover various "tonner" ratings similar to meter formula thinking with length, beam, bulk, and sail area are major factors involved.

*minimum evolution **controlled evolution ***control flexibility

2

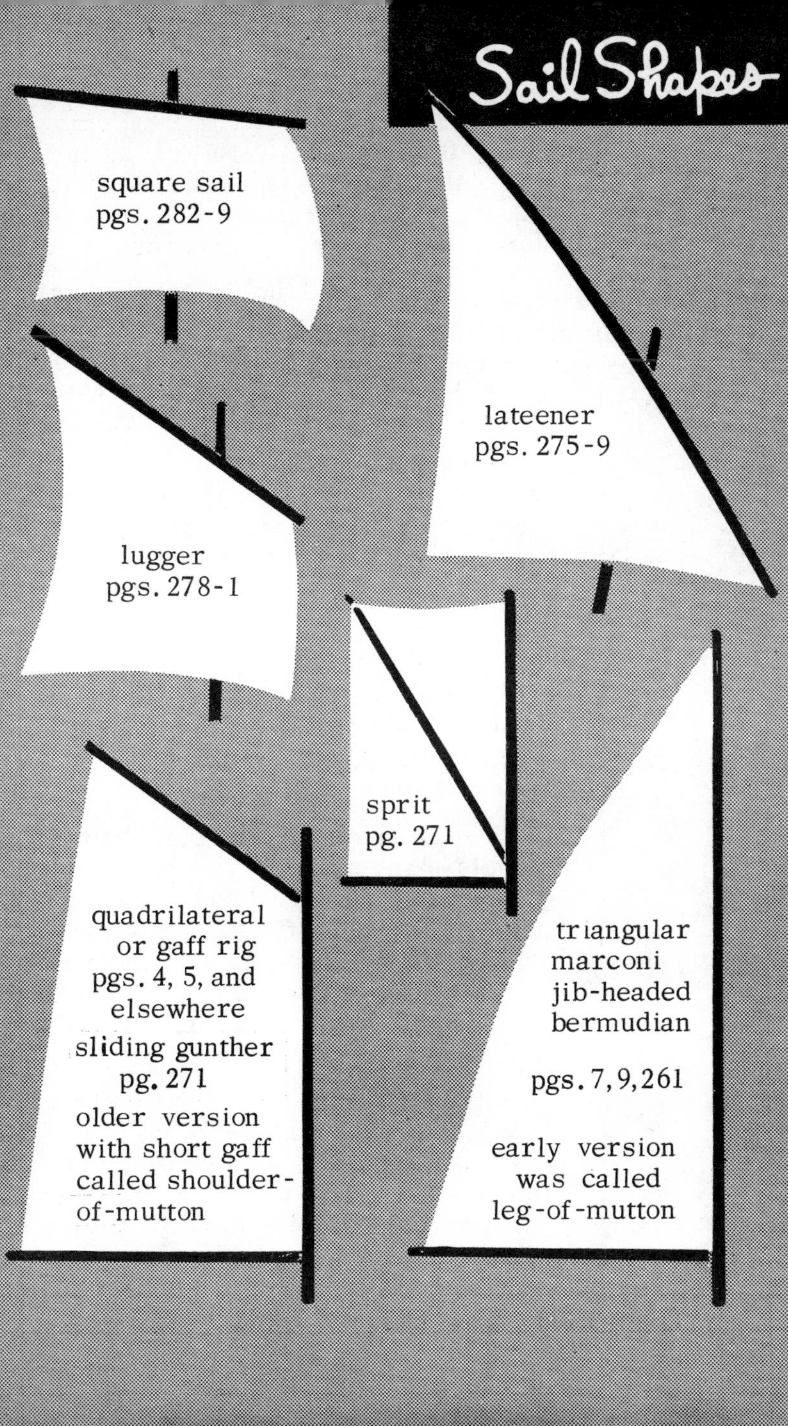

Sail Shapes

square sail
pgs. 282-9

lateener
pgs. 275-9

lugger
pgs. 278-1

sprit
pg. 271

quadrilateral
or gaff rig
pgs. 4, 5, and
elsewhere

sliding gunther
pg. 271

older version
with short gaff
called shoulder-
of-mutton

triangular
marconi
jib-headed
bermudian

pgs. 7, 9, 261

early version
was called
leg-of-mutton

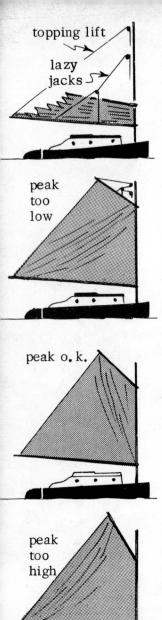

topping lift

lazy jacks

peak too low

peak o. k.

peak too high

QUADRILATERAL or GAFF RIG

The gaff rig was the first advancement over the lugger, the lateener and square rigs. It became the standard fore and aft rig up to the marconi rig.

A gaff rig was ideal for coastal trading and fishing when the wind was on the oceans surface and often abeam. Under these conditions the shorter masts requiring a minimum of staying.

A large catboat has been shown that was very popular around the turn of the century. Its primary advantage was for fishing with the large cockpit area ideal for handling nets and lines.

The large cat often has much to be desired in todays sailing. It may carry a lot of weather helm, while the long boom, round bottom, and huge rudder, are combination that make downwind sailing tricky.

With improved engineering and better metals, many of the gaff rigged boats have changed to the higher marconi rig eliminating gaffs, lazy jacks, and one of the halyards. An advantage of the gaff in a sudden blow, is that the sail may be "scandalized" pg. 148, to reduce excess wind pressure.

Traditional gaff sails were usually laced to gaff and boom, secured to mast with wooden hoops. Those desiring more information read "Gaff Rig" by John Leather, Int. Marine Pub. Co., Camden, Maine 04843, 272 pages.

Sailing Illustrated

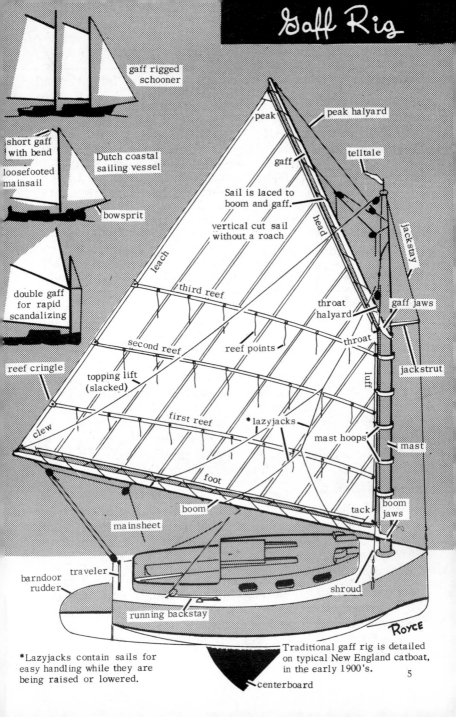

Gaff Rig

gaff rigged schooner

short gaff with bend

loosefooted mainsail

Dutch coastal sailing vessel

bowsprit

double gaff for rapid scandalizing

reef cringle

peak

peak halyard

telltale

gaff

head

Sail is laced to boom and gaff.

vertical cut sail without a roach

jackstay

leach

third reef

throat halyard

throat

gaff jaws

second reef

reef points

jackstrut

topping lift (slacked)

luff

first reef

*lazyjacks

mast hoops

clew

mast

foot

boom jaws

boom

tack

mainsheet

traveler

shroud

barndoor rudder

running backstay

Royce

*Lazyjacks contain sails for easy handling while they are being raised or lowered.

Traditional gaff rig is detailed on typical New England catboat, in the early 1900's.

centerboard

5

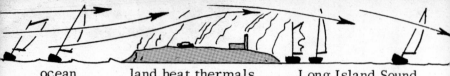

ocean   land heat thermals   Long Island Sound

The popular sailing rig with a triangular mainsail most commonly seen today is called the BERMUDIAN RIG by the British, the MARCONI RIG by most U. S. sailors, and JIB-HEADED RIG by others. As early examples of this type of craft were overstayed, the nickname resulted when they often resembled early marconi wireless towers.

The marconi rig is of major importance to both the racing and cruising sailor as the marconi rig will point higher than the gaff rig when sailing closehauled .. which averages more than half of your sailing time.

Most of our sailing is for short tacks with frequent tack changes by coming about or jibing. The marconi or jib-headed rig is adaptable for this kind of use with its simplicity of operation, eliminating the peak halyard and running backstays used by the gaff rig. Running backstays are still used on larger meter boats, and older sailing craft.

The taller mast of the marconi rig is an important factor to those sailing in inland areas where the wind isn't always on the water's surface. While the gaff rig with the shorter mast may operate successfully in the ocean side of Long Island, the taller marconi rig is preferred on the Long Island Sound where the useful wind may be a considerable distance above the waters surface in the daytime.

This phenomenon is due to HEAT THERMAL UPDRAFTS caused by daytime heating of the lands surface, plus heat emissions from autos and manufacturing plants. After dark as land temperature and other heat making methods are reduced, the wind drops lower to the surface of the Long Island Sound, and other inland sailing areas.

An early version of the Lightning class is shown at right. It is an excellent basic sailboat to study if you want to analyze the reasons behind the specialized racing hardware found on "Sea Fever", pages 34 through 37.

6   Sailing Illustrated

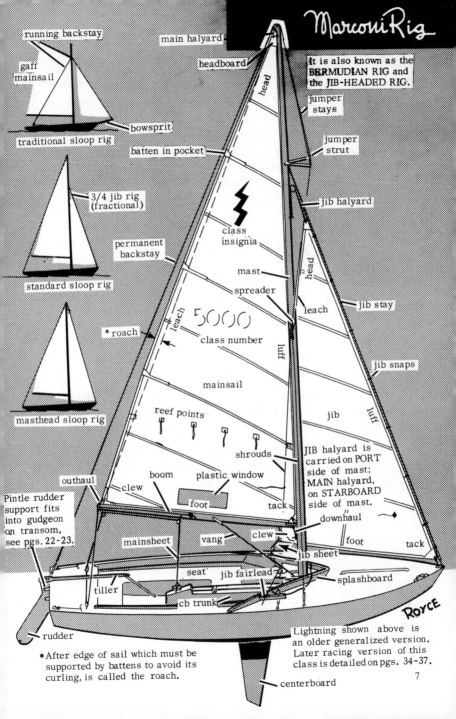

Marconi Rig

running backstay

gaff mainsail

traditional sloop rig

bowsprit

3/4 jib rig (fractional)

standard sloop rig

permanent backstay

masthead sloop rig

main halyard

headboard

head

It is also known as the BERMUDIAN RIG and the JIB-HEADED RIG.

jumper stays

jumper strut

jib halyard

batten in pocket

class insignia

mast

spreader

head

leach

jib stay

leach

5000

*roach

class number

luff

jib snaps

mainsail

jib

luff

reef points

shrouds

JIB halyard is carried on PORT side of mast; MAIN halyard, on STARBOARD side of mast.

outhaul

boom

plastic window

clew

foot

tack

downhaul

Pintle rudder support fits into gudgeon on transom, see pgs. 22-23.

mainsheet

vang

clew

foot

tack

jib sheet

seat

jib fairlead

splashboard

tiller

cb trunk

Royce

rudder

Lightning shown above is an older generalized version. Later racing version of this class is detailed on pgs. 34-37.

*After edge of sail which must be supported by battens to avoid its curling, is called the roach.

centerboard

7

Endless varieties of sail combinations are used for different sailing areas and interests. Common types are shown at right with page references for additional information.

We provide a considerable exposure to the MONOHULL (one hull) and the MULTIHULL (two hulls) catamarans from Hobies, to the Pacific Cat, to the large "Patty Cat" to help you understand both sides of the sailing world.

A sailboat with one sail regardless of size is generally called a catboat. The catamaran has two hulls and any variety of sail combinations, including if desired, the catboat rig.

Sloops, originally called knockabouts if they didn't have a bowsprit, are the most common type seen in the U.S., having a mainsail and jib. Jibstay or headstay goes to the top of the mast on a MASTHEAD rig, while it doesn't go to top of the mast on a STANDARD or FRACTIONAL sloop rig. A CUTTER basically has two headsails or jibs, with mast stepped further aft than on a sloop.

Two masted fore and aft rigged sailboats are generally recognized from distance by relationship of sails.... and when closer, by location of tiller and rudder post.

Yawl generally has small sail aft of tiller, while a ketch has masts of similar size, with the forward mast being taller, the tiller located aft of both masts. A schooner has both masts the same height, or after one taller.

Sail ASPECT RATIO. At right we show three sail craft with identical hulls and same total sail area. First boat has a short mast with long boom called LOW aspect ratio mainsail. Third boat has a HIGH aspect ratio with tall mast and short boom, increasing upwind drive area of mainsail shown by shaded area. The higher aspect ratio main has longer drive area with steadier wind currents aloft, minimizing wind disturbance on waters surface.

8   Sailing   Illustrated

1 pgs. 4-5

catboat

2 (highest mast)

standard sloop
jibstay part way
up the mast

If 2, 3, 4, have
identical hulls
and same total
sail area . . . .

3 pgs. 6-7,
260-1

masthead sloop
jibstay goes to
top of the mast

4 (shortest mast) pgs. 262-3

cutter with
two jibs

If 5, 6, 7, have
identical hulls
and same total
sail area . . .

5 pgs. 264-5

yawl

tiller between masts

6 pgs. 266-7

ketch

tiller aft of both masts,
with forward mast taller

7 pgs. 268-9

schooner

both masts same height,
or after mast is taller

8

standard schooner rig

9

staysail schooner

10 pgs. 282-7

traditional types

If hulls 11, 12, 13 are identical
with same total sail area . . . .

longest drive area

11
low
aspect
ratio

12
medium
aspect
ratio

13
high
aspect
ratio

9

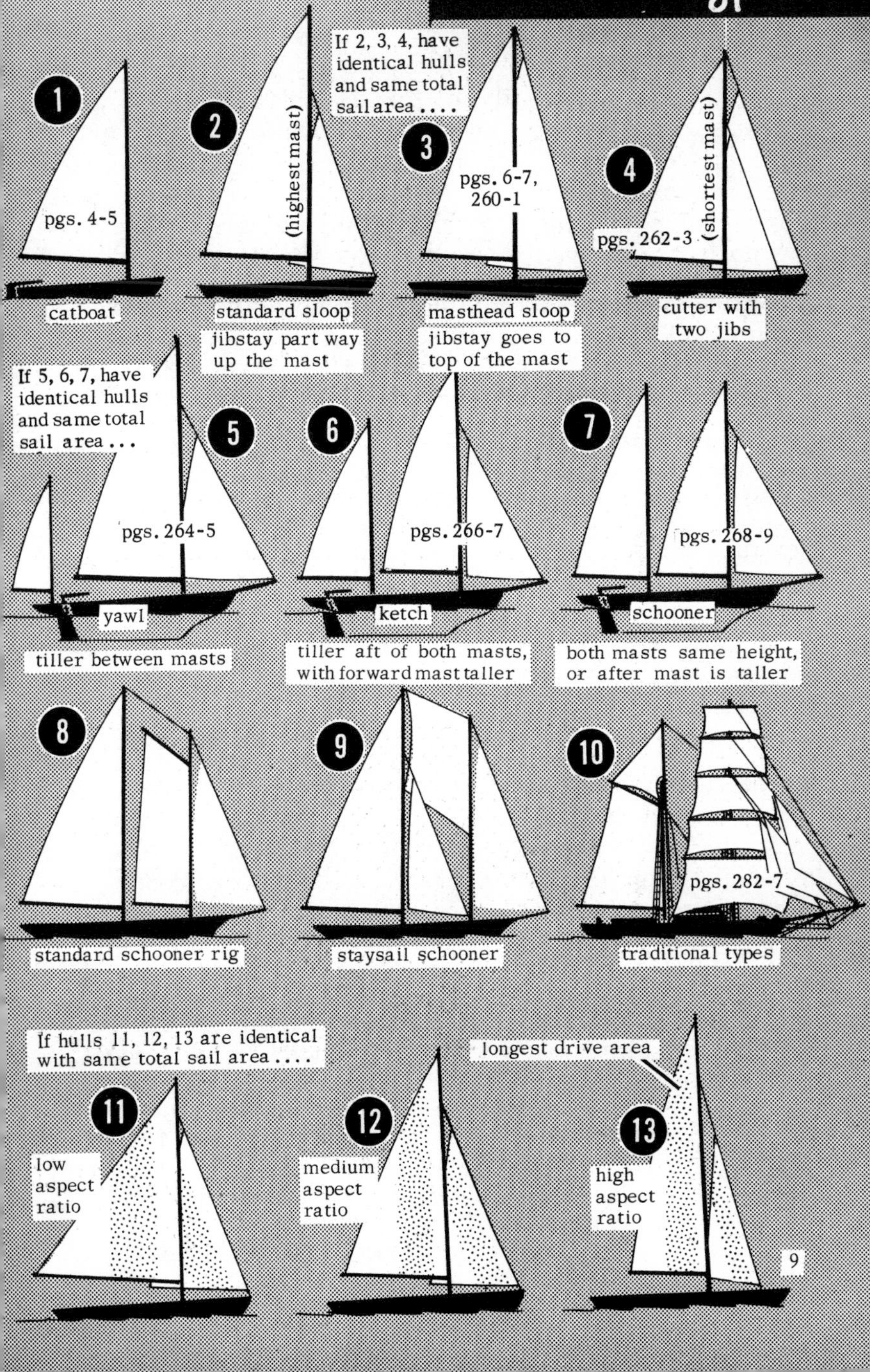

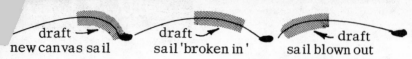

draft → new canvas sail   draft → sail 'broken in'   ← draft sail blown out

Draft was originally built into forward third of cotton and canvas sails. After a few hours use, draft would move aft somewhat to position shown, being classed as 'broken in'. After much use, or draft destroyed due to absence of topping lift pg. 97, the draft moved further aft with useful upwind life of mainsail coming to an abrupt end.

The jib seemed the main factor with upwind drive force in our 3rd Edition. The mainsail shortly received a lot more attention especially with draft control, pg. 117, improving the wind flow funnel between the main and jib.

Your sails may look good to you ... yet check your sails from another boat, or take photos underway checking trim, cut, wrinkles, etc., which may prove an eye opener.

New dacron sail cloth has been a great boon to sailmakers and sailors, having a lighter, stronger and more adaptable surface. Due to present stability of material, draft is now built into sail eliminating the 'break-in" period. Panels started with 18" widths, increasing until 36" panels are now standard. This cloth stability has also eliminated the need for the miter cut jib, pg. 13, for normal use.

In the last couple of years the miter cut jib and main have made a tremendous comeback in racing craft as they can be trimmed flatter than crosscut or miterless main and jib, yet sailmakers say lifespan is reduced. For information on battens see page 91.

Mainsails should be cut to fit your local wind conditions. Identical boats in our Southern California Newport Harbor will have a full draft due to light winds. Similar craft in San Francisco normally expecting much stronger winds, will have a flatter cut or flatter draft mainsail.

It has been fascinating to watch the change from canvas to Dacron and nylon sail cloth around 1960, followed by a continuous series of improvements in cloth and sailmaking techniques not available at any price twenty years ago.

Sail cloth may be made of a tight weave without a filler, or if it has a very smooth surface a filler has been added after the cloth comes off the loom.

Junks have used full length battens for hundreds of years. For use on larger boats read Yachting, pg. 49, May '68 issue.

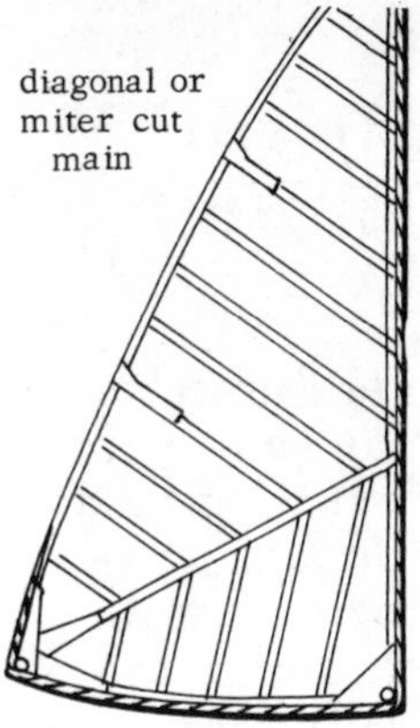

diagonal or miter cut main

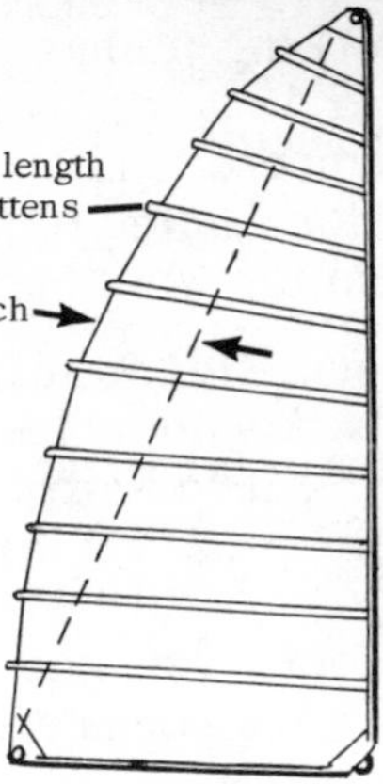

full length battens

roach

rigid headboard

head

head band

tabling

upper girthline measurement

strongest direction of cloth

Full batten mainsail with large roach

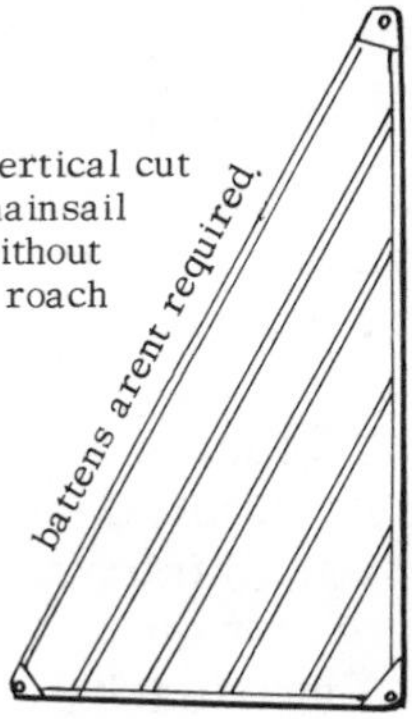

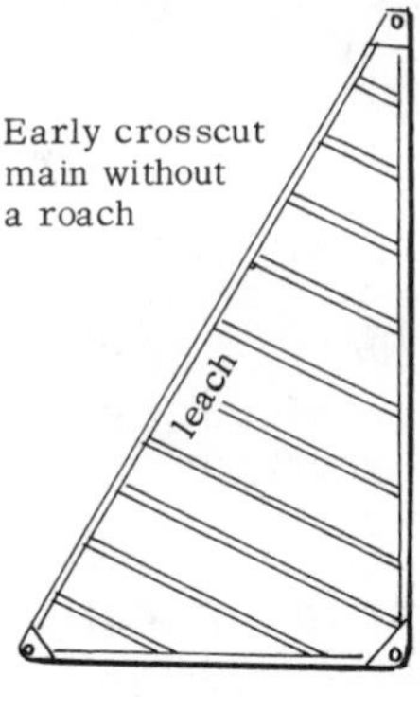

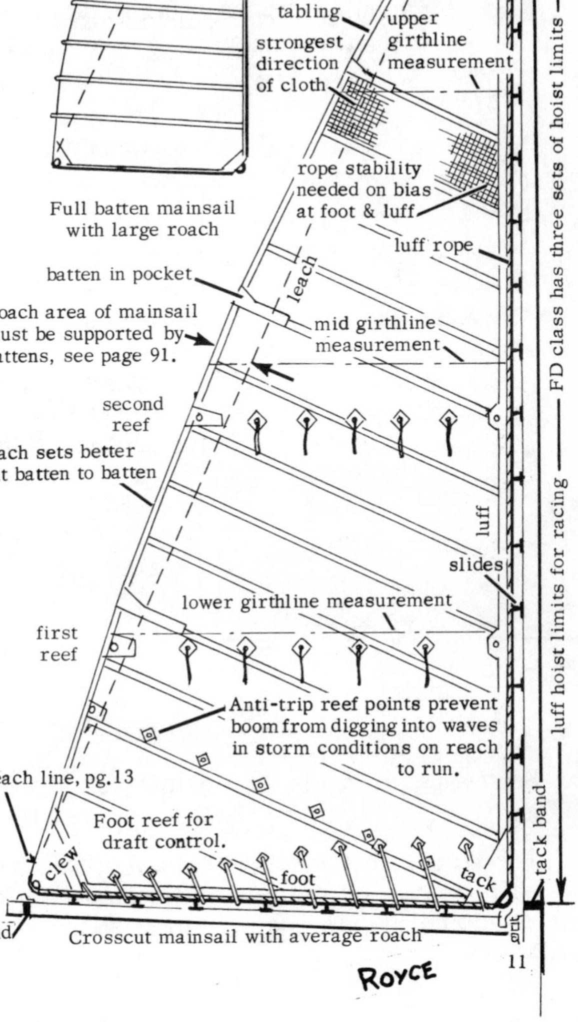

rope stability needed on bias at foot & luff

luff rope

Vertical cut mainsail without a roach

batten in pocket

leach

mid girthline measurement

batten arent required.

Roach area of mainsail must be supported by battens, see page 91.

second reef

leach sets better cut batten to batten

lower girthline measurement

luff

slides

FD class has three sets of hoist limits

luff hoist limits for racing

Early crosscut main without a roach

first reef

Anti-trip reef points prevent boom from digging into waves in storm conditions on reach to run.

leach

leach line, pg.13

clew

Foot reef for draft control.

clew band

foot

tack

tack band

Crosscut mainsail with average roach

ROYCE

11

Forward sail on a sloop is usually called a jib. A 100% working jib has area 1/2 I x J, see shaded area. 150% genoa is 50% larger, clew well aft of mast. Gennie and working jib are used for closehauled or beating. Reaching jib provides softer wind funnel for reaching.

#1 gennie usually has soft cloth, full draft for light winds. A same size #1 may be heavier with flatter cut for stronger wind. #2 gennie with reefed main, is smaller with higher clew permitting wave breaking aboard to drain under its foot. #3 gennie has a shorter luff with full length wire pennant, cut very flat for strong winds.

The working jib is often used for relaxing afternoon sailing, or for cruising especially if short handed. It is also called a lapper as it slightly overlaps the mast.

genoas and lapper

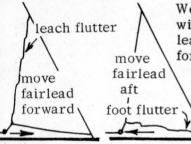

We've taught on many Lido 14's, with no two jibs cut identical. If leach broke first, move jib fairlead forward. If foot broke first, move fairlead aft till foot and leach break at same time as a boat heads into the wind.

1. correct trim   2. sail higher   3. pinching

Sew yarn telltales to jib luff, see location facing page, to analyze sail trim by air flowing past its surfaces.

1. Correct controlled flow. 2. Vertical leeward flow, stalled, sail higher, or harden jib sheet. 3. Pointing too high, found on narrow beam boats or ones with narrow sheeting base.

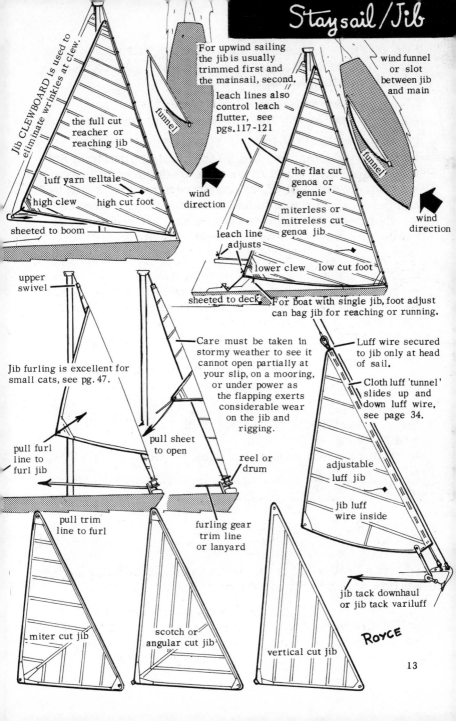

Jib CLEWBOARD is used to eliminate wrinkles at clew.

the full cut reacher or reaching jib

luff yarn telltale

high clew   high cut foot

sheeted to boom

'funnel'

wind direction

For upwind sailing the jib is usually trimmed first and the mainsail, second.

leach lines also control leach flutter, see pgs. 117-121

wind funnel or slot between jib and main

the flat cut genoa or 'gennie'

miterless or mitreless cut genoa jib

leach line adjusts

lower clew   low cut foot

sheeted to deck

'funnel'

wind direction

For boat with single jib, foot adjust can bag jib for reaching or running.

upper swivel

Jib furling is excellent for small cats, see pg. 47.

pull furl line to furl jib

pull trim line to furl

Care must be taken in stormy weather to see it cannot open partially at your slip, on a mooring, or under power as the flapping exerts considerable wear on the jib and rigging.

pull sheet to open

reel or drum

furling gear trim line or lanyard

Luff wire secured to jib only at head of sail.

Cloth luff 'tunnel' slides up and down luff wire, see page 34.

adjustable luff jib

jib luff wire inside

jib tack downhaul or jib tack variluff

miter cut jib

scotch or angular cut jib

vertical cut jib

ROYCE

13

For several years we puzzled over the best way to show the variety of cloth weights, and increasing kinds of sails available to the sailing public.

The folder at right produced by sailmaker Don McKibbin may provide many of the answers you are seeking.

Don feels the combination of sails and cloth weight will apply to sloops in the 24 to 30 foot range. Cloth weight listed under sail types will average out for that used on a 30' sloop. With such a foundation you may adjust the numbers up or down to fit the size of your boat, local weather conditions, and whether your major interest is racing, cruising, or a combination of both.

We thank Don for letting us use a reproduction of his chart on the facing page. As reduction is considerable write for a copy of his chart in its full 18" by 22" size. Also ask for his booklet discussing modern sail materials, uses, trim, and maintenance.

Send your request to McKibbin Sails, 1821 Reynolds Ave., Irvine Industrial Complex, Irvine, CA 92714.

•

Then we come to sails found on older boats, seldom seen today, though they may show up tomorrow as the latest breakthrough. A sample is the "spitfire", a heavy weather English jib, a name which has also been applied to drifters, reachers, etc., but doesn't stick for very long.

One of the humorous names of sails checked into, developed during a discussion many years ago with the manager of the Ratsey Sail Loft who made the first "mule". With a wry smile he said the term "mule" was the kindest term he could find for that sail.

George Mixter wanted a circus tent size sail for his "Teregram" he accidentally called a "gollywobbler", pg.269, which now goes only to the foremast of most schooners.

the "mule"
forestysl
or'jumbo'

George Mixter's
original
"gollywobbler"

14

After you have the basic mainsail, working jib, a 150% gennie jib, and an all-purpose chute, what is the next kind of sail to choose for your boat...and how heavy the cloth.

Various Sails

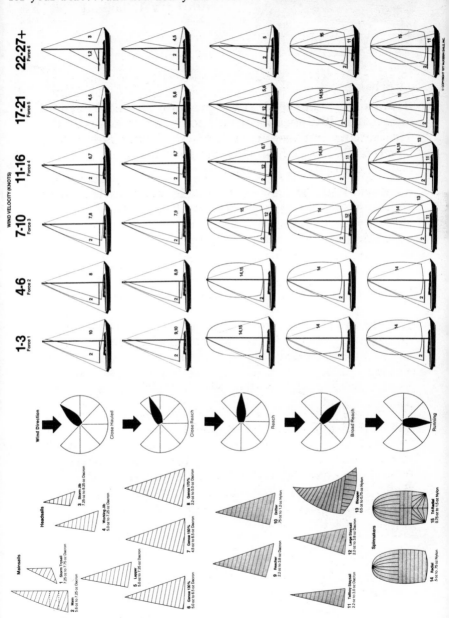

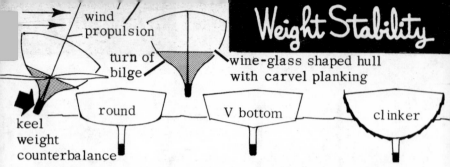

wind

propulsion

turn of
bilge

wine-glass shaped hull
with carvel planking

round

V bottom

clinker

keel
weight
counterbalance

Sailors have depended on weight stability in the form of cargo and movable ballast, since before the days of the Phoenicians. In todays sailing for pleasure, most weight is carried outside hull as part of keel.

Keel weight stability provides resistance to upset. Further a boat heels, the more effect the keel weight will provide to resist or counteract additional heel angle. Weight stability of narrow beam, wine-glass shaped hull, is often puzzling to the newcomer climbing aboard this kind of keel boat at the dock, seeming to have very little stability in the upright position.

Smooth hull with rounded or wine-glass section is usually preferred on larger boats for ocean use, as it will pound less than a keel boat with a hard chine. Small day racers with this type hull often have rolling tendencies, noted in downwind sailing. Many of todays open one-design having keels used on larger lakes and coastal waters, prefer the arc or V bottom with less rolling tendencies for downwind sailing.

The clinker-built hull was popular for a few years, but is seldom seen in boats being built today. Resistance of the overlapping planks not only proved unnecessarily noisy, but they also increased the hull drag .. which reduced its speed. When leaks developed between planks of this type hull and caulking is used, the opening may enlarge as the caulking swells.

Abbreviations commonly used throughout our book to conserve space are ... cb-centerboard, db-daggerboard, hlyd-halyard, fwd-forward, stbd-starboard, sp-spinnaker.

16

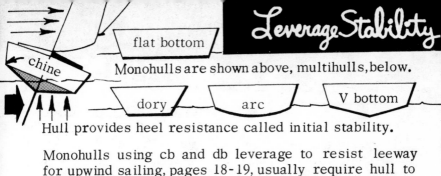

flat bottom

chine

Monohulls are shown above, multihulls, below.

dory   arc   V bottom

Hull provides heel resistance called initial stability.

Monohulls using cb and db leverage to resist leeway for upwind sailing, pages 18-19, usually require hull to also have initial stability for heel resistance. Many of these open one-designs as a result have flat bottoms, arc bottoms, and V bottoms. This hull shape also provides upset resistance in an upright condition... especially important when climbing aboard from the dock, pg.88.

After 45° to 50° heel angle has been exceeded, a neutral point is reached. Add a few more degrees of heel, and the cb and db craft finds itself more stable in the upset position. Best advice is to use an inclinometer with heel limitations of your craft clearly marked, pages 134,144.

Multihulls also use leverage stability to resist capsize or upset. The wide beam to length ratio of cats and tris, produces tremendous initial stability, also permitting them to keep weight to a minimum.

The high initial stability of a good cat, permits it to use the wind more efficiently on all courses than a monohull. The high initial stability of a good trimaran, is of some help on an upwind course, and especially advantageous when romping downwind such as in the Multihull Transpac to Hawaii.

Same length monohull sailing downwind under similar conditions, can't maintain same speed due to rolling motion, additional drag, additional frontal area, and its limiting waterline-length speed factor, page 141.

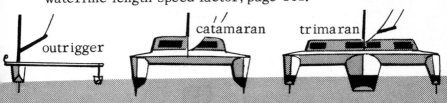

outrigger   catamaran   trimaran

Daggerboard

Daggerboard leverage stability is used on monohull dinghies, catamarans, and trimarans of varied sizes. Early Snipes had choice of daggerboard or centerboard. Daggerboard version pointed higher and footed faster than Snipe with centerboard, due to better aspect ratio. Cats improved this by carrying straight edge on fwd side.

Less cockpit space is required for db well, sailing upwind. It also decreases drag or turbulence of longer cb slot. Disadvantage becomes apparent sailing downwind, with board removed, becoming a wet, clumsy object to trip over. In larger multihulls, boards are raised out of the way in their own compartments. If rapidly moving craft using db hits solid object such as stump or rock, damage may result to daggerboard or well structure.

Leeboard

Leeboards pivot on sides of sailing vessel. They originated in Europe to minimize leeway for upwind sailing, and for flat bottom craft having to settle on marsh or mud flats without damage due to great tidal ranges common in the Netherlands.

Though still found on English Thames Sailing Barges and cargo vessels in Holland, the leeboard seems restricted to small dinghies such as the Sabot in the U. S.

Sailing   Illustrated

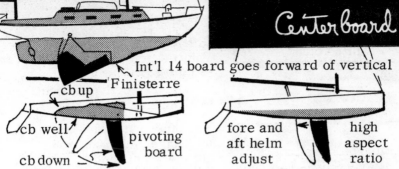

Int'l 14 board goes forward of vertical

cb up   Finisterre

cb well   pivoting board   fore and aft helm adjust   high aspect ratio

cb down

The centerboard started as a pivoted board for sailboats 20' or smaller, mainly used for shallow water or "dry sailing", stored on trailers when not in use. Purpose was to provide leverage against the water to reduce leeway when sailing upwind. If board hits a rock, stump, or sand, it may swing up without damage. The centerboard is raised up into its well to be out of the way for downwind sailing.

Designers started to add centerboards to keel boats to reduce weight and draft, also to reduce upwind weather helm, pg. 135. The board is all way down when beating in light breeze. As wind increases, board is raised sufficient amount to trim rudder for neutral helm, pages 132-3.

The Int'l 14 is a proving ground for many ideas in center-board usage. Newer boats have long slim boards for high aspect ratio leverage with minimum drag.

The 45' "Salty Tiger", a combination centerboard/keel boat, was designed by Bob Derecktor to race as a yawl or as a sloop. The centerboard pivot point was able to move fore and aft about six feet in down position, to balance the helm when changing from sloop to yawl rig, and to balance out minor weather helm variables. Int'l 14 has used a saddle to also permit fore and aft trim without raising its centerboard, see illus. above and page 250.

●

NOTE—a considerable number of references to products, manufacturers, class secretaries, etc., are listed as an additional reference service for our readers. They are not paid for . . . nor are they implied advertising.

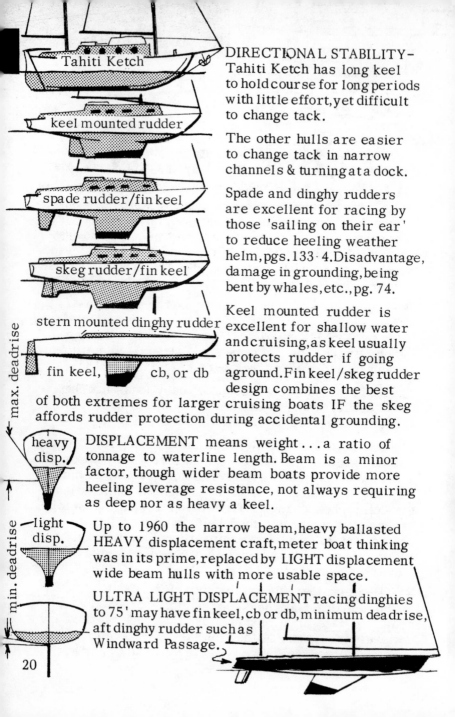

DIRECTIONAL STABILITY –
Tahiti Ketch has long keel
to hold course for long periods
with little effort, yet difficult
to change tack.

The other hulls are easier
to change tack in narrow
channels & turning at a dock.

Spade and dinghy rudders
are excellent for racing by
those 'sailing on their ear'
to reduce heeling weather
helm, pgs. 133-4. Disadvantage,
damage in grounding, being
bent by whales, etc., pg. 74.

Keel mounted rudder is
excellent for shallow water
and cruising, as keel usually
protects rudder if going
aground. Fin keel/skeg rudder
design combines the best
of both extremes for larger cruising boats IF the skeg
affords rudder protection during accidental grounding.

DISPLACEMENT means weight...a ratio of
tonnage to waterline length. Beam is a minor
factor, though wider beam boats provide more
heeling leverage resistance, not always requiring
as deep nor as heavy a keel.

Up to 1960 the narrow beam, heavy ballasted
HEAVY displacement craft, meter boat thinking
was in its prime, replaced by LIGHT displacement
wide beam hulls with more usable space.

ULTRA LIGHT DISPLACEMENT racing dinghies
to 75' may have fin keel, cb or db, minimum deadrise,
aft dinghy rudder such as
Windward Passage.

Labels on illustrations: Tahiti Ketch; keel mounted rudder; spade rudder/fin keel; skeg rudder/fin keel; stern mounted dinghy rudder; fin keel, cb, or db; max. deadrise; heavy disp.; light disp.; min. deadrise

20

Tempest   bulb keel   Star

ADVANTAGES. If your sailing area has enough deep water, you don't intend to do much trailering and hoists are available, the keel boat may be preferred. Major advantage is resistance to upset in strong wind.

Keel is standard for larger sailboats. Some wooden boats such as "Finisterre" use combination centerboard and keel for which all other factors equal, require more bracing as not all ribs are continuous in large centerboard hulls.

DISADVANTAGES. Keel boat may sink if swamped, so check flotation methods. Avoid shallow water on ebb tide, as keel boat may be left high and dry on its side. During winter in boatyard, have boat on adequate cradle stored well above hurricane high water limit, pg. 166.

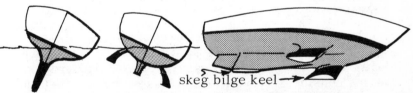

skeg bilge keel→

SINGLE vs TWIN KEEL. Around '64 the English developed twin keel sailboats for their tidal "mud flats" sailing. They required less water, had less rolling tendencies downwind, were easier to trailer. If caught aground they had a better chance to remain upright without support than single keel.

Then we come to the fleets of portable cabin sailboats without fixed keels starting a battle of semantics. Most dinghy centerboards are light providing leverage, while most centerboards used in cabin sailboats provide leverage AND weight in down position.

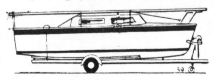

The most difficult part of sailing whether to learn to sail, or to read sea stories . . . is the "foreign" sailing language. Because of this we keep adding illustrations while reducing our text without adding pages, hoping one illustration is more helpful to you than an additional thousand words.

Our emphasis on visual terms to a wide variety of sailboats and operational standards of this new language, will make sailing easier for you to understand, pick up, and put to practice . . . starting with our enlarged dinghy section.

•

It is interesting to continually study the dinghy class trends for readers which vary considerably across our nation. Locally, for example, we've only seen a handful of Sunfish, and no Optimist Dinghies, the two largest sailing classes.

Take the time to study the varied controls and cockpit arrangements of the dinghies detailed, so with little preparation you may climb into any of them, make last minute adjustments, then enjoy a sail with an uneventful return to the dock. We have moved the complex Finn and International 14 to pages 248-251.

Southern California has huge fleets of Naples Sabots, with the similar daggerboard El Toro the Northern California leader (Sec'y, Box 487, San Leandro, CA 94577). Hardware varies considerably with these classes, our Sabot detailed covers basic hardware that may be installed with minimum tools such as screwdriver, drill, and wrenches.

•

We never considered detailing a Windsurfer, but . . . Our sailboat is docked across from a beach where endless board boats are launched, followed by a never ending series of splashes providing continuous entertainment. Between splashes we often try to ask the reason they chose this type of craft with ages ten through seventy. The dang board boats still don't make sense . . . but how can you question their popularity?

•

If you desire any class secretary address, write to USYRU, Box 209, Newport, RI 02840, or phone (401) 849-5200.

Sailing Illustrated

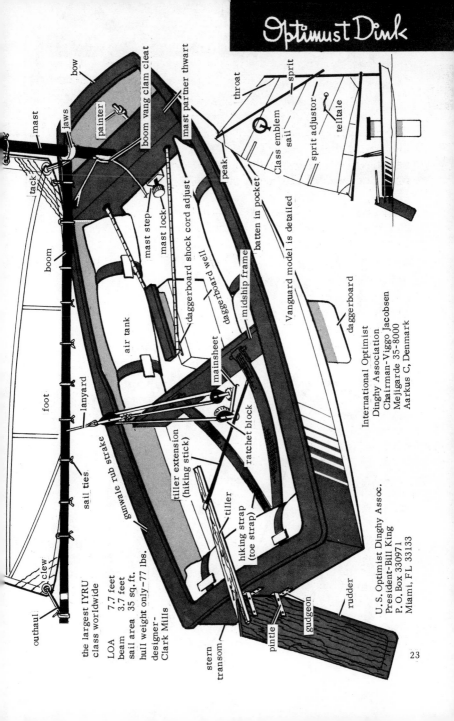

Optimust Dink

bow
mast
jaws
tack
painter
boom vang clam cleat
mast partner thwart
throat
sprit
Class emblem
sail
sprit adjustor
telltale
peak
batten in pocket
mast step
mast lock
daggerboard shock cord adjust
daggerboard well
midship frame
Vanguard model is detailed
daggerboard
boom
air tank
mainsheet
ratchet block
foot
lanyard
tiller extension
(hiking stick)
tiller
hiking strap
(toe strap)
gunwale rub strake
sail ties
clew
outhaul

the largest IYRU
class worldwide

LOA   7.7 feet
beam   3.7 feet
sail area 35 sq.ft.
hull weight only—77 lbs.
designer—
Clark Mills

International Optimist
Dinghy Association
Chairman-Viggo Jacobsen
Mejigarde 35-8000
Aarkus C, Denmark

U.S. Optimist Dinghy Assoc.
President-Bill King
P.O. Box 330971
Miami, FL 33133

rudder
stern
transom
pintle
gudgeon

23

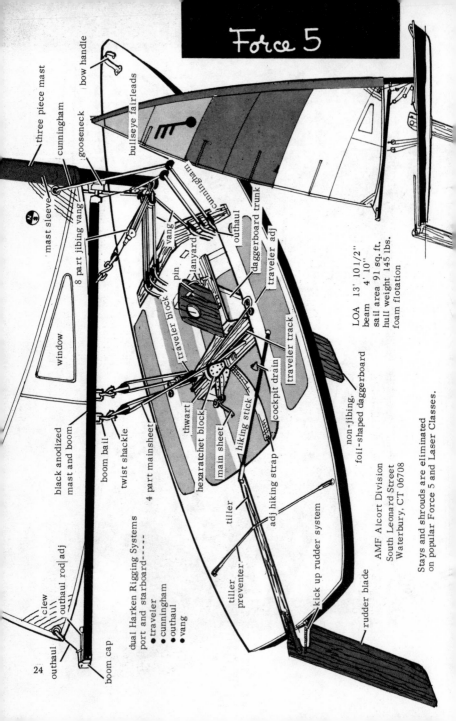

Force 5

three piece mast
cunningham
gooseneck
bow handle
mast sleeve
8 part jibing vang
bullseye fairleads
cunningham
vang
pin
lanyard
outhaul
daggerboard trunk
traveler adj
traveler block
window
traveler track
thwart
hexaratchet block
main sheet
hiking stick
cockpit drain
non-jibing, foil-shaped daggerboard
black anodized mast and boom
boom bail
twist shackle
4 part mainsheet
tiller
adj hiking strap
AMF Alcort Division
South Leonard Street
Waterbury, CT 06708

Stays and shrouds are eliminated on popular Force 5 and Laser Classes.

dual Harken Rigging Systems
port and starboard------
• traveler
• cunningham
• outhaul
• vang

clew
outhaul
outhaul rod adj
boom cap
outhaul

tiller preventer
kick up rudder system
rudder blade

LOA 13' 10 1/2"
beam 4' 10"
sail area 91 sq. ft.
hull weight 145 lbs.
foam flotation

24

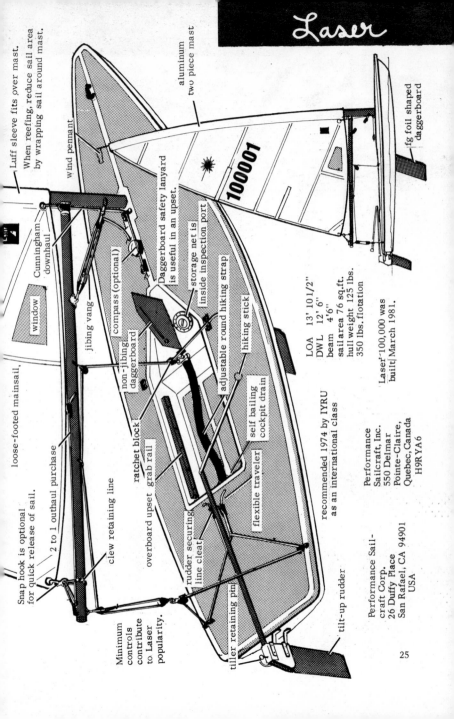

Laser

Luff sleeve fits over mast. When reefing, reduce sail area by wrapping sail around mast.

wind pennant

aluminum two piece mast

fg foil shaped daggerboard

100001

Cunningham downhaul

window

jibing vang

compass (optional)

Daggerboard safety lanyard is useful in an upset.

storage net is inside inspection port

non-jibing daggerboard

adjustable round hiking strap

hiking stick

LOA 13' 10 1/2"
DWL 12' 6"
beam 4'6"
sail area 76 sq.ft.
hull weight 125 lbs.
350 lbs. flotation

Laser 100,000 was built March 1981.

Snap hook is optional for quick release of sail.

loose-footed mainsail,

2 to 1 outhaul purchase

clew retaining line

ratchet block

overboard upset grab rail

rudder securing line cleat

self bailing cockpit drain

flexible traveler

recommended 1974 by IYRU as an international class

Performance Sailcraft, Inc.
550 Delmar
Pointe-Claire,
Quebec, Canada
H9RYA6

Minimum controls contribute to Laser popularity.

tiller retaining pin

tilt-up rudder

Performance Sailcraft Corp.
26 Duffy Place
San Rafael, CA 94901
USA

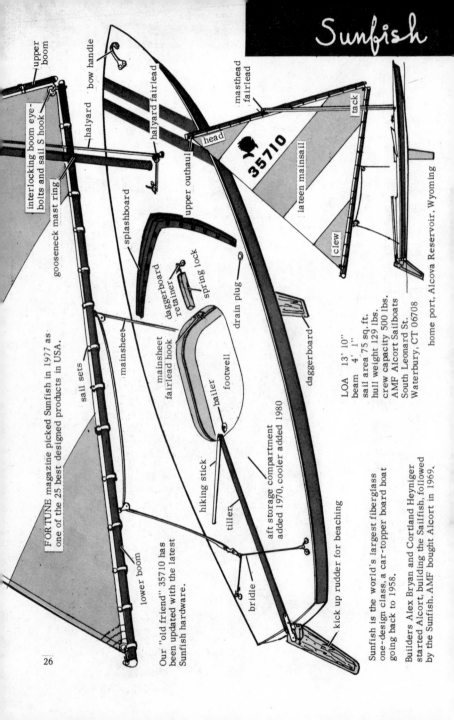

Sunfish

upper boom

bow handle

interlocking boom eye-bolts and sail S hook

halyard

masthead fairlead

tack

gooseneck mast ring

halyard fairlead

head

35710

lateen mainsail

upper outhaul

clew

splashboard

daggerboard retainer

spring lock

drain plug

daggerboard

sail sets

mainsheet

mainsheet fairlead hook

bailer

footwell

LOA 13' 10"
beam 4' 1"
sail area 75 sq. ft.
hull weight 129 lbs.
crew capacity 500 lbs.
AMF Alcort Sailboats
South Leonard St.
Waterbury, CT 06708

home port, Alcova Reservoir, Wyoming

FORTUNE magazine picked Sunfish in 1977 as one of the 25 best designed products in USA.

aft storage compartment added 1970, cooler added 1980

hiking stick

tiller

Our "old friend" 35710 has been updated with the latest Sunfish hardware.

lower boom

bridle

kick up rudder for beaching

Sunfish is the world's largest fiberglass one-design class, a car-topper board boat going back to 1958.

Builders Alex Bryan and Cortland Heyniger started Alcort, building the Sailfish, followed by the Sunfish. AMF bought Alcort in 1969.

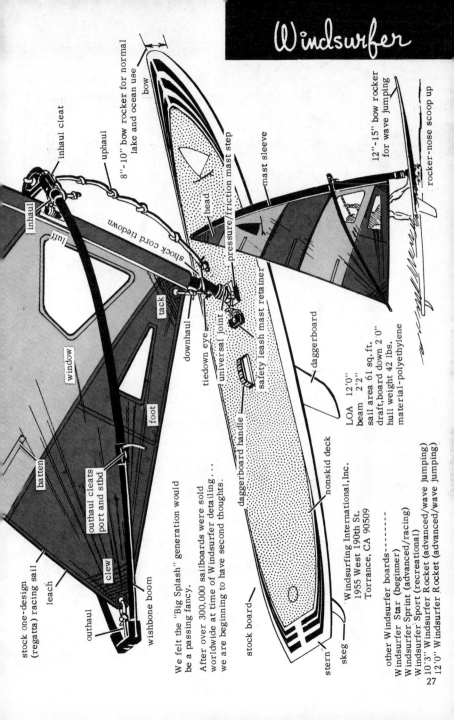

Windsurfer

inhaul cleat

uphaul

8"–10" bow rocker for normal lake and ocean use

bow

12"–15" bow rocker for wave jumping

rocker-nose scoop up

inhaul

luff

shock cord tiedown

mast sleeve

head

pressure/friction mast step

tack

downhaul

tiedown eye

universal joint

safety leash mast retainer

daggerboard

window

foot

daggerboard handle

nonskid deck

LOA   12'0"
beam   2'2"
sail area 61 sq.ft.
draft, board down 2 0"
hull weight 42 lbs.
material-polyethylene

batten

outhaul cleats
port and stbd

We felt the "Big Splash" generation would be a passing fancy.

After over 300,000 sailboards were sold worldwide at time of Windsurfer detailing... we are beginning to have second thoughts.

stock one-design
(regatta) racing sail

leach

clew

outhaul

wishbone boom

Windsurfing International, Inc.
1955 West 190th St.
Torrance, CA 90509

stock board

skeg

stern

other Windsurfer boards--------
Windsurfer Star (beginner)
Windsurfer Sprint (advanced/racing)
Windsurfer Sport (recreational)
10'3" Windsurfer Rocket (advanced/wave jumping)
12'0" Windsurfer Rocket (advanced/wave jumping)

27

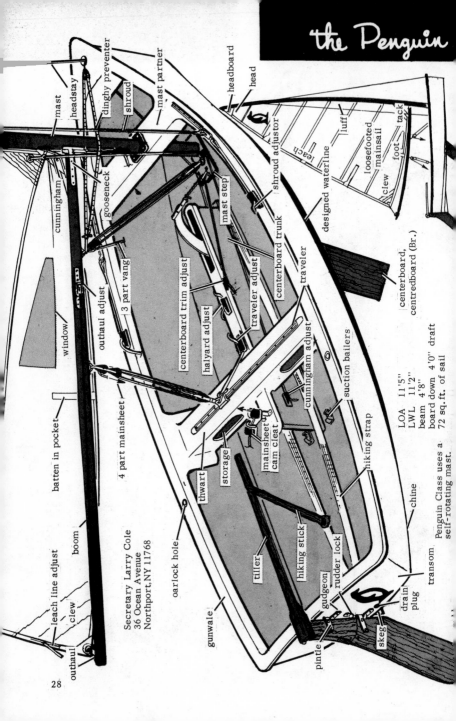

the Penguin

mast
headstay
dinghy preventer
shroud
mast partner
headboard
head

cunningham
gooseneck
mast step
shroud adjustor
leach
luff
loosefooted mainsail
clew
foot
tack
designed waterline

window
outhaul adjust
3 part vang
centerboard trim adjust
halyard adjust
traveler adjust
centerboard trunk
traveler
centerboard, centreboard (Br.)

leach line adjust
clew
outhaul
boom
batten in pocket
4 part mainsheet
thwart
storage
mainsheet cam cleat
cunningham adjust
suction bailers
hiking strap
chine

oarlock hole
tiller
hiking stick
rudder lock
gudgeon
pintle
skeg
drain plug
transom
gunwale

Secretary Larry Cole
36 Ocean Avenue
Northport, NY 11768

LOA   11'5"
LWL   11'2"
beam   4'8"
board down 4'0" draft
72 sq.ft. of sail

Penguin Class uses a
self-rotating mast.

28

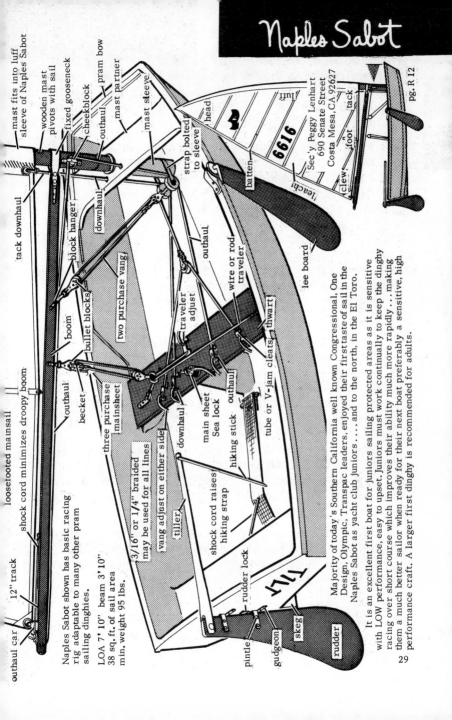

Naples Sabot

mast fits into luff sleeve of Naples Sabot

wooden mast pivots with sail

fixed gooseneck

cheekblock

outhaul

pram bow

mast partner

mast sleeve

tack downhaul

strap bolted to sleeve

head

luff

6199

Sec'y Peggy Lenhart
690 Senate Street
Costa Mesa, CA 92627

foot

tack

block hanger

downhaul

batten

leach

clew

outhaul

12" track

outhaul car

loosefooted mainsail

shock cord minimizes droopy boom

Naples Sabot shown has basic racing rig adaptable to many other pram sailing dinghies.

LOA 7' 10" beam 3' 10"
38 sq. ft. of sail area
min. weight 95 lbs.

boom

outhaul

becket

bullet blocks

three purchase mainsheet

two purchase vang

outhaul

wire or rod traveler

traveler adjust

thwart

lee board

3/16" or 1/4" braided may be used for all lines

vang adjust on either side

tiller

downhaul

hiking stick

main sheet
Sea lock

outhaul

tube or V-jam cleats

shock cord raises hiking strap

rudder lock

TILT

pintle

gudgeon

skeg

rudder

Majority of today's Southern California well known Congressional, One Design, Olympic, Transpac leaders, enjoyed their first taste of sail in the Naples Sabot as yacht club juniors.... and to the north, in the El Toro.

It is an excellent first boat for juniors sailing protected areas as it is sensitive with LOW performance, easy to upset. Juniors must work continually to keep the dinghy racing over short course which improves their ability much more rapidly ... making them a much better sailor when ready for their next boat preferably a sensitive, high performance craft. A larger first dinghy is recommended for adults.

29

The Lido 14 appeared locally in 1958, one of the first quality fiberglass dinghy hulls. The Lido is the standard of simplicity as rigging and controls are well designed, helping to make the Lido a happy boat to sail, delicate to the helm, and sensitive to weight placement.

When the wind comes up you have a spirited boat, ideal for the new boat owner, plus high school and college sailing instruction and racing. I've taught on over 40 of this class including one Lido which had three owners that gained enough experience to buy larger sailboats.

•

The Thistle, designed by Sandy Douglass, appeared in 1945. Growth has been slow but steady with Thistle sailors enjoying a comradery many classes dream about ... yet few realize. Over 6000 registered Thistles were in existence at time of printing, see details page 32.

Thistle is an open 17' dinghy with air tanks to keep it afloat during an upset. It planes easily and seems ready to take on her share of newcomers ... indicated by "The Green Thing" (#2744) first overall in the 1969 Yachting's OOAK races. A discussion whether Thistle could beat Lightning, gave impetus to first 1949 OOAK.

•

The Snipe, designed by William F. Crosby in 1931, was the largest one-design classic till the late sixties, with continuous class self improvement. We've had a Snipe in every edition of our book, starting with a basic one. The next two belonged to Earl Elms who dominated the Snipe Worlds for over a decade.

We asked its secretary for a late representative Snipe. He recommended one of a dozen identical boats being built for the 1979 Pan-American competition. We chose Snipe #24001 for detailing.

An owner helping with the Snipe detailed had spent ten years racing large boats on both coasts. Racing had became boring until buying his first Snipe ..."That class is where I found the REAL competition!"

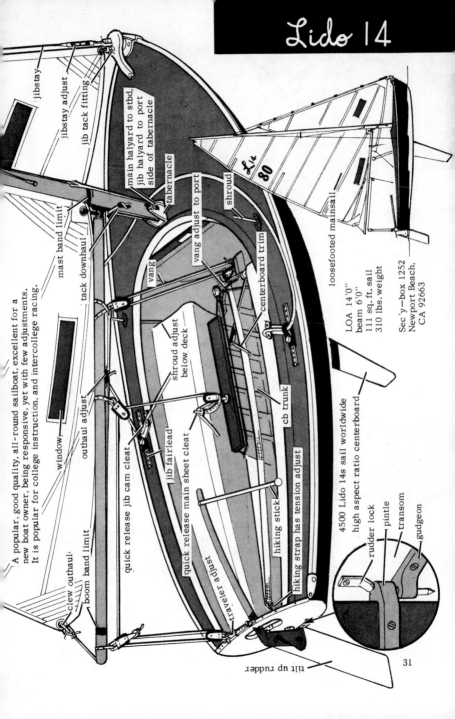

Lido 14

A popular, good quality, all-round sailboat, excellent for a new boat owner, being responsive, yet with few adjustments. It is popular for college instruction, and intercollege racing.

jibstay

jibstay adjust

jib tack fitting

main halyard to stbd, jib halyard to port side of tabernacle

tabernacle

shroud

vang adjust to port

centerboard trim

vang

loosefooted mainsail

mast band limit

tack downhaul

Lⁱ⁴ 80

window

outhaul adjust

shroud adjust below deck

cb trunk

clew outhaul

boom band limit

quick release jib cam cleat

jib fairlead

quick release main sheet cleat

hiking stick

traveler adjust

hiking strap has tension adjust

LOA 14'0"
beam 6'0"
111 sq. ft. sail
310 lbs. weight

Sec'y—box 1252
Newport Beach,
CA 92663

4500 Lido 14s sail worldwide

high aspect ratio centerboard

rudder lock

pintle

transom

gudgeon

tilt up rudder

31

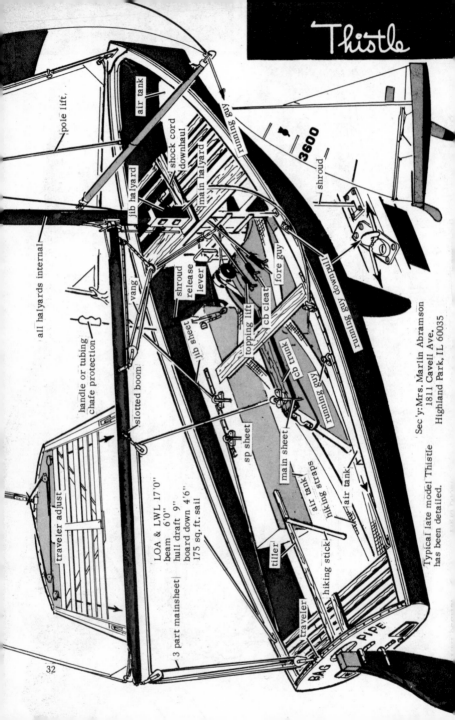

Thistle

pole lift

air tank

running guy

3600

shroud

all halyards internal

jib halyard

shock cord downhaul

main halyard

shroud release lever

fore guy

vang

cb cleat

handle or tubing chafe protection

jib sheet

topping lift

running guy downhaul

slotted boom

cb trunk

running guy

sp sheet

air tank

main sheet

traveler adjust

air tank

hiking straps

LOA & LWL 17'0"
beam   6'0"
hull draft 9"
board down 4'6"
175 sq.ft. sail

tiller

3 part mainsheet

hiking stick

traveler

BAG PIPE

Sec'y:Mrs.Marlin Abramson
1811 Cavell Ave.
Highland Park, IL 60035

Typical late model Thistle
has been detailed.

32

the Snipe

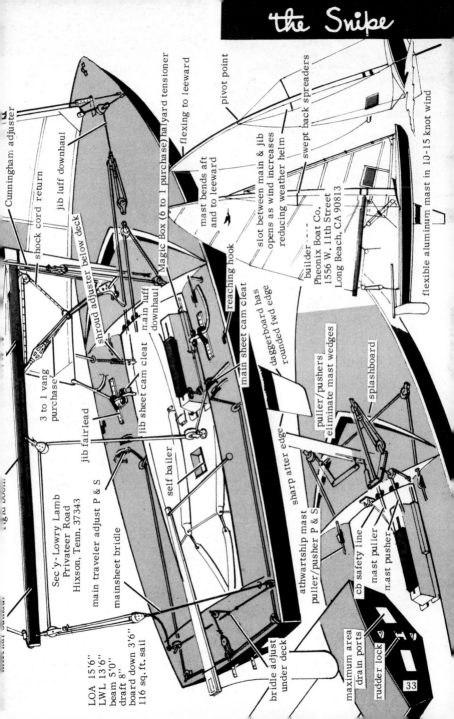

Cunningham adjuster

jib luff downhaul

shock cord return

halyard tensioner

flexing to leeward

pivot point

swept back spreaders

mast bends aft and to leeward

slot between main & jib opens as wind increases reducing weather helm

builder----
Pheonix Boat Co.
1556 W. 11th Street
Long Beach, CA 90813

flexible aluminum mast in 10-15 knot wind

Magic Box (6 to 1 purchase)

shroud adjuster below deck

main luff downhaul

reaching hook

main sheet cam cleat

daggerboard has rounded fwd edge

3 to 1 vang purchase

jib fairlead

jib sheet cam cleat

self bailer

sharp after edge

puller/pushers eliminate mast wedges

splashboard

Sec'y-Lowry Lamb
Privateer Road
Hixson, Tenn. 37343

main traveler adjust P & S

mainsheet bridle

athwartship mast
puller/pusher P & S

cb safety line

mast puller

mast pusher

maximum area

drain ports

rudder lock

bridle adjust
under deck

LOA 15'6"
LWL 13'6"
beam 5'0"
draft 8"
board down 3'6"
116 sq. ft. sail

33

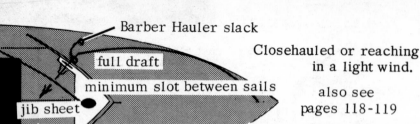

Barber Hauler slack

full draft

minimum slot between sails

jib sheet

Closehauled or reaching
in a light wind.

also see
pages 118-119

A controlled laminar air flow between main and jib is important to win races, the lack of such a funnel or slot eliminates catboats from sloop competition.

San Diego sailors, identical Barber twins Manning and Merritt, took their idea to Carl Eichenlaub who built their Lightning. The new hauler proved an instant success in heavy competition the following Saturday.

The air flow can be squeezed when sailing in light and/or disturbed air at the start, with jib sheet tension direct to jib fairlead as shown above.

As wind increases when reaching or closehauled, the slot is opened by hardening on the Barber hauler for a better laminar air flow without backing mainsail.

Jib wire and jib cloth adjusts are eased to squeeze the slot in light wind, and backstay eased to increase mainsail draft. Jib wire and jib cloth are hardened enough to remove luff wrinkles to open slot as wind increases.

The flexible aluminum mast is also important to slot control. As wind increases, so should the amount of rake or bend to flatten mainsail. This helps open the slot, reducing heel, changing most wind pressure into forward drive. In a very strong wind, excessive mast bend lets upper part of mainsail feather aft, which would otherwise overpower the boat, reducing excess heel and weather helm.

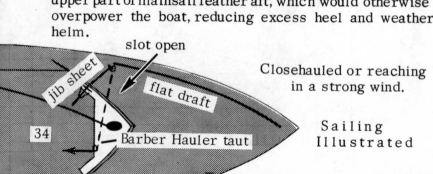

slot open

jib sheet

flat draft

Closehauled or reaching
in a strong wind.

34

Barber Hauler taut

Sailing
Illustrated

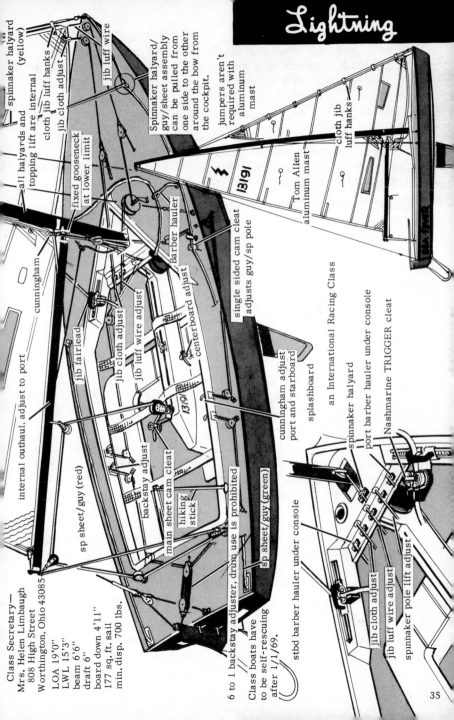

Lightning

Class Secretary—
Mrs. Helen Limbaugh
808 High Street
Worthington, Ohio 43085

LOA 19'0"
LWL 15'3"
beam 6'6"
draft 6"
board down 4'11"
177 sq. ft. sail
min. disp. 700 lbs.

6 to 1 backstay adjuster, drum use is prohibited

Class boats have to be self-rescuing after 1/1/69.

internal outhaul, adjust to port

cunningham

spinnaker halyard (yellow)

all halyards and topping lift are internal

cloth jib luff hanks

jib cloth adjust

jib luff wire

fixed gooseneck at lower limit

Spinnaker halyard/guy/sheet assembly can be pulled from one side to the other around the bow from the cockpit.

jumpers aren't required with aluminum mast

cloth jib luff hanks

Tom Allen aluminum mast

13191

jib fairlead

jib cloth adjust

jib luff wire adjust

Barber hauler

centerboard adjust

single sided cam cleat adjusts guy/sp pole

an International Racing Class

backstay adjust

main sheet cam cleat

hiking stick

13191

cunningham adjust port and starboard

splashboard

spinnaker halyard

port barber hauler under console

Nashmarine TRIGGER cleat

sp sheet/guy (red)

sp sheet/guy (green)

stbd barber hauler under console

port barber hauler under console

jib cloth adjust

jib luff wire adjust

spinnaker pole lift adjust

35

The Lightning has been the best-loved centerboarder worldwide, granted the status of an International Racing Class in 1962. The association has existed since 1939 with over 460 chartered fleets worldwide at present. The Lightning was designed by Sparkman and Stephens.

Lightning sailors are highly competitive, yet their boat is also comfortable for family afternoon sailing... while many other racing classes are not as comfortable, seldom leaving the dock except to race.

The Lightning Class spinnaker halyard/sheet/guy assembly is rigged together, page 35, then pulled out of the way, with a tang support at the bow. The crew can pull the assembly from one side to the other without leaving the cockpit.

The chute halyard/sheet/guy assembly is usually secured to the chute in a bag or basket to port, page 37, as most triangular course races leave marks to port. Pole is raised just before mark, halyard is raised as the mark is turned, then chute is raised, pulled to the pole with a running guy, then the sheet is set. Jib is dropped and secured as shown.

The mast has changed from wood to aluminum eliminating the jumpers. The new flexibility of controls allow the same crew weight to be used more effectively in a much wider variety of wind and water conditions.

This is the 3rd Lightning we've detailed, owned by Mike Boswell who said, "Owners love their boats staying with the association for a long time". Many factors involved to keep this worldwide class expanding, starts with its hard-working secretary of many years, Helen Limbaugh.

●

The Flying Dutchman was selected as the two man centerboarder for Olympic competition starting in 1960, the designer, U. van Essen of Holland. It is a fascinating class, with the challenge and attraction... the FD is an easy boat to sail, but very difficult to sail well.

Few changes have taken place since detailing the complex 1967 Plastrend FD, except a double bottom forward is 36 now standard, and its weight is increased to 374 pounds.

Sailing Illustrated

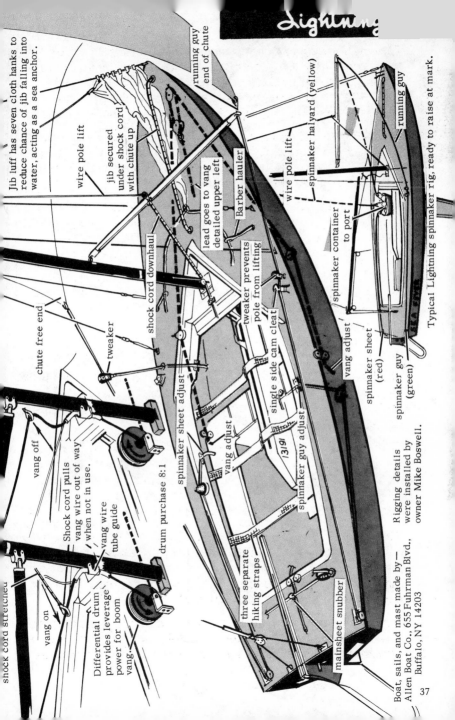

Lightning

Jib luff has seven cloth hanks to reduce chance of jib falling into water, acting as a sea anchor.

running guy end of chute

wire pole lift

jib secured under shock cord with chute up

running guy

spinnaker halyard (yellow)

Barber hauler

lead goes to vang detailed upper left

wire pole lift

tweaker prevents pole from lifting

spinnaker container to port

chute free end

tweaker

shock cord downhaul

vang adjust

spinnaker sheet (red)

spinnaker guy (green)

spinnaker sheet adjust

single side cam cleat

vang adjust

13/9

Typical Lightning spinnaker rig, ready to raise at mark.

vang off

spinnaker guy adjust

Shock cord pulls vang wire out of way when not in use.

vang wire tube guide

Rigging details were installed by owner Mike Boswell.

three separate hiking straps

drum purchase 8:1

shock cord stretched

vang on

Differential drum provides leverage power for boom vang.

mainsheet snubber

Boat, sails, and mast made by—
Allen Boat Co., 655 Fuhrman Blvd.,
Buffalo, NY 14203

37

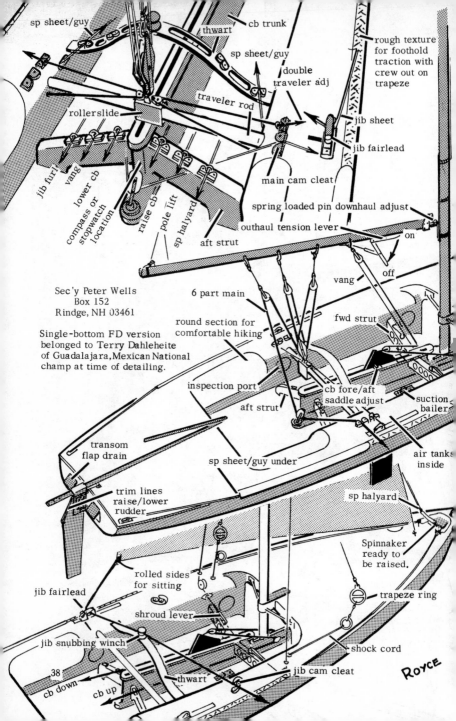

sp sheet/guy

cb trunk

thwart

sp sheet/guy

double traveler adj

rough texture for foothold traction with crew out on trapeze

traveler rod

rollerslide

jib sheet

jib fairlead

jib furl

vang

lower cb

compass or stopwatch location

raise cb

pole lift

sp halyard

aft strut

main cam cleat

spring loaded pin downhaul adjust

outhaul tension lever

on

off

vang

6 part main

fwd strut

Sec'y Peter Wells
Box 152
Rindge, NH 03461

Single-bottom FD version belonged to Terry Dahleheite of Guadalajara, Mexican National champ at time of detailing.

round section for comfortable hiking

inspection port

aft strut

cb fore/aft saddle adjust

suction bailer

sp sheet/guy under

air tanks inside

transom flap drain

sp halyard

trim lines raise/lower rudder

Spinnaker ready to be raised.

rolled sides for sitting

trapeze ring

jib fairlead

shroud lever

shock cord

jib snubbing winch

38

cb down

cb up

thwart

jib cam cleat

ROYCE

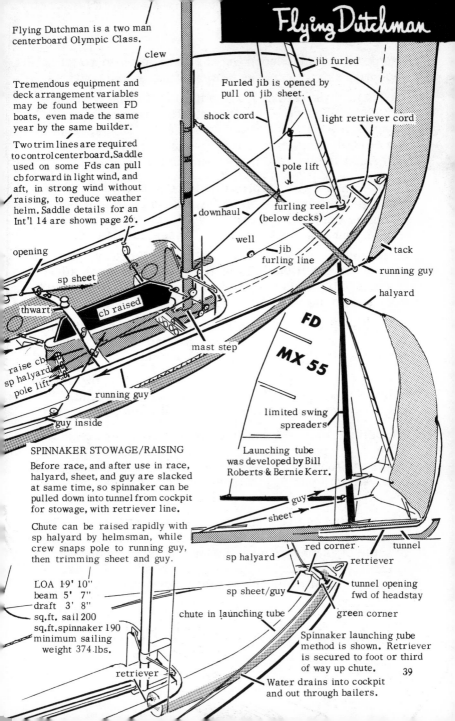

Flying Dutchman

Flying Dutchman is a two man centerboard Olympic Class.

clew

jib furled

Furled jib is opened by pull on jib sheet.

Tremendous equipment and deck arrangement variables may be found between FD boats, even made the same year by the same builder.

shock cord

light retriever cord

Two trim lines are required to control centerboard. Saddle used on some Fds can pull cb forward in light wind, and aft, in strong wind without raising, to reduce weather helm. Saddle details for an Int'l 14 are shown page 26.

pole lift

downhaul

furling reel (below decks)

well

jib furling line

tack

running guy

opening

halyard

sp sheet

thwart

cb raised

FD

MX 55

raise cb
sp halyard
pole lift

mast step

running guy

limited swing spreaders

guy inside

SPINNAKER STOWAGE/RAISING

Launching tube was developed by Bill Roberts & Bernie Kerr.

Before race, and after use in race, halyard, sheet, and guy are slacked at same time, so spinnaker can be pulled down into tunnel from cockpit for stowage, with retriever line.

guy

sheet

Chute can be raised rapidly with sp halyard by helmsman, while crew snaps pole to running guy, then trimming sheet and guy.

red corner

tunnel

sp halyard

retriever

LOA 19' 10"
beam 5' 7"
draft 3' 8"
sq.ft. sail 200
sq.ft. spinnaker 190
minimum sailing
weight 374 lbs.

sp sheet/guy

tunnel opening fwd of headstay

chute in launching tube

green corner

Spinnaker launching tube method is shown. Retriever is secured to foot or third of way up chute.

39

retriever

Water drains into cockpit and out through bailers.

Frank Butler introduced the C 15 in 1969 with strict hull, and sail restrictions, yet minimum hardware controls.

We detailed the C 15 in 1971 finding conflicting hardware versions. When we saw the new C 15 detailed at the 1981 Long Beach Sailboat Show, we found the hardware time tested with excellent results .. probably a nightmare for salesmen to explain to first time sailors.

●

The C 15 has comfortably rolled cockpit sides for your creature comfort, plus hiking straps, and a high boom to eliminate the need for excessive ducking when changing tack as found on decksweeping classes such as Finn.

Snipe and C 15 are almost identical in length, yet the C 15 carries an additional 23 sq. ft. of sail. This is an advantage in areas of light winds, with the crew out on the trapeze in stronger winds to sail the boat flat for best results.

The mainsheet traveler adjustment is important for the high boom. It is usually carried to windward for upwind sailing, with adjustments made by a continuous traveler.

A mast partner is added to improve control of the flexible mast. A downhaul pulls the boom to the mast band, with p & s cunningham controls to control main luff tension.

We believe the first pouches for halyards, sheets, etc., were developed in the early C 15 to eliminate the line snake pit found in some classes, also used on the Cat 38. The Snipe/Lightning shock cord retractor was added to the vang to retract it out of the way when not in use.

Centerboard can be trimmed to port or starboard. The high-aspect board is held down by a shock cord which lets the cb swing up when hitting an obstruction ... then returning the board to its original position. Rudder and centerboard are fully retracted for beaching.

●

The C 15 is a stimulating, spirited, highly competitive planing class which has matured. If I could convince the first mate we needed one more sailboat for the family, it might be the "Vin Rose".

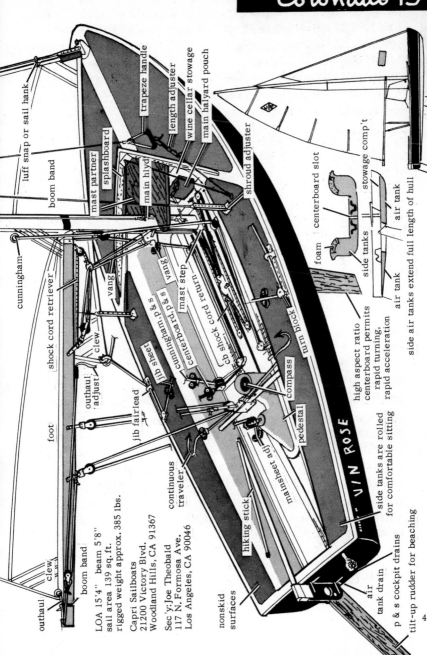

Coronado 15

luff snap or sail hank
boom band
mast partner
splashboard
main hyd'l
length adjuster
wine cellar stowage
trapeze handle
main halyard pouch
shroud adjuster
cunningham
shock cord retriever
vang
outhaul adjust
clew
jib fairlead
jib sheet
cunningham, p & s
centerboard, p & s
mast step
vang
cb shock cord return
turn block
compass
pedestal
mainsheet adj
hiking stick
foot
continuous traveler
nonskid surfaces
air tank drain
p & s cockpit drains
tilt-up rudder for beaching

foam   centerboard slot
stowage comp't
side tanks
air tank
air tank
side air tanks extend full length of hull

high aspect ratio centerboard permits rapid turning, rapid acceleration
side tanks are rolled for comfortable sitting

V/N ROSE

outhaul
clew
boom band

LOA 15'4" beam 5'8"
sail area 139 sq. ft.
rigged weight approx. 385 lbs.

Capri Sailboats
21200 Victory Blvd.
Woodland Hills, CA 91367

Sec'y: Joe Theobald
117 N. Formosa Ave.
Los Angeles, CA 90046

41

William Sweisguth designed the Star in 1911 as a poor man's boat. A late fully-equipped racing Star now starts at $10,000. Its high peaked gaff main was changed to a low headed marconi rig in 1921. As the version was too tame, the first flexible lofty rig was introduced in 1929 with a wooden mast, replaced by the super "wet noodle" aluminum mast, the best controlled of all flexible rigs.

We decided to include the Star only because it is involved in the 1984 Olympics, not the choice for a new boat owner. It gives equal trophies to crew and skipper even in local races, and owners say they have an excellent organization behind them. Our problem was to find and detail a late Star which would be most representative of its class.

Harrison Hine stepped forward offering his "Yawaes", then his later "Rapidamente", each with 130 blocks, with rigging in the middle, not to either extreme. Harrison is a marine hardware manufacturer*who has recorded all blocks by their catalog number, plus length, color, and diameters of rope for each of the 17 diverse rigging systems.

Harrison feels the Star a pleasure to sail upwind, and very exciting to sail downwind. It is extremely responsive to delicate tuning with everything adjustable. The Stars are so equally matched they normally race in a pack with any one of five leaders ready to take over the lead in an unexpected situation, or a slight wind shift.

Harrison has a clean deck layout for skipper and crew with dual controls port and starboard, except for outhaul and jibstay mast puller. Jib slot control is interesting as jib fairlead car adjusts fore and aft, inboard to outboard, acting as a barber hauler in outboard position.

Below deck rigging we've always shown on previous class sailboats has been eliminated as it was so complex many more detail pages would have been required. Anyone wanting the latest information in hardware for this 71 year young and other competitive one-design classes, ask for *Seaway Supply Catalog, 4201 Redwood Ave., Los Angeles, CA 90066.

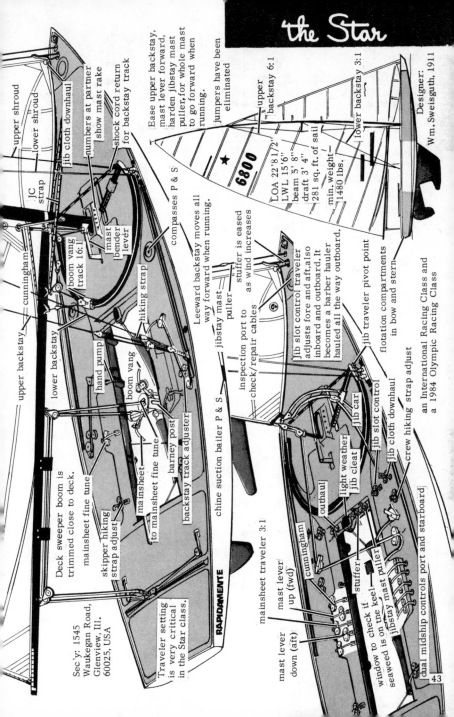

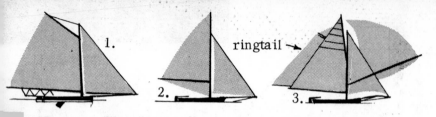

1.

ringtail →

2.

3.

Then we come to those not satisfied with ordinary sailing.

1. New York Harbor from 1870 to 1900 had 20'-30' boats often measuring 70' from jib tack to boomkin, with up to 1600 sq. ft. of sail called SANDBAGGERS. All ballast was inside .. with 600-700 lbs. required to keep them from capsizing at anchor. Canvas ballast bags with 50-60 lbs. of gravel each, were piled on the weather side of these tender centerboard hulls by large active crews when racing.

2. 14' BERMUDA RACING DINGHIES have three rigs to use according to weather, the largest includes a spinnaker of 700 sq. ft. Races are beats or runs with spinnaker, pole, and lines sometimes thrown overboard when rounding the last mark with live ballast expendable... can you swim? The order, "Would you like to bend on the jib?", bears second thoughts with a bowsprit sticking 9 1/2' past bow.

3. The New Zealand 18 FOOTER is a sportsman's dream with no limit to sail area. The jib and main may have up to 400 sq. ft. of sail, with a spinnaker, the total may increase to 1400 sq. ft. Some also use RINGTAILS, formerly spanker extensions to increase sail area on square riggers.

lateen rig

MALIBU OUTRIGGER was the first craft able to sail out, and return to Southern California beaches, replaced by the Hobie generation. We have many fond memories of the Malibu "Lot" club sailors and their gopher problems.

outrigger or ama

Pulse quickens when inland sailors hear the magic word SCOW, a wide beam, shallow draft craft with a square bow ... a light, lively, and extremely tender "souped up" machine for smooth water sailing at extreme heel angles. Crew stands on bilgeboard while hanging on a monkey bar to prevent capsize.

44

Sailing Illustrated

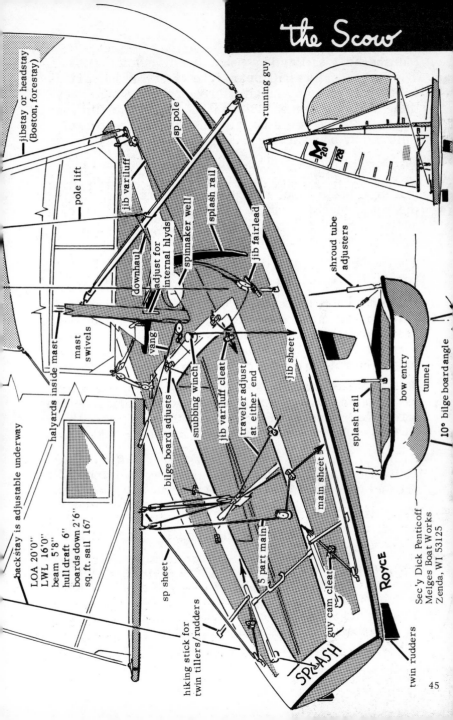

the Scow

jibstay or headstay
(Boston, forestay)

pole lift

jib variluff

sp pole

running guy

downhaul

spinnaker well

splash rail

adjust for
internal hlyds

jib fairlead

shroud tube
adjusters

mast
swivels

vang

jib sheet

halyards inside mast

bow entry

tunnel

backstay is adjustable underway

bilge board adjusts

splash rail

10° bilge board angle

LOA 20'0"
LWL 16'0"
beam 5'8"
hull draft 6"
boards down 2'6"
sq. ft. sail 167

snubbing winch

jib variluff cleat

traveler adjust
at either end

jib sheet

main sheet

5 part main

sp sheet

guy cam cleat

SPLASH

ROYCE

Sec'y Dick Penticoff
Melges Boat Works
Zenda, WI 53125

hiking stick for
twin tillers/rudders

twin rudders

45

Multihull day sailing is a specialized world of its own. The dream ... fly a hull clear of the water for long periods with wind and spray singing through the rigging. Everything is on the ragged edge. Will a sudden puff flip your cat, will the lee bow stub it's toe to cause a cartwheel, followed by boneyarding ... is not for the weak of heart.

● TRAMPOLINE CATS. The Hobie 14 appeared in 1968, a natural for surfers to sail from the beach, return, and trailer it home. Since the cat rig was somewhat clumsy, the owner may now obtain a factory conversion kit by adding the jib and hardware shown to make it more maneuverable, the 7th largest U.S. one-design class.

The Hobie 16 arrived in 1970, presently the 3rd most popular U.S. class, the 3rd fastest growing U.S. class boat.

Mainsheet rigging has been updated on the 14 and 16. It starts at the bitter end (see illus.), then goes to an eye in the main sheet block, returning to the traveler control cleat for traveler adjusting. It then goes to the main sheet cam cleat, controlling traveler and main sheet with one line.

Both Hobie 14* and 16 have continuous jib sheets, the 16 having a jib traveler adjust, while the 14, is fixed. Hobie production numbers at the end of 1981 were more than — Hobie 14-31,000, Hobie 16-66,000, Hobie 18-7000.

● RIGID CATS. There are a variety of these elite classes nationwide, yet class numbers aren't very large due to production/equipment costs, and trailering limitations.

The first successful small cat was the 1962 Pacific Cat so well designed and built by Carter Pyle that #1 is still supposed to be competitive.

The second generation P2/18, is a solid wing, highly complex machine produced by neighbor Owen Minney with a lifetime of racing around the buoys, plus almost all long distance west coast races ... yet his favorite is the P Cat. The chute is eliminated as in all but light breezes the P2/18 would sail faster than the spinnaker.

46   *Hobie 14 Turbo   Sailing   Illustrated

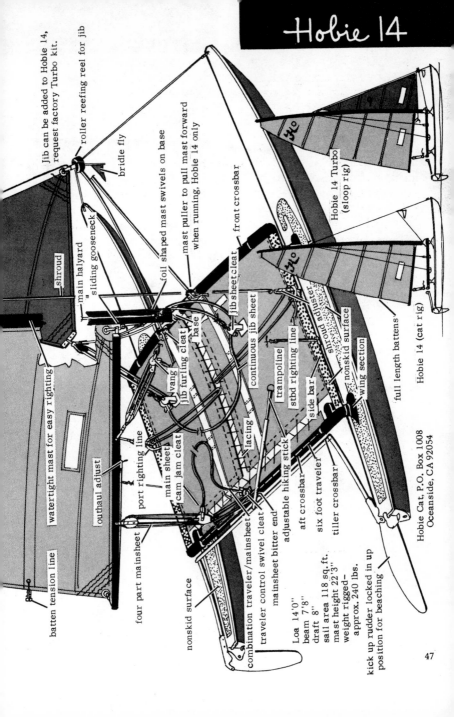

Hobie 14

jib can be added to Hobie 14, request factory Turbo kit.

roller reefing reel for jib

bridle fly

main halyard

sliding gooseneck

foil shaped mast swivels on base

mast puller to pull mast forward when running, Hobie 14 only

front crossbar

shroud

jib sheet cleat

base

watertight mast for easy righting

vang

jib furling cleat

continuous jib sheet

shroud adjuster

outhaul adjust

lacing

trampoline

stbd righting line

nonskid surface

wing section

batten tension line

port righting line

main sheet

cam jam cleat

side bar

adjustable hiking stick

full length battens

four part mainsheet

combination traveler/mainsheet

traveler control swivel cleat

mainsheet bitter end

aft crossbar

six foot traveler

tiller crossbar

nonskid surface

kick up rudder locked in up position for beaching

Loa 14'0"
beam 7'8"
draft 8"
sail area 118 sq.ft.
mast height 22'3"
weight rigged—
approx. 240 lbs.

Hobie 14 Turbo (sloop rig)

Hobie 14 (cat rig)

Hobie Cat, P.O. Box 1008
Oceanside, CA 92054

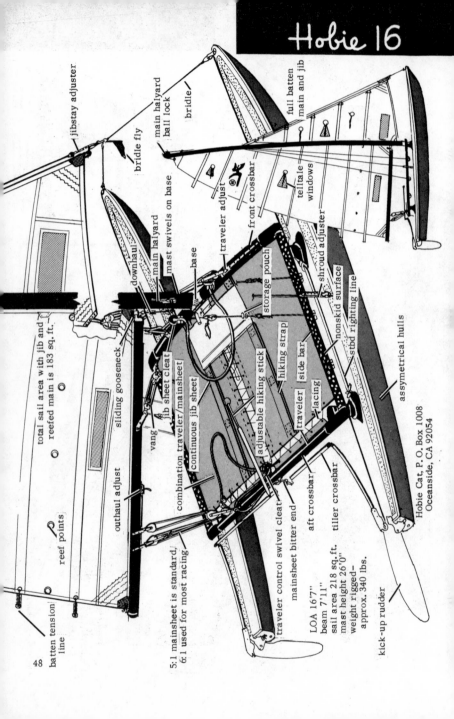

Hobie 16

jibstay adjuster

bridle fly

main halyard ball lock

bridle

full batten main and jib

mast swivels on base

main halyard

downhaul

traveler adjust

front crossbar

telltale windows

shroud adjuster

base

storage pouch

nonskid surface

stbd righting line

assymetrical hulls

total sail area with jib and reefed main is 183 sq. ft.

sliding gooseneck

vang

jib sheet cleat

combination traveler/mainsheet

continuous jib sheet

adjustable hiking stick

hiking strap

traveler

side bar

lacing

outhaul adjust

5:1 mainsheet is standard, 6:1 used for most racing

traveler control swivel cleat

mainsheet bitter end

aft crossbar

tiller crossbar

Hobie Cat, P. O. Box 1008
Oceanside, CA 92054

LOA 16'7"
beam 7'11"
sail area 218 sq. ft.
mast height 26'0"
weight rigged—
approx. 340 lbs.

kick-up rudder

reef points

batten tension line

48

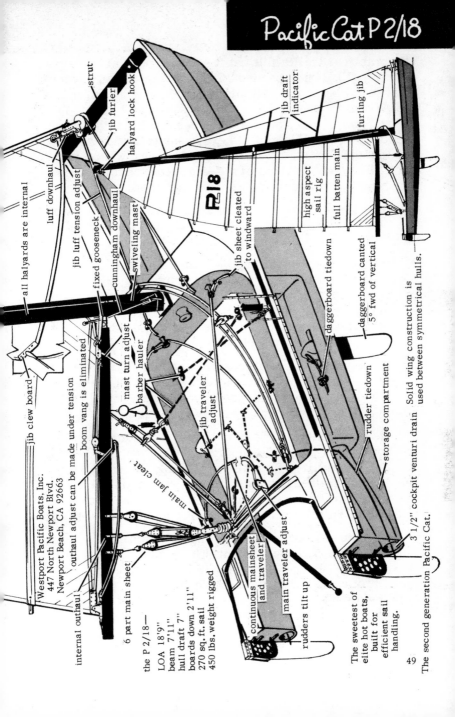

Pacific Cat P 2/18

strut

jib furler

halyard lock hook

jib draft indicator

furling jib

all halyards are internal

luff downhaul

jib luff tension adjust

fixed gooseneck

cunningham downhaul

swiveling mast

R18

jib sheet cleated to windward

high aspect sail rig

full batten main

daggerboard tiedown

daggerboard canted 5° fwd of vertical

jib clew board

internal outhaul outhaul adjust can be made under tension

boom vang is eliminated

Westport Pacific Boats, Inc.
447 North Newport Blvd.
Newport Beach, CA 92663

mast turn adjust

barber hauler

jib traveler adjust

main jam cleat

rudder tiedown

storage compartment

3 1/2" cockpit venturi drain

Solid wing construction is used between symmetrical hulls.

6 part main sheet

the P 2/18—

LOA 18'9"
beam 7'11"
hull draft 7"
boards down 2'11"
270 sq. ft. sail
450 lbs. weight rigged

continuous mainsheet and traveler

main traveler adjust

rudders tilt up

The sweetest of elite hot boats, built for efficient sail handling.

The second generation Pacific Cat.

49

The practical, trailerable cabin sailboat popularity began around 1970, then expanded at a faster rate than anyone anticipated. Many went to inland areas such as Oklahoma and Arkansas where the sailing bug was just beginning to bite, and to shallow water areas such as the Puget Sound and New England. Others went to Arizona, New Mexico, the Great Lakes, and other areas where the portability/vacation factors, along with the backyard home port storage became main advantages.

Three representative portable cabin sailboats are shown, the Catalina 22 now over 9000 strong, and the Balboa 21 and 23, formerly called Aquarius 21 and 23.

A wide variety of trailerable cabin sailboats from 20' to 28' are available. If you desire this kind of sailboat try to find the practical overnighter which can be towed behind the family auto or camper. Also consider the kind of sailing areas you expect to use, plus the kind of launching ramps or hoists you will be using.

Try to be as practical as possible and don't be oversold by advertising when it comes to looks vs size as some boats may look quite large in brochures, yet shrink considerably after spending a few days aboard.

Size is confusing. If all other factors are equal, the 24' sailboat is not just 4' longer than a 20' boat, but TWICE the cubic capacity...making it TWICE the size. While the larger sailboat is more comfortable on the water underway, the extra capacity or size must be reckoned with while launching, loading, trailering, and in storage.

Trailerable sailboats are often made much lighter than hefty full keel relatives designed for much more rugged ocean use. When the hull weight is reduced, so is the amount of material in the boat reducing its price. While this makes the portable cabin sailboat easier to launch, recover, and trailer, its use in coastal areas should be restricted to good weather sailing, though it opens new sailing areas not practical for their heftier and larger full keel relatives.

50

Catalina 22

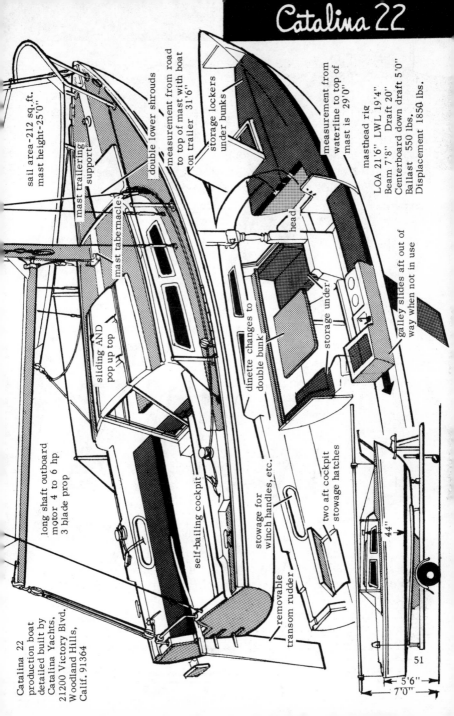

sail area-212 sq.ft.
mast height-25'0"

mast trailering support

double lower shrouds

measurement from road to top of mast with boat on trailer 31'6"

storage lockers under bunks

measurement from waterline to top of mast is 29'0"

masthead rig

LOA 21'6" LWL 19'4"
Beam 7'8"   Draft 20"
Centerboard down draft 5'0"
Ballast 550 lbs.
Displacement 1850 lbs.

head

mast tabernacle

galley slides aft out of way when not in use

sliding AND pop up top

dinette changes to double bunk

storage under

long shaft outboard motor 4 to 6 hp. 3 blade prop

self-bailing cockpit

stowage for winch handles, etc.

two aft cockpit stowage hatches

removable transom rudder

Catalina 22
production boat
detailed built by
Catalina Yachts,
21200 Victory Blvd.
Woodland Hills,
Calif. 91364

44"

51

5'6"
7'0"

Balboa 21

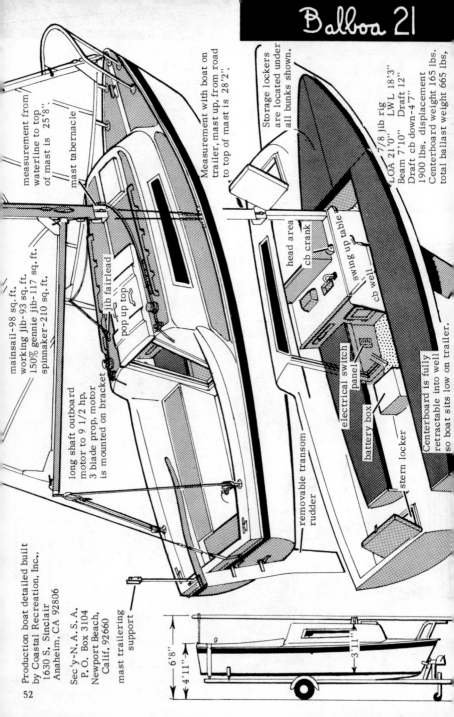

measurement from waterline to top of mast is 25'8".

mast tabernacle

Measurement with boat on trailer, mast up, from road to top of mast is 28'2".

Storage lockers are located under all bunks shown.

LOA 21'0"   7/8 jib rig
Beam 7'10"   LWL 18'3"
Draft cb down-4'7"   Draft 12"
1900 lbs. displacement
Centerboard weight 165 lbs.
total ballast weight 665 lbs.

mainsail-98 sq.ft.
working jib-93 sq.ft.
150% gennie jib-117 sq.ft.
spinnaker-210 sq.ft.

jib fairlead

pop up top

head area

cb crank

swing up table

cb well

long shaft outboard motor to 9 1/2 hp. 3 blade prop, motor is mounted on bracket

electrical switch panel

battery box

stern locker

Centerboard is fully retractable into well so boat sits low on trailer.

removable transom rudder

Production boat detailed built by Coastal Recreation, Inc., 1630 S. Sinclair Anaheim, CA 92806

Sec'y-N.A.S.A.
P.O. Box 3104
Newport Beach,
Calif. 92660

mast trailering support

6'8"
4'11"
3'11"

52

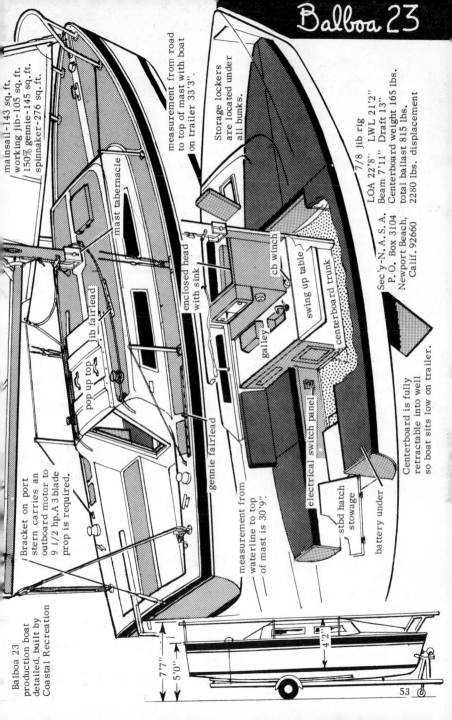

Balboa 23

mainsail-143 sq. ft.
working jib-105 sq. ft.
150% gennie-145 sq. ft.
spinnaker-276 sq. ft.

measurement from road
to top of mast with boat
on trailer 33'3''.

Storage lockers
are located under
all bunks.

7/8 jib rig

LOA 22'8''   LWL 21'2''
Beam 7'11''   Draft 13''
Centerboard weight 165 lbs.
total ballast 815 lbs.
2280 lbs. displacement

Sec'y-N.A.S.A.
P.O. Box 3104
Newport Beach,
Calif. 92660

mast tabernacle

enclosed head
with sink

cb winch

swing up table

centerboard trunk

galley

electrical switch panel

pop up top

jib fairlead

gennie fairlead

stbd hatch
stowage

battery under

Centerboard is fully
retractable into well
so boat sits low on trailer.

measurement from
waterline to top
of mast is 30'9''.

Bracket on port
stern carries an
outboard motor to
9 1/2 hp. A 3 blade
prop is required.

Balboa 23
production boat
detailed, built by
Coastal Recreation

7'7''   5'0''   4'2''

53

Weight is as important and critical to the trailerable cabin sailboat as it is to a light airplane ... if either is overloaded or the weight improperly located.

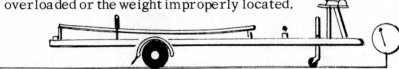

1. Weigh trailer without boat on local public scales.

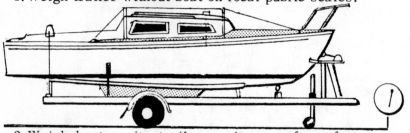

2. Weigh boat on its trailer as it came from factory, then subtract trailer weight to find boat weight.

3. Weigh loaded boat on trailer with outboard motor, full fuel and water tanks (see weight pg. 144), tool kit, anchors and anchor line, sails, radio, cooking gear, etc. Subtract #2 from #3 for weight of equipment aboard which normally increases the longer you own the boat.

Does weight of boat with full equipment weigh more than maximum weight capacity for trailer? If considering a boat/trailer rig with trailer having a 15% or so safe load factor when boat is empty ... the boat fully loaded may exceed listed maximum weight which not only reduces useful lifespan of trailer and tires, but may also become a hazard. A stronger trailer with a larger load weight capacity factor should be considered.

After you know the weight of your boat relatively empty, then when it's loaded, this will help develop a sensitivity to know if your boat is dull and listless on the water if it is overloaded, OR if you have a light crew, to add extra weight below to improve your boat speed. Keep your portable cabin sailboat on a continual diet to perform to its best ability.

Sailing Illustrated

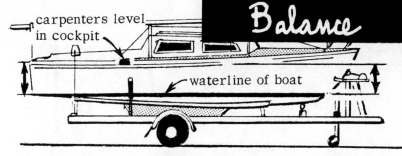

carpenters level
in cockpit

waterline of boat

Sailboat fore and aft balance, is delicate especially on light portable cabin sailboats. If the boat is out of balance it begins to slow down, often dragging the rudder as it is no longer sailing on its lines.

Sail your boat on its lines by installing a simple carpenters level the helsman can easily see when he is steering the boat... by having it parallel to waterline.

Weight DISTRIBUTION is important as a sailboat is a floating teeter totter. Trim your sails, and trim the weight so it sails itself with rudder only used for minor steering corrections (pg. 115) using two light fingers on tiller.

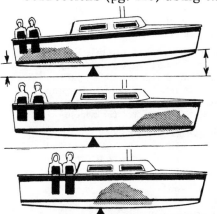

Bow up, stern down. Boat is off its lines, out of balance, reducing speed and pointing ability.

Excessive teeter–totter action, improper balance. Confused boat hesitates, reducing speed.

Sailboat balanced, on its lines. It has rapid recovery with minimum hesitation to meet new wave angle.

As wind increases when flying chute, gennie, or with working jib in storm (pg. 123), pull on mast depresses bow. Move crew weight aft till carpenters level indicates your boat is again sailing on its fore and aft lines.

Sailing   Illustrated   55

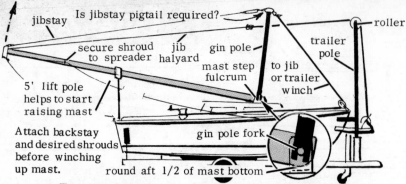

jibstay

Is jibstay pigtail required?

roller

secure shroud jib gin pole
to spreader halyard

trailer pole

mast step to jib
fulcrum or trailer
winch

5' lift pole
helps to start
raising mast

Attach backstay
and desired shrouds
before winching
up mast.

gin pole fork

round aft 1/2 of mast bottom

Too many hazards exist when a mast is raised by physical force instead of using simple, easily available pole leverage on a sailboat on its trailer at the launching ramp as concrete isn't the softest landing pad if you trip on the cabin top.

- GIN POLE. The first time we faced this problem was in 1964 on Islander 24 #1. We added a line to the jibstay turnbuckle, then led it forward through a bow block, and back to the jibsheet winch, providing full control while lowering the mast.

Before raising, we noticed an unusual saddle fitting a short way up the mast, and a strange pole lashed to the deck. One end of the pole slid into the saddle, the outer end had a ring. We secured the jibstay turnbuckle to the ring, then tied a line to the ring which led forward to a block on the bow, and back to the jibsheet winch...or it can also go to the trailer winch, making it easy to raise the mast single handed.

- TRAILER POLE. Secure bottom of mast to step or tabernacle, then connect backstay and upper shroud to their deck fittings. Secure bitter end of jib halyard to port/mast cleat, and tie a line to the jibstay snap. Put this line over pole roller, and install pole in trailer frame fitting with V shaped collar resting against bow, then raise mast with trailer winch.

After the mast is vertical, reach jibstay turnbuckle with a boat hook, then lock it to bow tang. Flip line off roller, remove and secure pole to trailer frame for use the next time.

sail
cover

Have sailmaker add slugs to mainsail luff and foot, pg. 87. Add sail to boom and secure with gaskets, then add sail cover to keep sail clean.

After mast is up and secured, add boom gooseneck to mast, feed luff slugs into mast slot, then add stop so slugs won't fall out of mast slot.

stop

- When lowering mast using either method, add a line to the jibstay turnbuckle, run it through a bow block, then take it
56 back to jib sheet winch for full control when lowering mast.

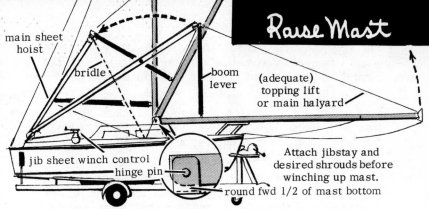

main sheet hoist

bridle

boom lever

(adequate) topping lift or main halyard

jib sheet winch control

hinge pin

Attach jibstay and desired shrouds before winching up mast.

round fwd 1/2 of mast bottom

● The Dutch mast raising method is popular for sailboats entering Huntington Harbor in Southern California which unfortunately has a low bridge across its entrance.

We asked Fred Lanting making this installation on our "Pink Cloud" why he preferred a mast to tilt forward.

"When I was a boy in Holland I often worked on my fathers general merchandise floating store. He didn't want to pay endless bridge keepers to raise their bridges as he made his monthly rounds. He could use this method to lower and raise the mast singlehanded from the cockpit using the main sheet as leverage on his 60' boat to go under the bridges".

Our upper shroud has a 3" spacer added with a hinge pin, forming a pivot point in line with the pivot of the mast, (other methods prefer using a lower shroud) with a bridle above to prevent boom from swinging while raising and lowering. Quick disconnect hardware is necessary for both backstay and lower shrouds. A longer mainsheet is required which sometimes gets in the way when teaching sailing. Forward bottom half of mast must be rounded as shown.

●

● Dockside raising-the gin pole is good for boats to 25', while the Dutch method is efficient for full keel sailboats to 60' to lower and raise a mast to go under a bridge, to replace burned out light bulbs, to check and/or replace mast fittings, and to paint the mast.

● Launching ramp raising -the trailer pole seems to have an edge for the trailerable sailboat since the only time a person has to spend on the cabin top is to secure the base of the deck-stepped mast to its shoe, step, or tabernacle, considerably reducing the chance of a person falling off the cabin top of his boat on its trailer.

Others prefer the gin pole method requiring a little more rigging time on top of the cabin before raising the mast.

The size and cost of a sailboat are secondary factors to how often it is used. Systematically rig your boat with all controls coming to the cockpit so your sailboat will be used a lot more . . . as it is much more fun to sail.

Endless fleets of trailerable cabin sailboats have been launched since 1970. Many were equipped with minimum hardware to cut cost. It can become a blessing in disguise as we face a new economic world.

Most of these boats are light compared to same size full length keel sailboats. When a fast moving storm moves in they heel considerably. It then becomes a hazard to go forward to drop sails or lower anchor.

Take your time to rerig these sailboats so all controls lead to the cockpit. Take your time to analyze each installation so hardware and leads are simple, practical, and easy to use.

When a storm hits, drop the mainsail, with the main halyard to starboard coming to its pouch so surplus line is out of the way. Shock cord installed along boom is flipped over main so sail is secured out of way, pg. 86, and cannot break open.

Many boats now sail under jib only. If it still has too much sail area, jib halyard can be released to drop jib, requiring jib downhaul so jib stays on deck . . . otherwise jib might lift and fill periodically causing erratic steering action.

The option is to run before a storm up to broad reach under bare poles, or drop anchor which can be handled from cockpit.

Jam cleats jam under pressure, the reason they have to be replaced with cam cleats for main and jib sheets under pressure, pg. 144. Probably the best cam cleat tested recently is the highly versatile Nashmarine TRIGGER cleat, page 35, 32906 Avenida Descanso, San Juan Capistrano, CA 92675.

All fittings must be able to operate under storm pressures needing wooden or stainless backing plates, page 190, to spread fitting stress on fiberglass over a larger area.

Token cleats are monted on bow of many boats for anchor and dock lines. Replace with bitt, pg. 190, requiring less space, also handling larger diameter lines. Also replace standard chocks with larger Skene chocks, pg. 188, which are able to secure and handle larger diameter lines. If you want to enjoy your sailboat, good cockpit controls should be considered.

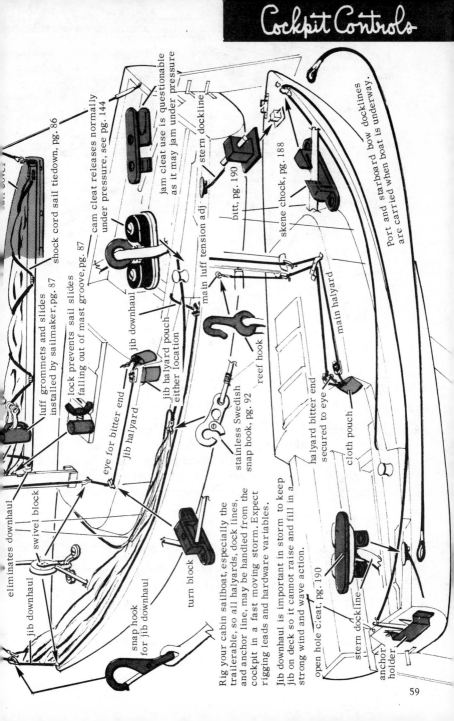

shock cord sail tiedown, pg. 86

cam cleat releases normally under pressure, see pg. 144

jam cleat use is questionable as it may jam under pressure

stern dockline

luff grommets and slides installed by sailmaker, pg. 87

cam cleat releases normally under pressure, pg. 87

lock prevents sail slides falling out of mast groove, pg. 87

jib downhaul

bitt, pg. 190

main luff tension adj.

skene chock, pg. 188

Port and starboard bow docklines are carried when boat is underway.

jib halyard pouch either location

eye for bitter end

jib halyard

jib downhaul

reef hook

stainless Swedish snap hook, pg. 92

main halyard

eliminates downhaul

halyard bitter end secured to eye

cloth pouch

swivel block

jib downhaul

turn block

snap hook for jib downhaul

Rig your cabin sailboat, especially the trailerable, so all halyards, dock lines, and anchor line, may be handled from the cockpit in a fast moving storm. Expect rigging leads and hardware variables.

Jib downhaul is important in storm to keep jib on deck so it cannot raise and fill in a strong wind and wave action.

open hole cleat, pg. 190

stern dockline

anchor holder

59

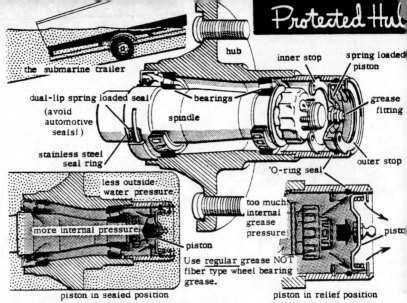

the submarine trailer

dual-lip spring loaded seal
(avoid automotive seals!)

stainless steel seal ring

hub   inner stop   spring loaded piston

bearings

spindle

grease fitting

'O-ring seal   outer stop

less outside water pressure

more internal pressure

piston

piston in sealed position

too much internal grease pressure

piston

Use regular grease NOT fiber type wheel bearing grease.

piston in relief position

Many boat trailers use automotive hubs which do an excellent job IF the hubs are never submerged. If the hubs are submerged in salt or fresh water, water leaks in to mix with the hub grease, corroding metals, and/or causing a water/grease emulsion pressure restricting heat release. If the hubs are submerged, the races and bearings need to be cleaned and the hub repacked.

The Bearing Buddy® concept for "submarine trailer hubs" uses outboard motor or outdrive lower unit grease to protect bearings, hubs, and inner surfaces. Their basic concept... maintain internal hub pressure (3 p.s.i.) more than outside water pressure, to keep out water.

Protected hub above can't be overpacked. Grease is added through spring-loaded piston. When hub is full, the piston is forced outward to release excess grease, then returns to make a seal against its "O" ring.

A warning... avoid automotive inner seals through which grease may leak... use only dual-lip spring loaded seals made by Bearing Buddy® having a much tighter fit.

Aquappliances, Inc., 135 Sunshine Lane, San Marcos, CA 9206

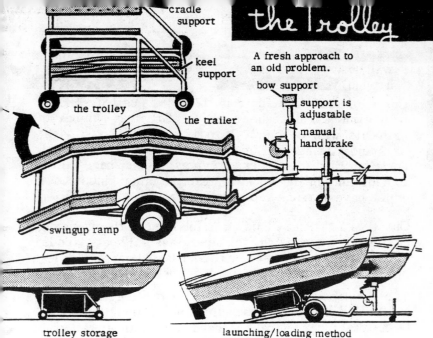

A fresh approach to an old problem.

cradle support

keel support

the trolley

bow support

support is adjustable

the trailer

manual hand brake

swingup ramp

trolley storage

launching/loading method

The 21'4" Varianta Class and special trolley/trailer were designed by E. B. van de Stadt (also FD designer). Both are made at the Dehler Factory, Germany's present top yacht builder. The "Menina" and its trolley/trailer shown are owned by our sailing language expert, Karl Freudenstein of Bonn, Germany.

Several Varianta Class boats are in his area, with one trailer serving several of these class boats. Winch cable is secured to eye on keel, then boat on trolley, is winched aboard trailer till bow rests on Y shaped support. After part of ramp is vertically raised and locked, boat tiedowns are secured, and the rig is ready for trailering without submerging trailer hubs and tail lights.

We do not know if the trolley/trailer concept has been used in the U.S. The idea seems to have excellent potentials to launch and load sailboats easily in a wide variety of situations without submerging trailer tire hubs, also providing more flexibility for storage.

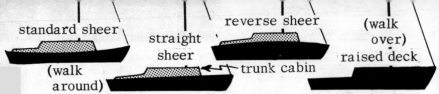

standard sheer | straight sheer | reverse sheer | (walk over) raised deck

(walk around) | trunk cabin

Curve of deck viewed from the side is called SHEER, with various kinds shown above. Greatest number of sailboats with cabins built today, use either a straight or standard sheer. For boats under 30', the raised deck or walk-over deck provides more space below, topside and in the cockpit, than the other kinds shown which have a trunk cabin walk-around deck.

•

Our 1964 24'"Pink Cloud" was the first of the new small, comfortable ocean cruising fiberglass sailboats. Wooden sailboats this size existed with poor layouts, also with less practical space below due to wood construction frames, etc.

The newness of the idea proved a challenge in which MINIATURIZATION was required on all installations to be built to closer tolerances than found on larger sailboats.

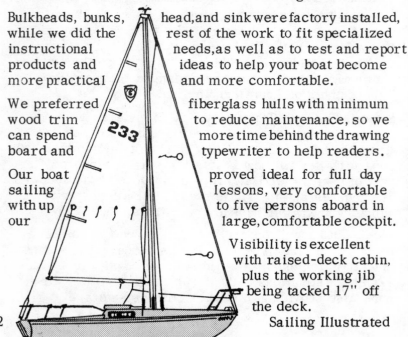

Bulkheads, bunks, head, and sink were factory installed, while we did the rest of the work to fit specialized instructional needs, as well as to test and report products and ideas to help your boat become more practical and more comfortable.

We preferred fiberglass hulls with minimum wood trim to reduce maintenance, so we can spend more time behind the drawing board and typewriter to help readers.

Our boat proved ideal for full day sailing lessons, very comfortable with up to five persons aboard in our large, comfortable cockpit.

Visibility is excellent with raised-deck cabin, plus the working jib being tacked 17" off the deck.

Sailing Illustrated

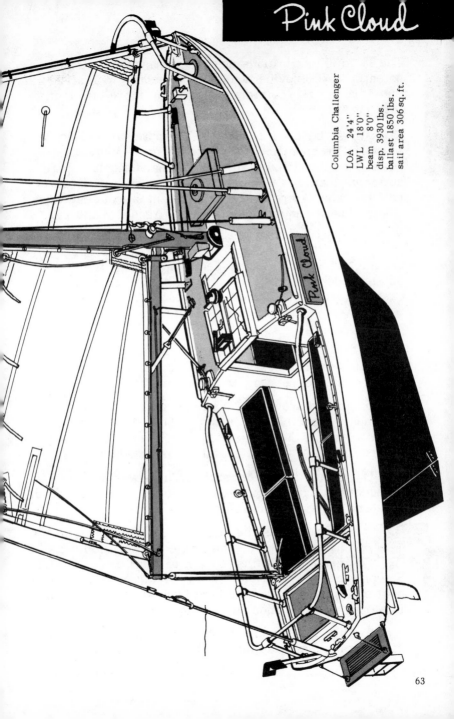

Pink Cloud

Columbia Challenger

LOA   24'4"
LWL   18'0"
beam   8'0"
disp. 3930 lbs.
ballast 1850 lbs.
sail area 306 sq. ft.

63

The 24' to 30' ocean cruising sailboat has many unexplored potentials.We provide two pages of details to analyze as the more built-in comfort it has,and the more efficiently it is rigged, the more you will want to use your sailboat.

•

Sails must be easy to handle. The mainsail should be stored on the boom under a sail cover,pg. 87,with a topping lift and a boom lift, pg. 96, easy to reach. Replace plain and jam cleats for main and jib sheets with cam cleats, pg.59,so sheets are easily released in storm conditions. The mainsail requires a jiffy reef, pages 148 and 149.

Various instruments add to ocean cruising flexibility with a depth sounder, pgs. 222,and 245, the rdf, pg. 245,a barometer,pg. 213, the Sea Temp, pg. 228,and the speed-ometer/odometer installed in the cabin for protection,yet easy to read from the cockpit. The humidity indicator, pg.213,requires an outside protected location.

Two High Tensile Danforth anchors, 5 lb. and 12 lb., plus two 300' 1/2" braided lines, and 5' of heavy chain are adequate for ocean use,pg. 162.A Para-Anchor, pg. 161, and flopper stoppers,pg. 162,have important special uses.

Electrical requirements are important, with a 110-115 amp hour capacity battery, with a built-in charger for dockside use.If the engine doesn't have a built-in charger, a portable generator is useful for isolated anchorages.

Autopilot potentials under sail and/or power will seldom be understood until you see one in operation.The "Tiller Master" is the second autopilot used on our sailboat.

Storage must be organized. Each person should have one bulkhead storage bag for clothing,add grommet drains to eliminate mildew potentials. Sleeping bags are stored in pillow bolsters when not in use. Seat belt straps make excellent bunk straps for sleeping in sloppy weather underway or at anchor.

Avoid white cockpit sun shades due to glare; choose red, green, or blue Acrilan®material to eliminate the glare.

Installations

Pink Cloud

pulpit
working jib
telltale
jib foot adjust
17" jib pennant
main hlyd to stbd
jib hlyd to port
whisker/spinnaker pole
bitt
shroud roller
tabernacle
humidity indicator
compass
chart
rdf
downhaul
cunningham
midship cleat
double lower shrouds
stowage for flopper stoppers, Para-Anchor, etc.
bulkhead storage bags
15 gal. water tank
head
clinometer
bunk straps
alcohol stove
Sea Temp
preserver locker
mast step
barometer
depth sounder transducer
extinguisher
odometer and speedometer
outboard controls
"Tiller Master" auto pilot
boom vang/preventer
jib sheet cam cleat
cockpit railing
genoa fairlead
outhaul
jiffy reef
topping lift
topping lift cleat
boom lift
telltale
stern light
main sheet cam cleat
mainsheet
traveler adjust
skene chocks
swim, dive platform
dockside power inlet
electrical switch panel
12v 110 amp battery
rope locker below
Lewco battery charger
shock cord tiedown
7 1/2 hp outboard pg. 180
vents

65

Papeete is the crossroads of the Pacific. When the first mate and I visited it in 1973 there were 53 tired sailboats stern to the quay-52 wooden sailboats, one excellent concrete sailboat, yet no fiberglass sailboats ... showing the popularity of wooden sailboats for cruising sailors.

You can find many good wooden sailboats in various ocean ports as salt water is kind to wood if the boat is well designed and adequately maintained. Avoid buying any wooden OR fiberglass sailboat that will not pass a competent marine survey to avoid unnecessary problems.

The "Finisterre" (Spanish—"End of Land") detailed was launched in 1954, spawning an endless number of larger versions to 55' sailing worldwide. All of these we've seen are ageless classics in mint condition, including a 40' version, "The Dreamer", on a mooring near our slip after its return from a three year cruise of the South Seas.

"Finisterre" was called an ugly duckling by traditionalists, those with sleek, narrow beams, wet, heavy displacement sailboats standard at that time. Owners did an about face when this multipurpose craft became the first to win the Bermuda Race first overall in three consecutive races.

She was beamy and heavy with 10 tons displacement. Her centerboard provided 7'7" draft when down, which was trimmed to reduce weather helm. It had 4'0" draft when up for crossing reefs, and shallow water inshore docking.

Pages 70-73 detail "Iris", built for and owned by John Martucci of Brooklyn. It received the 1939 "Blue Water Cruising Award" for sailing to Italy. She was featured in many magazine articles to 1956 when John was alive.

John asked us to detail the early gaff cruising rig carried for over 20 years when preparing his illustrations in 1954.

What wonderful memories we have of "Iris" in 1947 when we used to paddle in our Folbot kayak around her moored near Sheepshead Bay ... a mysterious world we couldn't fathom. Little did we realize we would meet its owner, then
66 detail his boat which has been in every printing since 1956.

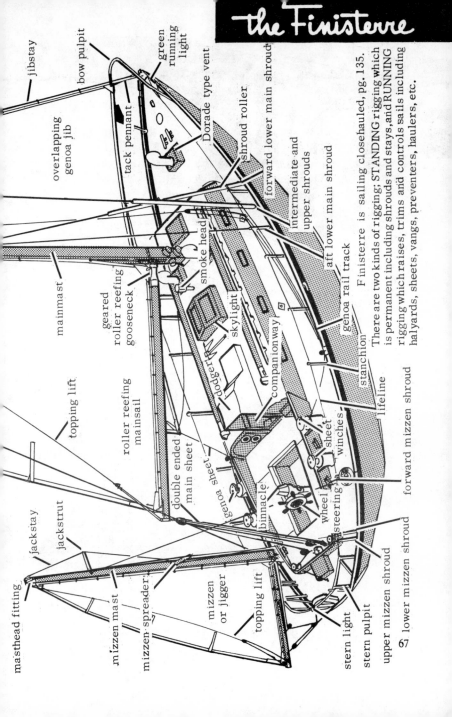

the Finisterre

jibstay
bow pulpit
green running light
overlapping genoa jib
tack pennant
Dorade type vent
shroud roller
forward lower main shroud
intermediate and upper shrouds
aft lower main shroud
mainmast
geared roller reefing gooseneck
smoke head
genoa rail track
topping lift
skylight
dodger
companionway
stanchion
lifeline

Finisterre is sailing closehauled, pg. 135. There are two kinds of rigging; STANDING rigging which is permanent including shrouds and stays, and RUNNING rigging which raises, trims and controls sails including halyards, sheets, vangs, preventers, haulers, etc.

roller reefing mainsail
double ended main sheet
genoa sheet
jib sheet
winches
binnacle
wheel steering
forward mizzen shroud

masthead fitting
jackstay
jackstrut
mizzen mast
mizzen spreader
mizzen or jigger
topping lift
stern light
stern pulpit
upper mizzen shroud
lower mizzen shroud

67

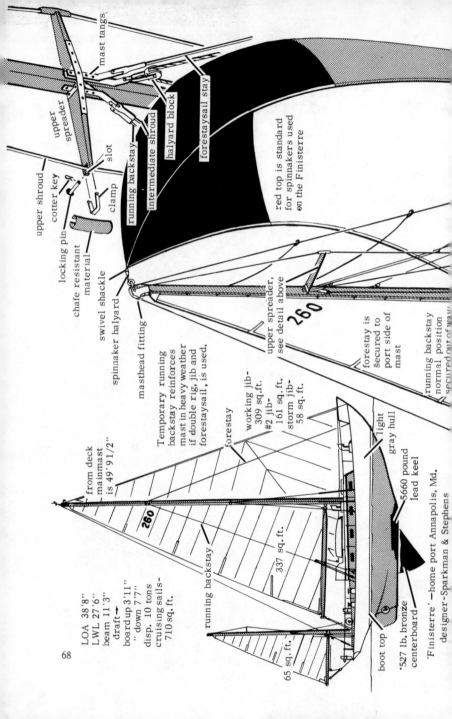

mast tangs

upper spreader

upper shroud

cotter key

locking pin

chafe resistant material

swivel shackle

spinnaker halyard

masthead fitting

slot

clamp

running backstay

intermediate shroud

halyard block

forestaysail stay

red top is standard for spinnakers used on the Finisterre

upper spreader, see detail above

260

forestay is secured to port side of mast

running backstay normal position secured out of way.

from deck mainmast is 49'9 1/2"

Temporary running backstay reinforces mast in heavy weather if double rig, jib and forestaysail, is used.

forestay

working jib– 309 sq. ft.

#2 jib– 161 sq. ft.

storm jib– 58 sq. ft.

260

running backstay

337 sq. ft.

light gray hull

5660 pound lead keel

65 sq. ft.

boot top

527 lb. bronze centerboard

'Finisterre'–home port Annapolis, Md. designer–Sparkman & Stephens

LOA 38'8"
LWL 27'6"
beam 11'3"
draft—
board up 3'11"
" down 7'7"
disp. 10 tons
cruising sails–
710 sq. ft.

68

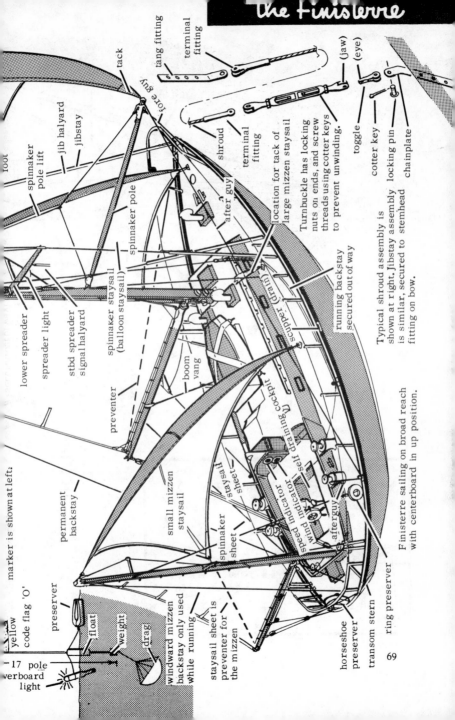

the Finisterre

tang fitting

terminal fitting

foot

jib halyard

jibstay

spinaker pole lift

tack

fore guy

terminal fitting

shroud

(jaw)

(eye)

toggle

cotter key

locking pin

chainplate

after guy

location for tack of large mizzen staysail

Turnbuckle has locking nuts on ends, and screw threads using cotter keys to prevent unwinding.

lower spreader

spreader light

stbd spreader signal halyard

spinnaker staysail (balloon staysail)

spinnaker pole

running backstay secured out of way

Typical shroud assembly is shown at right. Jibstay assembly is similar, secured to stemhead fitting on bow.

preventer

boom vang

scupper (drain)

permanent backstay

small mizzen staysail

spinnaker sheet

staysail staysail sheet

speed indicator self draining cockpit

wind indicator

afterguy

Finisterre sailing on broad reach with centerboard in up position.

marker is shown at left.

yellow code flag 'O'

preserver

float

weight

drag

horseshoe preserver

transom stern

ring preserver

17 pole overboard light

windward mizzen backstay only used while running

staysail sheet is preventer for the mizzen

69

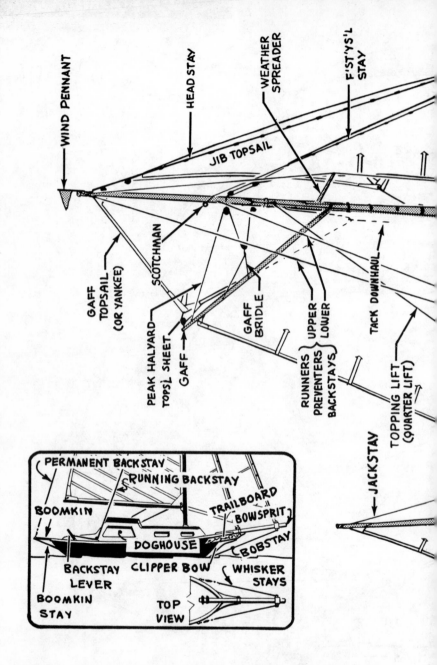

WIND PENNANT

HEAD STAY

WEATHER SPREADER

F'ST'YS'L STAY

JIB TOPSAIL

GAFF TOPSAIL (OR YANKEE)

SCOTCHMAN

PEAK HALYARD

TOPS'L SHEET

GAFF

GAFF BRIDLE

RUNNERS
PREVENTERS } UPPER
BACKSTAYS } LOWER

TACK DOWNHAUL

JACKSTAY

TOPPING LIFT (QUARTER LIFT)

PERMANENT BACK STAY

RUNNING BACKSTAY

BOOMKIN

TRAILBOARD

BOWSPRIT

DOGHOUSE

BOBSTAY

BACKSTAY LEVER

CLIPPER BOW

WHISKER STAYS

BOOMKIN STAY

TOP VIEW

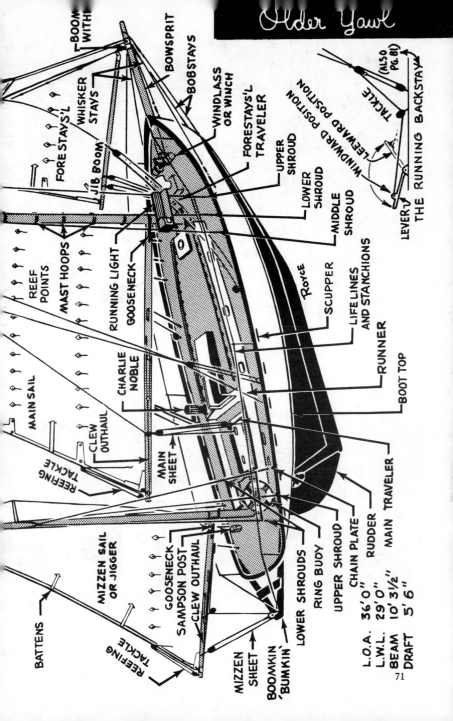

Older Yawl

BOOM WITH

BOWSPRIT

BOBSTAYS

WHISKER STAYS

FORE STAYS'L

JIB BOOM

WINDLASS OR WINCH

FORESTAYS'L TRAVELER

UPPER SHROUD

LOWER SHROUD

MIDDLE SHROUD

(ALSO PG. 81)

TACKLE

WINDWARD POSITION

LEEWARD POSITION

LEVER

THE RUNNING BACKSTAY

REEF POINTS

MAST HOOPS

RUNNING LIGHT

GOOSENECK

CHARLIE NOBLE

Royce

SCUPPER

LIFE LINES AND STANCHIONS

RUNNER

BOOT TOP

MAIN SAIL

CLEW OUTHAUL

REEFING TACKLE

MAIN SHEET

BATTENS

MIZZEN SAIL OR JIGGER

MIZZEN SHEET

BOOMKIN 'BUMKIN'

GOOSENECK

SAMPSON POST

CLEW OUTHAUL

REEFING TACKLE

LOWER SHROUDS

RING BUOY

UPPER SHROUD

CHAIN PLATE

RUDDER

MAIN TRAVELER

L.O.A.   36'0"
L.W.L.   29'0"
BEAM   10'3½"
DRAFT   5'6"

71

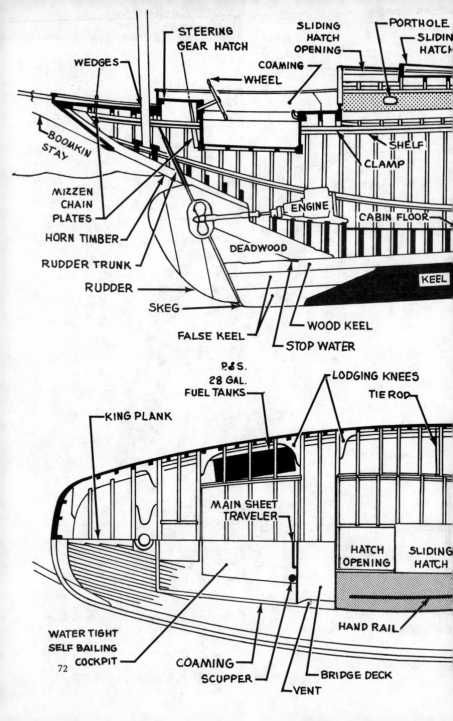

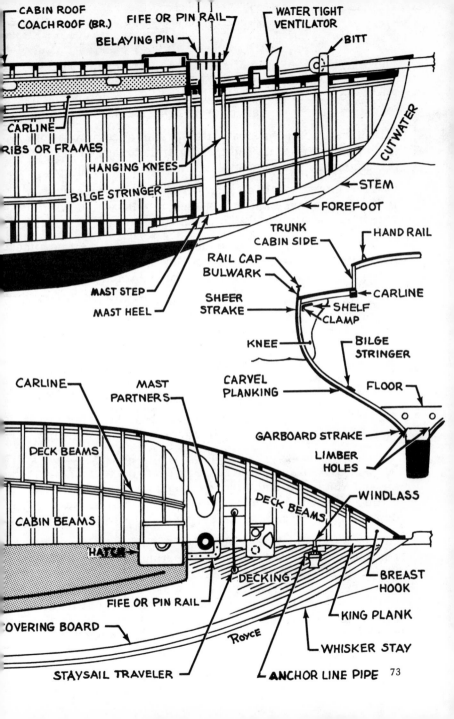

CABIN ROOF
COACH ROOF (BR.)
FIFE OR PIN RAIL
WATER TIGHT VENTILATOR
BELAYING PIN
BITT
CARLINE
RIBS OR FRAMES
HANGING KNEES
BILGE STRINGER
CUTWATER
STEM
FOREFOOT
TRUNK CABIN SIDE
HAND RAIL
RAIL CAP
BULWARK
CARLINE
MAST STEP
MAST HEEL
SHEER STRAKE
SHELF
CLAMP
KNEE
BILGE STRINGER
CARLINE
MAST PARTNERS
CARVEL PLANKING
FLOOR
DECK BEAMS
GARBOARD STRAKE
LIMBER HOLES
CABIN BEAMS
DECK BEAMS
WINDLASS
HATCH
FIFE OR PIN RAIL
DECKING
BREAST HOOK
KING PLANK
COVERING BOARD
Royce
WHISKER STAY
STAYSAIL TRAVELER
ANCHOR LINE PIPE
73

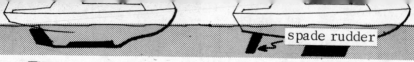
spade rudder

There are three kinds of sailboats...the open boat, the weekender, and the larger combination racing/cruising boat. Let us compare the latter with a 1 to 10 ratio comparison to analyze the wide variables in cruising sailboats.

A lean, wet, racing sailboat with spartan accommodations is on one extreme, its tight living and storage areas soon producing temper clashes...a minimum 1 rating.

On the other extreme is a heavy, sluggish, undercanvassed gaff rigger, cranky, and dull upwind, moving well downwind in a blow, mostly for dockside sailing with a 0-0-0 rating.

If we had a large bank account and endless time to cruise the South Seas, we'd choose the Newporter at right with a cutter rig, sailing better upwind than the ketch rig.

"Ack" Ackerman spent three years sailing the South Seas for preparation to design his ideal, the first comfortable and practical cruising sailboat. We have spent much time on a variety of Newporters cruising, vacationing, and partying, plus a considerable share of stormy weather. Newporter was the first sailboat we know specifically designed for cruising ...with a maximum rating of 10.

A wide variety of cruising/racing sailboats have been built since 1970 for which you will have to provide a rating.

Cruising boats need considerable living space, comfortable bunks, and storage areas for extended periods of living aboard which increase windage, reducing upwind ability. Galley layout is important to separate and protect the cook from crew coming below, or going topside.

Sail handling must be designed for one person operation raising and lowering sails, and reefing in heavy weather. SEAWORTHINESS is important so the boat takes care of itself in a storm...after its crew has quit. AVOID the spade rudder (above) as the active cruising boat must expect to occasionally go aground. Will the keel be able to protect the rudder in a temporary grounding?

74   Sailing Illustrated

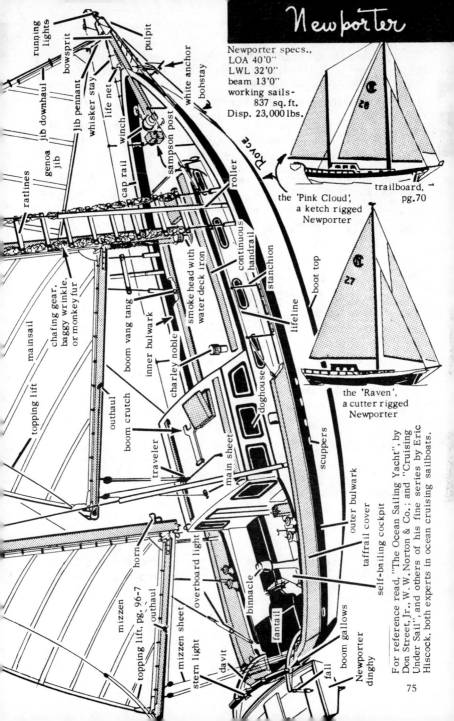

Newporter

Newporter specs.,
LOA 40'0"
LWL 32'0"
beam 13'0"
working sails-
837 sq. ft.
Disp. 23,000 lbs.

the 'Pink Cloud', a ketch rigged Newporter

ROYCE

trailboard, pg.70

the 'Raven', a cutter rigged Newporter

running lights
bowsprit
jib downhaul
jib pennant
whisker stay
genoa jib
life net
winch
sampson post
cap rail
ratlines
pulpit
white anchor
bohstay
roller
continuous handrail
stanchion
lifeline
boot top
scuppers
outer bulwark
taffrail cover
self-bailing cockpit

mainsail
chafing gear, baggy wrinkle, or monkey fur
topping lift
outhaul
boom crutch
traveler
boom vang tang
inner bulwark
smoke head with water deck iron
charley noble
doghouse
main sheet

mizzen
horn
mizzen sheet
stern light
topping lift, pg. 96-7
outhaul
davit
overboard light
binnacle
fantail
boom gallows
Newporter dinghy
fall

For reference read, "The Ocean Sailing Yacht", by Don Street, Jr., W. W. Norton & Co.; and "Cruising Under Sail", and others of his fine series by Eric Hiscock, both experts in ocean cruising sailboats.

75

The combination racing/cruising type fiberglass production sailboat grew to maturity from 1960 to 1970.Then the IOR rule was introduced in which each sailboat was measured individually to the new IOR formula,the all-out goal,racing.

A wide variety of one-off,and low production number IOR sailboats with tall rigs and pinched sterns appeared for short periods in the quest for first place.

Frank Butler of Catalina Yachts took the best of IOR design requirements putting them into a one design racer-cruiser,the Catalina 38,to insure its future. The Cat 38 has been chosen for the Congressional Cup Series since 1979,replacing the Cal 40 which is no longer in production, an outstanding two decade racer.Over 150 Cat 38's were produced by the end of 1981.

Ten years after the IOR philosophy was introduced, the Cat 30 can race as a one-design, P.H.R.F., IOR, SORD, and a variety of other rules. It is a sensitive, well-balanced boat in light airs that gains stability as the breeze picks up, carrying a racing crew of six or seven. Five sails are allowed for class racing,while additional sails may be added such as the light Mylar jib, the blooper, and the daisy or wind seeker for open fleet racing,

The Catalina 38's are active in local,weekend,and long distance racing with a good record,such as "Defiance", owned by Richard and Barbara Nowling,winning first in the SORD Class 1981 annual race to Ensenada,Mexico, the largest race in numbers of sailboats held worldwide.

The Catalina 38 is at least 3000 pounds displacement heavier than similar length stripped down IOR competitors, the extra weight involved in practical creature comforts below for staying aboard overnight, weekends, weekend sailing, harbor hopping, and leisurely vacations.

The Catalina 38 leads the way proving creature comfort can be compatible with IOR racing philosophy for the young active sailors ... while local stripped down IOR competitors seldom leave the dock if not to race.

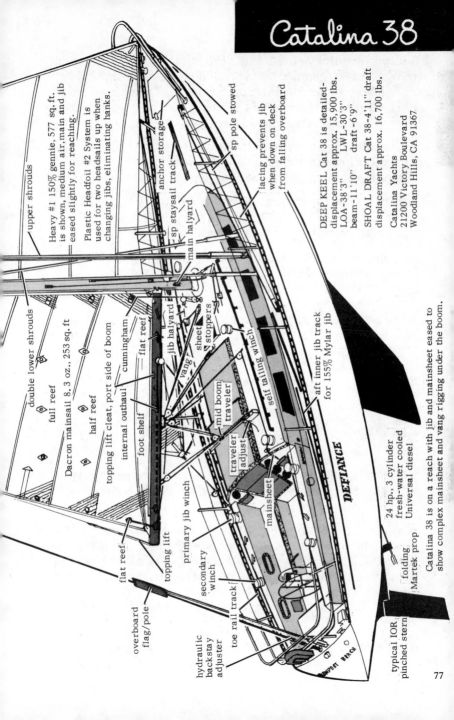

Catalina 38

upper shrouds

Heavy #1 150% gennie, 577 sq. ft.
is shown, medium air, main and jib
eased slightly for reaching.

Plastic Headfoil #2 System is
used for two headsails up when
changing jibs, eliminating hanks.

anchor storage

sp pole stowed

lacing prevents jib
when down on deck
from falling overboard

sp staysail track

main halyard

jib halyard

vang

sheet
stoppers

mid boom
traveler

traveler
adjust

mainsheet

self tailing winch

aft inner jib track
for 155% Mylar jib

DEFIANCE

double lower shrouds

full reef

Dacron mainsail 8.3 oz., 253 sq. ft

half reef

topping lift cleat, port side of boom

internal outhaul — cunningham

foot shelf — flat reef

flat reef

topping lift

primary jib winch

secondary
winch

hydraulic
backstay
adjuster

toe rail track

overboard
flag/pole

typical IOR
pinched stern

folding
Martek prop

24 hp, 3 cylinder
fresh-water cooled
Universal diesel

DEEP KEEL Cat 38 is detailed-
displacement approx. 15,900 lbs.
LOA-38'3"   LWL-30'3"
beam-11'10"   draft-6'9"

SHOAL DRAFT Cat 38-4'11" draft
displacement approx. 16,700 lbs.

Catalina Yachts
21200 Victory Boulevard
Woodland Hills, CA 91367

Catalina 38 is on a reach with jib and mainsheet eased to
show complex mainsheet and vang rigging under the boom.

77

- Racing Inventory—mainsail, 253 sq. ft., 8.3 oz. Dacron
  155% light #1 gennie, Mylar*, 588 sq. ft., 2.6 oz.
  150% heavy #1 gennie, Dacron, 577 sq.ft., 7.7 oz., med. air
  130% #2 gennie, Dacron, 474 Sq.ft., 7.7 oz., heavy air, beating
  100% #3 gennie, Dacron, 333 sq. ft.

  Tri-radial chute, nylon, 1.5 oz., 1384 sq.ft.
  Tri-radial chute, nylon, 3/4 oz., 1384 sq. ft.
  blooper-nylon, 1.23 oz., 583 sq. ft.

- Additional Sails - Tri-radial chute, nylon, 3.4 oz., 1384 sq.ft.
  daisy—nylon, 3/4 oz., 391 sq. ft., very light windseeker
  110% spinnaker staysail-Dacron, 4.1 oz., 385 sq. ft.

  Jib top-Mylar*, 3.4 oz., 577 sq. ft., reaching medium air
  Genoa Staysail, Mylar*, 3.4 oz., 270 sq. ft.
  *Bainbridge Temperkote Mylar material is used
  ●

The high aspect rig Cat 38 detailed is a very sensitive
racing sailboat for Southern California with light, steady
wind patterns. Yet it likes a stiff breeze when the hull
hardens down with tremendous pointing ability to 30°
heel when beating with reefed main and smaller jib...
with minimum leeway.

The 100% gennie isn't standard for local racing, though
recommended for San Francisco racing, and returning
from long races to Hawaii and Acapulco.

For winds over 20 knots, the #2 gennie is used to avoid
excess heel, with jib fairlead snatch block located on the
forward jib track.

The plastic Headfoil #2 System helps to change jibs in
minimum time as one can be raised while the other is
lowered. If the jib is sheeted before it is all the way up,
or allowed overlong to luff in a strong wind before being
sheeted, it may come out of the plastic jib track requiring
better teamwork timing. Otherwise it is necessary to
rethread the jib luff and raise the jib a second time.

The hydraulic backstay adjuster when beating may carry

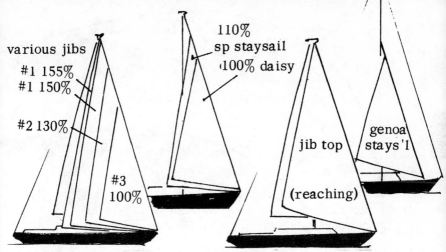

various jibs

#1 155%
#1 150%

#2 130%

#3 100%

110% sp staysail
100% daisy

jib top
(reaching)

genoa stays'l

Catalina 38 owners have an ample supply of sails to choose from for a wide variety of racing and sailing conditions.

•

2200 pounds pressure raised to 3500 pounds in heavy air. This pulls the masthead aft, straightening the jibstay so the Cat 38 may point higher and foot faster. The adjuster is eased all the way for downwind sailing.

In light airs the crew is stationed on or near the rail, aft of the mast and forward of the companionway. The lightest crew members go forward of the mast to raise or lower the chute, as the speed reduction is quite obvious on the digital knotmeter reading in hundredths of a knot.

Owners have varied ideas on additional sails. One owner avoids a spinnaker staysail as the foredeck movement to handle one may offset its potential performance advantage. A blooper is avoided in light winds for the same reason, coming into its own in medium to strong winds to improve downwind steering with chute up.

The small 100% daisy is preferred in light drifting wind conditions, to the 155% drifter which may hang vertically due to sail cloth weight. After hull speed reaches three knots, the 155% Mylar gennie is raised.

We wish we had 30 more pages to fully cover the Cat 38.

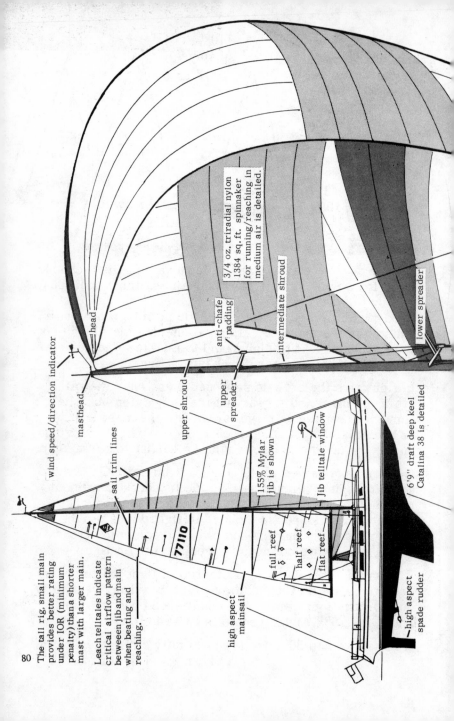

The tall rig, small main provides better rating under IOR (minimum penalty) than a shorter mast with larger main.

Leach telltales indicate critical airflow pattern between jib and main when beating and reaching.

wind speed/direction indicator

masthead

head

anti-chafe padding

3/4 oz. triradial nylon 1384 sq. ft. spinnaker for running/reaching in medium air is detailed.

intermediate shroud

lower spreader

upper shroud

upper spreader

sail trim lines

77110

high aspect mainsail

155% Mylar jib is shown

Jib telltale window

full reef

half reef

flat reef

6'9" draft deep keel
Catalina 38 is detailed

high aspect spade rudder

80

Double spinaker halyards, primary and secondary, are carried for changing chutes, to carry chute and blooper, chute and spinnaker staysail, or replacement for lost halyards.

Due to huge chute called "Patches" by owner (24 at time of detailing), we worked closely with sailmaker using aerial photos to help for accurate detailing.

When the sailmaker analyzed the final art, he studied it closely, finally remarking, "The chute is accurate but it certainly makes the boat look small".

pole topping lift

jibstay

Dip pole jibe method is used, page 130. Pole is raised high enough up mast, to allow outer end of pole to go under jibstay, and clear pulpit area.

tack

spinnaker pole

stays'l track

pole foreguy

spinnaker pole

traveler adjust

knotmeter

mainsheet

prevang

apparent wind

depth sounder

wind speed

double lower shrouds

cunningham eased

outhaul eased

prevang

primary sp hlyd

secondary sp hlyd

clinometer

companionway controls

sp sheet

lazy sheet

after guy

lazy guy

line storage
organizer

DEFIANCE

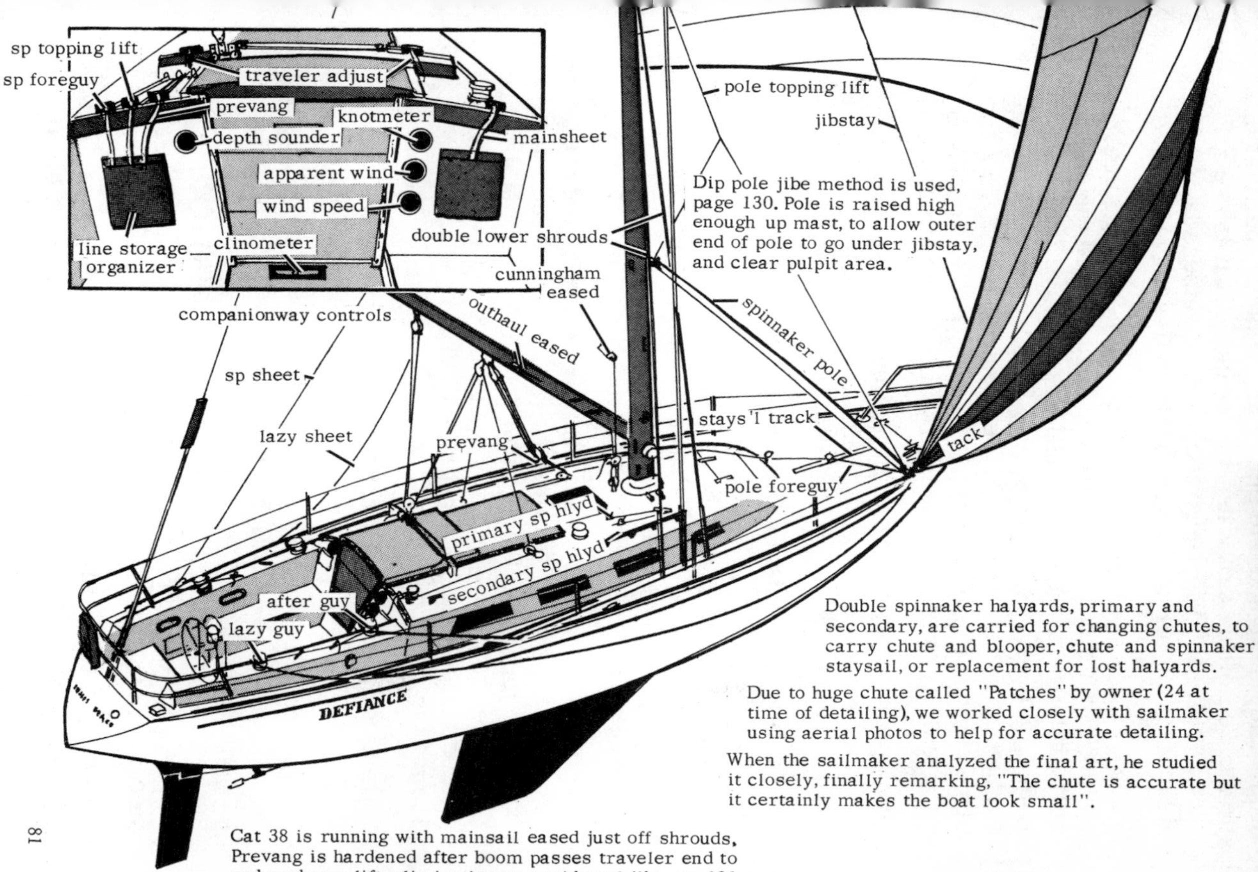

sp topping lift

sp foreguy

Cat 38 is running with mainsail eased just off shrouds. Prevang is hardened after boom passes traveler end to reduce boom lift, eliminating an accidental jibe, pg. 121.

Rudy Choy designed and built the "Aikane", the first of a new breed of big cat. When two weeks old it broke all records in the 1957 Newport Beach, to Ensenada, Mexico Race, leaving all committee boats wallowing in its wake.

Rudy is the leader in light hull construction for ocean racing for his big cats with long, lean, twin displacement hulls, eliminating the monohull speed/wave limitation trap, pages 140-141. It was over a decade later that these engineering concepts started to be used in the long, thin ultra light sailboats, registering continuous speeds in racing never previously seen in similar length monohulls.

His specialty was asymmetrical hulls, using twin hull stability leverage with minimum displacement, permitting lighter construction without dead weight ballast.

We've enjoyed cruising and racing on Rudy's designs from 26' to 57', with "Patty Cat" our favorite. Soft water support with slim, double-ended hulls provide a comfortable ride under ocean conditions with minimum water lift. Absence of a wake, yet a roostertail at 20 knots with one finger steering, is an eyeopener to monohull sailors.

The monohull has an automatic heel safety valve releasing excess wind pressure, while the big cat with considerable heel resistance makes much more use of available wind pressure. In strong or puffy winds on a big cat, a SHEET safety valve is used by rapidly slacking the main sheet from 3' to 5'...then resheeting immediately.

Catamarans may flip and float, while a monohull may be holed and sink...a choice which is up to the buyer.

We've seen Rudy's cats while racing, even his 26' design, easily outpoint and outfoot local 10 meter monohulls. In a 12 meter challenge, the race committee suddenly cancelled the race in the middle of the afternoon when the 35' cat was ready to catch and pass the 12 meter barely making steerageway...raising many interesting questions.

The sailing fraternity lost much when Rudy chose to move back to Hawaii, a designer/leader way ahead of his time.

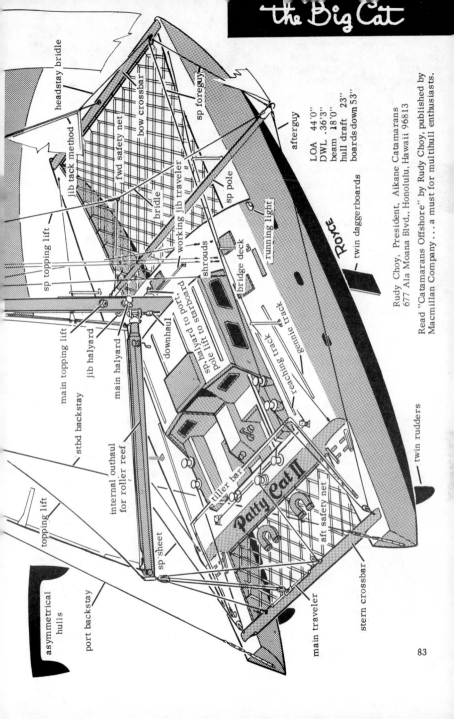

the Big Cat

headstay bridle

jib tack method

fwd safety net

bow crossbar

bridle

sp topping lift

working jib traveler

sp foreguy

afterguy

LOA 44'0"
DWL 36'3"
beam 18'0"
hull draft 23"
boards down 53"

sp pole

running light

ROYCE

twin daggerboards

main topping lift

stbd backstay

jib halyard

main halyard

downhaul

sp. halyard to port,
jib halyard to starboard

pole lift to port
sp. pole lift to starboard

shrouds

bridge deck

reaching track

gennie track

internal outhaul
for roller reef

tiller bar

Patty Cat II

topping lift

aft safety net

twin rudders

asymmetrical
hulls

sp sheet

port backstay

main traveler

stern crossbar

Rudy Choy, President, Aikane Catamarans
677 Ala Moana Blvd., Honolulu, Hawaii 96813

Read "Catamarans Offshore" by Rudy Choy, published by
Macmillan Company...a must for multihull enthusiasts.

83

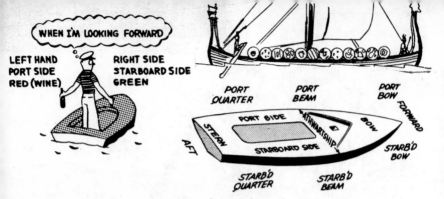

The captain of a square rigger had to be a man of few words. His commands were specific, clear, and concise, as they had to be understood and put to use in seconds by crews from various nations barely able to communicate with each other. Thus the universal language of the sea was developed to fit this specific need.

Today's sailing vocabulary is a functional, colorful, spoken language developed from technical slang terms some more than a thousand years old. The term starboard comes from Scandinavian stjørn-bordi, the side (board) where the steering oar was hung. To protect it, ships were tied to docks lade-board, or "laddeborde" side later pronounced larboard. Since this term was easily confused in a storm with starboard, the British replaced it with the term port in the mid 1700's*.

Your sailing language is a spoken one ... rather than the written language of scholars. A puzzled newcomer as a result will find various terms used for one and the same function such as sail courses ... and according to choice writers may spell halyard one of three different ways.

Considerable effort is required to learn the sailing language, yet it is your only effective communication means to explain your intentions to other sailors, and to get exact answers from them. And without it you would feel lost trying to expand your sailing knowledge by reading books about Christopher Columbus, Horatio Hornblower, and other maritime gems. (*Thanks to Karl Freudenstein's
84 multilanguage research to redefine the definition of port.)

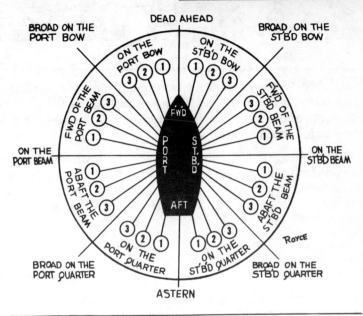

DEAD AHEAD

BROAD ON THE
PORT BOW

ON THE
PORT BOW
3 2 1

ON THE
STB'D BOW
1 2 3

BROAD ON THE
STB'D BOW

FWD OF THE
PORT BEAM
3
2
1

FWD OF THE
STB'D BEAM
3
2
1

FWD

PORT ST.B'D.

AFT

ON THE
PORT BEAM

ON THE
STB'D BEAM

ABAFT THE
PORT BEAM
1
2
3

ABAFT THE
STB'D BEAM
1
2
3

ON THE
PORT QUARTER
3 2 1

ON THE
STB'D QUARTER
1 2 3

ROYCE

BROAD ON THE
PORT QUARTER

BROAD ON THE
STB'D QUARTER

ASTERN

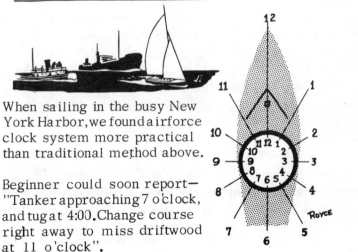

When sailing in the busy New York Harbor, we found a airforce clock system more practical than traditional method above.

Beginner could soon report— "Tanker approaching 7 o'clock, and tug at 4:00. Change course right away to miss driftwood at 11 o'clock".

ROYCE

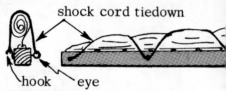

furling method

gasket tiedowns   hook   eye   shock cord tiedown

In the days when canvas sails reigned supreme, standard procedure was to stuff sails into a sailbag, being sure to leave lots of air pockets. If stuffed in too tight especially when damp, the canvas sails mildewed rapidly.

Common practice for many one-design owners today is to fold their dacron sails, using similar sequence to that shown at right. Reason is to keep wrinkle formation to a minimum, as some sailors feel wrinkles cause minute areas of drag, hindering racing performance, see pg. 88.

Folding a mainsail on a dock or lawn is not always an easy task. On some small boats, battens are removed, sail is rolled around boom, then boom and sail stowed.

On larger craft with mainsail stowed on boom, two methods are used. For those with standard reefing, see page 149, eyes are mounted on one side of boom with hooks on the other for a shock cord sail tiedown.

If hook and eye method were used with roller reefing, the sharp metal parts would chafe or cut sail. The older gasket procedure as result, is used to secure sail to top of boom.

When our new sails on the "Pink Cloud" were lowered, the luff rope of the main would fall out of the mast track, spilling mainsail onto the deck. We took the sail back to the sailmakers. Plastic slugs were installed on both the luff and foot, permitting storage shown at right.

When furling a sail for boom storage, pull AFT with each tug of sail so battens will lay parallel to boom and not be broken. Sail can be furled as shown upper left, or pocket made next to boom, then mainsail rolled and secured with either gasket or shock cord method, so it will stay neatly on top of the boom. The sail is ready to be raised in a few seconds, the next time you go sailing.

remove battens

folds

Accordian or loft fold is shown so creases are PARALLEL to foot since horizontal folds disturb less air flow than vertical folds. For more information see 'Junior Sailing Illustrated'

Accordian fold

head

ff

clew

rolling-luff to clew

clew

Typical folding sequence for mainsail after battens are removed.

When sail is stuffed into sailbag, the corner you want to come out first...is stored last.

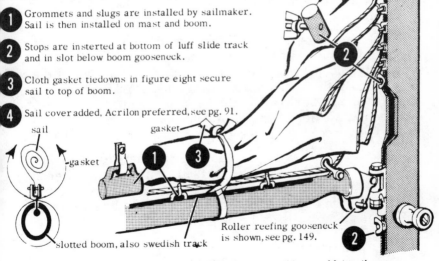

1. Grommets and slugs are installed by sailmaker. Sail is then installed on mast and boom.

2. Stops are insterted at bottom of luff slide track and in slot below boom gooseneck.

3. Cloth gasket tiedowns in figure eight secure sail to top of boom.

4. Sail cover added, Acrilon preferred, see pg. 91.

sail

gasket

gasket

slotted boom, also swedish track

Roller reefing gooseneck is shown, see pg. 149.

Many sailboats over 20' have slotted aluminum masts and booms. Mainsail may be stored on boom when not in use, and luff prevented from falling out onto deck in heavy weather when a reef is applied, page 149, if slugs are installed on luff and foot of sail by sailmaker. Carry spare slugs aboard as they break from time to time needing replacement.

87

Lower centerboard or daggerboard before raising sails, to stabilize boat reducing chance of persons falling overboard.

Sailboat at right is on mooring, pointing into the wind. First sail to be raised is mainsail. For a boat to 15', the head is often secured to main HALYARD, then raised directly from sailbag. Pull foot of sail aft along boom setting OUTHAUL, then pulling boom down with DOWNHAUL.

Other sailors prefer to secure mainsail to boom before raising. Much depends on kind and condition of boat, though this method is usually second choice, as sail has more chance of falling into the bilge and/or being walked on.

On larger boats with mainsail normally stowed on boom, shock cord or gaskets are released, page 86, the head raised with main halyard, then the downhaul hardened and secured. Boom lift or topping lift is released, pages 61 and 97. A word of caution...have the sheet SLACK. Otherwise the mainsail may fill, and the boat start sailing on its own.

Sailmakers should stamp labels on corners of sails, or use coding such as ■ for tack, and ● for head. This helps to identify the part of the sail you are pulling out of the sailbag. If this hasn't been done, add markings to your sail, which otherwise might be raised 'upside down'. Somehow we feel the sailor who has not had this kind of experience, has never taken a boat from the dock.

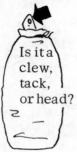

Is it a clew, tack, or head?

Stow sails in REVERSE order to that in which they are raised. If they are lowered directly into the sailbag, areas will be stowed in correct sequence for raising directly from the sailbag the next time out.

If sails are stuffed instead of being folded, extra sailing time should be considered to smoothen out the wrinkles on the surface of your sails before a race.

Sailing Illustrated

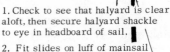

Bending a Main

1. Check to see that halyard is clear aloft, then secure halyard shackle to eye in headboard of sail.

2. Fit slides on luff of mainsail into track on aft side of mast.

3. Add stop at bottom of sail track on mast to secure slides.

4. Run slides out boom.

5. Secure outhaul to clew of sail.

6. Secure tack with pin to gooseneck fitting.

7. Add battens.

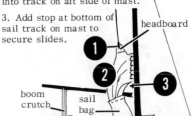

headboard

boom crutch

sail bag

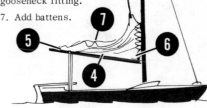

Sequence above may be reversed with mainsail first secured to boom on small open sailboat, yet it provides more tendency for sail to fall into bilge where it may be stained with dirt or water, or walked on by the crew.

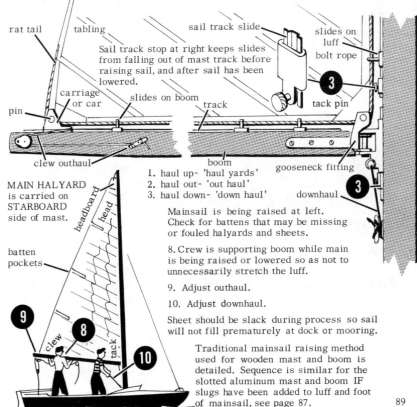

rat tail

tabling

sail track slide

slides on luff

bolt rope

Sail track stop at right keeps slides from falling out of mast track before raising sail, and after sail has been lowered.

carriage or car

slides on boom

track

tack pin

pin

clew outhaul

boom

gooseneck fitting

downhaul

MAIN HALYARD is carried on STARBOARD side of mast.

headboard

head

1. haul up- 'haul yards'
2. haul out- 'out haul'
3. haul down- 'down haul'

Mainsail is being raised at left. Check for battens that may be missing or fouled halyards and sheets.

batten pockets

8. Crew is supporting boom while main is being raised or lowered so as not to unnecessarily stretch the luff.

9. Adjust outhaul.

10. Adjust downhaul.

Sheet should be slack during process so sail will not fill prematurely at dock or mooring.

clew

tack

Traditional mainsail raising method used for wooden mast and boom is detailed. Sequence is similar for the slotted aluminum mast and boom IF slugs have been added to luff and foot of mainsail, see page 87.

89

The flexible aluminum mast used on many classes, is designed to bend to a continuous predetermined arc, pages 114, 117, 119, 121, with the mainsail cut to fit this arc. On classes having the flexible mast, the sequence for raising the mainsail will follow either sequence discussed on the previous page. Some of the classes using a fixed boom position, will have the tack tension set instead of outhaul, see Int'l 14, Finn, Snipe, Star and Tempest details, using this method.

The three basic tension factors covered, plus vang and traveler, pgs. 116-121, are eased or increased depending on course chosen ... and whether the wind strength is diminishing or increasing.

While beating to windward with wind strength increasing, all of these adjustments may be hardened. Tension increase on sail in addition to resulting bend of mast, helps to produce a flatter draft or flatter airfoil contour. If beating to windward and the wind is easing, the tension factors are often eased to increase the draft, or increase the airfoil or depth of the mainsail.

Various boats have been specifically detailed to help you study adjustments currently used ... which will vary considerably from class to class, and to a lesser amount, within the class. Study and practice are required till you have the normal feel and touch of these adjustments .... part of the challenge and fun of sailing.

Similar yet different tension and draft factors result when comparing flexible and rigid booms. Those favoring the flexible boom feel it decreases leach pressure, helping minimize strong wind weather helm, pgs. 116-7, 132-5 . Those in favor of rigid boom feel they can accomplish sufficient similar adjustments with leach line, pgs. 117-8.

At the end of the season, how about leaving your sails with your sailmaker? He will have more time to do a better job checking, repairing, and/or washing your sails than the following spring when he is swamped with rush orders.

Best way to check setting and trim of sails, is to take photos of your boat underway, from another boat.

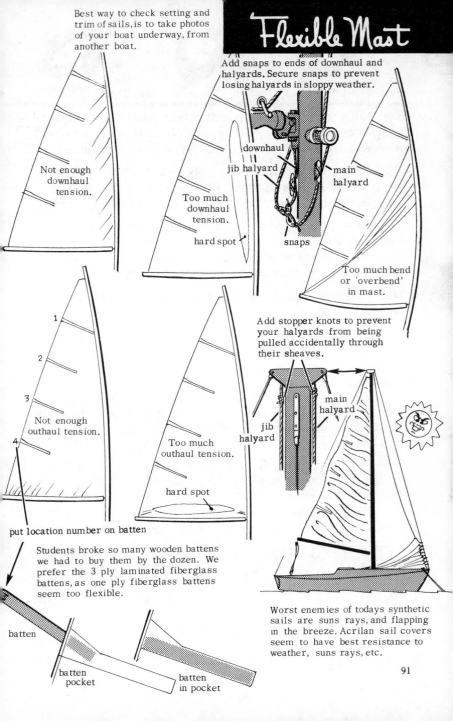

Flexible Mast

Add snaps to ends of downhaul and halyards. Secure snaps to prevent losing halyards in sloppy weather.

downhaul

jib halyard

main halyard

snaps

Not enough downhaul tension.

Too much downhaul tension.

hard spot

Too much bend or 'overbend' in mast.

Add stopper knots to prevent your halyards from being pulled accidentally through their sheaves.

main halyard

jib halyard

Not enough outhaul tension.

Too much outhaul tension.

hard spot

put location number on batten

Students broke so many wooden battens we had to buy them by the dozen. We prefer the 3 ply laminated fiberglass battens, as one ply fiberglass battens seem too flexible.

batten

batten pocket

batten in pocket

Worst enemies of todays synthetic sails are suns rays, and flapping in the breeze. Acrilan sail covers seem to have best resistance to weather, suns rays, etc.

Swedish snap hook   see below*   blackjack–AVOID!

Returning to 15' sailboat pointing into wind, after mainsail is up, bend on (secure) jib to jibstay (small boat), headstay a New York term, or the forestay, a Boston term.

The "Pink Cloud" jib is snapped onto jibstay at dock, page 96, without attaching jib sheet. It is dropped and stuffed into sailbag to keep from filling or falling overboard.

When time comes to raise jib, sailbag is removed and jib halyard raises head rapidly as practical. Jib sheet is then secured to jib clew with Swedish snap hook above instead of bowlines, customary procedure on large sailboats.

When approaching dock upwind in tight quarters, release button is pushed, disengaging jib sheet from clew of jib, preventing sudden fluky wind puff off buildings filling or backing jib at last critical moment when docking.

When dropping jib, we prefer to lower it directly into sailbag, to be raised directly from sailbag the next time it is used. If dropped to deck first then put into sailbag, chances increase for dirt, grease, footprints, etc., to stain jib. Sailmakers disagree with this practice using Dacron material feeling it adds extra wrinkles to sail cloth.

Swedish snap hook above is ideal for 20' to 28' sailboats. *NICRO FICO makes a jib clew fitting for sailboats in four sizes with load capacities from 3000 to 14,000 lbs. AVOID large snap shackle above . . . this author found it a blackjack when testing a new boat in a force 8 storm.

JIB HALYARD TENSION is critical varying in boat size. Jib halyard is set so luff wire tension is tighter than jibstay on most boats under 20'. On sailboats to 35', jibstay, jib halyard, and wire luff tension may be similar. On larger sailboats, major tension is carried on jibstay instead of luff wire and jib halyard.

*Nico Corp., 2065H West Ave. 140th, San Leandro, CA 94577

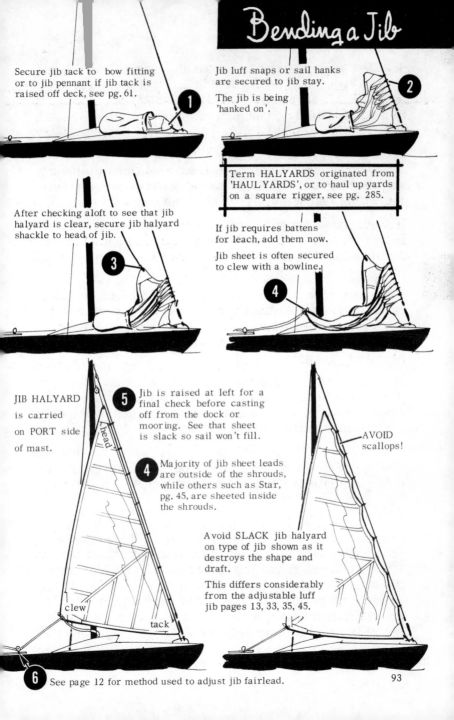

1 Secure jib tack to bow fitting or to jib pennant if jib tack is raised off deck, see pg. 61.

2 Jib luff snaps or sail hanks are secured to jib stay.

The jib is being 'hanked on'.

Term HALYARDS originated from 'HAUL YARDS', or to haul up yards on a square rigger, see pg. 285.

3 After checking aloft to see that jib halyard is clear, secure jib halyard shackle to head of jib.

4 If jib requires battens for leach, add them now.

Jib sheet is often secured to clew with a bowline.

JIB HALYARD is carried on PORT side of mast.

5 Jib is raised at left for a final check before casting off from the dock or mooring. See that sheet is slack so sail won't fill.

4 Majority of jib sheet leads are outside of the shrouds, while others such as Star, pg. 45, are sheeted inside the shrouds.

AVOID scallops!

Avoid SLACK jib halyard on type of jib shown as it destroys the shape and draft.

This differs considerably from the adjustable luff jib pages 13, 33, 35, 45.

head

clew

tack

6 See page 12 for method used to adjust jib fairlead.

93

Suppose sailboat has centerboard or daggerboard down, rudder secured & sails raised. The next step may seem to be to cast off and start sailing. A note of caution at this point should be considered however.

Have you checked the sails to see if they are set properly; are the halyards stowed neatly yet ready for instant use; and have you checked the weather conditions. Following are some of our favorite stories about sailors in a hurry... forgetting that important last moment check.

We were just ready to cast off from a mooring at Staten Island when a storm hit. We had been so intent on raising sails that we overlooked the advancing storm.

Then we have the matter of a meticulous west coast sailor. He thought he had taken care of every detail... as he cast off from the dock to start an important three day race. It wasn't until twenty minutes later that a crew member realized the owners' wife, a very good cook, had been left at the dock.

A crew member pulled the wrong halyard and raised the jib in a crowded mooring area. The sail filled, & the bow swung to a broad reach before the boat finally responded to the tiller... after narrowly missing a new 50' cruiser.

The owner of a large boat decided to sail from the dock with a large group of guests aboard. Everything went nicely... until he found the hard way that a stern line was still secured to the dock.

Just before race time a Star skipper realized his regular crew member hadn't been notified of the race, so his friend who was head of the race committee volunteered. Since time was short, his new crew hurriedly raised the mainsail upside down. The sail filled and the boat sailed into the breaker line. After standing upright for two full minutes it finally toppled over... in full view of his race committee colleagues.

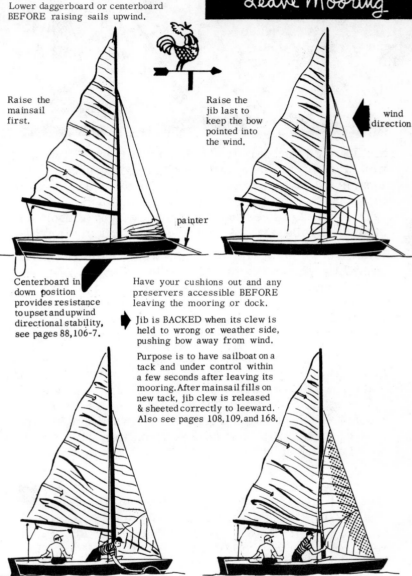

Lower daggerboard or centerboard BEFORE raising sails upwind.

Raise the mainsail first.

Raise the jib last to keep the bow pointed into the wind.

wind direction

painter

Centerboard in down position provides resistance to upset and upwind directional stability, see pages 88,106-7.

Have your cushions out and any preservers accessible BEFORE leaving the mooring or dock.

Jib is BACKED when its clew is held to wrong or weather side, pushing bow away from wind.

Purpose is to have sailboat on a tack and under control within a few seconds after leaving its mooring. After mainsail fills on new tack, jib clew is released & sheeted correctly to leeward. Also see pages 108,109, and 168.

Is your paddle ready if the wind suddenly stops? When your course is clear have crew cast off painter, then BACKWIND JIB shown at right for a quick controlled start.

ROYCE

Put rudder hard over to make use of sternway. When sailboat falls onto tack crew will sheet in jib on correct side. Give rigging, halyards a final check. 95

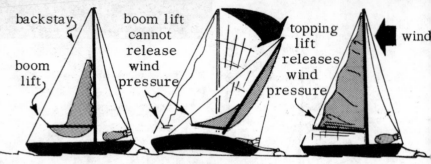

backstay

boom lift
cannot
release
wind
pressure

boom
lift

topping
lift
releases
wind
pressure

wind

Sailboats 22' and larger should have a boom lift to hold weight of boom when sails are not being used, and a topping lift or temporary line from outer end of boom to top of mast. Topping lift carries weight of boom while sails are being raised and lowered, as weight of boom will stretch sail material, damaging sails airfoil; also pg. 149.

In a light breeze with bow into wind, mainsail may be raised with boom lift carrying weight of boom. After sail is up, boom lift is released. Use of boom lift is dangerous in strong or puffy wind as sail may fill before lift is released...causing a serious knockdown at the dock or mooring, and an embarrassing situation.

If weight of boom is supported by a topping lift instead, boom is able to swing to either side of boat releasing sudden wind pressures. After sail is up, topping lift is released, and downhaul hardened. On boats under 30', topping-lift boom-attach may be released and secured next to shrouds. Jib is usually secured to jibstay and put back into bag beforehand, pg. 92, ready for raising.

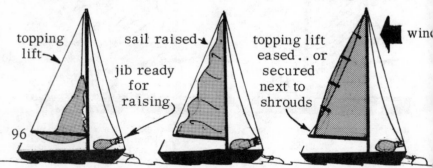

topping
lift

sail raised

jib ready
for
raising

topping lift
eased .. or
secured
next to
shrouds

wind

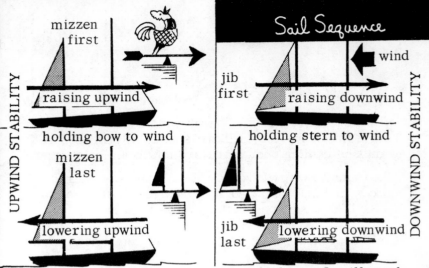

(Figure labels, clockwise): UPWIND STABILITY — mizzen first — raising upwind — holding bow to wind — mizzen last — lowering upwind — Sail Sequence — wind — jib first — raising downwind — holding stern to wind — jib last — lowering downwind — DOWNWIND STABILITY

Watch a wind indicator on a nearby home. It will catch an object on the aft side of the arrow, causing the other end to pivot and point directly into the wind.

An identical situation occurs when raising and lowering sails. You want to weathercock the boat so it will have RESISTANCE to TURNING or directional stability while sails are being raised...and lowered. If above process is reversed, directional stability is lost. The boat out of control and out of balance may change course abruptly.

The BOW is weathercocked into wind with AFTERMOST sail raised first, the main second and jib last. Sequence is reversed for lowering with the aftermost sail the last to come down, also weathercocking the bow into the wind.

The sails may be raised DOWNWIND in light winds with the JIB first, the main second, and mizzen third, weathercocking STERN so the boat maintains downwind course.

The sequence is reversed for lowering with the JIB the last sail to come down, weathercocking STERN to the wind. This is seldom practiced except in light airs as slides stick and bind, the halyards get tangled, and sails may catch in spreaders breaking battens and ripping batten pockets.

97

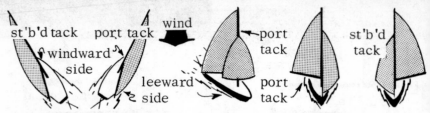

st'b'd tack   port tack   wind   port tack   st'b'd tack

windward side

leeward side   port tack   port tack

Sailboat is on PORT TACK with wind coming over port bow, beam, or quarter. Sailboat is on STARBOARD TACK with wind coming over starboard bow, beam, or quarter.

When running with wind dead aft, sailboat is on starboard tack with BOOM carried to port...as boat is on tack OPPOSITE to side on which main boom is carried.

Course of sailboat is determined by angle at which it is sailing into, or away from the wind. We have included many course terms no longer used in todays' sailing but still found in square rigger movies. For todays' sailing we suggest the following terms:

- CLOSEHAULED (beating is preferred for racing)
- RUNNING (before the wind with sails wing and wing)
- REACHING (all courses between closehauled and running)

Man was able to sail up to a beam reach with his square sails for many centuries. Pointing, or ability to sail closer to eye of wind, slowly improved till square rigger could point about 20° higher, or 70° away from eye of wind if it had a clean bottom; 90° to 120°, with a fouled bottom.

Todays' cruising sailboats may point to within 50-54° of the winds eye, while many well designed fore and afters can steadily maintain a 45° course from eye of wind. Racing machines such as Int'l 110 and meter boats may point to within 30-35° from eye of the wind.

If fore and afters or square riggers point higher than these limits enforced by nature, the sails then become air BRAKES instead of providing propulsion. When sails hit this barrier they lift...their flexible airfoil breaks, with the wind pressure now hitting BOTH sides of sail, called luffing. Boat stops, goes into irons, then begins to drift backward.

Sailing Illustrated

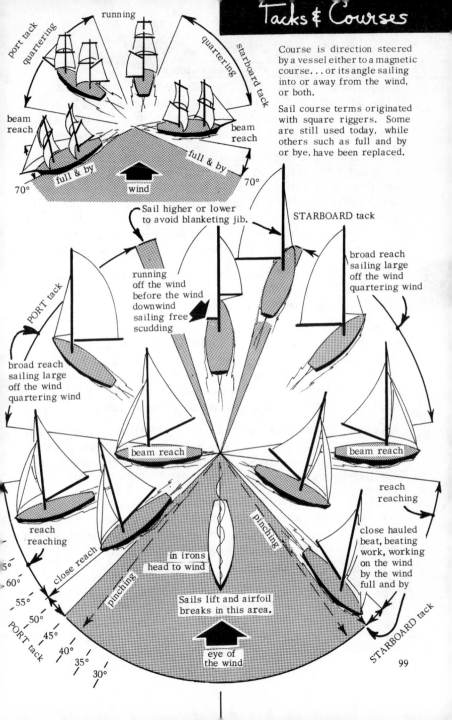

Tacks & Courses

Course is direction steered by a vessel either to a magnetic course... or its angle sailing into or away from the wind, or both.

Sail course terms originated with square riggers. Some are still used today, while others such as full and by or bye, have been replaced.

running

port tack quartering

quartering

starboard tack

beam reach

beam reach

full & by

full & by

70°

70°

wind

Sail higher or lower to avoid blanketing jib.

STARBOARD tack

broad reach sailing large off the wind quartering wind

PORT tack

running off the wind before the wind downwind sailing free scudding

broad reach sailing large off the wind quartering wind

beam reach

beam reach

reach reaching

reach reaching

close reach

pinching

in irons head to wind

pinching

close hauled beat, beating work, working on the wind by the wind full and by

5°

60°

55°

50°

Sails lift and airfoil breaks in this area.

PORT tack

45°

40°

35°

30°

eye of the wind

STARBOARD tack

99

sailboat is HEELING,
   not keeling

Wind direction is of vital importance to sailboat operation. First factor to study is stationary TRUE wind indicators on shore which are flags, movement of trees, bushes, and grass, as well as smoke coming from chimneys.

Second factor is APPARENT wind direction found on your sailboat underway. For daytime, yellow/orange threads, or ribbons, and especially in light weather, feathers, are most effective for shrouds showing direction & strength of wind entering sails...especially in any kind of wave action. In smooth water the masthead telltale is effective but may produce a stiff neck if watching it constantly.

Night sailing finds white shroud telltales easier to see. Masthead telltale may be illuminated by turning on the masthead light directly beneath it.

A modern sailboat advances or works its way to windward on a closehauled course about 45° away from eye of wind. The sailboat changes wind to the other side of boat or changes tack by coming about, while advancing to windward. If the sailboat points above closehauled, the boom lifts, the vertical airfoil breaks, and sailboat slows to a stop.

As wind increases on upwind course, a sailboat heels which is a natural pressure-release valve. As angle increases you "hike" to the high side to reduce pressure being spilled from sails.

Square rigger sailing followed tradewind ocean currents for centuries maintaining tacks for long periods with the wind aft to abeam. The wearing method shown at right was used to change tack under most conditions.

"Tacking Ship" by changing the wind over the bow was only used in ideal conditions as all sails are caught back momentarily.... causing dismastings, and knockdowns in heavy weather, a probable cause for the disappearance of many square riggers.

caught aback

Sailing   Illustrated

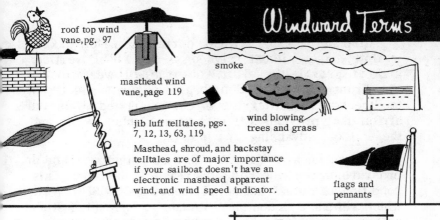

roof top wind vane, pg. 97

masthead wind vane, page 119

jib luff telltales, pgs. 7, 12, 13, 63, 119

smoke

wind blowing trees and grass

Masthead, shroud, and backstay telltales are of major importance if your sailboat doesn't have an electronic masthead apparent wind, and wind speed indicator.

flags and pennants

Square riggers were ideally designed to sail the tradewind/ocean current patterns around the world with the wind aft to abeam.

After square riggers began to close with the land they faced land breezes, pg. 211, often having to sail to windward to reach port sailing full and by about 70° from the apparent wind.

When it came time to change to the other tack they often had to change the tack by changing the wind over the stern of the vessel, called wearing, or to wear ship. The wearing procedure was also used on traditional lateeners, page 277.

Over 50% of today's sailing for pleasure is closehauled, hard on the wind, beating, or working to windward.

The remaining 25% of the time is spent reaching...with 25% running downwind or on a broad reach.

wind direction

sailing upwind, closehauled, or beating

closehauled at 70° to the wind, sailing full and by (or bye)

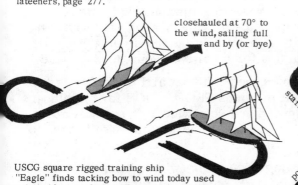

port tack

coming about

short leg or short board

starboard tack

coming about

port tack

coming about (tacking is the commonly used racing term)

USCG square rigged training ship "Eagle" finds tacking bow to wind today used only in ideal conditions. Wearing above must still be used in light winds...and in strong winds with heavy seas where it is dangerous and even impossible to back the square sails to change the wind over the bow of the vessel, see "Eagle Seamanship", pg. 286.

1819 traditional "Waring" methods are covered in Lever's".. Sheet Anchor", see page 184.

long tack or long board

starboard tack

101

The airplane relys on a RIGID horizontal airfoil to keep it aloft... the sailboat relys on a FLEXIBLE vertical airfoil to provide upwind lift. While engine power provides air thrust for one, wind fuel provides lift and thrust for the sailboat. After the thrust is applied, it is the airfoil that provides LIFT to keep airplane aloft, and the sailboat advancing to windward.

The lift of an airfoil is developed from an increase in pressure on one side, and a decrease on the other. This condition is often inadequately described as SUCTION, which refers to a complete vacuum... instead of slight but adequate differences in pressure.

Between these two extremes are the high speed ice boat airfoil, and at a lower speed, the sailing catamaran. Due to greater surface speeds than sailboat, the full batten sails develop a SHALLOW semi-rigid airfoil for upwind sailing. (A May '68 Yachting article pg. 49, on full batten sail seems to indicate that they have many unexplored potentials for all kinds of sailing craft.)

Note how much greater a curve exists in LOW SPEED AIRFOIL of monohull sailing upwind. While the entire sail area is required, it is the shaded area having the maximum curvature providing the maximum upwind airfoil lift or propulsion for a sailboat going to windward.

The FLEXIBLE low speed sailboat airfoil performs two major functions. It provides PROPULSION for a sailboat underway both upwind and downwind. For sailboat about to stop at dock or mooring, the airfoils are broken to provide an AIR BRAKE to bring sailboat to a stop, 168-9.

A FLAT rigid wing without lift (without airfoil).. would cause a vertical STALL on most aircraft. A sailboat trying to use a flat rigid sail above a broad reach will experience a parallel condition, a horizontal STALL. For downwind sailing it will be second best to the flexible sail retarded by rolling action of boat, causing unstable flow or air disturbance surging back and forth across flat surface and around its edges.

Windward Theory

● LIFT FORCE
AIRPLANE WING
rigid horizontal airfoil

decreased pressure

increased pressure

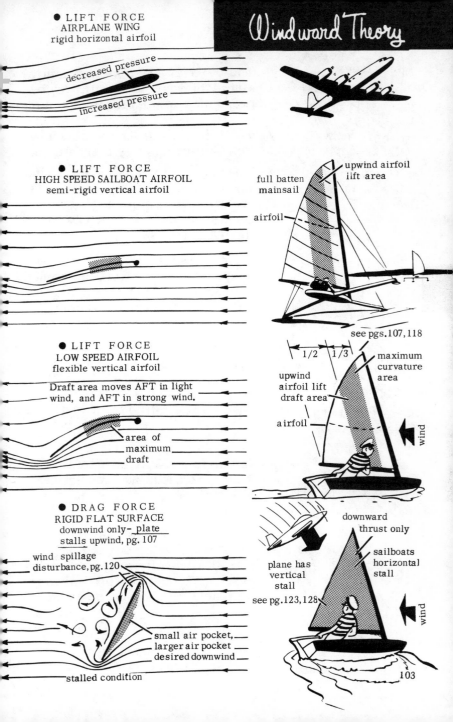

● LIFT FORCE
HIGH SPEED SAILBOAT AIRFOIL
semi-rigid vertical airfoil

full batten
mainsail

airfoil

upwind airfoil
lift area

see pgs.107, 118

● LIFT FORCE
LOW SPEED AIRFOIL
flexible vertical airfoil

Draft area moves AFT in light
wind, and AFT in strong wind.

area of
maximum
draft

1/2   1/3

upwind
airfoil lift
draft area

airfoil

maximum
curvature
area

wind

● DRAG FORCE
RIGID FLAT SURFACE
downwind only- plate
stalls upwind, pg. 107

wind spillage
disturbance, pg.120

small air pocket,
larger air pocket
desired downwind

stalled condition

plane has
vertical
stall
see pg.123, 128

downward
thrust only

sailboats
horizontal
stall

wind

103

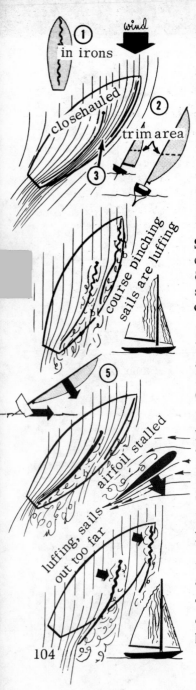

1 in irons
wind

2 closehauled
trim area
3

course pinching sails are luffing

5

airfoil stalled

luffing, sails out too far

The flexible, sensitive and natural airfoil of your sails will provide propulsion or airbrakes. Example of latter is sailboat head to wind or IN IRONS, with laminar airflow past sails completely broken down.

When sailboat points close to wind as efficiency permits, and sails are trimmed as close as efficiency permits, vessel is on a CLOSE—HAULED course.

Slight course deviation is req'd to compensate for variables in strength & direction of wind. Due to sag of sail material, boom is trimmed closer on larger sailboat, see (2).

If sailboat points too high it is PINCHING. The boat slows down as drive area (forward half, pg. 9) is broken, becoming an air brake (also see sail telltale pgs. 12, 119).

If sailboat is on closehauled course yet sails are trimmed in too far, airfoil is in STALLED condition. Result is obvious by excessive heel & leeway (a condition similar to STALL angle of airplane wing).

If sailboat is on closehauled course yet sails slacked out too far, a LUFFING condition results helping to reduce a vessels speed when it approaches a dock or mooring.

Try operating just above a LUFF condition so maximum drive results producing minimum heel & leeway.

Sailing Illustrated

close hauled

wind funnel

All factors equal, a sloop has an advantage over catboat due to WIND FUNNEL or slot effect of wind flow past leeward side of main. As a result correct setting of a genoa jib is most important to avoid destroying the luff or drive area of main. Situation on ketch is increased as jib may backwind main, & main backwind the mizzen.

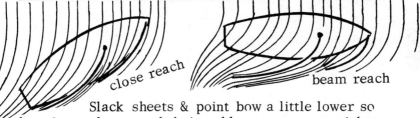

close reach

beam reach

Slack sheets & point bow a little lower so boat is on close reach, being able to steer a straighter course. From that & down to beam reach, sheets have to be let out to maintain maximum airfoil efficiency. If not slacked far enough, stall condition will result.

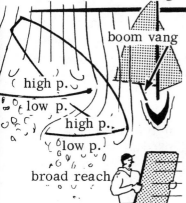

boom vang

high p.

low p.

high p.

low p.

broad reach

The boom vang, pg. 120, should be hardened to flatten mainsail by preventing boom from lifting when sailing downwind, and also sometimes when sailing as high as a close reach.

If vang isn't used, the boom will lift with mainsail developing into shape of a wind funnel, releasing useful wind pressure.

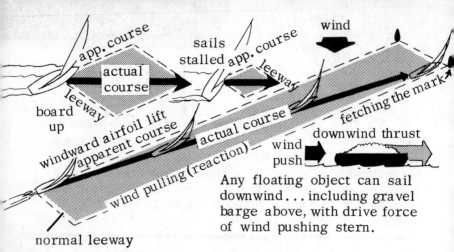

board up

normal leeway

sails stalled

wind

fetching the mark

windward airfoil lift

apparent course

wind pulling (reaction)

actual course

leeway

app. course

actual course

downwind thrust

wind push

Any floating object can sail downwind... including gravel barge above, with drive force of wind pushing stern.

- DOWNWIND THRUST. Anything with buoyancy can float downwind. Sails should be at right angles to apparent wind (felt on the boat underway) with a slight cup to reduce air surge back and forth across sail area, pg. 120.

  This world of sailing is noticeable in smooth water with a well balanced keel hull. Boat can operate through this range without sails up due to wind pressure on hull, mast, etc. Slightly below beam reach a barrier is reached in which hull stalls out, falls back to run to regain speed.

- UPWIND AIRFOIL LIFT. To sail higher to windward the sails become a major factor to provide upwind lift, with an opposing force of sideways drift compensated by hull shape, centerboards, etc.

  The higher a boat sails to windward, the greater becomes the increase in sideways force, with decrease in forward drive forces.

- AIR BRAKES. Sails at minimum angle to wind underway stall out with remaining forces producing leeway as forward drive is eliminated, hull also stalls out. Point a little higher and the sails lift, and airfoils break.... providing an air brake to stop your boat, 98, 102, 168-9.

  Designers are continually experimenting with methods to sail efficiently at a higher angle to windward without
106 losing speed. Closehauled sailing is a continuous challenge.

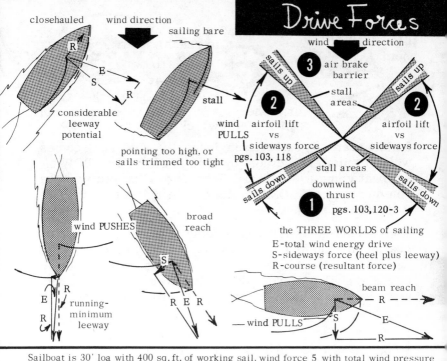

closehauled wind direction
sailing bare

Drive Forces

wind ⬛ direction

considerable leeway potential

pointing too high, or sails trimmed too tight

3 air brake barrier

stall areas

2 airfoil lift vs sideways force
pgs. 103, 118

2 airfoil lift vs sideways force

stall areas

1 downwind thrust
pgs. 103, 120-3

wind PUSHES

broad reach

running-minimum leeway

the THREE WORLDS of sailing
E - total wind energy drive
S - sideways force (heel plus leeway)
R - course (resultant force)

beam reach

wind PULLS

Sailboat is 30' loa with 400 sq. ft. of working sail, wind force 5 with total wind pressure available of from 384 to 560 lbs. (approximately .96-1.4 lbs pressure per sq. ft., pg. 137).

Wind pressure above is INCREASED by upwind AIRFOIL LIFT. The sails push the mast, pulling stays, shrouds, and sheets forward to propel the boat.

On the minus side are the sideways force factors of heel and leeway, parasitic drag of underbody, wave trap-pg. 141, also drag factors of mast, stays, shrouds, plus hull and cabin exposed to wind not providing airfoil lift.

SAFETY FACTOR. In sudden wind puff boat has heeling safety valve action to help spill extra wind pressure from sails.

Wind pressure is LESS since speed of boat away from wind must be subtracted.

TOTAL AREA of boat above waterline including sails, mast, shrouds, stays, hull, cabin, people in cockpit, which wind can push against, provides DOWNWIND THRUST for sailboat below, see pg. 120.

Minus factors are parasitic drag of hull, bow and stern wave trap.

Most DISMASTINGS occur sailing downwind as boat doesn't have normal method to spill excessive wind pressure which demands more awareness of crew.

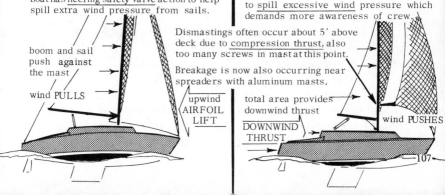

boom and sail push against the mast

wind PULLS

upwind AIRFOIL LIFT

Dismastings often occur about 5' above deck due to compression thrust, also too many screws in mast at this point.

Breakage is now also occurring near spreaders with aluminum masts.

total area provides downwind thrust

DOWNWIND THRUST

wind PUSHES

—107—

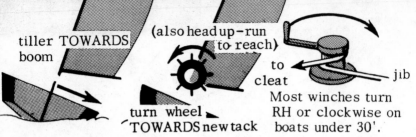

tiller TOWARDS boom

(also head up – run to reach)

to cleat

jib

turn wheel TOWARDS new tack

Most winches turn RH or clockwise on boats under 30'.

Sailboat can only sail at an angle into the wind. Time comes when it must change tack by changing wind over BOW of sailboat going to windward. Procedure required is more commonly called COMING ABOUT, though in racing rules it is defined as tacking.

Page 104 defines wind as providing propulsion . . . or if the boat points too high, it becomes an air brake or wall. Sailboat must change course from one tack to other, by swinging bow across dead wind area, and falling onto new closehauled tack, till sails are full and pulling.

Variables are considerable in timing required for sailing craft to come about, due to wind strength, wave action, weight of boat, beam and underbody shape.

Traditional long, narrow HEAVY DISPLACEMENT craft normally has considerable inertia, permitting it to easily coast through eye of wind from one tack to other. On larger craft such as meter boats having large gennies difficult to winch in after sail is pulling, the sheet is often released and taken in on new side, BEFORE gennie fills.

Newer WIDE beam LIGHT DISPLACEMENT sail craft commonly found today in centerboard or the short keel weekenders, normally have minimum drive or inertia to take them through and past the dead wind area.

Light-displacement short-keel craft should change tack rapidly. AFTER mainsail fills on new tack, THEN release jib sheet and rapidly sheet it in for new tack . . . called "backing the jib". This method keeps sailboat under control while maneuvering in tight docking and mooring areas. We've taught on long keel motor sailers up to 50', also requiring jib to be backed continually when coming about 108 while sailing in a harbor or on the ocean.

Coming About is method used to change wind's direction over bow of a sailboat going to windward.

Command "Ready About" 1., is given to alert crew and passengers. Depending on size of craft, jib may or may not be uncleated and hand held. Helmsman 2., gives command "Helms Alee" moment he turns craft by pushing tiller TOWARDS boom.

After boat is slightly past eye of wind, the wind 3., starts to fill jib on wrong side, pulling bow over to new tack. Command "Cut" 4., or "Over", is given moment the boom swings to other side of boat, indicating craft is on new tack with main filling. Helmsman at the same time pushes tiller amidship 5., and jib sheet 6., is rapidly released and cleated at 7., for new tack.

Note: MAIN SHEET on monohull should automatically tend or adjust itself when changing from one closehauled tack to other when coming about. It is standard procedure on most multihulls to back jib and SLACK main sheet while coming about. Both sails are sheeted to new side after changing tack.

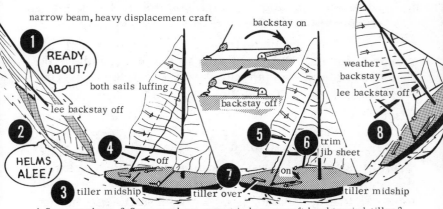

1. Same as above. 2. Same as above, except in larger craft head to wind, tiller 3., is pulled to midship position. Old backstay 4., is slacked, and new backstay 5., is taken in. Jib sheet especially with gennie on larger craft 6., is released, taken in, then cleated for new tack BEFORE jib can fill. Tiller is pushed over again 7., so bow will fall off from eye of wind, and sails fill on new tack, with tiller again in midship position 8.

(also bear off—
reach to run)

CRACK

| Will boom clear backstay? | Tiller AWAY from boom. | Wheel turns TOWARD boom or new tack. |

Jibing is method used to change wind direction over STERN of fore and aft rigged vessel, changing from one downwind tack to the other. Three types of jibing are controlled jibe, the flying or North River Jibe, and the accidental jibe to be avoided.

Controlled jibe is standard for down wind use in light to medium winds. In light airs boom may be pulled amidship, and pushed to other side as main fills. In stronger winds with rolling sea, main sheet may be temporarily snubbed around cleat to take punch out of boom swinging to end of its arc, on new tack.

Flying jibe is standard racing procedure when turning marks, and often used in afternoon sailing. In strong wind the rapid course change helps absorb punch of swinging boom, eliminating damage that otherwise might result. Flying jibe was developed to high state of perfection in upper reaches of the Hudson & North River, see pg. 274.

In strong or puffy winds it may be more practical to change from one downwind tack to the other, with wind changed over the bow instead. We have adapted the term "Chicken Jibe" to describe this maneuver.

In tight channel with strong wind, with insufficient room to wear, and jibing isn't practical, drop head of mainsail to avoid damaging uncontrolled accidental jibe.

Personal experience with endless students prompted us to use command, "Jibe-O –DUCK", which we feel is more practical than command "Jibe-O." With sufficient practice jibing becomes as normal a method to change from one tack to the other, as coming about. The accidental jibe is discussed on page 122.

Sailing Illustrated

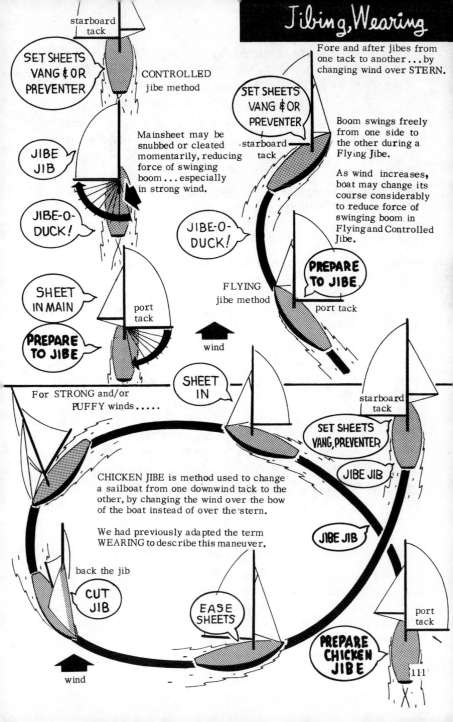

Wind power is transmitted to the hull from the sails, mast, and sheets, providing sailboat propulsion. If the sails, mast, and rigging try to go faster than the hull, the result is a dismasting.

• If your one-design sailboat has a flexible mast, obtain rigging standards from the class secretary, then compare these tension standards with the shroud and stay tension of the reigning fleet champion.

• Tall IOR rigs, pg. 80, are under considerable pressure at all times. Hydraulic backstay pressure, pg. 78, is increased when beating to reduce the jibstay from sagging. This tall rig should be set up by professionals.

Many 20' to 30' masthead and fractional rigs with rigid masts have similar rigging patterns. The common mistake is to set up the stays and shrouds way too tight, trying to force the mast step through the cabin top or out through the keel, or to pull up the chain plates, which also reduces hull speed in medium aspect ratio rigs.

The opposite extreme is a rig too slack with the mast bouncing up and down in a sloppy sea like a pile driver.

The tension compromise you are looking for is between these extremes. We recommend sufficient tension to keep the mast in position with any additional tension usually unnecessary, except to reduce jibstay sag when beating.

Many boats under 30' have been built with single lower shrouds causing a mast pumping action in rough water which may contribute to a dismasting. If they are changed to double lower shrouds, pg. 63, it provides better support with less potential equipment damage if you are caught out in a blow as most mast pumping action is eliminated.

Shroud rollers should roll with the jib when changing tack, pg. 65. Avoid snug or tight rollers into which hygroscopic salt crystals may collect, coupled with blocked air flow producing oxygen starvation, which can contribute to stainless steel intergranular corrosion failure indicated by broken strands.

Sailing Illustrated

Rigging Tension

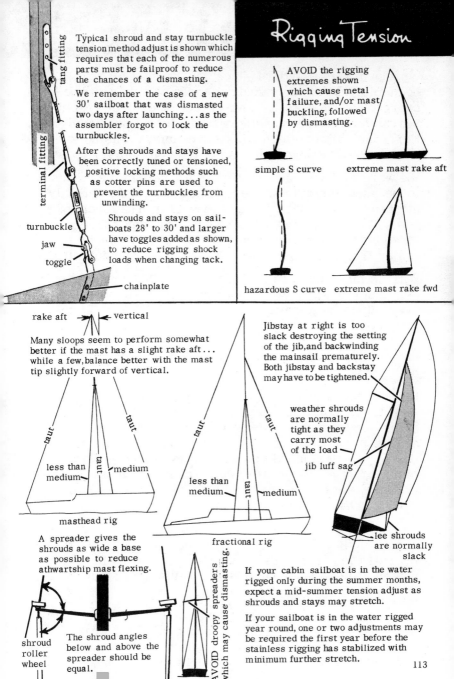

Typical shroud and stay turnbuckle tension method adjust is shown which requires that each of the numerous parts must be failproof to reduce the chances of a dismasting.

We remember the case of a new 30' sailboat that was dismasted two days after launching...as the assembler forgot to lock the turnbuckles.

After the shrouds and stays have been correctly tuned or tensioned, positive locking methods such as cotter pins are used to prevent the turnbuckles from unwinding.

Shrouds and stays on sailboats 28' to 30' and larger have toggles added as shown, to reduce rigging shock loads when changing tack.

tang fitting

terminal fitting

turnbuckle

jaw

toggle

chainplate

AVOID the rigging extremes shown which cause metal failure, and/or mast buckling, followed by dismasting.

simple S curve

extreme mast rake aft

hazardous S curve

extreme mast rake fwd

rake aft → ← vertical

Many sloops seem to perform somewhat better if the mast has a slight rake aft... while a few, balance better with the mast tip slightly forward of vertical.

taut

taut

less than medium

taut

medium

masthead rig

taut

taut

less than medium

taut

medium

fractional rig

A spreader gives the shrouds as wide a base as possible to reduce athwartship mast flexing.

shroud roller wheel

The shroud angles below and above the spreader should be equal.

AVOID droopy spreaders which may cause dismasting.

Jibstay at right is too slack destroying the setting of the jib, and backwinding the mainsail prematurely. Both jibstay and backstay may have to be tightened.

weather shrouds are normally tight as they carry most of the load

jib luff sag

lee shrouds are normally slack

If your cabin sailboat is in the water rigged only during the summer months, expect a mid-summer tension adjust as shrouds and stays may stretch.

If your sailboat is in the water rigged year round, one or two adjustments may be required the first year before the stainless rigging has stabilized with minimum further stretch.

113

Wooden masts, standard since the dawn of history, are becoming increasingly scarce, especially those made from evergreens such as fir and spruce, due to the publics yearly demand for Christmas trees. It was predicted by Herreshoff before the turn of the century...as he tried his best to discourage the use of trees for this purpose.

We were told Vikings grew trees for several centuries to be used for masts. They planted a tree, then shortly afterwards, a circle of trees around it. The circle of trees acted as a wind break to help the center tree grow straighter, also reducing number of lower limbs as the center tree tried to outgrow the trees surrounding it.

What is most interesting, was to find that until the new aluminum mast, no two wooden masts in history were ever supposed to be identical. Advantages of the aluminum mast common today, are standardization which produced predictability...with controlled flexibility. John Powell of Sparlight Ltd., was the aluminum mast pioneer in large boats, Ian Proctor, the leader in one-design classes.

It was interesting to watch the change in the Snipe class when the Proctor aluminum mast was first tested against Snipe wooden masts. When a puff moved in, the boat with a wooden mast heeled first, then started moving, while those with flexible aluminum masts heeled less, adding more effort to accelerating forward speed. In a stronger wind the slot opened more with the flexible mast, which reduced chance of jib backwinding mainsail.

While both advantages in the aluminum Snipe mast may seem small, a flexible aluminum mast provided the edge, the extra few feet at the finish line separating boats that placed...and those which also raced.

Major cause for dismasting a couple of feet above the deck is the same for both kinds of masts...too many screws and fittings in that area, providing a weak spot in the mast. Internal halyard pulleys should be staggered 114 vertically to reduce a weak spot in this area of the mast.

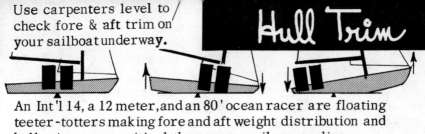

Use carpenters level to check fore & aft trim on your sailboat underway.

Hull Trim

An Int'l 14, a 12 meter, and an 80' ocean racer are floating teeter-totters making fore and aft weight distribution and hull trim more critical than many sailors realize.

Boat should be kept on its fore and aft lines on beat, reach, and run, to present minimal frontal area with minimum hull resistance, going through the water. If stern or bow is down, frontal area increases reducing speed, producing erratic steering action sometimes due to changing bow entry. Check fore & aft trim underway with carpenters level.

Have hull weight trim distribution near center of boat while beating. We trimmed sails on a 25 year old 40' ketch for self steering. A half hour later its 125 lb. owner walked a few feet forward bringing bow down, and pulling bow up into the wind. If he'd walked aft, the bow would raise slightly, and swung further away from the eye of the wind causing lee helm.

Sailing downwind with spinnaker, pg.123, move weight aft to counteract bows downward thrust as wind increases, also to keep bow from digging in on smaller craft. If boat has up/down movement downwind, it may be reduced or dampened by moving weight apart.

Best athwartship trim while beating is _7° to 15° heel_ .... check with inclinometer, & neutral helm. Weight may be shifted slightly to leeward in weak breeze, and moved to windward in strong breeze to maintain the same ideal heel angle. If monohulls heel more, the lee bow wave pressure increases, page 133, increasing weather helm drag which should be kept to minimum for best hull trim weight distribution.

HULL trim vs SAIL trim vs HEEL trim=performance (balance)

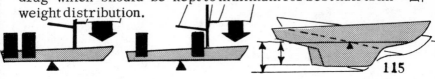

115

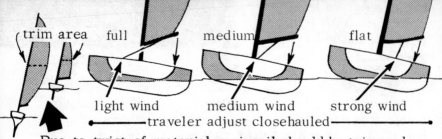

trim area full   medium   flat

light wind   medium wind   strong wind

•————————traveler adjust closehauled————————•

Due to twist of material, mainsail should be trimmed half way up sail. 12 meter boom closehauled as result is almost amidship, while dink carries boom over quarter.

Start with reference point on transom to trim boom. In light wind traveler car may be carried upwind increasing airfoil, and to leeward in strong wind flattening mainsail and reducing heel. Downpull of boom by vang may also be used to minimize twist of sail with large roach.

Traveler is normally eased to leeward for reach through run. Tension is increased on vang to reduce sail twist, with depth maintained by easing outhaul and downhaul.

Flexible rig with mid-boom sheet attach, provides built in draft variables. The flexing can provide fuller draft for light winds and rougher water, or flatten main trim for stronger winds and smoother water ... with variables between for a wide range of wind and wave conditions. Shallow draft gennie (pg. 13), excels for closehauled, while the fuller-cut reaching jib is more efficient for a reach.

Masthead rig with end boom attach, uses traveler and vang shown right, to adjust main for varied conditions. Draft can be flattened by using zipper or reef points on foot of sail, and by easing leach line (roach line) pg. 118.

40' sloop "Dolphin" uses loosefooted main for racing. Wide variety of draft conditions are possible using outhaul, and topping lift. This main is restricted to an afternoon race as rules permit only one mainsail for a long distance race.

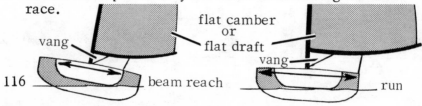

vang   flat camber
                   or
                flat draft
                        vang

116 ———————— beam reach   run

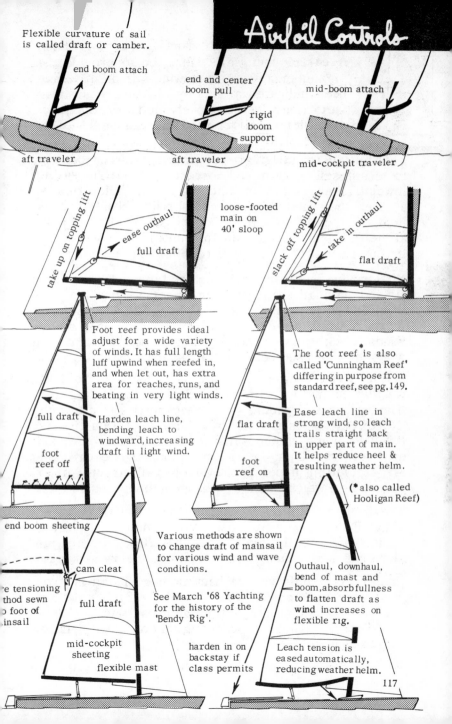

Flexible curvature of sail is called draft or camber.

end boom attach

end and center boom pull

rigid boom support

mid-boom attach

aft traveler

aft traveler

mid-cockpit traveler

take up on topping lift

ease outhaul

full draft

loose-footed main on 40' sloop

slack off topping lift

take in outhaul

flat draft

Foot reef provides ideal adjust for a wide variety of winds. It has full length luff upwind when reefed in, and when let out, has extra area for reaches, runs, and beating in very light winds.

full draft

Harden leach line, bending leach to windward, increasing draft in light wind.

foot reef off

The foot reef is also called 'Cunningham Reef' differing in purpose from standard reef, see pg.149.

flat draft

Ease leach line in strong wind, so leach trails straight back in upper part of main. It helps reduce heel & resulting weather helm.

flat draft

foot reef on

(* also called Hooligan Reef)

end boom sheeting

cam cleat

re tensioning
thod sewn
o foot of
insail

full draft

mid-cockpit sheeting

flexible mast

Various methods are shown to change draft of mainsail for various wind and wave conditions.

See March '68 Yachting for the history of the 'Bendy Rig'.

harden in on backstay if class permits

Outhaul, downhaul, bend of mast and boom, absorb fullness to flatten draft as wind increases on flexible rig.

Leach tension is eased automatically, reducing weather helm.

117

Draft is further aft in light winds and strong winds. Areas of your sails supposed to provide the maximum amount of upwind airfoil lift have been indicated at left by shaded areas. Major factors involved in closehauled upwind sailing are efficient sail trim and hull balance, 115, 133.

trim jib first ●

Yarn telltales on jib luff are very important when beating, to tell if sail is trimmed correctly, if boat is sailing lower than necessary, or pinching. Sailing below this on a reach, the speed indicator and shroud telltale become primary factors to watch. For broad reach to run, the aft telltale and speed indicator should be checked. . . . if you are to obtain best sail trim for maximum speed.

Numerous adjustments are required to produce the best jib and mainsail shape and trim under a wide variety of wind and wave conditions. In light winds they help to increase draft of the mainsail, or to flatten it in strong winds...with a wide variety of sail settings and trim which may be used between the two extremes.

Major consideration as wind increases, is to keep weather helm to a minimum. To accomplish this, the "Daring" uses a saddle to move centerboard aft, while "North Star"pulls the jib stay forward. Leach line is found on some racing sails to cup the leach, increasing draft for light winds. In stronger winds the leach line is slacked, letting upper part of main trail directly aft to reduce heel which causes weather helm, pages 132-135.

The Barber Hauler was invented by the Barber twins of San Diego. It was first used on Lightnings to open wind funnel between sails, for best laminar flow on reach, just above point at which boat was able to carry spinnaker.

Hauler also helps reduce backwinding of main in strong wind. Star has considerable use of the Barber Hauler, to control and adjust the jib trim and resulting wind flow between sails, which is considerably different between light and heavy winds, see page 34.

118   Sailing   Illustrated

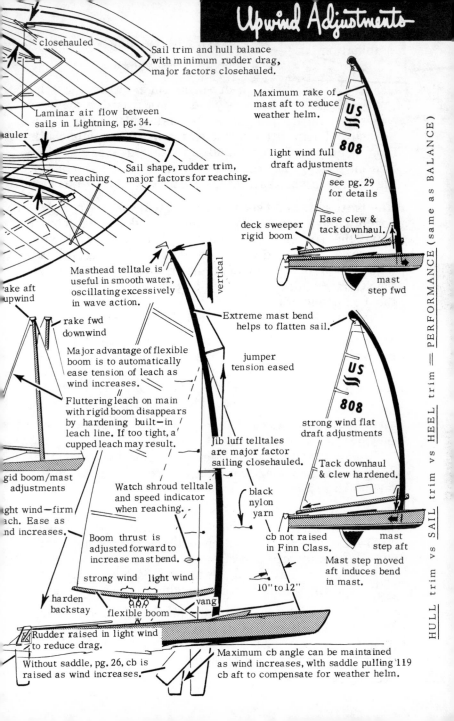

closehauled

Sail trim and hull balance with minimum rudder drag, major factors closehauled.

Maximum rake of mast aft to reduce weather helm.

Laminar air flow between sails in Lightning, pg. 34.

hauler

light wind full draft adjustments

see pg. 29 for details

Sail shape, rudder trim, major factors for reaching.

reaching

deck sweeper rigid boom

Ease clew & tack downhaul.

mast step fwd

rake aft upwind

Masthead telltale is useful in smooth water, oscillating excessively in wave action.

vertical

rake fwd downwind

Extreme mast bend helps to flatten sail.

Major advantage of flexible boom is to automatically ease tension of leach as wind increases.

jumper tension eased

Fluttering leach on main with rigid boom disappears by hardening built—in leach line. If too tight, a cupped leach may result.

strong wind flat draft adjustments

Jib luff telltales are major factor sailing closehauled.

gid boom/mast adjustments

Tack downhaul & clew hardened.

Watch shroud telltale and speed indicator when reaching.

black nylon yarn

ght wind—firm ach. Ease as nd increases.

cb not raised in Finn Class.

mast step aft

Boom thrust is adjusted forward to increase mast bend.

Mast step moved aft induces bend in mast.

strong wind   light wind

10" to 12"

harden backstay

flexible boom

vang

Rudder raised in light wind to reduce drag.

Without saddle, pg. 26, cb is raised as wind increases.

Maximum cb angle can be maintained as wind increases, with saddle pulling 119 cb aft to compensate for weather helm.

HULL trim vs SAIL trim vs HEEL trim = PERFORMANCE (same as BALANCE)

preventer/vang combination — boom without vang

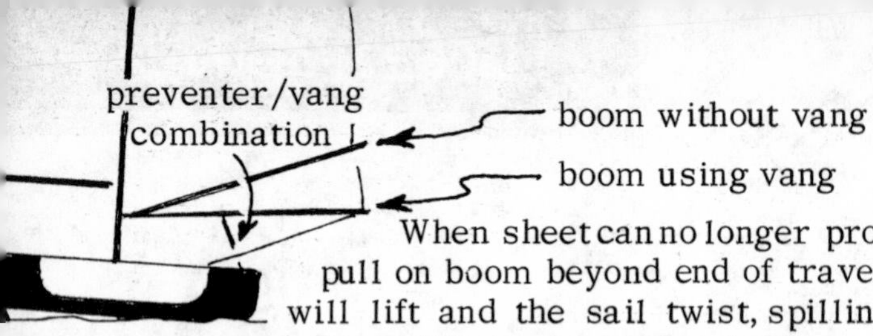

boom using vang

When sheet can no longer provide vertical pull on boom beyond end of traveler, the boom will lift and the sail twist, spilling useful wind pressure. Boom lift tendency is obvious on monohulls from beam reach to run, and on a reach in stronger winds. The Int'l 14, pg. 26, requires a vang to be used most of the time even when sailing closehauled, with its full roach.

Illustration at right shows extreme twist of main on beam reach without vang. Only the small shaded area provides drive, the remaining confused sail area spilling wind pressure from head to clew to tack due to extreme twist, with sail disturbed by continual movement of boom. A VANG is required to provide vertical pull to stabilize the boom and the boats movement, which increases sail drive because of the additional thrust area.

Mainsail rides on lee shroud downwind in Thistle and FD classes, breaking sail surface into two areas, producing unnecessary chafe. This tendency is minimized by allowing lee shroud lever release shown at right. Plastic tube or bicycle type handle reduces shroud chafe against boom.

PREVENTER is a line leading forward to oppose aft pull of sheet, to prevent an accidental jibe when sailing down-wind, pg. 123. We usually prefer a combination preventer/vang shown above and at right, eliminating the need for a person to go forward to set or release a bow preventer.

Sails provide airfoil for upwind sailing drive, and wind cup or bag for sailing downwind with thrust areas shown below. Due to rolling action, outhaul and downhaul are eased to help cup effect, reducing disturbance of wind spilling to either side, pgs. 102-3. Total exposure of sail area is major downwind performance factor.

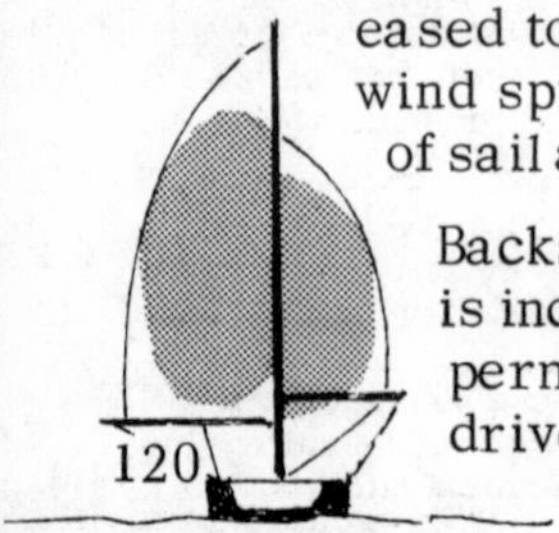

Backstay tension is slacked, and jumper tension is increased in classes such as Int'l 14, and 5.5, permitting top of mast to move forward. increasing drive and easing helm.

120

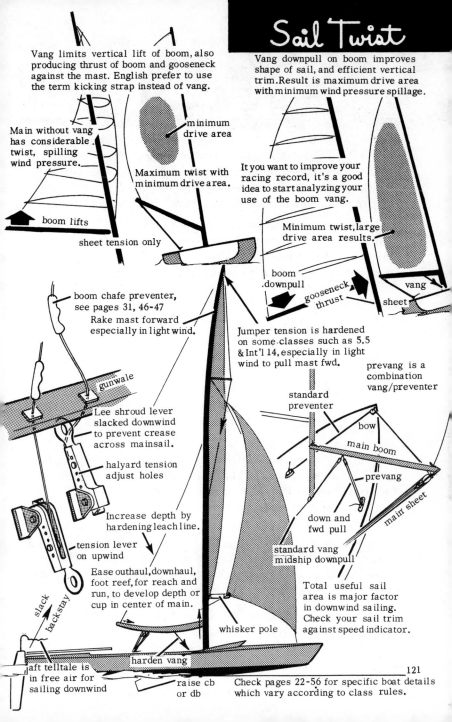

Sail Twist

Vang limits vertical lift of boom, also producing thrust of boom and gooseneck against the mast. English prefer to use the term kicking strap instead of vang.

Vang downpull on boom improves shape of sail, and efficient vertical trim. Result is maximum drive area with minimum wind pressure spillage.

Main without vang has considerable twist, spilling wind pressure.

minimum drive area

Maximum twist with minimum drive area.

If you want to improve your racing record, it's a good idea to start analyzing your use of the boom vang.

boom lifts

sheet tension only

Minimum twist, large drive area results.

boom downpull

gooseneck thrust

vang

sheet

boom chafe preventer, see pages 31, 46-47

Rake mast forward especially in light wind.

gunwale

Lee shroud lever slacked downwind to prevent crease across mainsail.

halyard tension adjust holes

Increase depth by hardening leach line.

tension lever on upwind

Ease outhaul, downhaul, foot reef, for reach and run, to develop depth or cup in center of main.

slack backstay

aft telltale is in free air for sailing downwind

Jumper tension is hardened on some classes such as 5.5 & Int'l 14, especially in light wind to pull mast fwd.

prevang is a combination vang/preventer

standard preventer

bow

main boom

prevang

down and fwd pull

standard vang midship downpull

main sheet

Total useful sail area is major factor in downwind sailing. Check your sail trim against speed indicator.

whisker pole

harden vang

raise cb or db

Check pages 22-56 for specific boat details which vary according to class rules.

Now that's what I call a jibe!

Jibing is as normal a sailing procedure as coming about, yet as our friend above found out the hard way, not all jibes come out as planned. While vang and preventer help reduce potentials of accidental jibe, main factor is skipper awareness to avoid one in the developing stage.

Skipper should be aware of dangers when running before the wind and swells, since rolling and broaching could lead to an accidental jibe. Avoid sailing by the lee in a cb or db boat, see right, which can contribute to jibe with upset. Storms also take unnecessary toll often due to sudden violent winds and windshifts, pages 206-213.

Disturbed wind flow can also cause anxious and some-times humorous moments. If you sail close to high bluffs, steep hills, or tall buildings, sudden wind shifts and/or DOWNDRAFTS may result. Not aware of this we sailed too close to a support pillar of the George Washington Bridge one peaceful afternoon. A knockdown with two accidental jibes resulted . . . rearranging the furniture.

We expected a drawbridge to open as we approached it near Jones Beach without success, requiring our boat to jibe in a strong wind. The boom jibed . . . but the top of the mainsail didn't jibe, producing a GOOSEWING jibe. It was necessary to rejibe the boom and make a second try to produce a successful jibe.

When running in light wind you may sometimes find the faster course between two points by tacking downwind. As wind increases, the boat sailing straight downwind may finish earlier than the sailboat tacking downwind.

Spinnaker is a lifting sail, yet pull on mast, sheet, etc., depresses bow, lifting stern. Move weight aft in strong wind to improve rudder control, and to keep bow from 122 digging in . . . especially critical on centerboard boat.

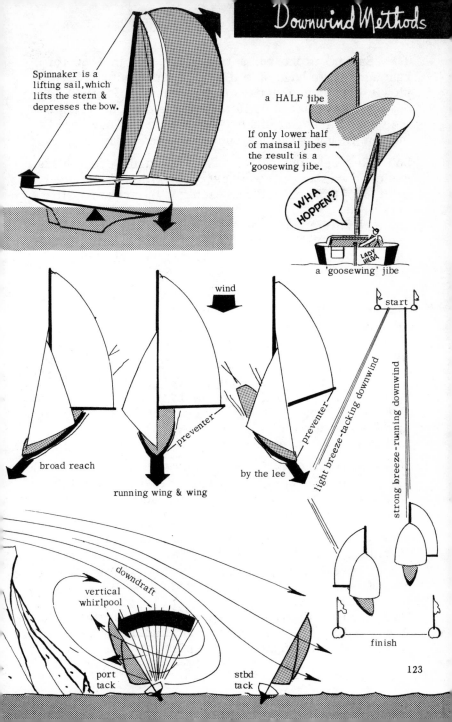

Spinnaker is a lifting sail, which lifts the stern & depresses the bow.

a HALF jibe

If only lower half of mainsail jibes — the result is a 'goosewing' jibe.

WHA HOPPEN?

LADY HILDA

a 'goosewing' jibe

wind

broad reach

running wing & wing

preventer

preventer

by the lee

start

light breeze-tacking downwind

strong breeze-running downwind

downdraft

vertical whirlpool

port tack

stbd tack

finish

123

The "Sphinx" broke out a triangular sail in 1886 for running. Due to huge size it was called "Sphinx's Acre", slowly changing to todays term spinnaker. It might be described as a large drifter with pole often dragging in the water. Early flat "Sphinnaxer" eventually developed into the lifting parachute spinnaker used today.

Spinnaker development has been rapid in recent years. Basically we start with a full cut chute with wide shoulders limited to running. A flat cut reacher with narrow shoulders may be used from broad reach to a beam reach. A storm chute, similar but smaller without shoulders, reduces oscillation, cause of many spinnaker wraps around jib stay. One design classes permit only one chute, a compromise version with major emphasis on reaching.

The star cut chute fills the awkward area between the reaching spinnaker and the gennie for sailing closehauled as it operates up to a close reach. Some find it useful as a heavy weather chute for running because of its flat cut which reduces oscillation, also its strong construction.

Then enters rapidly changing technology of tonner and twelve meter competition. In the 1974 twelve meter trials, "Intrepid" introduced the new tri-radial as an all purpose chute, out maneuvering "Courageous' which continually lost ground as it had to change reaching and running chutes.

"Courageous" then used the tri-radial in the American Cup Series. This is a complex spinnaker to develop and build. Stresses theoretically fall on the thread lines, loading and unloading throughout the entire chute at the same time.

Loose side of chute is trimmed with sheet, while pole side is trimmed with after guy leading aft from pole, a foreguy leads forward from pole end on most boats over 20'. Pole weight is supported by spinnaker topping lift. Above a broad reach with spinnaker pole well forward, a reaching strut is used to reduce chafe of afterguy against shrouds. After dealing with the spinnaker off and on for twenty years, 124 it can best be describe as an "emotional" sail.

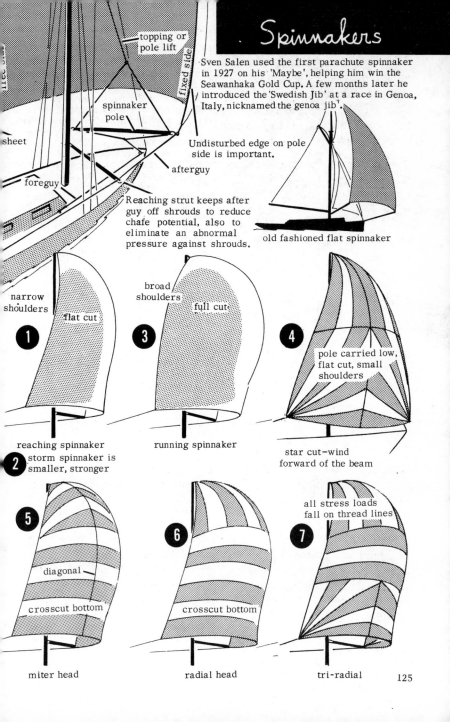

Spinnakers

topping or pole lift

fixed side

spinnaker pole

sheet

foreguy

afterguy

Undisturbed edge on pole side is important.

Reaching strut keeps after guy off shrouds to reduce chafe potential, also to eliminate an abnormal pressure against shrouds.

Sven Salen used the first parachute spinnaker in 1927 on his 'Maybe', helping him win the Seawanhaka Gold Cup. A few months later he introduced the 'Swedish Jib' at a race in Genoa, Italy, nicknamed the genoa jib.

old fashioned flat spinnaker

1 narrow shoulders — flat cut

reaching spinnaker

2 storm spinnaker is smaller, stronger

3 broad shoulders — full cut

running spinnaker

4 pole carried low, flat cut, small shoulders

star cut—wind forward of the beam

5 diagonal — crosscut bottom

miter head

6 crosscut bottom

radial head

7 all stress loads fall on thread lines

tri-radial

125

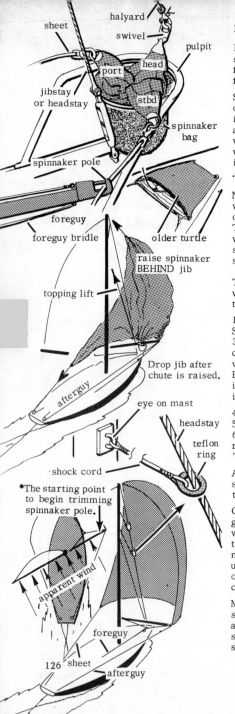

sheet
halyard
swivel
pulpit
port — head
jibstay or headstay
stbd
spinnaker bag
spinnaker pole
foreguy
foreguy bridle
older turtle
raise spinnaker BEHIND jib
topping lift
Drop jib after chute is raised.
afterguy
eye on mast
headstay
teflon ring
shock cord
*The starting point to begin trimming spinnaker pole.
apparent wind
foreguy
126 sheet
afterguy

For larger sailboats ...

LIGHT WINDS. Majority of sailboats to 50' set spinnaker flying, by raising it directly from spinnaker bag secured to the pulpit, forward of jibstay or headstay as shown.

STRONG WINDS. Raise chute behind the jib, or set up in STOPS before raising. After chute is up, it opens and fills after tug on sheet and afterguy. This method is important with large spinnakers which may fill part way up, if set flying. Pressure may make it difficult to winch halyard rest of way .. or may pull crew member up the mast.

* * * * * * * *

Net is required to reduce chances of chute wrapping around headstay. Two slides are often used, secured to mast with shock cord. This permits slide to ride to top of headstay when gennie is used ... then drop down as shown by gravity, for spinnaker use. Rope spinnaker net page 128, may also be used.

* * * * * * * * * *

To set spinnaker flying. Rig lines as shown with pole carried to windward side for new tack. When order is given ......

1, 2. Raise HALYARD and pull back on SHEET simultaneously to reduce wrap.
3. Start winching AFTER GUY aft when chute is about 2/3 up, so pole is parallel with boom, at right angle to apparent wind. Experiment with varied settings as this is just the starting point, due to variables in wind and wave action, kind of boat, etc.

4. Adjust and set TOPPING LIFT.
5. Adjust and set FOREGUY.
6. Adjust SHEET so luff is full without reverse curve or spillage, referred to as 'sailing just above a catastrophe'.

A trained crew goes through this sequence so rapidly a new sailor must watch closely to follow the sequence listed above.

Considerable practice is required to become good friends with a spinnaker. Use a stop watch to check raising, lowering & stowing time so chute is set for next use. Light, medium and heavy sheets and guys, are used for different wind strengths. Light ones are used in light winds to keep chute clews from drooping.

Much practice will be required to perfect spinnaker handling. Have well defined jobs, and stick to basic terminology. Talking should be kept to a minimum when flying spinnakers ... or expect snafus.

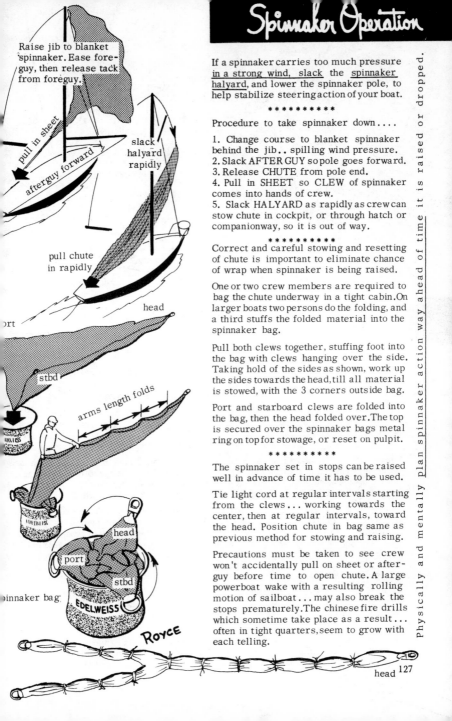

Raise jib to blanket spinnaker. Ease fore-guy, then release tack from foreguy.

pull in sheet

afterguy forward

slack halyard rapidly

pull chute in rapidly

head

ort

stbd

arms length folds

innaker bag

head

port

stbd

EDELWEISS

ROYCE

head 127

If a spinnaker carries too much pressure in a strong wind, slack the spinnaker halyard, and lower the spinnaker pole, to help stabilize steering action of your boat.

* * * * * * * * * *

Procedure to take spinnaker down....

1. Change course to blanket spinnaker behind the jib.. spilling wind pressure.
2. Slack AFTER GUY so pole goes forward.
3. Release CHUTE from pole end.
4. Pull in SHEET so CLEW of spinnaker comes into hands of crew.
5. Slack HALYARD as rapidly as crew can stow chute in cockpit, or through hatch or companionway, so it is out of way.

* * * * * * * * * *

Correct and careful stowing and resetting of chute is important to eliminate chance of wrap when spinnaker is being raised.

One or two crew members are required to bag the chute underway in a tight cabin. On larger boats two persons do the folding, and a third stuffs the folded material into the spinnaker bag.

Pull both clews together, stuffing foot into the bag with clews hanging over the side. Taking hold of the sides as shown, work up the sides towards the head, till all material is stowed, with the 3 corners outside bag.

Port and starboard clews are folded into the bag, then the head folded over. The top is secured over the spinnaker bags metal ring on top for stowage, or reset on pulpit.

* * * * * * * * * *

The spinnaker set in stops can be raised well in advance of time it has to be used.

Tie light cord at regular intervals starting from the clews ... working towards the center, then at regular intervals, toward the head. Position chute in bag same as previous method for stowing and raising.

Precautions must be taken to see crew won't accidentally pull on sheet or after-guy before time to open chute. A large powerboat wake with a resulting rolling motion of sailboat ... may also break the stops prematurely. The chinese fire drills which sometime take place as a result ... often in tight quarters, seem to grow with each telling.

Physically and mentally plan spinnaker action way ahead of time it is raised or dropped.

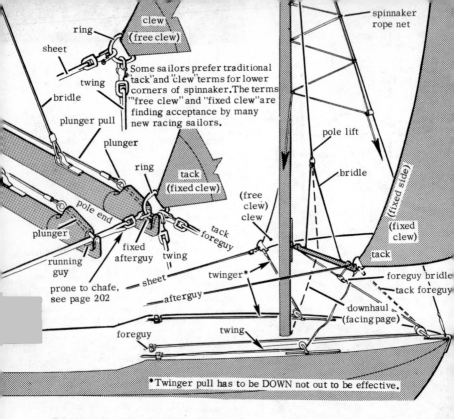

clew
(free clew)

ring

sheet

twing

bridle

plunger pull

Some sailors prefer traditional "tack" and "clew" terms for lower corners of spinnaker. The terms "free clew" and "fixed clew" are finding acceptance by many new racing sailors.

plunger

ring

tack
(fixed clew)

pole end

plunger

running guy

fixed afterguy

twing

tack foreguy

prone to chafe, see page 202

sheet

afterguy

foreguy

twing

spinnaker rope net

pole lift

bridle

(free clew)
clew

(fixed side)

(fixed clew)

tack

twinger*

foreguy bridle

tack foreguy

downhaul
(facing page)

*Twinger pull has to be DOWN not out to be effective.

Double-ended pole, or end-for-end jibing method is used for most boats to 40'. Large boats may use the dip pole method shown pg. 130. Method shown right, is used for one-design boats, with pole downhaul coming back to lower part of mast.

Similar jibing method is used on boats to 40', except foreguy must also be changed secured to ring on corner of chute. Foreguy coming to bridle under the pole, eliminate this extra operation. Running guy seems used on majority of boats for short races. long ocean races, afterguy is secured to ring on chute, reducing chafe on afterguy.

Discussion of "twing" or "tweaker" will produce varied reactions. We've had considerab luck with it on wide beam monohulls over 30' to make chute trim changes in preferenc to sheet, yet with little luck, on narrow beam hulls. We used a stout shock cord 'twing' on wide deck "Tri Star" pg. 81, providing better trim, also eliminating spinnaker net. Wra potentials are maximum on rolling monohull, running in sloppy seas with puffy wind while multihull beam reduces rolling, minimizing wrap in same conditions. Spinnake net made of rope above has stowage problem, minimized if it is wrapped in a cloth roll.

Balance of sailboat carrying spinnaker is critical in all winds, yet most obvious o monohull rolling considerably in strong winds with tendency to bury bow, pg. 123, causing erratic steering action. Steering action may be reduced by moving crew af to level hull under these conditions, see page 115.

When people wander around the deck with spinnaker up, extra rudder compensations are required, reducing boat speed. If twinger & foreguy adjustments may be made fro cockpit in a short race instead of on the foredeck, it may improve your racing record

128

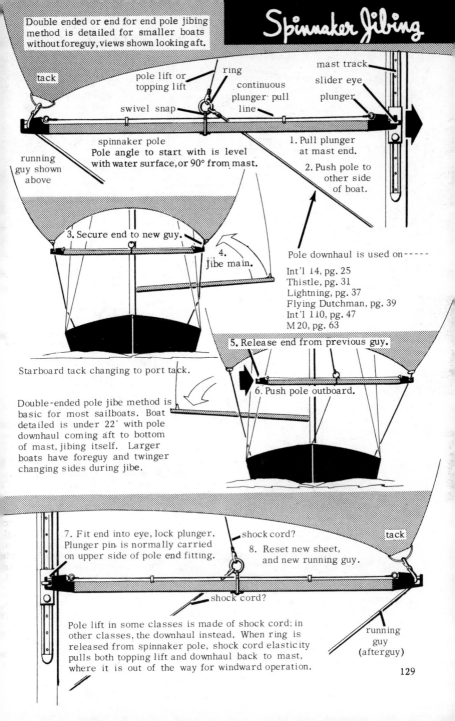

Spinnaker Jibing

Double ended or end for end pole jibing method is detailed for smaller boats without foreguy, views shown looking aft.

tack

pole lift or topping lift

ring

continuous plunger pull line

mast track

slider eye

plunger

swivel snap

spinnaker pole
Pole angle to start with is level with water surface, or 90° from mast.

running guy shown above

1. Pull plunger at mast end.

2. Push pole to other side of boat.

3. Secure end to new guy.

4. Jibe main.

Pole downhaul is used on - - - - -
Int'l 14, pg. 25
Thistle, pg. 31
Lightning, pg. 37
Flying Dutchman, pg. 39
Int'l 110, pg. 47
M 20, pg. 63

Starboard tack changing to port tack.

Double-ended pole jibe method is basic for most sailboats. Boat detailed is under 22' with pole downhaul coming aft to bottom of mast, jibing itself. Larger boats have foreguy and twinger changing sides during jibe.

5. Release end from previous guy.

6. Push pole outboard.

7. Fit end into eye, lock plunger. Plunger pin is normally carried on upper side of pole end fitting.

shock cord?

8. Reset new sheet, and new running guy.

tack

shock cord?

Pole lift in some classes is made of shock cord; in other classes, the downhaul instead. When ring is released from spinnaker pole, shock cord elasticity pulls both topping lift and downhaul back to mast, where it is out of the way for windward operation.

running guy (afterguy)

129

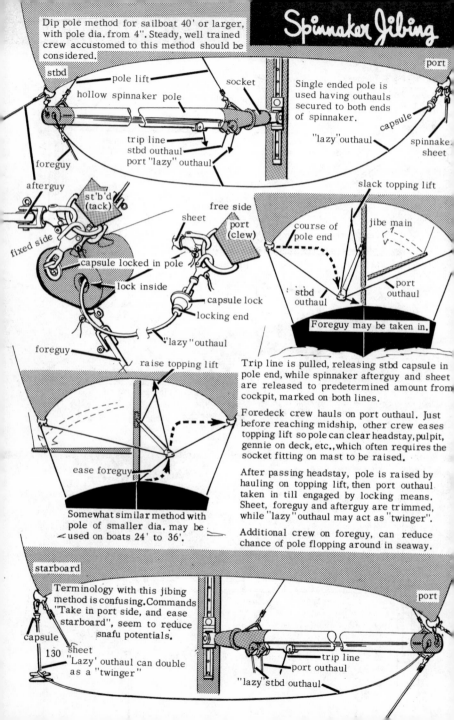

Dip pole method for sailboat 40' or larger, with pole dia. from 4". Steady, well trained crew accustomed to this method should be considered.

stbd

pole lift

hollow spinnaker pole

socket

port

Single ended pole is used having outhauls secured to both ends of spinnaker.

"lazy" outhaul

capsule

spinnaker sheet

trip line
stbd outhaul
port "lazy" outhaul

foreguy

afterguy

st'b'd (tack)

free side
port (clew)

sheet

fixed side

capsule locked in pole

lock inside

capsule lock

locking end

"lazy" outhaul

foreguy

raise topping lift

slack topping lift

course of pole end

jibe main

stbd outhaul

port outhaul

Foreguy may be taken in.

Trip line is pulled, releasing stbd capsule in pole end, while spinnaker afterguy and sheet are released to predetermined amount from cockpit, marked on both lines.

Foredeck crew hauls on port outhaul. Just before reaching midship, other crew eases topping lift so pole can clear headstay, pulpit, gennie on deck, etc., which often requires the socket fitting on mast to be raised.

ease foreguy

Somewhat similar method with pole of smaller dia. may be used on boats 24' to 36'.

After passing headstay, pole is raised by hauling on topping lift, then port outhaul taken in till engaged by locking means. Sheet, foreguy and afterguy are trimmed, while "lazy" outhaul may act as "twinger".

Additional crew on foreguy, can reduce chance of pole flopping around in seaway.

starboard

Terminology with this jibing method is confusing. Commands "Take in port side, and ease starboard", seem to reduce snafu potentials.

port

capsule

130 sheet
"Lazy" outhaul can double as a "twinger"

trip line
port outhaul

"lazy" stbd outhaul

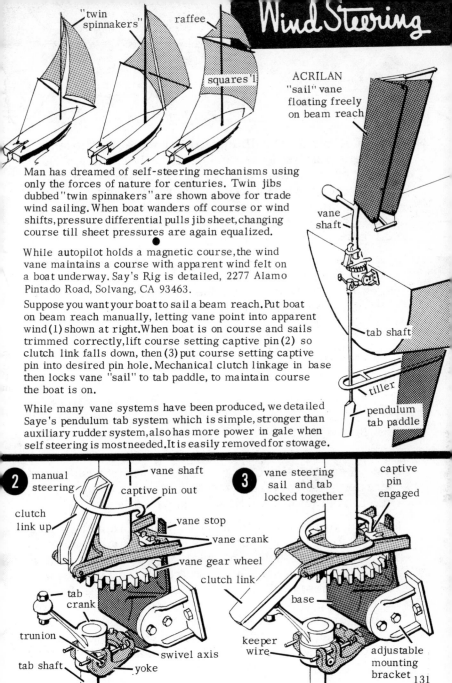

"twin spinnakers"

raffee

squares'l

ACRILAN "sail" vane floating freely on beam reach

vane shaft

tab shaft

tiller

pendulum tab paddle

Man has dreamed of self-steering mechanisms using only the forces of nature for centuries. Twin jibs dubbed "twin spinnakers" are shown above for trade wind sailing. When boat wanders off course or wind shifts, pressure differential pulls jib sheet, changing course till sheet pressures are again equalized.

While autopilot holds a magnetic course, the wind vane maintains a course with apparent wind felt on a boat underway. Say's Rig is detailed, 2277 Alamo Pintado Road, Solvang, CA 93463.

Suppose you want your boat to sail a beam reach. Put boat on beam reach manually, letting vane point into apparent wind (1) shown at right. When boat is on course and sails trimmed correctly, lift course setting captive pin (2) so clutch link falls down, then (3) put course setting captive pin into desired pin hole. Mechanical clutch linkage in base then locks vane "sail" to tab paddle, to maintain course the boat is on.

While many vane systems have been produced, we detailed Saye's pendulum tab system which is simple, stronger than auxiliary rudder system, also has more power in gale when self steering is most needed. It is easily removed for stowage.

2 manual steering

vane shaft

captive pin out

clutch link up

vane stop

vane crank

vane gear wheel

tab crank

trunion

tab shaft

swivel axis

yoke

3 vane steering sail and tab locked together

captive pin engaged

clutch link

base

keeper wire

adjustable mounting bracket

131

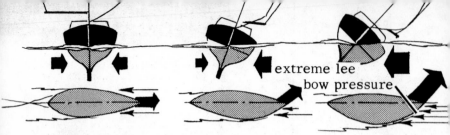

extreme lee bow pressure

Monohull balance of hulls and sails trimmed for closehauled course is very delicate and continually changing, due to amount of heel with resulting change in immersed shape of hull, see above. Imbalance due to increasing heel can be compensated for with rudder, producing unnecessary drag... or corrected with sail changes, to produce self-steering neutral helm.

A new sailor, depending only on rudder trim corrections for heel, soon finds the rudder produces tremendous drag which reduces boat speed, due to water density being over 800 times that of the air.

Under light conditions closehauled, DOWNWIND lee helm is produced if sloop is only sailed with jib; and UPWIND weather helm, with boat wanting to go up into the wind or into irons, if only sailed with the mainsail up.

(1). Sloop closehauled is carrying gennie for self steering, replaced by a working jib at (2)., as wind strength and heel increases, to still maintain neutral helm.

(3). At considerable heel angle in strong wind, unequal bow pressures and CLR moving forward as result, have increased tendency to force bow up into the wind. It is time to reef main for self steering, to balance boat.

(4). In an April '65 storm in the Catalina Channel moving from a force 6 to 9, our 24' sailboat maintained self-steering neutral helm on reach to close reach, with a working jib for over five hours ... requiring a fishermans reef over most of jib at peak of storm. The tiller was held in place and adjusted, while secured by shock cord. This experience plus endless questions by students prompted our reevaluation of storm operational conditions, especially with the popular, small, wide beam craft.

132

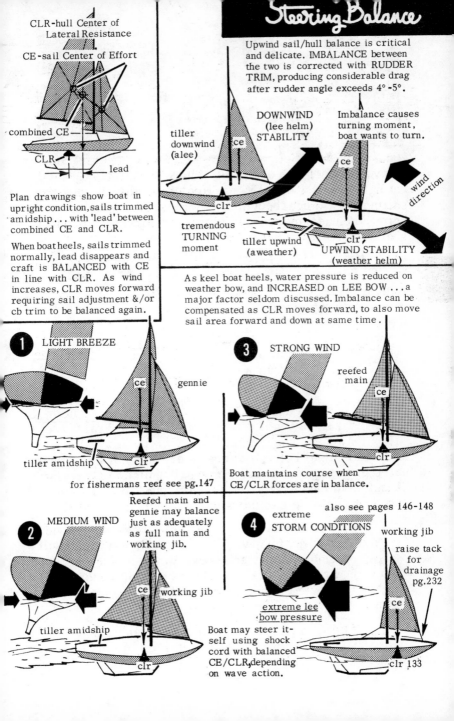

CLR-hull Center of
Lateral Resistance

CE-sail Center of Effort

combined CE —

CLR — lead

Plan drawings show boat in
upright condition, sails trimmed
amidship... with 'lead' between
combined CE and CLR.

When boat heels, sails trimmed
normally, lead disappears and
craft is BALANCED with CE
in line with CLR. As wind
increases, CLR moves forward
requiring sail adjustment &/or
cb trim to be balanced again.

Upwind sail/hull balance is critical
and delicate. IMBALANCE between
the two is corrected with RUDDER
TRIM, producing considerable drag
after rudder angle exceeds 4°-5°.

DOWNWIND
(lee helm)
STABILITY

Imbalance causes
turning moment,
boat wants to turn.

tiller
downwind
(alee)

ce

ce

wind
direction

clr

tremendous
TURNING
moment

tiller upwind
(aweather)

UPWIND STABILITY
(weather helm)

clr

As keel boat heels, water pressure is reduced on
weather bow, and INCREASED on LEE BOW ... a
major factor seldom discussed. Imbalance can be
compensated as CLR moves forward, to also move
sail area forward and down at same time.

1 LIGHT BREEZE

ce gennie

tiller amidship

clr

for fishermans reef see pg.147

3 STRONG WIND

reefed
main

ce

clr

Boat maintains course when
CE/CLR forces are in balance.

Reefed main and
gennie may balance
just as adequately
as full main and
working jib.

2 MEDIUM WIND

ce working jib

tiller amidship

clr

also see pages 146-148

4 extreme
STORM CONDITIONS

working jib

raise tack
for
drainage
pg.232

extreme lee
bow pressure

ce

Boat may steer it-
self using shock
cord with balanced
CE/CLR, depending
on wave action.

clr 133

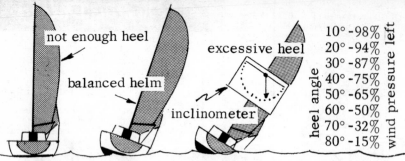

heel angle	wind pressure left
10°	-98%
20°	-94%
30°	-87%
40°	-75%
50°	-65%
60°	-50%
70°	-32%
80°	-15%

not enough heel

excessive heel

balanced helm

inclinometer

Many sailboats are designed to have a neutral balanced helm between 7° to 15°. In lighter wind with less heel sailing upwind, boat becomes cranky producing downwind helm. When heel increases beyond ideal angle, underwater shape of hull, pg. 132, wants to force it to go up into irons if compensation isn't made. drag — rudder

With too much heel comes a little tiller pressure.... which exerts tremendous rudder pressure, the only way the boat out of balance can fight back. Rudder beyond 5° produces tremendous drag due to water density being over 800 TIMES that of air. This drag reduces boat speed and pointing ability, as well as producing very strong & unnecessary pressure on rudder and its fittings.

When forces are in balance you can trim sails and hull so the boat sails itself. Crew of 60' 10 meter "Branta" prefer tiller to wheel. They watch tiller continually trimming sails for neutral helm. If rudder were lost 'Branta' could sail triangular course relying on sail choice and hull trim. Turns would naturally be wider around buoys without rudder to provide rapid change of course.

We often hear weather helm helps to provide maximum upwind lift for sailboat going to windward. Due to leeway, water flowing around windward side of keel or board and rudder, helps provide lifting action with balanced helm.

After sail/hull balance, try minute changes with rudder trim, sail trim, weight trim, and adjusting standing rigging while checking against speedometer or other boat of class to find your boats peculiarities for maximum speed.

134

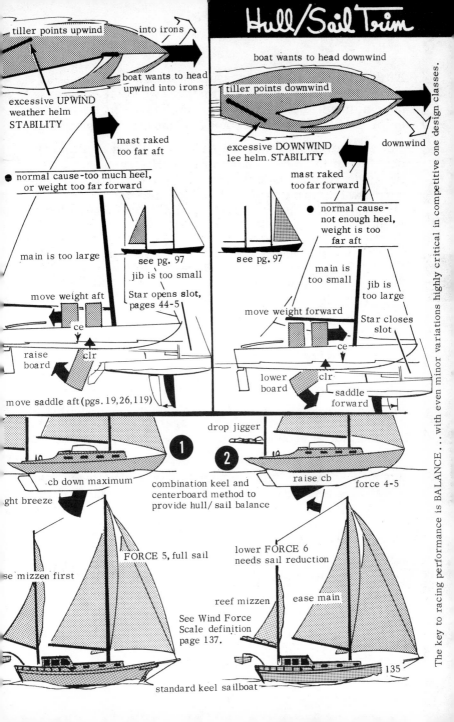

Hull/Sail Trim

tiller points upwind — into irons

boat wants to head upwind into irons

excessive UPWIND weather helm STABILITY

mast raked too far aft

● normal cause - too much heel, or weight too far forward

main is too large

see pg. 97

jib is too small

Star opens slot, pages 44-5

move weight aft

ce

raise board

clr

move saddle aft (pgs. 19, 26, 119)

boat wants to head downwind

tiller points downwind

downwind

excessive DOWNWIND lee helm STABILITY

mast raked too far forward

● normal cause - not enough heel, weight is too far aft

main is too small

jib is too large

see pg. 97

move weight forward

Star closes slot

ce

lower board

clr

saddle forward

drop jigger

1 combination keel and centerboard method to provide hull/sail balance **2**

cb down maximum

raise cb

force 4-5

ght breeze

FORCE 5, full sail

lower FORCE 6 needs sail reduction

se mizzen first

reef mizzen

ease main

See Wind Force Scale definition page 137.

135

standard keel sailboat

The key to racing performance is BALANCE...with even minor variations highly critical in competitive one design classes.

After the wind force pressure patterns and variables are understood and applied, the ocean and lake sailors have a useful tool. It makes sailing more fun, easier and safer, as wind changes become obvious in developing stage

Our wind force pressure scale was developed by Admiral Beaufort of the British navy in 1806. His purpose was to first record the rudder action of square riggers in light winds when trying to develop steerageway. At force 5 his square riggers reached hull speed, and above that a reduction in sail area shown at right, was required.

While weather bureau reports wind speed in mph, the sailors primary need is know wave action (RESULTANT) and (CAUSE), wind pressure strength. Once understood it may be applied to a 9' or 190' sailboat.

● Memorizing this scale is easy...forces 1-2, ripples; 3-4, waves; 5-6, whitecaps; 7, whitecaps and swells—the small craft warning (see page 139).

This wind pressure scale was developed for use on the open ocean. It is a flexible yardstick with variables that need to be understood for our use. In currents, the wave action will be greater blowing against than with the current, while ground swells also develop wave patterns to be compensated for. '

Suppose a force 6 wind suddenly starts blowing across a smooth stretch of ocean, then several hours later quits abruptly. It takes time in the beginning for the wave action to catch up with the pressure pattern. Afterwards it takes time for the old seas to smoothen out.

On inland lakes where wind pressure has insufficient area to develop this visual ocean pattern, one or two forces are often added. While wave action may be force 5, you have force 7 pressures acting on boat, sails and rigging.

Wind FORCE or pressure scale is probably the most important, yet the least understood item facing the new sailor IF he wants to stay out of trouble.

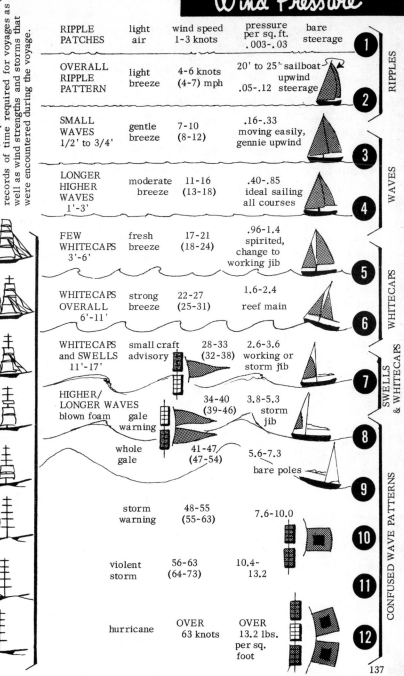

Wind Pressure

by British Admiral Beaufort to detail exact amount of sail carried on a square rigger, shown below, to provide accurate admiralty records of time required for voyages as well as wind strengths and storms that were encountered during the voyage.

		wind speed	pressure per sq. ft.	bare steerage		
RIPPLE PATCHES	light air	1-3 knots	.003-.03	bare steerage	1	RIPPLES
OVERALL RIPPLE PATTERN	light breeze	4-6 knots (4-7) mph	.05-.12	20' to 25' sailboat upwind steerage	2	RIPPLES
SMALL WAVES 1/2' to 3/4'	gentle breeze	7-10 (8-12)	.16-.33 moving easily, gennie upwind		3	WAVES
LONGER HIGHER WAVES 1'-3'	moderate breeze	11-16 (13-18)	.40-.85 ideal sailing all courses		4	WAVES
FEW WHITECAPS 3'-6'	fresh breeze	17-21 (18-24)	.96-1.4 spirited, change to working jib		5	WHITECAPS
WHITECAPS OVERALL 6'-11'	strong breeze	22-27 (25-31)	1.6-2.4 reef main		6	WHITECAPS
WHITECAPS and SWELLS 11'-17'	small craft advisory	28-33 (32-38)	2.6-3.6 working or storm jib		7	SWELLS & WHITECAPS
HIGHER/ LONGER WAVES blown foam	gale warning	34-40 (39-46)	3.8-5.3 storm jib		8	SWELLS & WHITECAPS
	whole gale	41-47 (47-54)	5.6-7.3 bare poles		9	CONFUSED WAVE PATTERNS
	storm warning	48-55 (55-63)	7.6-10.0		10	CONFUSED WAVE PATTERNS
	violent storm	56-63 (64-73)	10.4-13.2		11	CONFUSED WAVE PATTERNS
	hurricane	OVER 63 knots	OVER 13.2 lbs. per sq. foot		12	CONFUSED WAVE PATTERNS

In 1958 a new type of storm warnings were introduced, that have proven quite successful when correctly used. Of most concern to us is the small craft warning...for vessels under 300', that is calibrated in wind force.

Page 137 covers the cause of wind PRESSURE, with the resultant action upon water. The pressure as you notice, doubles per square foot from force 5 to force 7 .... requiring a reduction of more than half in sail area.

From force 7 to 9, the pressure again doubles. This will not only require another half reduction in sail, but the dynamic action of the water has greatly increased.

Force 12 which originated with square riggers not being able to carry any sail, the axiom still applies as the pressure on the hull, spars, etc., is enough to keep a boat going. In one case we checked, it was sufficient to put an elderly gaff headed sloop without sail on a plane during a white squall. Their only protection was to start dragging anchors to slow the boat down to a safer speed.

One night in an ocean race, we experienced a sudden wind increase from force 6 to 10 or 11; only 3 of 13 entries finished that race. We had a knockdown and were unable to carry any sail. With the engine on, we had excessive sternway & a wild rolling boat without rudder control.

Finally I analyzed the pressure ... and the high doghouse. Turning the Newporter Ketch beam to wind, it took off like a scared jackrabbit. We later referred to it as a "doghouse reach", a sensation you'd rather read about.

Another time we moored in an open roadstead with a force 5 wind increasing to force 8 after dark. Following the USCG advisory broadcast the next morning...the two pennant signal was raised! While the system is good, it is up to the sailor in the final analysis to anticipate stormy weather and protect himself...secondly to rely on the storm warning signals. P. S., the new owners hair color changed from black to gray during that wild night.

See page 136 for definitions of Wind Force.

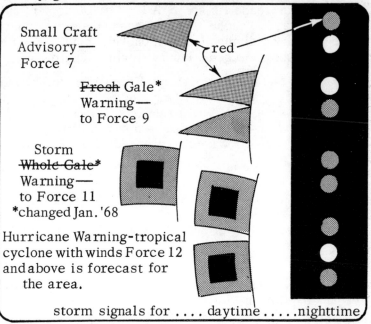

Small Craft
Advisory—
Force 7

red

~~Fresh~~ Gale*
Warning—
to Force 9

Storm
~~Whole Gale*~~
Warning—
to Force 11
*changed Jan. '68

Hurricane Warning-tropical
cyclone with winds Force 12
and above is forecast for
the area.

storm signals for .... daytime.....nighttime

P.S....due to lack of space elsewhere, we would like to
mention a few causes of head failure which
seems a major factor in sailboat sinkings.

Basic parts used in the head have a practical
yet limited useful life span. For a boat used
year-round, all parts contained in a repair
kit should be replaced every two years.

Avoid putting water-resistant facial tissues
into the head. We've found they ball up in the
overboard valve, permitting water to back
into a boat underway. Carry a coat hanger
to unplug overboard valve from outside.

A tennis ball should be standard equipment
for boats with heads, as it can usually plug
bowl opening when everything else fails.   139

If hull speed of a light planing hull is exceeded, the boat
will lift and increase its speed. A light displacement hull
may temporarily reach surfing speeds in the same situation,
while a heavy displacement monohull may be sailed
under if its speed exceeds $1.6\sqrt{\text{waterline length}}$.

|←——30'——→|
|←—20'—→|

|←——27'——→|

deep trough
little free-
board

Nature made strict limitations for ocean
operation, a primary one being HULL SPEED
or speed/length ratio. Hull speed of sailboat
with 20' waterline is 6 knots. This coincides
with 20' wave length speed ... going 6 knots.

Increase speed to 7 knots ... crest to crest
distance is now approx. 27'. Unless boat has
tremendous overhangs, a deep TROUGH
develops. Without water support, boat may
sink lower ... and eventually sail under.

(left margin, vertical:) $1.34\sqrt{\text{waterline length}}=\text{max.eff.hull speed}$

wave speed knots	wave-len. feet
6	20.0
7	27.2
8	35.6
9	45.0
10	55.6
11	67.3
12	80.1
14	109.0
16	142.4
20	222.5
25	347.7
30	500.6

Some square riggers may have disappeared,
being unable to douse sail quick enough in a
storm. As speed increased, the hull floated
lower ... and sailed under.

According to WAVE SPEED SCALE at left, a
heavy disp. sailboat requires 220' waterline
to maintain efficient 20 knot hull speed.

Wave length/boat-speed scale, has plagued
man for centuries in his use of monohull
power & sailboat hulls. Todays oceangoing
vessels are not only restricted to speeds
caused by WAVE trap ... but RESISTANCE of
water. Most tankers & freighters will seldom
exceed 0.7, or liners 1.0 waterline length speed
as fuel consumption becomes prohibitive.

As hull speed is reached, a PRESSURE pocket develops
UNDER vessel, causing monohull bow/stern wave trap. As
wind increases, pressure must be sufficient to lift and plane
a light hull, or dig a deep trough and sail heavy vessel
under. "Sailing Theory and Practice" by C.A. Marchaj has
140 detailed information on sailboat hull hydrodynamics.

Heavy displacement monohull sailboat speed is limited by its basic hull design with the resulting water resistance. Skin friction is major resistance factor to $0.8\sqrt{wl}$.

0.6 to $0.8\sqrt{wl}$

stern wave   bow wave

Freighters and tankers* cruise around $0.6\sqrt{wl}$, moving easily at this speed with minimum fuel consumption. Maximum speed of liners and battleships is about $1.0\sqrt{wl}$, after which friction and wave action produce excessive fuel consumption.

The 'theoretical' maximum efficient hull speed is reached at $1.34\sqrt{\text{Waterline Length}}$. The controlling or limiting force is the bow/stern wave trap.

$1.34\sqrt{wl}$ speed (approx.)

stern wave crest   trough amidship   bow wave crest

Water pressure pocket under hull, produces hydraulic action with bow/stern wave trap as resultant.

The 'Patty Cat II' hull design, pgs. 76-79, practically eliminates water pressure buildup. Wave action is nil at 20 knots.

As speed and wake increases, bow and stern wave pattern moves aft, developing a deep trough between. Stern squats due to minimum water support aft.

1.5 – $1.6\sqrt{wl}$ speed

Freeboard generally reduced.

stern wave crest   deep trough aft   bow wave crest

pressure pocket

Hydraulic lift results in planing lift of light craft, after displacement speed has been exceeded.

wake reduced

pressure leakage

The water 'hardens' as resistance increases rapidly with boat speed, providing water lift. Water density providing this hydraulic lift, is approximately 835 times that of air.

hydraulic water lift

Separation point should be sharp to avoid drag!

attack angle

PRESSURE TRAP

PRESSURE LIFT

ROYCE
141

* For additional information on power vessel speed limitations, read 'Naval Architecture of Small Craft' by D. Phillips-Birt.

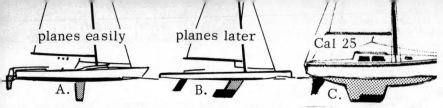

planes easily   planes later   Cal 25

A.   B.   C.

A. Light sailboats with ample sail area and good bottom support such as Int'l 14, 505, Finn, Thistle, FD, etc., may permit planing speeds to 5.0*, limited by crew experience, condition of equipment, and wave action.

B. Light keel Tempest, Int'l 110, centerboard Lightning, etc., are heavier with less relative sail area, which may produce speeds under normal conditions to 3.0*.

C. We've had our heavy 24' sailboat exceed the bow/stern wave trap on a beam reach, hard on the 10 knot peg for over an hour, which was exhilarating but uncomfortable. Yet we have been able to make the Cal 25 surf easily with little fuss. The Cal 40 was the first of the large ocean racing fleet to surf consistently for long periods in the Transpac to Hawaii. In recent years many large ultra light dinghies up to the 70' 'Merlin' consistently exceed the heavy displacement bow/stern wave trap.

•

Sequence details method to put FD on plane in adequate wind. Keep boat flat and watch jib luff closely so sails are full. Bear off rapidly as speed increases, not to run out of apparent wind moving forward. Weight is important factor to keep boat on planing lines, while vang tension becomes critical to produce a flatter high-speed airfoil.

Another planing method is to have boat on course. As puff hits, pump and/or trim sails rapidly, and if possible catch a good wave to keep bow up and out of front wave . . . so bow won't dig in and stop with stern still moving, the cause of broaching, or cartwheeling and boneyarding.

The FD automatically drops off plane while jibing, as it rounds the mark. If you want to drop off a plane earlier when not racing, use the methods shown. Planing methods detailed, are similar for other classes.

* Speed factor refers to $1.34\sqrt{\text{waterline length}}$, pgs. 140, 146.

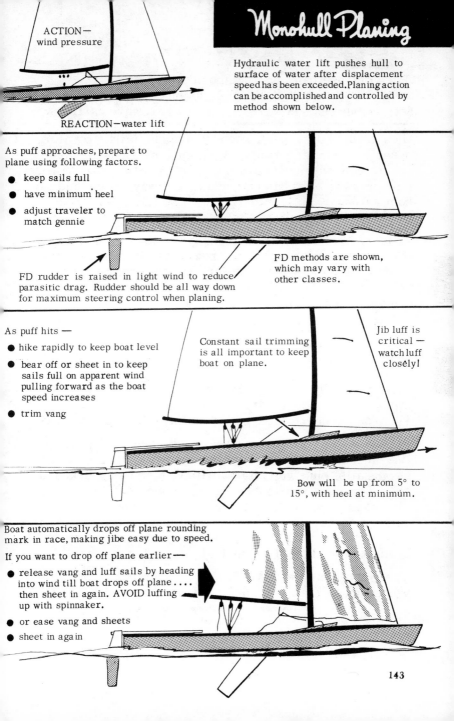

Monohull Planing

ACTION— wind pressure

REACTION—water lift

Hydraulic water lift pushes hull to surface of water after displacement speed has been exceeded. Planing action can be accomplished and controlled by method shown below.

As puff approaches, prepare to plane using following factors.

- keep sails full
- have minimum heel
- adjust traveler to match gennie

FD rudder is raised in light wind to reduce parasitic drag. Rudder should be all way down for maximum steering control when planing.

FD methods are shown, which may vary with other classes.

As puff hits —

- hike rapidly to keep boat level
- bear off or sheet in to keep sails full on apparent wind pulling forward as the boat speed increases
- trim vang

Constant sail trimming is all important to keep boat on plane.

Jib luff is critical — watch luff closely!

Bow will be up from 5° to 15°, with heel at minimum.

Boat automatically drops off plane rounding mark in race, making jibe easy due to speed.

If you want to drop off plane earlier—

- release vang and luff sails by heading into wind till boat drops off plane .... then sheet in again. AVOID luffing up with spinnaker.
- or ease vang and sheets
- sheet in again

143

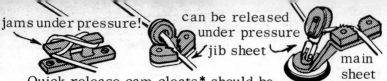

jams under pressure! can be released under pressure
/jib sheet
main sheet

Quick release cam cleats* should be standard on cb and db boats, reducing chance of upset. See various kinds in various marine hardware catalogs.

CB and DB boats upset when equipment fails, operator doesn't recognize changing weather conditions, or come about too slowly and are caught in irons. After sails fill their forward lift has changed to sideway thrust, and the boat trips over cb.

Boats using boards for leverage stability have inverse ratio to keel boat. Hull form provides more initial stability. After 45°-50° is reached, the centers pass each other, and the boat becomes more stable in upset .position. The C of G can be changed if a person puts his weight on the centerboard or daggerboard.

When boat has 90° upset, check crew, then have them lash all floating objects to boat. Slack main halyard, then swim to top of mast. Unshackle head of sail, secure float to main halyard to prevent 180° upset (turning turtle) while sails are being dropped. For wind or current situation it might be advised to drop anchor. After boat is righted PLUG centerboard or daggerboard well ... start bailing.

In 180° upset, check crew, then slack sheets all way. Rig line across bottom of boat, use body as righting lever. Drop sails, plug well, start bailing. Metal daggerboard should be secured to boat after leaving dock, as it can sink in capsize. After salt water upset, hose down metal parts, then dry and wax them to reduce corrosion. Boat may be dismasted during recovery if towed in upset condition, or righted without sheets being released.

The further a keel boat heels, greater effect of keels weight to restrict heeling ... but it can sink if boat fills.

●Movable ballast can hasten upset chances-----------
fresh water weighs approx. 8.3lbs. per gallon; regular
144 gasoline, 6.6lbs. per gallon; diesel oil, 7.3lbs. per gallon.

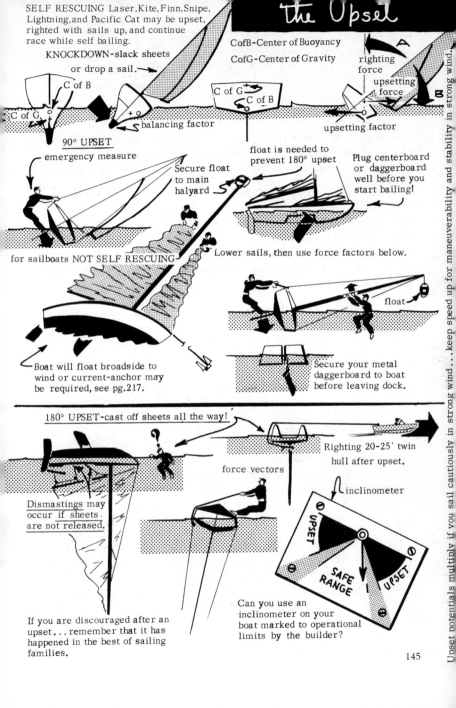

SELF RESCUING Laser, Kite, Finn, Snipe, Lightning, and Pacific Cat may be upset, righted with sails up, and continue race while self bailing.

KNOCKDOWN-slack sheets or drop a sail.→

the Upset

CofB-Center of Buoyancy
CofG-Center of Gravity

righting force

upsetting force

C of B

C of G
C of B

balancing factor

upsetting factor

90° UPSET
emergency measure

float is needed to prevent 180° upset

Plug centerboard or daggerboard well before you start bailing!

Secure float to main halyard

for sailboats NOT SELF RESCUING

Lower sails, then use force factors below.

float

Boat will float broadside to wind or current-anchor may be required, see pg. 217.

Secure your metal daggerboard to boat before leaving dock.

180° UPSET-cast off sheets all the way!

Righting 20-25' twin hull after upset.

force vectors

inclinometer

Dismastings may occur if sheets are not released.

UPSET

SAFE RANGE

UPSET

If you are discouraged after an upset... remember that it has happened in the best of sailing families.

Can you use an inclinometer on your boat marked to operational limits by the builder?

145

Upset potentials multiply if you sail cautiously in strong wind...keep speed up for maneuverability and stability in strong wind.

* Heavy disp. hull speed scale based on boats waterline length

1.34 maximum eff. hull speed
*danger zone
surfing planing
0
0.5
1.0
1.5
2.0
lb/ton pressure 4 10 15 30 60 120 150 180
water resistance in pounds for each ton of vessel weight

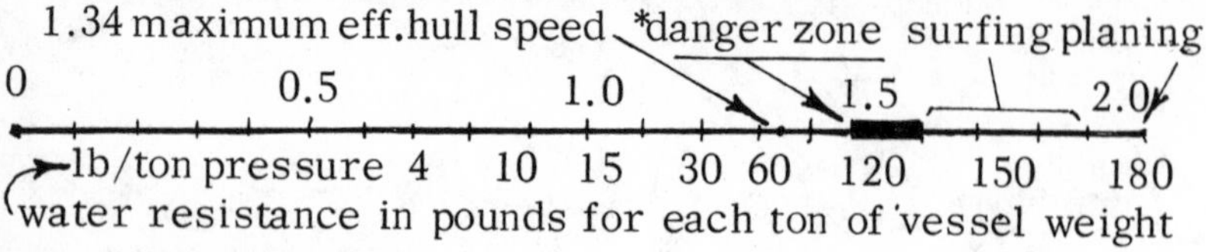

Yawl and sloop sail reduction methods are quite similar. At force 5 they carry sufficient wind pressure (.96–1.4 lbs. per sq. ft) to maintain maximum efficient hull speed.

When wind increases it is necessary to reduce sail area to still maintain same total pressure in sails as before. If the wind jumps from force 5 to 7, the wind pressure DOUBLES, requiring sail area reduction to half of #2. In a sudden temporary puff, use FISHERMANS REEF by easing or releasing main sheet, also heading higher to reduce heel producing abnormal upwind helm, pg. 133.

pressure trap

In a sudden violent storm a *heavy displacement sailboat such as narrow 10 meter, may be sailed under in its own wave trap... the probable cause of many unexplained square rigger disappearances, page 140.

pressure lift

Current light to medium displacement wide beam boats have little chance of being sailed under. When overpowered past wind pressure to reach hull speed, they may heel excessively, have equipment failure as the sails try to go faster than the boat... or temporarily surf or plane as they exceed the speed trap (see graph above), an exceptionally rare phenomenon before 1960 in ocean racing sailboats larger than open one-design craft.

Some of todays glass boats are cranky at surfing speeds, others under certain conditions are quite efficient. When instructing off Santa Barbara in '68 on a Cal 25, the wind suddenly increased from force 5 to a weak 7. The main was dropped and we returned to the harbor under jib alone on beam reach never under 10 knots, and often up to 14 and 15 knots. Conditions were ideal to produce this wild and wonderful experience to our students who were not novices, wanting this type of exposure. Larger boats such as Cal 40, "Windward Passage", "Blackfin", and others in increasing numbers surf in favorable conditions.

Reefing

FISHERMANS REEF is used in sudden strong wind puff. Ease or release main sheet to reduce excessive upwind helm caused by heeling, pg.133.

ease main sheet, harden in on jib sheet

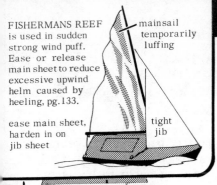

mainsail temporarily luffing

tight jib

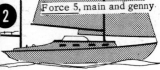

2 Force 5, main and genny.

For #1, see page 135.

3 Twin headsails (see upper right).

Wind force pressure DOUBLES when the wind force changes from 5 to 7, 6 to 8, etc., requiring HALF the total sail AREA to maintain the same wind pressure on sails required, see Wind Force, pg.137.

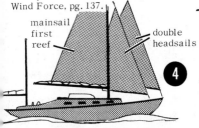

mainsail first reef

double headsails

4

Force 6 at #4. Wind pressure increases by half, requiring a 1/3 sail reduction in area to maintain similar pressure as at #2, not to overpower boat and cause abnormal pressure on sails, hull, rigging.

Force 7 at #5. Wind pressure doubles that of #2, requiring HALF sail area of #2 to maintain same total sail pressure and not overpower boat.

mainsail second reef

small jib

5

Reefing method shown below is for a 40 yawl with a 27' waterline to develop a maximum normal hull speed of 7-8 knots (see pg. 140). At #2 it is carrying a force 5 wind with jigger down. As the wind increases (see pgs. 14,15) the first change is to DOUBLE HEADSAILS at #3, reducing wind flow on lee side of main.

As wind pressure increases, sail area has to be decreased proportional amount not to exceed sail pressures of force 5 required for 7 knot hull speed.

Loosefooted storm trysail to take sting out of jibing, is laced to mast so sail cannot pull out mast track in sudden blow. On the other hand it can only be raised to the first projection on mast such as lower spreader.

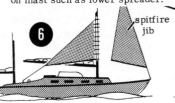

spitfire jib

6

Both sketches #6 and #7 show yawl riding to storm sails in force 7 through 9, with different trysail methods.

Switch track permits main to be lowered and storm trysail raised immediately. In rare instances to prevent being becalmed in deep troughs the sail below can be raised higher than at #6.

storm trysail

7

When overpowered at #6 or #7 on light, wide beam hulls the next step seems to be to sail under jib alone, page 133.

If wind still increases and boat cannot carry any sails, see pages 154 to 157 Also study pages 150 on heave to methods, and pg. 152, the broach to be avoided.

147

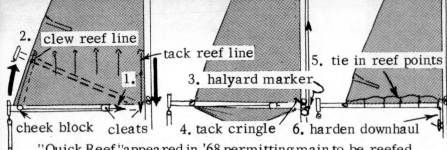

2. clew reef line
tack reef line
5. tie in reef points
1.
3. halyard marker
cheek block   cleats   4. tack cringle   6. harden downhaul

"Quick Reef" appeared in '68 permitting main to be reefed underway without dropping or using roller reef. 1. Pull clew reef line tight and cleat, raising boom to #2. Drop halyard marker #3 to predetermined point. 4. Snap hook secured to boom through luff eye cringle, or haul down and cleat tack reef line. 5. Tie reef points or zipper shut to secure bunt. 6. Harden downhaul, sheet in main.

First demonstration I saw required 3 seconds to complete. For single 1/3 reef we feel it has no competition. For larger boats or heavier booms, add winch to clew reef line. Aft pull of clew reef line flattens airfoil for strong wind, wire may be sewn into sail across reef area for extra support. Reef lines dead end on other side of boom.

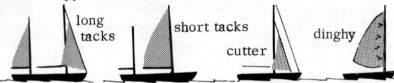

long tacks   short tacks
                              dinghy
                  cutter

For long tacks on ketch, it may sail straighter course easier under jib and mizzen, yet for tacking up narrow harbor it may turn easier under main alone. Cutter often operates under inner jib (forestays'l) in storm.

Dinghy has little defense in strong wind. If boom is removed and sailed loosefooted, damage from accidental jibe is reduced. Next step is to slack halyard to reduce sail luff efficiency. Final step is secure sail and mast to bow line and use it as a storm anchor.   peak halyard

Gaff rigged sail can be SCANDALIZED in a   lift →
strong puff reducing sail area by half. After
topping lift is set up, release PEAK halyard
148 (on port). This is a temporary measure only.

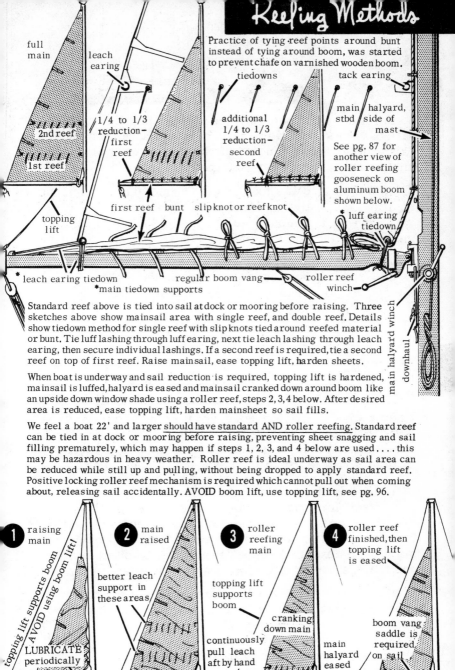

full main

leach earing

2nd reef

1st reef

1/4 to 1/3 reduction– first reef

topping lift

first reef

Practice of tying reef points around bunt instead of tying around boom, was started to prevent chafe on varnished wooden boom.

tiedowns

additional 1/4 to 1/3 reduction– second reef

bunt   slip knot or reef knot

tack earing

main halyard, stbd side of mast

See pg. 87 for another view of roller reefing gooseneck on aluminum boom shown below.

* luff earing tiedown

* leach earing tiedown   regular boom vang   roller reef
      *main tiedown supports   winch

main halyard winch   downhaul

Standard reef above is tied into sail at dock or mooring before raising. Three sketches above show mainsail area with single reef, and double reef. Details show tiedown method for single reef with slip knots tied around reefed material or bunt. Tie luff lashing through luff earing, next tie leach lashing through leach earing, then secure individual lashings. If a second reef is required, tie a second reef on top of first reef. Raise mainsail, ease topping lift, harden sheets.

When boat is underway and sail reduction is required, topping lift is hardened, mainsail is luffed, halyard is eased and mainsail cranked down around boom like an upside down window shade using a roller reef, steps 2, 3, 4 below. After desired area is reduced, ease topping lift, harden mainsheet so sail fills.

We feel a boat 22' and larger should have standard AND roller reefing. Standard reef can be tied in at dock or mooring before raising, preventing sheet snagging and sail filling prematurely, which may happen if steps 1, 2, 3, and 4 below are used .... this may be hazardous in heavy weather. Roller reef is ideal underway as sail area can be reduced while still up and pulling, without being dropped to apply standard reef. Positive locking roller reef mechanism is required which cannot pull out when coming about, releasing sail accidentally. AVOID boom lift, use topping lift, see pg. 96.

1 raising main

topping lift supports boom
AVOID using boom lift!
LUBRICATE periodically

2 main raised

better leach support in these areas

3 roller reefing main

topping lift supports boom

cranking down main

continuously pull leach aft by hand

main halyard eased

4 roller reef finished, then topping lift is eased

boom vang saddle is required on sail

149

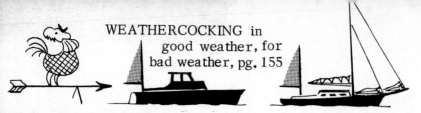

Before stout parachute surface anchors pgs.156-7,160-1, sailboats in storm were forced to run downwind under bare poles towing lengths of chain or hawser as canvas storm anchors were often prone to failure.

The other method was to HEAVE TO, maintaining drifting position with sails and rudder counterbalancing each other. It was common practice making lunch in light to medium weather, or for single handers riding out storm.

Above we see the aft sail which enables lobster boats to go into irons and stay head to wind in wind condition while their operators pick up or replace their lobster pots. The aft sail on a ketch or yawl can also accomplish this by providing upwind helm or directional stability, pg.97.

Illustrations at right show balancing method combining sail and rudder trim fighting each other, Their purpose, to cancel forward movement of vessel in deep water as it slowly drifts to leeward without coming about.

Practice heaving to in good weather to understand the basic principles involved if it must be used in storm conditions. We enjoy trolling for fish under sail. Main difficulty was learning to heave to on short notice.

Long keel cruising boat pg.152, can heave to and look after itself for long periods of time if need be. This is a wonderful way to ease movement to reduce the noise factor and make the boat more comfortable. Heaving to may cause abnormal rudder pressures so check rudder and fittings periodically for wear or potential failure.

The popular wide-beam light-displacement sailboat with short keel isn't generally able to look after itself in a storm or confused seaway if hove to. It should LAY TO parachute anchor using methods shown pgs. 156-7, 161, providing it is sufficiently offshore to do so.

150

Square rigger is hove to with
sails aback to maintain position.

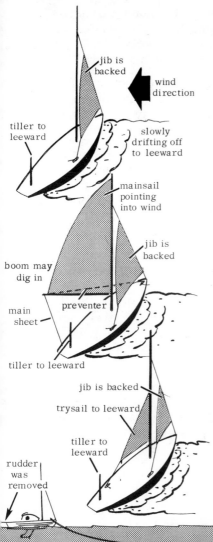

Heave To

The ancient art of "heaving to" to maintain position in good weather or survive a storm in bad weather is by balancing the sails AGAINST the rudder.

The boat is balanced so that the bow will fall off, then point up a little as the boat gathers headway, and fall off or fall back to original position without coming about.

The reason, is to reduce sailboats speed till it is making little or no headway. The boat is then able to ride up and over the waves off her bow, yielding to them easily so they don't break aboard. It permits her to "roll with the punch".

Try heaving your boat to in good weather to understand the factors involved. First start with jib backed, tiller pointing the other way or to leeward #1.

Now raise the main and rig a preventer so the mainsail acts as a wind vane to help hold boat in this position.

Two masted boats are generally easier to "heave to" due to a wider variety of sail combinations.

Older boats may often be easier to "heave to" because of long keels, see sketch at top of page at left which will resist turning in bad weather, 20,152.

Many of todays glass boats with short keels which are excellent for easy turning in tight harbors are difficult to "heave to" except in conditions which are ideal. Because of the short keel they are too active and can easily be thrown around by wave action in a storm, instead of being able to maintain position by ability to "heave to".

Much of the present edition is devoted to ample coverage of the popular, wide beam, light displacement craft. See following pages for heavy weather operational methods.

Robert Manry has delighted thousands of Americans by sailing his 14 foot "Tinkerbelle" from Falmouth in the U.S. to Falmouth, England.

At night he 'parked' his boat to a canvas bucket with a 150' length of 1/2" nylon. A float with a 15' line was secured to the bucket to keep it from sinking any deeper.

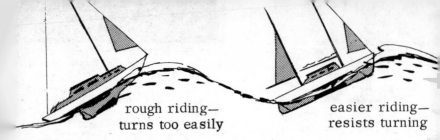

rough riding—
turns too easily

easier riding—
resists turning

Tremendous wind and wave pressure potentials exist in a seaway. Up and down bouncing, chafing of sheets, gear, and sails, plus abnormal pressures against rudder and rudder fittings bear close observation and study.

If headway can be maintained, jog along an easy 2 to 3 knot forward speed to ease action, reducing boat rolling. It also minimizes chafe which is always present, also reducing pressures on rudder due to forward motion.

Action won't be as pronounced on long keel cruising boat above. Popular wide beam light displacement sailboat with short keel will be much more active in storm. If latter should heave to, abnormal wave pattern may knock bow off course. Boat may jibe or come about with tiller and sails lashed down at worst possible moment, pg.151.

By its very nature light displacement craft wants to go faster than heavy cruising boat in storm, and must be slowed down. This type boat is more subject to surface wave action which is a great safety factor as it allows boat to roll with punch. On the other hand the lively action may be more fatiguing on crew, requiring shorter watches. If waves are short and steep, an upwind course may be desired as downwind course may present more hazards.

With majority of cases a downwind jetty entrance should be avoided in considerable wave action. In other instances a "Mexican Hat" pg. 162, towed behind a sailboat with a little chain and trip line, may provide sufficient drag to permit steerage control to enter some jetties without broaching or other similar problems.

trip line

Mexican Hat

chain

Wave action provides drive downwind, resistance upwind.

①

An easy BALANCED helm is important in good weather ... yet more important in bad weather to protect the rudder and its fittings, also to not unnecessarily fatigue the helmsman.

(continuation of pg. 147)

If boat can still efficiently carry storm sails, keep boat jogging along moving easily so it is always able to respond to rudder. If the boat points too high, it rapidly loses rudder control at the worst possible time, till it is able to fall off and fill sails to again be able to respond to rudder.

Short watches are best as fatigue can produce bad judgment at critical moment. We recommend Bonine® or Bucladin® (a prescription pill) to avoid seasickness. Avoid pills that make you sleepy ... and avoid OVER MEDICATION as it is the worst time to fight side effects produced.

wind

②

Avoid sailing a beam reach in cresting wave action as a large wave breaking aboard may roll the boat.

Lightning, Snipe, etc., can broach and upset in smooth water if wind rapidly increases over stern.

BROACH TO. Boat above is sailing downwind with main up ... out of balance. Boat wants to slew around into wind, catching a wave on the beam and rolling. The boat should have downwind helm, jib only. If steering is difficult and boat still wants to slew around, add drag such as rope, chain, or Turboflow element shown lower left.

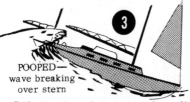

③

POOPED— wave breaking over stern

④

Stern may keep going as it pivots around or over bow.

PITCHPOLE— bow trips digging in, coming down steep wave

bow stops

Both situations above are product of sailing downwind in a storm. If pooped, stern may slew around beam to wind, producing a broach and roll. Causes are boat going SLOWER than wave speed, or shallow water with steep waves.

PITCHPOLE is often caused by boat going FASTER than wave speed, coming over top of steep wave, and having bow dig in before flotation can lift bow. How far the bow digs in, and if boat is rolled by the next wave depends on situation. The narrow beam deep draft hull seems more prone to bow digging in, pg. 155. Avoid sailing downwind especially in shallow water where vertical development increases.

WAVE ACTION. Try to stay in deep water where waves may look mountainous but boat can often ride them like a duck. As waves move into shallow water they become steeper as they are retarded at their base. When crest to trough ratio is 7 to 1 they break, releasing considerable energy. They are most dangerous at 8 or 9 to 1 ratio just before breaking with steep almost vertical fronts. Read 'Ocean Sciences', Annapolis.

Mariners Library, Rupert Hart-Davis Limited, (London) publishes over 40 books ... the classics of long distance cruising, heavy weather, etc.

⑤

7 to 1 or less

breaking crests

crest to crest   trough

steep front

153

Downwind sailing in storm has many hazards, upwind sailing more protection. Downwind must respond to rudder—don't overly reef. Boat must respond to rudder.

The seaworthy boat is one that will take care of you, after you can no longer take care of the boat. A bottle can ride out the wildest hurricane if the top is sealed, and if the bottle doesn't hit a solid object.

Heavy weather sailboat operation is almost identical. Seal the boat, then keep it in deep water so boat cannot be thrust against solid objects such as a rock, heavy driftwood, a shoreline, etc.

If boat is holed in collision, use sail as shown above, so pressure of water against hole helps seal opening. Before shoring up inside, have everything ready, then shove rapidly into position. If done slowly, inward pressure on sail ceases, with water beginning to flow between sail and hull.

Hull form and keel length is critical in storm as longer keel resists turning, while popular short keel boat can be overly active, fatiguing helmsman. Keep body warm and dry as possible. If you are cold and wet, it drains body heat, which increases mental fatigue, decreasing analytical ability.

An ocean boat should always be prepared, so when a storm hits, the boat is ready to take care of itself. Avoid wood screws, bolting everything possible such as cleats, bitts, lifeline supports, etc., with corrosion resistant metals.

Shock cord mounts should be provided to secure movable objects, and bunk straps provided to keep you in your bunk in a seaway... also to contain BATTERY in a roll.

It is a good idea to use double clamps on most hoses, or replace clamps periodically, including stainless clamps. Pay special attention to maintenance and care of head... which we feel has been major factor in boat sinkings. The positive action sea cock valves on the head are preferred to gate valves without positive sealing in closed position.

MASTHEAD LIGHT may provide maximum visibility in questionable situation, as deck mounted side and stern lights and vessel silhouette are almost impossible for lookout on large vessel to see looking DOWN at water.

154

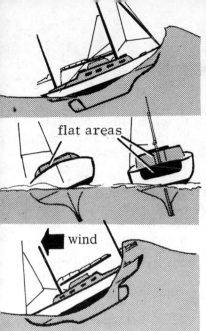

flat areas

wind

Keep jogging along on reach or close reach if possible, with water draining easily under high-tacked jib.

BOW ENTRY is better prepared to take storm, wind and wave action, due to minimum flat surfaces for nature to thrust against.

If broad reach or run are chosen in hurricane, waves have flat areas to thrust against, which can cause dismasting, pitchpoling, etc. Stern is also open to waves breaking and filling cockpit.

In the spring of '64 off Carolina coast, 39' keel/cb yawl "Doubloon" ran under bare poles with winds 60-80 knots. Changing to broad reach, it had a beams end knockdown.

After righting, course was changed 60° to 70° from wind, later experiencing two 360° rolls and one beams end knockdown.

Makeshift sea anchor was then used comprising sails, sailbag, and anchor, to keep bow 50°-60° from wind with 45° desired, mattresses lashed to stern pulpit to help weathercock bow into wind.

A couple of months later owner of "Mambo" purchased a "Para-Anchor" for use in a similar situation. Both boats are practically identical to "Finisterre", pgs. 66-69.

Shallow draft boats are drier and more active, responding faster to surface wave action. Designer/builder Bob Derecktor, Apr. '67 Yachting, pg. 122, states . ". . a deep keel boat is more likely to trip on a steep wave and roll over" (see pg. 153). Main cause of "Doubloon" roll probably was to tripping over centerboard in down position.   155

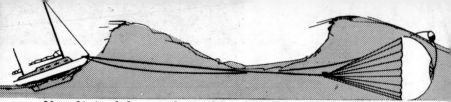

Unsolicited letter from Mambo owner tells first use of "Para'Anchor" in Gulf Stream with winds 40 to 60 knots, with seas probably 25' high. 120' of 1" diameter nylon line, and similar length 5/16" dacron trip line were used.

Main problem was <u>chafe</u> of nylon line going through chock. Owner said only one man was required in heavy seas afterwards to take in "Para-Anchor" with trip line. No knockdowns or 360° rolls experienced by "Doubloon", were encountered by "Mambo" in similar weather.

Within its first year "Para-Anchor" was used by fishing fleets worldwide. After a severe loss of fishing vessels in a '64 typhoon, it was tested by and became standard of the Japanese fishing fleets; also see pages 160-161.

In '69 we tested the "Two Pennant Storm Anchor*". Though only 6' dia. storing size of a pillow, its heavy nylon open weave made minute bleed holes, releasing small streams of water for stability, producing minimal drift. We call it a storm anchor for heavy weather, though it could be broken open in light weather under power.

Traditional iron hoop, canvas storm anchor is shown at right which should be restricted to powerboats providing <u>considerable backwards drift</u> with bow into wind.

Sailboats generally have large rudders only designed for forward motion. Traditional storm anchor may produce excessive sternway tearing rudder loose... or causing abnormal pressures on rudder fittings. <u>Sail craft should consider parachute</u> surface <u>anchors</u> providing minimum drift <u>to protect their rudders</u> under severe conditions.

Bucket makes ideal dinghy anchor going into lee shore through breakers. Secure bucket to bow line so dinghy keeps bow into breakers... without turning sideways, rolling, broaching, or pitchpoling.

*Lissaur Co., 2529 Chambers St., Vernon, CA 90058

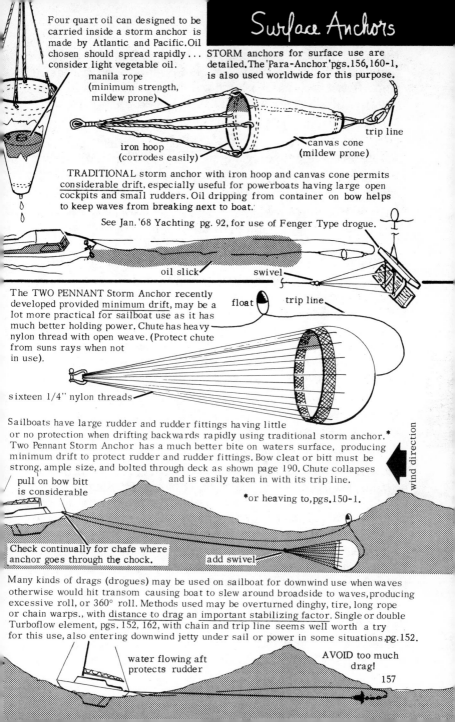

Four quart oil can designed to be carried inside a storm anchor is made by Atlantic and Pacific. Oil chosen should spread rapidly... consider light vegetable oil.

STORM anchors for surface use are detailed. The 'Para-Anchor' pgs. 156, 160-1, is also used worldwide for this purpose.

manila rope (minimum strength, mildew prone)

trip line

iron hoop (corrodes easily)

canvas cone (mildew prone)

TRADITIONAL storm anchor with iron hoop and canvas cone permits considerable drift, especially useful for powerboats having large open cockpits and small rudders. Oil dripping from container on bow helps to keep waves from breaking next to boat.

See Jan. '68 Yachting pg. 92, for use of Fenger Type drogue.

oil slick   swivel

The TWO PENNANT Storm Anchor recently developed provided minimum drift, may be a lot more practical for sailboat use as it has much better holding power. Chute has heavy nylon thread with open weave. (Protect chute from suns rays when not in use).

float   trip line

sixteen 1/4" nylon threads

Sailboats have large rudder and rudder fittings having little or no protection when drifting backwards rapidly using traditional storm anchor.* Two Pennant Storm Anchor has a much better bite on waters surface, producing minimum drift to protect rudder and rudder fittings. Bow cleat or bitt must be strong, ample size, and bolted through deck as shown page 190. Chute collapses and is easily taken in with its trip line.

wind direction

pull on bow bitt is considerable

*or heaving to, pgs. 150-1.

Check continually for chafe where anchor goes through the chock.   add swivel

Many kinds of drags (drogues) may be used on sailboat for downwind use when waves otherwise would hit transom causing boat to slew around broadside to waves, producing excessive roll, or 360° roll. Methods used may be overturned dinghy, tire, long rope or chain warps., with distance to drag an important stabilizing factor. Single or double Turboflow element, pgs. 152, 162, with chain and trip line seems well worth a try for this use, also entering downwind jetty under sail or power in some situations, pg. 152.

water flowing aft protects rudder

AVOID too much drag!

157

History of the mud hook or bottom anchor requiring thousands of years of development is shown on the facing page. If todays' modern anchors were available centuries ago, world history would have changed tremendously.

DANFORTH and NORTHILL anchors due to tremendous purchase power with light weight have much to recommend in todays use if properly dug in. The PLOW anchor seems to be favored by many of our cruising sailors today. Obtain sizes, specs., from the anchor manufacturers listed.

Paint all of these anchors WHITE so they are easier to see if properly dug in underwater... fouled, or wrapped around a rock, as the gray galvanize finish rapidly disappears as it merges with color of rocks, mud, etc.

Large MUSHROOM is a pivot center for chain to swivel on, as permanent mooring in all but loose sandy bottoms. With sufficient chain and properly dug in .. it has good holding power. Enough chain, scope, etc., required, pg. 167, for hurricane high water, yet must be compromised with local restrictions in New York area. Our only use for the small mushroom is shown page 161, not as an anchor.

Grapnels are used for anchoring in rocky or, coral formations, or to pick up mooring chain in the spring of the year if left in the water year round.

STOCKLESS or Navy type is used on large vessels with purchase depending mostly on WEIGHT. If a ship were shelled (WWI thinking) the vessel could steam out dragging anchor due to its inefficient holding power. Until modern lightweight anchors were produced, the YACHTSMAN anchor was preferred due to light size and easy stowage.

●

Care should be used to see anchor pin doesn't unwind when anchor line is shackled to anchor. For temporary use, monofilament fishing line is more practical than hemp, wire, etc. To lock pin for permanent use, a punch may be applied to cut the threads which lock the shackle to the pin.

Some anchors don't require stock, others require one to prevent rolling sideways.

DANFORTH anchor, also pg. 162; Navy lightweight (LWT) anchor.

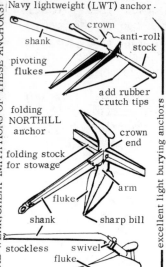

crown
anti-roll stock
shank
pivoting flukes
add rubber crutch tips

folding NORTHILL anchor
crown end
folding stock for stowage
arm
fluke
shank
sharp bill

stockless swivel fluke

Woolsey PLOWRIGHT anchor

(vertical text at left: excellent light burying anchors)

For specific information on Danforth and Northill anchors write to Danforth, Portland, Maine 04103; for the Plowright, Woolsey Marine Industries, 201 East 42nd St., New York, New York 10017.

Three anchors shown are excellent for temporary anchoring, while large mushroom is used in many areas for a permanent mooring, pages 166, 167. A good anchor has imitators with varying quality, so check look alikes closely. The shear pin anchor is questionable as we've seen the pins shear too often at the wrong time.

The Danforth is used by many sailors. Danforths' Bob Ogg uses the twelve pound Hi-Tensile for all purpose use on his 64' Huckins, with better strength for weight ratio than their Standard anchor. Large party fishing boats in our area which anchor numerous times daily seem to prefer the Northill.

The plow anchor designed by an Englishman is better known and more widely used in Europe. As more Americans are exposed to it, they are also developing a strong preference for this anchor.

Contact manufacturers above for the best light lunch hook, working anchor, and storm anchor, along with their recommended anchor rode specs., (combination fiber line and chain) for your boat.

Ground tackle term includes anchor, chain, line, shackle assembly.

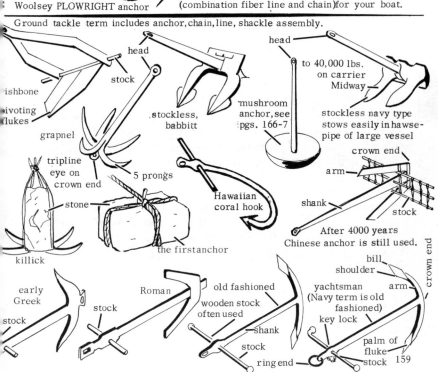

head
stock

fishbone
pivoting flukes
grapnel
tripline eye on crown end
stone
killick

5 prongs
the first anchor

stockless, babbitt

head
to 40,000 lbs. on carrier Midway

mushroom anchor, see pgs. 166-7

stockless navy type stows easily in hawse-pipe of large vessel

crown end
arm
shank
stock
After 4000 years Chinese anchor is still used.

Hawaiian coral hook

early Greek
stock

Roman
stock

old fashioned
wooden stock often used
shank
stock
ring end

yachtsman (Navy term is old fashioned)
bill
shoulder
arm
crown end
key lock
palm of fluke
stock

159

Size of anchor depends on type of boating area. If boat is over 18' in an exposed sailing area, two anchors are preferred. One may be a light lunch hook handled with minimum effort; the other one larger permitting your boat to ride out any kind of expected storm in your area.

Follow anchor lowering procedure shown, yet consider emergency heaving method discussed pgs.162.-3. Carry more than enough anchor line for a strong blow in your area. In many locations it means 15' of heavy chain, with 300' of anchor line. Length is to provide enough scope in shallow area, so anchor will dig in deep and stay.

A 3 or 4 to 1 scope is common for good weather, while in deep water say 600', a 2 to 1 scope is supposedly sufficient also if enough chain is used. The 8 to 1 scope theory often provides wry remarks in our area with 1000' to 3000' depths a short distance off shore. The volume, weight, cost, etc., make the 8 to 1 scope quite impractical.

Are your anchors painted? We've seen <u>white anchors</u> we felt dug in correctly, fouled at depths to 100', yet still visible in clear water. In murky water we've seen white anchors visible to 20', galvanized ones, to 4'. A scuba diving course proved invaluable to check anchors, which might be a good winter project to consider. The training not only proved ideal for this purpose but provided a lot of fun for underwater sight seeing. Friends presented us with an elderly anchor drag alarm. Anchor and weight dragging at same time, actuates battery-powered alarm.

The "Para-Anchor" and "Two Pennant Storm Anchor" were developed and tested by your author as a result of several unpleasant heavy weather experiences on power-boats and sailboats. The 'Para-Anchor' at right is an ideal all-purpose deep-water surface anchor known and used worldwide, pg.156. While we've found 50' to 75' of anchor line and trip line sufficient for good weather, both lines should be considerably longer for heavy weather use, pages 155-156.

An anchor may be fouled by swinging around her anchor when the wind, tide, or both change direction. A two anchor system may be used to avoid this, page 162.

Drop anchor slowly and gently to reduce chance of fouling anchor or line in all but emergency conditions, see pages 162-3.

SCOPE is ratio of anchor rode, page 159, paid out, to water depth which changes with the tidal stage.

2 to 1 scope may be sufficient for light weather, temporary anchoring.

We often find that a 4 to 1 scope is adequate for many anchoring conditions.

A scope of 7 or 8 to 1 is usually recommended for storm action in SHALLOW water, while less scope may be sufficient for deeper water.

1/4 holding power

1/2 holding power

7 or 8 to 1 scope   chafe
maximum holding power

Tape lower end of fiber anchor line to reduce chafe from sand rocks barnacles.

Heavy chain should be used on anchor end of line to improve anchor digging angle.

← chafe area

Anchor line was traditionally called a CABLE, generally 120 fathoms or 720 feet long, named by anchor to which it belonged as the SHEET cable, Bower cable, etc., on square riggers.

Use a buoyed trip line when anchoring in a rocky area. This will make it easier to locate anchor if caught in rocks.

float or plastic bottle

Alarm indicates anchor is dragging.

BRRRRING

If you have to anchor with short scope in rough weather, use as much chain as possible, and/or send weight down anchor line to reduce pull angle on the anchor, also easing shock on anchor line in wave action.

sag (catenary) in line
weight is about half way down anchor line

light line

rocks

Check for chafe where the anchor line goes through chock.

Traditional name for weight above on anchor line was called 'kellet' or 'sentinel'. Small mushroom anchor is practical for this use.

float

trip line

anchor line

'Para-Anchor' is a deep water surface anchor for light weather conditions as well as riding out a major storm, pages 155-6.

swivel

24' diameter parachute

161

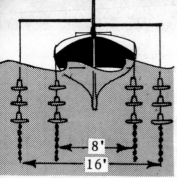

The rock and roll of a bad anchorage is good to mix martinis, but difficult on tempers. We use ROCKER STOPPERS*® ("Mexican hats") with chain, secured to our boat amidship, to reduce the excessive motion. If distance between them is doubled, the motion is again reduced by a half.

A Tahiti ketch entering a Mexican port ahead of a storm, had engine failure just before reaching the jetty. The owner heaved a 5 lb. hi-tensile Danforth which dug in immediately. It saved the boat, while holding for 18 hours with winds 35 to 50 knots, and ground swells often breaking under the stern. P. S., it gave the anchor a bent fluke.

Majority of boats put ashore or sunk in the South Seas, seems due to a minor unexpected engine failure such as the one mentioned. In '66 our engine quit in the breaker line. I heaved our 5 lb. Danforth using double braided anchor line, in a similar manner to our heaving line. The anchor dug in immediately, saving our boat.

A light Danforth ready for heaving in a tight spot, may also save your boat some day, but it requires special practice. As 3 strand has more tendency to kink when heaving, we recommend braided line stowed as discussed on page 186.

We enjoy taking the neighborhood kids fishing. The anchor line is led through the bow chock and back to the jib winch. The anchor is lowered from the cockpit, and raised by cranking it in with the jib winch.

Twin bow anchors can hold a boat in a changeable condition of tidal current or wind, as either anchor will hold the boat. The boat is first anchored bow and stern, then the stern line walked forward and secured to the bow cleat.

*Pastime Prod. Inc., 419 Park Ave. South, New York, NY 10016

162

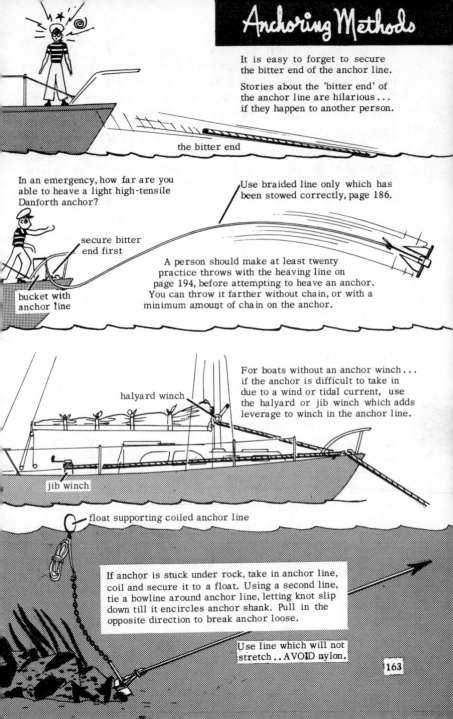

It is easy to forget to secure the bitter end of the anchor line.

Stories about the 'bitter end' of the anchor line are hilarious... if they happen to another person.

the bitter end

In an emergency, how far are you able to heave a light high-tensile Danforth anchor?

Use braided line only which has been stowed correctly, page 186.

secure bitter end first

bucket with anchor line

A person should make at least twenty practice throws with the heaving line on page 194, before attempting to heave an anchor. You can throw it farther without chain, or with a minimum amount of chain on the anchor.

For boats without an anchor winch... if the anchor is difficult to take in due to a wind or tidal current, use the halyard or jib winch which adds leverage to winch in the anchor line.

halyard winch

jib winch

float supporting coiled anchor line

If anchor is stuck under rock, take in anchor line, coil and secure it to a float. Using a second line, tie a bowline around anchor line, letting knot slip down till it encircles anchor shank. Pull in the opposite direction to break anchor loose.

Use line which will not stretch .. AVOID nylon.

163

For the sailor having luxury of ample mooring area, the only problem is to know right moment to point bow of boat into wind so it will stop next to mooring can. Forward inertia will carry boat to stop close enough so crew may grab pickup ring with his hands or with a boat hook.

In crowded areas, sailboat when possible should be luffed up to mooring instead, so if swimmer or other obstacle appears at last moment, the boat may be brought back into control by pulling in sheets. Otherwise the jib has to be backwinded before boat will respond to tiller.

The skipper at right has choice to approach mooring on either beam reach or close reach, the idea being to approach mooring upwind, using the sails as an airbrake at required moment, to stop forward motion. If downwind approach is made in any type of wind, the sails should be lowered to reduce inertia, then drop a BUCKET off stern at last moment to act as a water or hydraulic brake . . . if it is secured to the boat.

Always remember to have constant lookout for any other boats that may intercept your course though they may be temporarily hidden behind another boat.

When going through single moorings, the SAFE side to approach a boat or mooring is on the boats STERN . . while its bow is the DANGEROUS or windward side. If a sudden puff hits, it may blow your boat into the mooring, mooring line, or bow of moored boat. If you are close to its stern, a sudden puff of wind will blow you away from the moored boat; the exception, is a sudden wind shift.

If you have to cross in front of moored craft and your boat can't point high enough to clear it, get as much way on as possible. Now turn into the wind and coast until it is safe to pay off on a tack. This is called SHOOTING, and should not be tried unless your boat can easily clear the obstructions, mooring float and chain. Shooting should be avoided in small light sailboat that has minimum inertia.

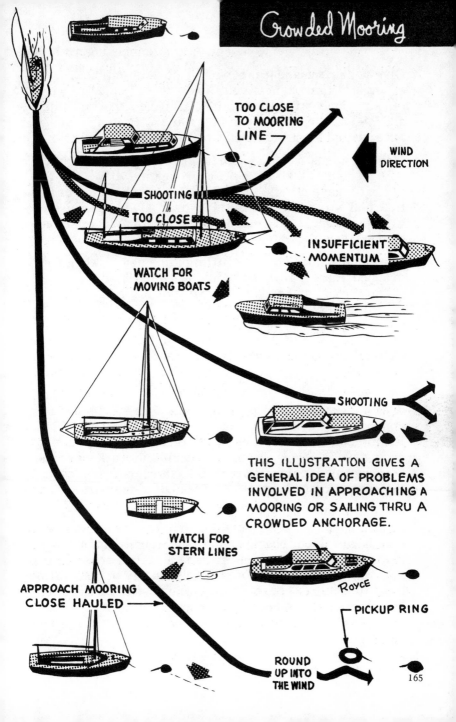

Crowded Mooring

TOO CLOSE TO MOORING LINE

WIND DIRECTION

SHOOTING TOO CLOSE

INSUFFICIENT MOMENTUM

WATCH FOR MOVING BOATS

SHOOTING

THIS ILLUSTRATION GIVES A GENERAL IDEA OF PROBLEMS INVOLVED IN APPROACHING A MOORING OR SAILING THRU A CROWDED ANCHORAGE.

WATCH FOR STERN LINES

ROYCE

APPROACH MOORING CLOSE HAULED

PICKUP RING

ROUND UP INTO THE WIND

165

Give your permanent mooring serious attention. This is especially important if your area is subjected to winds of hurricane strength and its resulting abnormal tides, and also if your boat can only have a limited amount of area or arc to swing through.

Plan the needs of your mooring on east coast, so that it will be able to take your boat through the above situation, yet still have a little slack left. The combination of high tide and strong winds blowing over a wide expanse of water can make an anchorage difficult. Add a strong current and the situation becomes quite serious.

The mushroom anchor has little holding power when first dropped. Have a rowboat riding to the painter for a week or so for the mushroom to have time to dig in. Since it is basically a pivot instead of anchor, the heavy chain is the mushroom anchors greatest need. If it has adequate chain, the snap of a boats pull will be absorbed by the chain, the mushroom will be most difficult to break out.

A good mushroom anchor in a good holding bottom with adequate heavy chain, is the best boat insurance. Main area to watch for is the painter, and as storm seasons approach, always try to have two painters to a mooring. Examine and replace any worn links, shackles, and pins once a year. Since the pins are able to work loose and set a boat adrift, always wire them, taking into due account the corrosion with eventual breakage of the wire.

Makeshift anchors such as locomotive wheels, chunks of concrete, etc., are wonderful on a calm day. When a storm hits the area, your boat may take that weight for a very expensive ride through a crowded mooring area. The cup shaped mushroom anchor that is properly dug in will be most difficult to break loose . . . IF the boat has sufficient heavy chain with adequate scope, to swivel on.

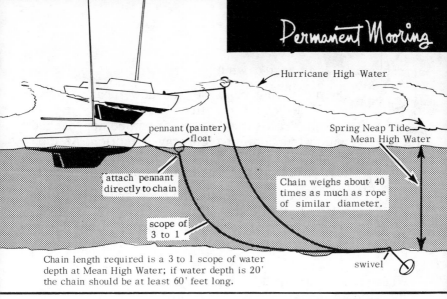

Hurricane High Water

pennant (painter)
float

Spring Neap Tide
Mean High Water

attach pennant
directly to chain

Chain weighs about 40
times as much as rope
of similar diameter.

scope of
3 to 1

swivel

Chain length required is a 3 to 1 scope of water
depth at Mean High Water; if water depth is 20'
the chain should be at least 60' feet long.

boat length	chain size	anchor weight	pennant length	pennant strength	notes
up to 15	5/16"	100 lbs.	4'	400 lbs.	Anchor weight
16' to 20'	3/8"	150 lbs.	8'	600 lbs.	is increased at the rate of 10 lbs.
21' to 25'	3/8"	200 lbs.	10'	800 lbs.	per foot on boats
30'	1/2"	300 lbs.	10'	1200 lbs.	26' and over.
35'	1/2"	350 lbs.	10'	1400 lbs.	Safe working load
40'	5/8"	400 lbs.	10'	1600 lbs.	of pennant is four times the weight of
45'	5/8"	450 lbs.	10'	1800 lbs.	the anchor used.
50'	5/8"	500 lbs.	10'	2000 lbs.	

Specifications shown above are the MINIMUM standards for the Port of New York,
also including the areas of Western Long Island to Larchmont and Huntington Harbor,
excepting narrow Sheepshead Bay which requires two anchors for each mooring buoy.

Mooring must be raised at intervals not to exceed TWO years, so it can be inspected
for damage from bottom chafing, corrosion, and destructive water conditions.

Authors note: Shackles with screw pins require the eye of the pin to be secured to
the shackle (see page 158) to prevent pin from unwinding. After mooring is in water
a couple of months corrosion generally expands galvanized steel screw pins, also
shrinking the eye of the shackle, making it more difficult for screw pin to unwind.

Periodically check mooring fittings from the surface to five feet below. Corrosion
rate is usually more rapid in this area due to warmer surface temperature and a
larger oxygen content in the water. Stainless fittings are ideal for above the waters
surface use, but they should be AVOIDED at the waters surface and below. Due to
oxygen starvation crevice corrosion may result with stainless shackles, etc., which
is indicated by stress cracks.

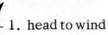

1. head to wind

2. luffing

On the facing page we see how ideal a three sided dock is for sailboats. Providing it has enough draft for sailboats, it can be approached with wind coming from any direction. At the proper moment a boat can point into the wind, turn on the sail airbrakes, and stop at the dock.

If one or two sides of the dock are blocked, or a boat has to come off and return to a lee dock, it becomes more of a sporting proposition. These variables are covered in the following pages.

●

When approaching dock or mooring under ideal conditions, the skipper usually has a choice of two approaches. In one he will round up into the wind breaking the airfoil, or putting the boat in irons. This will reduce the inertia so the sailboat will drift up and stop at the desired spot next to dock or mooring. Since the boat is weathercocked into the wind, page 96, all sheets must be slacked.

For the second approach, the mooring or dock will be directly on sailboats course. The airfoil is broken by luffing or slacking off on the sheets. To balance the boat the jib sheet is let fly first, then the main slowly slacked as the boat reduces speed.

In crowded areas it is especially important to keep a boat under control all way by luffing up to a dock or mooring. If a swimmer, boat, or other object has to be avoided, the sheets can be trimmed in for immediate rudder control.

Suppose a sailboat approaches a dock or mooring buoy by turning head to wind, losing inertia and response to rudder. The quickest method to get under way again, is to have crew member back the jib on opposite side to the tack you want to put boat on, see page 95.

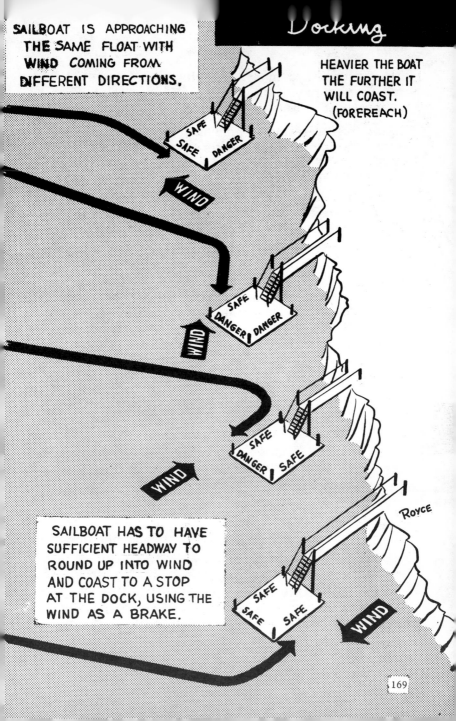

The lee dock has many variables to be considered all the way from methods to approach it, and the individual response of a boat due to weight and hull design.

In the first situation a sloop has to sail into a downwind dock. The main is the first sail lowered some way out, followed by the jib to keep it weathercocked on downwind course. Enough steerageway must be maintained so boat will respond to rudder all way into slip. The boat is then stopped by dropping a bucket off the stern to provide a momentary hydraulic water brake.

In the second situation a sailboat rounds up head to wind with jib lowered first, followed by main. A bucket is dropped over bow, so boat will slowly drift backwards stern to dock. The galvanized iron bucket with a stout handle is recommended for both situations, instead of a weak canvas bucket, or a small storm anchor that only has a purchase on the water in heavy weather.

The third method of anchoring and backing into an adverse dock has a lot to be recommended if you want to go sailing shortly, and the anchor doesn't foul or drag during this maneuver.

While variables exist on facing page due to hull inertia and design, it becomes even more obvious stopping in tight downwind slip at left.

Under normal conditions a light 14' sailboat may sail into the slip, stopping boat at last moment by suddenly turning the bow 180°. This kills its minimum inertia & the boat suddenly stops.

A heavy keel boat same size or larger on the same course usually approaches same dock with bare poles Lower main first, later jib to weather-cock boat downwind. The craft is then stopped in slip by suddenly turning the bow 180°.

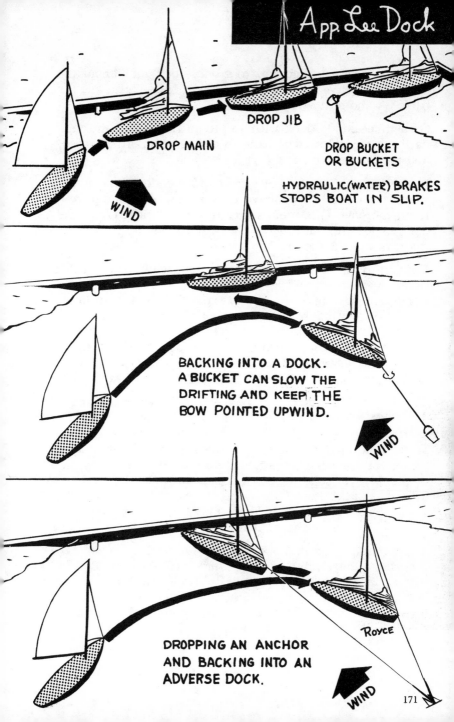

App. Lee Dock

DROP JIB

DROP MAIN

DROP BUCKET
OR BUCKETS

HYDRAULIC (WATER) BRAKES
STOPS BOAT IN SLIP.

WIND

BACKING INTO A DOCK.
A BUCKET CAN SLOW THE
DRIFTING AND KEEP THE
BOW POINTED UPWIND.

WIND

DROPPING AN ANCHOR
AND BACKING INTO AN
ADVERSE DOCK.

ROYCE

WIND

171

With the wind straight on to a one sided dock, about the best way to leave it is kedge out, raise sails, raise anchor, back jib and sail away.

On a three sided dock with ample sailing water, the same sailboat can be towed by hand to either side, sails raised, and the boat sailed away.

If the wind is coming directly off the dock, or on the sailboats quarter, you have to weathercock boat, page 96, from the bow. This means that it will be sailed from the dock under jib. Out a ways the boat rounds up into wind, main is raised, then sailed away.

Especially when encountering a lee dock to be sailed from, study the existing cleats, buoys, etc., that if used correctly will take you away from dock with minimum fuss. Quite often by towing a boat to another cleat, or turning it around with spring lines, lee dock problems may be eliminated. A heaving line requires little space can be used as a lead line to test depth, & provide method to take sailboat from lee dock across into windward dock.

To be sure the tack a catboat will take when leaving a dock or mooring, back the mainsail to opposite side. This unbalanced force will shove bow out. Approaching a dock from a downwind course provides a couple outstanding variables. In a light racing hull such as the Finn, the daggerboard must be down for it to round up and stop at the dock. A heavy cruising cat on same course, may raise centerboard, pivot 180° so boat will settle right up to dock . . . due to different inertia and hull design.

Slip lines may prove to advantage for pivots, etc., to take a sailboat out from a lee dock under power or sail, or to pivot boat at dock by hand. While slip lines have many uses, they should not have knots or other increased dia. at end that might catch in a cleat, causing more than a normal share of undocking comedy.

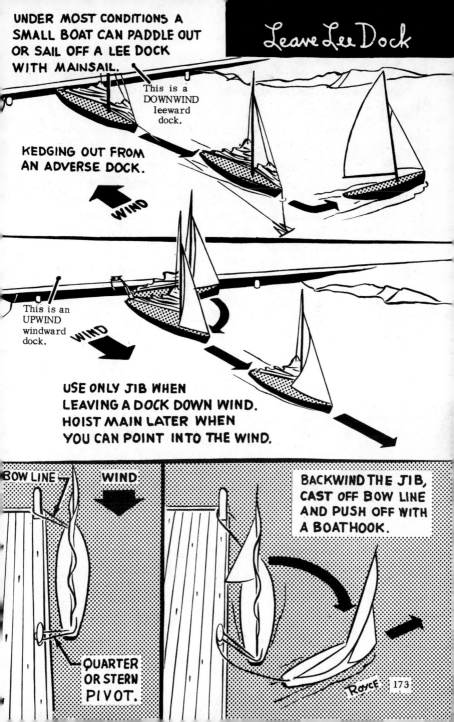

UNDER MOST CONDITIONS A SMALL BOAT CAN PADDLE OUT OR SAIL OFF A LEE DOCK WITH MAINSAIL.

Leave Lee Dock

This is a DOWNWIND leeward dock.

KEDGING OUT FROM AN ADVERSE DOCK.

WIND

This is an UPWIND windward dock.

WIND

USE ONLY JIB WHEN LEAVING A DOCK DOWN WIND. HOIST MAIN LATER WHEN YOU CAN POINT INTO THE WIND.

BOW LINE

WIND

BACKWIND THE JIB, CAST OFF BOW LINE AND PUSH OFF WITH A BOATHOOK.

QUARTER OR STERN PIVOT.

ROYCE 173

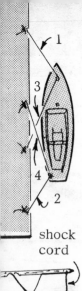

shock
cord

1. Bow line, 2. stern line; 3. after bow spring, 4. forward stern spring.

The bow line leads forward from the boats bow to the dock; a stern line from the stern or aft quarter to the dock.

Spring lines are used that lead forward from the stern, or aft from the bow. Purpose of these are to reduce fore and aft movement of boat at dock without strapping boat too close to dock. Another advantage of spring lines, is to act as pivots for turning a boat at the dock by hand, under sail, or under power.

Our first sailboat was too active at its mooring, especially in a tidal current. In many conditions it wanted to climb up and over the float. While it damaged the paint, the continual banging and clanging through the night was hardly pleasant.

Our first attempt to drop a bucket over the stern worked with great success for two nights keeping the boat off the mooring float. The pressures soon pulled the cleat out of the deck, the bucket disappeared, and we were back where we started... banging against the metal float.

A temporary bowsprit or holdoff pole lashed to your boat, with a shock cord extending from its outer end to the mooring can, is a practical method to eliminate the problem. Since it sticks out beyond the buoy, it stands a good chance of being hit and/or broken by another boat. This practice may be reduced by carving a rather sharp point on the outer end of the temporary bowsprit or pole.

About the only disagreeable aspect of the holdoff pole, is that it usually goes overboard when you cast off from the mooring. If not picked up for a couple of weeks, it may collect a considerable barnacle and grass growth if it has not had a coating of bottom paint.

short dock   stern in   bow in

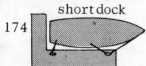
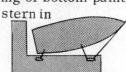
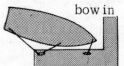

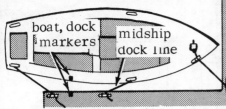

boat, dock markers
midship dock line

After adjustment, add permanent markings.

Sailing through tight mooring areas may become quite challenging. If a person isn't adequately trained, it may also be expensive since he is self convicted, if his boat underway collides with another that is moored.

It is easier to go through sailboats swinging to single moorings than double moorings. Since the moored sailboat

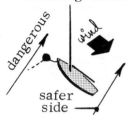

dangerous

wind

safer side

will point into the wind or current whichever is stronger, the safest side to pass is usually under its stern.

If a sudden wind puff hits, it should blow your boat away from the moored ones stern. If you were passing near the bow or danger side, a sudden wind puff might lay your boat over right into the moored one.

Another factor to consider, is that sailboats and power boats do not always lay the same to a mooring. A sailboat with more wetted area usually swings to the current while a nearby powerboat with more windage and less bottom area, may swing with the wind and be more restless.

In areas having little mooring space, boats often have to tie up between double moorings. Instead of sailing under the stern of these, you sail between the mooring buoy lanes. Again you have to sail closer to the windward one than the leeward, to protect your boat in a sudden wind puff.

While sailing through tight anchorages, you also have to take into account the wind variables. In a light wind on a centerboard boat with little way on, you must stay farther away from moored boats than in a stronger steady breeze.

Our boat above has three sets of docklines mounted on both sides of boat, which are a great aid while instructing students in docking under a wide variety of conditions. Markers on boat and dock make it easier to position a boat having a short dock or slip, such as shown above. 175

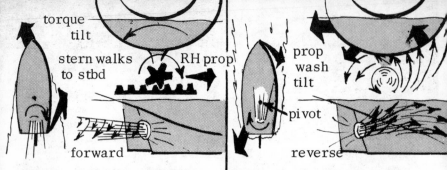

torque tilt

stern walks to stbd   RH prop

prop wash tilt

pivot

forward   reverse

| Maximum flow across rudder, maximum steering response. | Minimum flow past rudder, minimum steering response. |

Especially when accelerating, a boat doesn't track straight ahead. RH prop walks stern to stbd, pulling bow to port, note hull pivot. Compensate, correct with rudder.

When accelerating in reverse with minimum flow across rudder, the major factor is rotary prop wash pushing up against stbd hull bottom depressing port side, producing list which pulls stern to port, bow to starboard.

Back your boat for 100 yards. After reaching speed in reverse, inertia overcomes prop wash forces. Port stern pull may temporarily reverse or neutralize itself. For a sailboat steering with rudder, RH prop on outboard motor locked so motor won't turn, it also follows inboard pattern.

LH prop produces opposite stern walking/pulling factors. Offset and folding racing props are more individualized and complicated to understand.

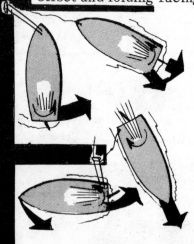

Boat left is using bow pivot line to pull stern out from dock to compensate for stbd prop wash. Bow line is slipped when stern is far enough out from dock.

Off center stern pivot line may be used to walk stern around dock. Pull line in rapidly when slipped not to foul prop. Use forward spurts till dock is cleared to minimize fwd stbd stern walking potential when accelerating.

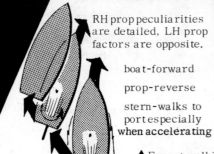

RH prop peculiarities are detailed, LH prop factors are opposite.

boat-forward

prop-reverse

stern-walks to port especially **when accelerating**

Single Screw

boat-reverse

prop-forward

stern-may swing to stbd if wind or current isn't present

▲ <u>Expect</u> walking/pulling <u>variables</u> due to weight, hull underbody, size of propeller, windage, current, etc.

boat-forward

prop-reverse

rudder-to port

stern-first stbd, then rapidly to port.

boat-reverse

prop-forward

stern-rapidly to stbd, bow may hit the dock

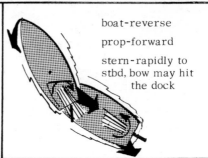

Approach slowly with less angle to dock

boat-forward

prop-reverse

stern-to port. straighten out with short bursts fwd throttle

boat-reverse

prop-forward then reverse

stern-rapidly to port

bow-rapidly to stbd, bow may hit dock

Boat/prop in reverse-stern only to port, bow to starboard.

Boat below is backing out long slip. Stern pulls to port in reverse. Counteract with short sudden burst of forward swinging stern to stbd. Then reverse again, drift out in neutral. While boat is still backing, use rudder, prop forward to pivot boat in short turning radius.

A simple meter is needed.

Carbon Monoxide

The average person living in modern society has been exposed to more carbon monoxide than he realizes due to theoretical training in high school physics that carbon monoxide is tasteless, colorless, and odorless.

Develop a positive attitude that you will recognize the smell of exhaust fumes coming from all gasoline engines. This is the smell from partially burned hydrocarbons. Any time you are able to smell these fumes...carbon monoxide is also present inside a garage, car, boat, or plane.

You have to be continually on guard for this deadly, sweet, gentle, numbing, mind crippler, as its awareness will only last a short time before the scent organ loses its sensitivity.

Carbon monoxide is a DEOXIDIZER since it is absorbed into the blood stream to 250 times faster and easier than oxygen. It unites with the hemoglobin in the blood...to prevent oxygen from going to the skin tissues.

SYMPTOMS. If you wake up with a 5 martini hangover yet you haven't had an alcoholic drink for several days, check for carbon monoxide. If your boat is underway and you feel like you have had a stiff drink, are drowsy, or irritable, yet the strongest drink you've had is coffee, check right away for the carbon monoxide source.

As a victim becomes sleepy, he may have a red face, headache, dizziness, and loss of balance or vertigo. As he becomes sleepy the heart may pound or flutter, and the oxygen starvation may soon cause irreversible damage to the brain. A person may be confused or incoherent in the early stages, similar to drinking too much alcoholic beverages.

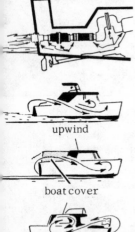

upwind

boat cover

downwind

Powerboat carbon monoxide problems are shown as they are similar, yet more obvious than on a sailboat. When you smell these gasoline exhaust fumes in a cabin going upwind, open a forward hatch, or if downwind, stay out of the cabin. Check for the source such as exhaust clamps, hoses, and manifold leaks.

If you have had a bout with carbon monoxide, blood transfusions may help, but be sure none of the donors have hepatitus, making it worse.

DIESEL engines produce unpleasant fumes, yet no carbon monoxide. The proof... only diesel engines are permitted deep in mines. Though they use up precious oxygen, carbon monoxide exhausts for miners in confined areas aren't classed as a health hazard.

Sailing Illustrated

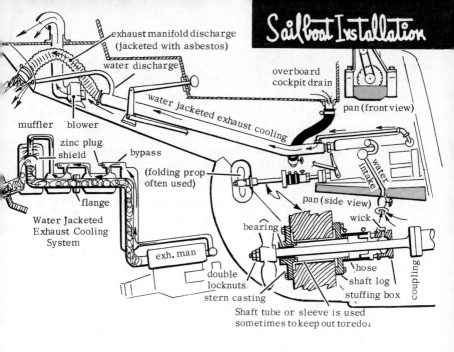

exhaust manifold discharge
(jacketed with asbestos)

water discharge

overboard
cockpit drain

pan (front view)

water jacketed exhaust cooling

muffler blower

zinc plug
shield

bypass

(folding prop
often used)

flange

Water Jacketed
Exhaust Cooling
System

water intake

pan (side view)

wick

bearing

exh. man

double
locknuts

stern casting

hose

shaft log

stuffing box

coupling

Shaft tube or sleeve is used
sometimes to keep out toredo

The 4 cycle low-performance sailboat engine operating at displacement speeds may operate almost troublefree for many years if it is adequately understood and properly maintained.

As compression isn't critical in the 18 to 40 hp engine, the 35' sailboat above normally uses a 25 hp engine, they are able to operate on lower octane fuel than needed for many autos. The main problems though are sporatic operation, and then often at full throttle for long periods, is that of fuel storage, and condensation inside the tanks, especially if stored out of the water during the winter months. Check with your dealer, engine manufacturer, and refiner, for the latest products to be used in this rapidly changing field.

The schematic shows a diesel engine exhaust system for a 40' sailboat. When flanges are used, it is necessary to make a BYPASS to carry water from one water jacket chamber to the next. Exhaust gases rise in the muffler while water is sprayed into the exhaust chamber through a series of holes or orifices. The engine water and exhaust gases finally combine to drain overboard.

The sailboat engine often operates cold, sometimes under 135°, using the free flowing outside water cooling source, without causing boiler scale to precipitate in the water passages, which can build up, strangle, and cause severe overheating in raw outside cooling water with thermostat temperatures above 150°.

Since the low water cooling temperature also causes insufficient heat to boil off oil contaminents of sulfur, condensation, and sludge, more frequent oil changes are required to reduce sulfuric acid, a product of sulfur and water.

The full length DRIP PAN is seldom found on inboard power boats, is a commendable item to keep a clean bilge. They are often found on ocean-going sailboats requiring clean bilges for food and storage on a long race or cruise.

The 7 1/2 hp long-shaft "aluminum spinnaker" installed in the aft lazarette of our "Pink Cloud" required much time to install, proving more practical than we had anticipated.

The motor is seldom used during instruction, except if the wind goes down. On trips to Catalina over 26 miles away, we call our boat a motor sailer, as the motor is used about half the time if we are to follow a schedule.

A plate form-fitted to the outboard motor, is bolted to the top of the outboard well to seal off the compartment from ocean water. We wish outboard manufacturers had templates showing contour of outboard at this intersection.

Correct fuel is important for 2 cycle operation. We use a good premix outboard fuel and run it out of carburetor after use, so motor starts with a couple of pulls.

Ventilation of the closed compartment is important to pass USCG requirements. Ventilation is also required to retard corrosion rate on bottom of metal outboard fuel tanks, detailed at right. Frame on platform restricts horizontal movement of tank, while stout shock cord restricts up and down movement in a seaway.

Maintenance of our motor left in the water year-round is rather easy. It has a yearly tuneup and the water pump is replaced yearly. Check grease level in lower end occasionally, and lubricate exposed connections often with WD-40®. Three or four times a year an organic bottom paint (TBTO) is painted on the immersed portion of the outboard motor to retard ocean growth which is quite rapid . . . AVOID corrosive copper bottom paints.

We feel a 7 1/2 hp long-shaft motor most adequate for our sailboat. Due to the extra 5" shaft length, the prop stays submerged even in considerable seas. When towing a heavy 28' powerboat with engine failure, we had about a knot loss in speed while towing it both with sail and outboard power.

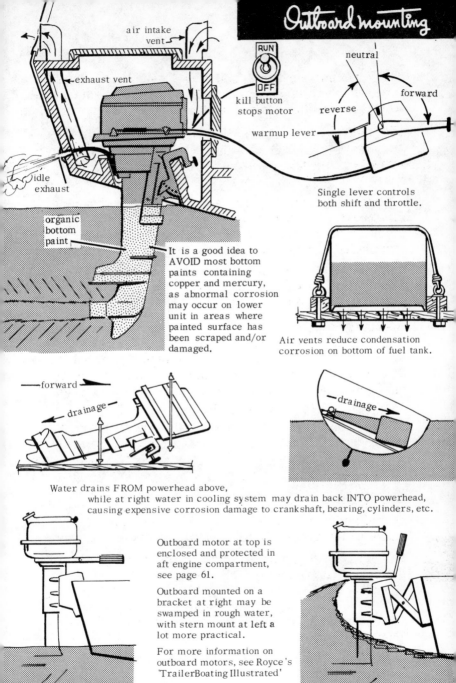

air intake vent

exhaust vent

RUN
OFF

kill button
stops motor

idle exhaust

organic bottom paint

neutral

forward

reverse

warmup lever

Single lever controls
both shift and throttle.

It is a good idea to
AVOID most bottom
paints containing
copper and mercury,
as abnormal corrosion
may occur on lower
unit in areas where
painted surface has
been scraped and/or
damaged.

Air vents reduce condensation
corrosion on bottom of fuel tank.

forward

drainage

drainage

Water drains FROM powerhead above,
while at right water in cooling system may drain back INTO powerhead,
causing expensive corrosion damage to crankshaft, bearing, cylinders, etc.

Outboard motor at top is
enclosed and protected in
aft engine compartment,
see page 61.

Outboard mounted on a
bracket at right may be
swamped in rough water,
with stern mount at left a
lot more practical.

For more information on
outboard motors, see Royce's
'TrailerBoating Illustrated'

We are pleased to announce a new "Sailing Illustrated Course" workbook.

The course combines a variety of ideas tested during our evening public sail classes, available in our area for around 7 years, plus our full-day year-round private sailing lessons offered from 1960 to 1972 (shown above) when we ran out of time to continue such a service.

During this period we developed a "bare bones" workbook for classroom use and our private sailing lessons which continually had the acid test, especially on the water as anything that could go wrong...did! This helped to update our "Sailing Illustrated" and our sail course.

When we found the majority of orders for the sail course workbook eventually came from individuals instead of classroom use, it was time to revise and expand our workbook to be equally useful for homestudy use.

We have included perspective illustrations of a wide variety of sailboats from Sunfish, Laser, and Force 5, up through Penguin, Snipe, Coronado 15, and Lightning, to the P2/18, Hobie 14, and Hobie 16 catamarans, to add the terms to pick up the new foreign sailing language. Students may then apply these terms to the 1954 "Finisterre", and the ultra modern Catalina 38.

If you want to teach sailing to your family with our new course material, build a simple model sailboat with a mast 12" to 15" tall, using model airplane silk for sails . . . then operate this model in front of an electric fan.

The simple boat model will make it easy to pick up the miniature operation of sail raising, coming about, jibing, backing the jib, and spinnaker handling. You can also test various ways to approach an upwind or downwind mooring as covered in our sail course.

● The FOUNDATION. We are the first to say our 128 page sail course does not have ALL the answers.

Its purpose is to provide the foundation to the most difficult part of sailing which is the new sailing language, which is needed to understand sailboat operation underway.

After students add sufficient terms to their new workbook, plus key words to operational questions, they begin to be able to understand and use the new sailing language.

Sailing instructors will check the course material quite thoroughly, eventually realizing that due to its flexibility, they can use it to apply their own ideas and techniques, choosing only what they want to cover, plus pages to assign for homework study for the next lesson.

The goal is to turn out better, more thoroughly qualified sailing students with the continually illustrated coverage of a sport in which each person can find the amount of simplicity . . . or complexity he or she desires.

You will find the new "Sailing Illustrated Course" in an efficiently programmed sequence, an easier way to learn to sail than by previous methods.

Our "Sailing Illustrated" is a handy reference book to use with our course material, as well as being the key to locate those hard to find answers on the water when underway.

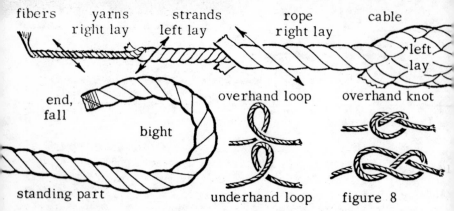

fibers — yarns right lay — strands left lay — rope right lay — cable left lay

end, fall — bight — overhand loop — overhand knot

standing part — underhand loop — figure 8

The navy defines ROPE as wire rope, LINE as fiber rope. Our sailing fraternity defines rope as becoming line only when used in boat operation including standing and running rigging, anchor line, etc., and rope when used to secure an object. See glossary pg. G25 for square rigger rope terms.

SYNTHETIC vs ORGANIC rope. Many changes have taken place since our book was first published. Synthetic rope obsoleted manila having more resistance to the elements, with greater strength for the same diameter rope.

Three strand nylon became popular for anchor lines, yet chafed easily and became brittle when subjected to the suns rays. Its elasticity proved a disadvantage for towing, and even hazardous when taking in anchor during storm.

During continuous testing of boating products we found BRAIDED rope equal and superior to three strand nylon in all areas except waist lifeline, pg. 229. Braided line is also easier on hands for sheets and halyards than three strand Dacron or polypropylene.

● Best photographic book of three strand knots and splicing we've found is "The Art of Knotting and Splicing" by Cyrus Day, pub. by U.S. Naval Institute, Baltimore, Md. 21402.

● For 1819 knots, splicing, gaskets, mats, blocks, tackles, and other methods, extremely well illustrated to fully rig and operate square riggers is "Lever's Young Sea Officers Sheet

Anchor", Sweetman Co., Box 1509, Largo, Florida 33540.

Strength shown is new
rope under test conditions.

| diameter | | traditional | controlled stretch | | minimum stretch | | galvanized chain |
| metric | inches | 3 strand | 3 strand | braided | 3 strand | braided | |
		manila	nylon	Gold-N-Braid	Dacron & polypro	Yacht Braid	
6mm	1/4	600	1850	2100	1750	2300	2700
8mm	5/16	1000	2850	3500	2650	3450	3700
9mm	3/8	1350	4000	4800	3600	4950	4600
10.5mm	7/16	1750	5500	6500	4800	6600	6200
12mm	1/2	2650	7100	8300	6100	8600	8200
14mm	9/16	3400	8350	11200	7400	11700	10200
16mm	5/8	4400	10500	14500	9000	15200	12500
18mm	3/4	5400	14200	18000	12500	19100	17700
22mm	7/8	7700	19000	26500	16000	28300	24000
24mm	1"	9000	24600	31300	20000	33600	31000

Braided rope strength provided by Samson Ocean Systems, Inc.;
variables exist with 3 strand rope specifications.

Rope and chain strength table listed above is "minimum" or
lowest tension under which it may break at any given point,
exclusive of damage from chafe, sharp edges, etc.

The safe working load of rope is computed with a safety factor
of 5 to 1, providing maximum security where life and property
are involved. A rope with a safe working load of 2000 pounds
without chafe should require one with a ratio on the above
table of 10,000 pounds or more.

This large safety factor is recommended by rope manufacturers
due to unusual conditions of extreme wind and wave action,
sudden jerks, or strains your boat may be exposed to from
time to time.

While chafe such as a dock line going through a small chock
with sharp edges will rapidly reduce its operational strength,
pg. 188, the safety factor may also be reduced to 80-85% by an
eye splice...and to 50% with a square knot with compression
and shearing action. A bowline on braided rope may reduce
rope strength to 70%, and to 60% with a bowline on 3 strand.

The cost of quality synthetic rope increases daily, yet it is
still a bargain in strength, chafe resistance, and long life, if
compared to manila rope which was the standard in 1960.

high points — chafe areas

minimum bearing surfaces   continuous bearing surface

Nylon rope is three times stronger than Manila which deteriorates rapidly, losing strength in boating use. Braided rope is up to 15% stronger than three strand synthetic rope of same diameter, varying with rope size.

Rope diameter shrinks as it stretches. At about 50% stretch 3 strand nylon may part, a hazard as end snaps back under load. A cleat pulled out under tow, snapping back to kill Coast Guard operator providing rescue tow service. Braided rope has 30% less stretch, reducing snapback in same situation, making it easier to tow another boat.

More time is required to know if anchor has dug in with 3 strand anchor line. 'Rubber band' action makes anchor difficult to break out in storm, or if caught under log it may fly back towards boat when suddenly released.

A major surprise came when testing 3 strand and braided anchor line. HIGH POINTS of 3 strand chafed rapidly against rocks, coral, chocks, breaking threads, reducing strength from minimum bearing surface. Resistance to abrasion of Samson Gold-N-Braid was surprising.

Age hardening is a factor to analyze when buying rope. We've seen imported synthetic rope which hardened and became brittle in two years, yet after considerable use Samson Braid still seems to have excellent flexibility... though both may look the same at boat shows when new.

Braided Dacron is preferred to 3 strand Dacron for sheets and halyards with longer life, easier on hands, 50% better gripping surface on sheaves, plus stronger for same dia.

Avoid coiling braided anchor line like 3 strand due to NEUTRAL LAY. We drop our 300' 7/16" braided anchor line into a plastic bucket to avoid hitches. We store another anchor line in a nylon sail bag with GROMMETS added for ventilation and drainage when stowed wet, also useful for storing wet storm
186 anchors, pages 156-7.   drains beneath↗ grommets

TWISTED LAY

3 strand is RIGHT lay

rotational, will unwind

always under stress with itself

spliceable

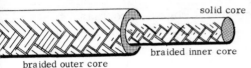

solid core

braided inner core

braided outer core

DOUBLE BRAIDED

non-rotational

neutral lay

not under stress with itself

spliceable

excellent for halyards, sheets, anchor line

hollow center, no core

HOLLOW BRAIDED

non-rotational

neutral lay

not under stress with itself

less efficient splice

usually polypropolene

good for towing as it floats

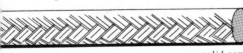

solid core

SOLID BRAIDED

non-rotational

neutral lay

not under stress with itself

seldom used for boating

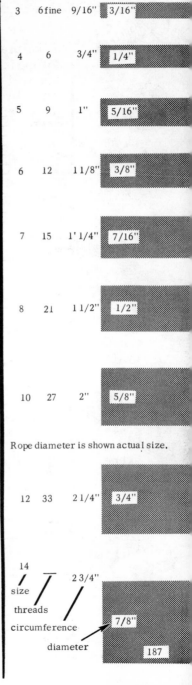

3	6 fine	9/16"	3/16"
4	6	3/4"	1/4"
5	9	1"	5/16"
6	12	1 1/8"	3/8"
7	15	1' 1/4"	7/16"
8	21	1 1/2"	1/2"
10	27	2"	5/8"

Rope diameter is shown actual size.

| 12 | 33 | 2 1/4" | 3/4" |

14 / size

/ threads

2 3/4" / circumference

7/8" ← diameter

187

tremendous
chafe..
AVOID!

skene
chock

leather gives
maximum
protection

Take braided rope from freely moving spool letting it fall into container pg. 186, so neutral lay will be maintained without kinks. Three strand rope is removed from coil by pulling inside end. Failure to do this, and coil three strand rope clockwise, will result in kinks.

Razors, knives.... and <u>small chocks,</u> are basically <u>cutting wedges</u>. Too many boats are lost at anchor or at the dock when the anchor line or dock lines have been chafed and cut through as a result of wind and wave action... setting the boats adrift.

Good rope is expensive. With normal care it may have a long useful life. If sharp edges are present for it to rub or chafe against, the useful life may be shortened considerably. Manila chafes easily especially if wet, while nylon has more chafe resistance. Braided rope has considerable resistance to chafe.

Adequate size skene chock lower left, of a larger size than first considered will not only reduce chafe action, but it will also help to prevent dock and anchor lines from jumping out of the chock in wave action.

A manila dinghy painter chafed, breaking twice in three days on a vacation. After resplicing, area was wrapped with <u>plastic</u> electricians tape. Very little chafe was evident at the same spot when we returned to the dock two weeks afterwards. We recommend you tape the eye and first two feet of anchor line, to extend its useful life and maximum strength, pg. 186.

First practical dock line chafe kits we've seen with sized/punched leathers, needle, thread, are manufactured by Svendsen Products, Box 1465, Torrance, Calif., 90505. They are excellent!

The fishermans knot is used to join fishline, twine, and small rope.

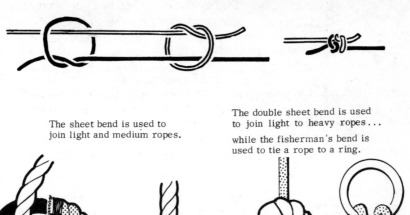

The sheet bend is used to join light and medium ropes.

The double sheet bend is used to join light to heavy ropes...

while the fisherman's bend is used to tie a rope to a ring.

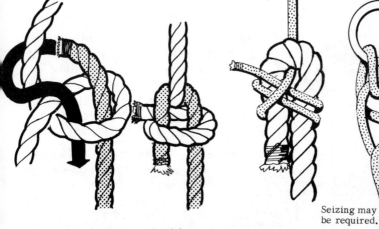

Seizing may be required.

The carrick bend is used to join heavy ropes, hawsers, and cables.

Rolling hitch is used to provide a lengthwise pull to a mast, spar, etc. A stopper knot may be needed if tow line has slippery surface.

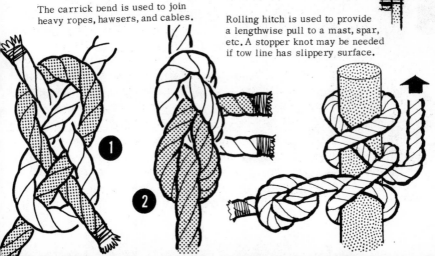

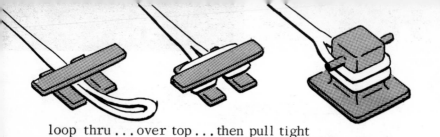

loop thru . . . over top . . . then pull tight

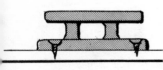

avoid wood
screws

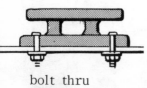

bolt thru
is better

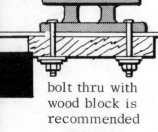

bolt thru with
wood block is
recommended

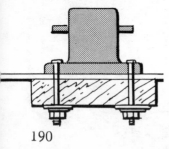

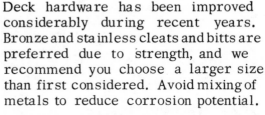

Deck hardware has been improved considerably during recent years. Bronze and stainless cleats and bitts are preferred due to strength, and we recommend you choose a larger size than first considered. Avoid mixing of metals to reduce corrosion potential.

Stronger dock lines of smaller diameter are used, which due to light weight often jump off cleats and bitts. Instead of the single loop, come through cleat (upper left) then put loop over top as shown. Use two loops around bitt to overcome tendency to jump off small bitts.

Wood screw cleat installation should be avoided on wooden and glass boats since the cleat can be ripped loose.

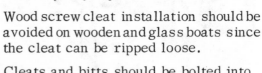

Cleats and bitts should be bolted into deck with wood block backing, & using washers of different sizes so stress will be spread over larger area, both on wooden and fiberglass boats.

●

If you have a sailboat 24' or larger, it may be a good idea to add a midship cleat for a spring line. With three dock lines looped as shown at top of page, and backed up correctly, a boat owner can recover a lot easier from a docking misjudgement . . . . which occasionally may happen to the best of sailors; see illustration top of page 175.

"ballit" (bollard) bitt cleat

Use two or three half hitches on cleat with three-strand synthetic line.

Use several half hitches on cleat with braided line, especially in the smaller diameters.

dock line

ock cord

Elvstrom compensator eases dock line pull in a surge.

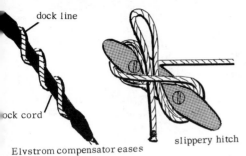

slippery hitch

the adjustable hitch

One or two loops are often used around object, when making the adjustable hitch.

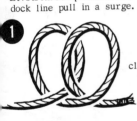

1

2 clove hitch

a slipped clove hitch

1 The jam hitch... it does the same job as a rolling hitch.

2

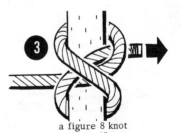

3 a figure 8 knot

The sheepshank is used to shorten a line. It must remain under tension to avoid slippage.

The BOWLINE has a wide variety of uses.

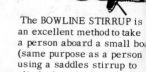

"MAN OVERBOARD"

The BOWLINE STIRRUP is an excellent method to take a person aboard a small boa (same purpose as a person using a saddles stirrup to climb aboard a horse).

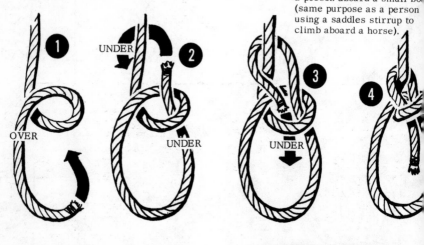

1 OVER UNDER **2** UNDER **3** UNDER **4**

The SQUARE KNOT was originally called a Reef Knot.

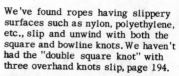

We've found ropes having slippery surfaces such as nylon, polyethylene, etc., slip and unwind with both the square and bowline knots. We haven't had the "double square knot" with three overhand knots slip, page 194.

192 Read "Lever's Sheet Anchor", pg. 284, for 1819 marlinspike practices.

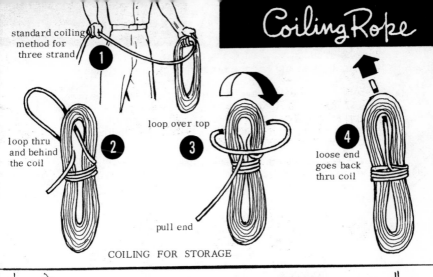

standard coiling method for three strand

1

loop thru and behind the coil **2**

loop over top **3**

pull end

4 loose end goes back thru coil

COILING FOR STORAGE

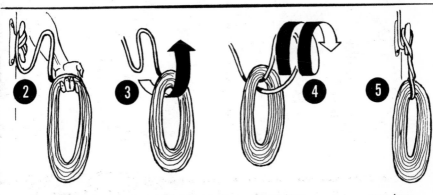

cleat halyard then coil line **2**

loop behind, then pull pull loop thru center **3**

rotate loop 2 or 3 times **4**

pass loop over cleat **5**

COILING A HALYARD

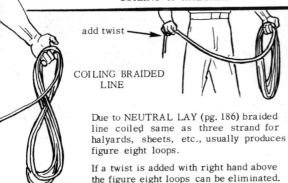

add twist

COILING BRAIDED LINE

Due to NEUTRAL LAY (pg. 186) braided line coiled same as three strand for halyards, sheets, etc., usually produces figure eight loops.

If a twist is added with right hand above the figure eight loops can be eliminated.

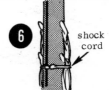

6

shock cord

Halyard cleats seem to be smaller each year. In sloppy weather add shock cord around mast to keep halyards in place.

Coiling Rope

193

Your boat should carry a practical heaving line such as the one above which requires little stowage space. We have pulled tired swimmers to our boat with it, we've towed dinghies and rowboats, and used it as the method to pull across a heavier tow line from another boat. It is also useful on a crowded launching ramp for handling a trailerable sailboat or powerboat.

The yellow polyethylene line is easy to see and handle, and it floats, protecting the prop. The "soft" softball is heavy enough for heaving, yet soft enough not to hurt a person hit by the ball.

We use two heaving lines, the first with 50' of 1/4" polypro braided line with 1100 lbs. breaking strength which uses the ball above. The second, is 75' long of 1/4" polypro which uses a heavier small fender which can be thrown further.

The secret of a practical heaving line is to use braided rope with a NEUTRAL lay or resistance to coiling. If you drop braided line into the container at left, the line will stow itself ready for use without producing snarls and snafus though being stowed for a long time. It can also be thrown as easily by left handers and right handers.

AVOID 3 strand heaving lines. They require much practice, often producing kinks and hitches when used by weekend sailors. Fouling seems unavoidable if coiled by a right hander then used by a left hander. If professionals coil a heaving line in the morning, yet find they won't use it till the evening, they often recoil the line to eliminate potential half hitches.

●

Ocean racing and cruising sailors have found the best way to avoid drowning, is to stay on the boat. Many deep water sailors prefer the shoulder harness for maximum protection in stormy weather, while the waist lifeline is easier to use and is less confining for a short summer squall, we carry both kinds on our boat.

Start with a ten foot length of 1/2" three strand nylon, and a #3 bronze boat snap. The eye splice end should go through the eyel of the snap twice. Add whipping to the other end, burning any loose fibers.

The waist lifeline should be tied long enough so it can encircle the waist a second time, yet remain snug and out of the way when snapped on itself when going below.

Use the double square knot, page 192, made of three overhand knots instead of a bowline which may have slipping tendencies when used on nylon rope.

Double braided eye splice method is considerably different from the three strand eye splice sailors have been making for centuries. After studying the following items listed below, then use splicing sequence detailed on the next pages.

Practice ONLY with NEW ROPE when learning to make a braided eye splice as tension on used line tends to shrink its diameter in use, increasing friction between cover and core. This makes it difficult to splice, requiring a smaller size fid, tapering point, after lubricating internally with "Fluid Film", or similar product.

TAPE. Plastic electrical tape is ideal. Limit to two wraps as additional tape makes splicing more difficult.

FID. Be sure it is CORRECT size. Next larger size will be almost impossible to push through rope, and smaller size fid hardly provides sufficient opening to PULL inner and outer core and cover through.

MARKING PENS. The bamboo tip pen is ideal. Use TWO colors though second pen is only used for step 5 in the beginning... which is important to locate point for step 20.

Angle of PUSHER and FID is important. A slight angle provides best leverage to pull cover and core behind fid. If push is almost parallel to fid, pusher may instead go through tape or rope, only pushing the fid. We feel this awkward holding/pushing action the most difficult part to become accustomed to when making a double braided eye splice.

Order a SPLICING KIT from Samson Ocean Systems, Inc., Pleasure Boating Division, 99 High Street, Boston, MA 02110; or buy 18' of 3/8" braided rope which can be cut into three 6' lengths for six smaller diameter eye splices, plus a fid and pusher. An ice pick makes a good pusher, yet always watch out for the sharp point.

The important idea is to make your first braided eye splice soon as possible. If you follow the steps detailed methodically as shown, they will seem puzzling yet you have at least an 80% chance of making a good braided splice on your first try.

During a free for all discussion at Avalon one afternoon the topic switched to splicing. The four guests aboard reluctantly admitted to each other making a perfect splice the first time using the following sequence, after unsuccessfully trying other braided eye splice methods. Sailing Illustrated 195

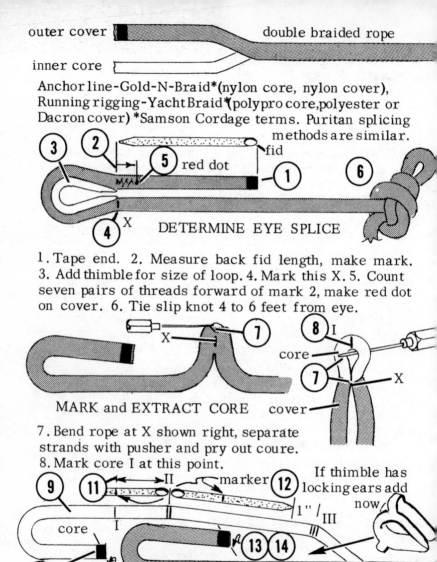

outer cover | double braided rope

inner core

Anchor line-Gold-N-Braid*(nylon core, nylon cover),
Running rigging-Yacht Braid*(polypro core, polyester or
Dacron cover) *Samson Cordage terms. Puritan splicing
methods are similar.

red dot · fid

X   DETERMINE EYE SPLICE

1. Tape end. 2. Measure back fid length, make mark.
3. Add thimble for size of loop. 4. Mark this X. 5. Count
seven pairs of threads forward of mark 2, make red dot
on cover. 6. Tie slip knot 4 to 6 feet from eye.

X   core   X

MARK and EXTRACT CORE   cover

7. Bend rope at X shown right, separate
strands with pusher and pry out coure.
8. Mark core I at this point.

II   marker   If thimble has
locking ears add
now

1" / III

core   I

MARKING INNER CORE   X

9. Pull out core. 10. Tape core end. 11. Measure back from I
amount of fid shown, mark it II. 12. Measure a fid length
from II, add an inch, mark it III. 13. Cut taped ends for taper
to fit eye in fid. 14. Retape cut ends with electrical tape.

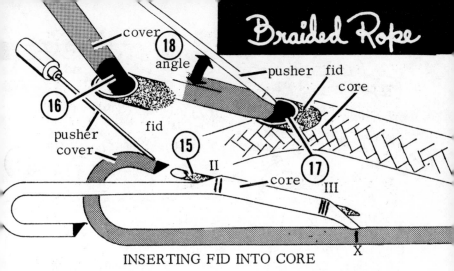

cover

Braided Rope

16

pusher
cover

angle

18

pusher fid

core

fid

15

16

II

core

17

III

X

INSERTING FID INTO CORE

15. Insert fid into core at II, out at III. 16. Insert taped
end of cover into eye of fid. 17.Angle taped end forward
locking cover into fid eye. Push fid at slight angle BEHIND
taped cover end at 18, till the cover comes out of core
at 19, see below.

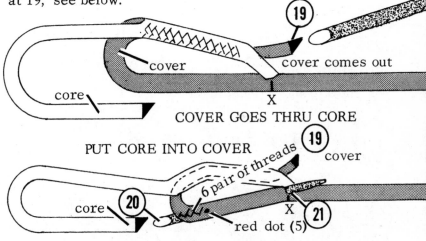

19

cover

cover comes out

core

X

COVER GOES THRU CORE

PUT CORE INTO COVER

6 pair of threads

19

cover

core

20

X

21

red dot (5)

20. Insert fid 6 pair threads after RED dot, coming out at X.
21. Push core into fid so it comes out at X, by using
the same holding, pushing method shown 16, 17, and 18,
to pull the core through the cover (see next page).

Sailing Illustrated

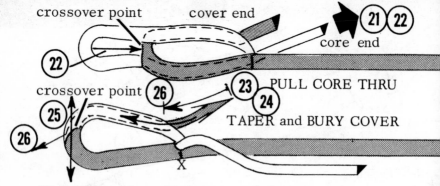

crossover point   cover end

22

core end

21 22

crossover point   26   23   PULL CORE THRU

25

24

26   TAPER and BURY COVER

X

22. Pull core thru till the two ends become one.
23. Remove tape. 24 . Tease, spread threads on cover end
then cut groups of strands at intervals for taper.
25. Pull both directions at crossover to eliminate slack.
26. Pull direction shown so cover barely disappears into
core. If not pulled tight at 25, cover may go in too far
to cause bunching, see 29 below.

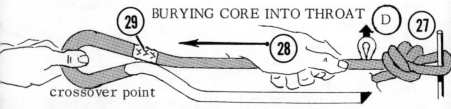

BURYING CORE INTO THROAT   D   27

29   28

crossover point

27. Put slip knot around peg, hook, etc. 28. Hold eye splice
with one hand, pull other hand towards eye splice so
cover slides over marks II, III, and crossover, so core
is buried into throat at 30.

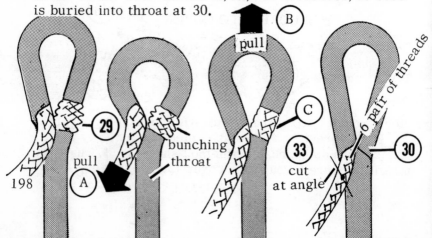

B

pull

29   C

bunching
throat

33

pull

cut
at angle

6 pair of threads

30

198

A

A. Pull on core tail as shown.
B. Pull out loop to smoothen crossover area.
C. If it doesn't bury, insufficient pull was made at #25.
D. If it still doesn't bury, open at D. Pull out core to bury
bunching, then pull in direction of #28 to bury core at D.
E. If it still doesn't bury, pull out cover, return to #20.

31. Open loop and position thimble.
32. Close loop after thimble is in position.
33. Count 6 pair threads out on core tail, then cut at angle
leaving small tuft.. not to pull core inside making a hollow.

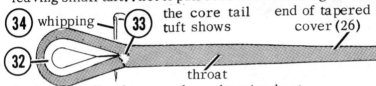

whipping — (33)   the core tail   end of tapered
(34)   tuft shows   cover (26)
(32)   throat

34. Pull needle thru as shown burying knot.
35. Wrap throat several times with Dacron (polyester) for
halyards, sheets, etc., or nylon whipping for anchor line
subject to stretch. In periods of extreme pressure, thimble
with ears, pg. 196, has less chance of jumping out of the
thimble as anchor line stretches.

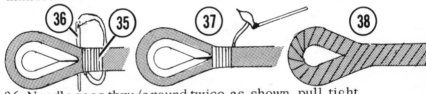

36. Needle goes thru/around twice as shown, pull tight.
37. Cut whipping with ample tail. Burn it back to splice
which will lock whipping in place with a good anchor.
38. For anchor line, tape eye plus a foot or more of throat
with plastic electricians tape to reduce chafe, page 161.
39. Untie slip knot and have a "Compōz"®.". or a martini.

We hope you will try to make a braided splice soon. If
sequence is followed exactly with NEW rope, you will be
able to make a professional splice the first or second
try. For USED rope, wash thoroughly to eliminate salts
and sand. Then lubricate thoroughly with FLUID FILM
or WD-40, let set for a while to soak through to reduce
the internal friction between core and cover, and splice. 199

Whipping

Traditional whipping thread found in marine stores is quite practical for many applications.

Nylon whipping thread is useful for other applications such as found in the excellent sail repair kit from West Marine Products, 850 San Antonio Road, Palo Alto, CA 94303. Send for catalog.

Double Thread Whipping will take tremendous punishment, the reason it is recommended.

whipping end of braided line

short matches have insufficient heat for fusing

1 Tape line an inch from the end.

2 Cut end about 3/16 from tape.

3 Fuse end with long matches rolling melted end to maintain same diameter.

4 After end cools remove tape.

The extra steps above eliminate chances of burning whipping twine if end is fused AFTER it has been whipped, using synthetic line. If you don't decide to whip end of line, soldering iron can fuse strands or double braid together. In some instances the 12" match may provide sufficient heat for permanent fusing.

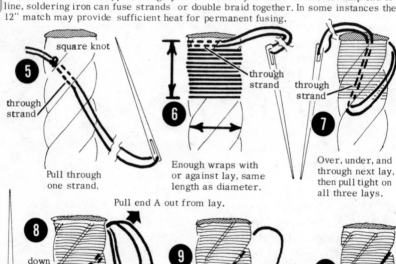

5 square knot — through strand — Pull through one strand.

6 through strand — Enough wraps with or against lay, same length as diameter.

7 through strand — Over, under, and through next lay, then pull tight on all three lays.

Pull end A out from lay.

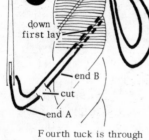

8 down first lay — end B — cut — end A — Fourth tuck is through first lay, then cut as is shown above.

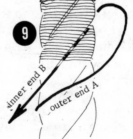

9 inner end B — outer end A — Pull end B tight.

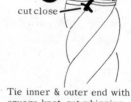

10 cut close — Tie inner & outer end with square knot, cut whipping tails close to knot.

200

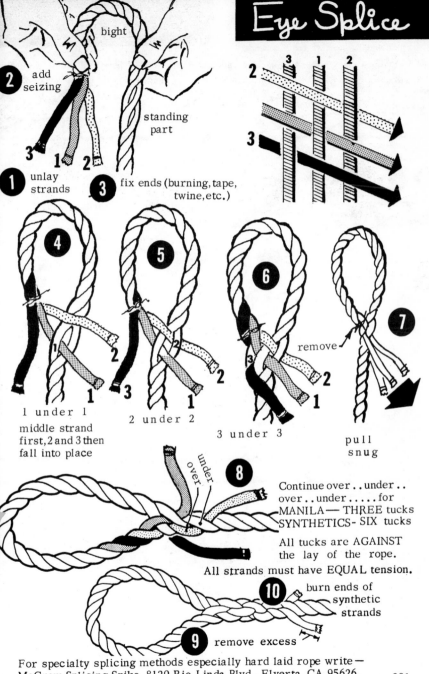

Eye Splice

2 add seizing

bight

1 unlay strands

3 fix ends (burning, tape, twine, etc.)

standing part

4

1 under 1

middle strand first, 2 and 3 then fall into place

5

2 under 2

6

3 under 3

remove

7

pull snug

8 under / over

Continue over..under..over..under.....for
MANILA — THREE tucks
SYNTHETICS- SIX tucks

All tucks are AGAINST the lay of the rope.

All strands must have EQUAL tension.

9 remove excess

10 burn ends of synthetic strands

For specialty splicing methods especially hard laid rope write —
McGrew Splicing Spike, 8120 Rio Linda Blvd., Elverta, CA 95626.

1. Fuse ends of small dia. synthetic strands and/or tape large dia. strands.

2. Unravel as many strands as desired. . add extra turns for slippery synthetic line.

3. Tie off at these points to prevent further strand unwinding.

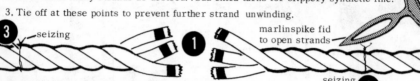

4. Splice ends together using sequence below . . . one tuck only.

5. Pull strands together so they are snug against each other.

6. Tie seizing around meeting point of the six strands.

7. Remove seizings at #3.

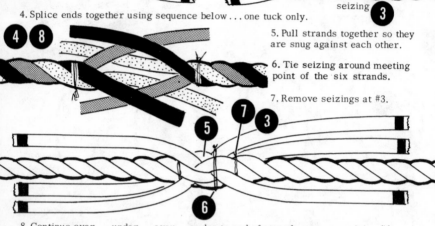

8. Continue over . . . under . . . over . . . under to end of strands, remove seizing #6.

9. If taper is required, cut some threads back, otherwise have ends show.

10. Roll and pound on hard surface.   11. Add whipping if desired.

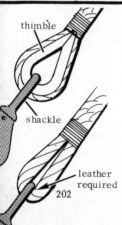

thimble

shackle

leather required

202

Major causes of equipment failure in equipment busting 1969 monohull Honolulu Transpac were----

1. Metal overloading or metal fatigue.

2. Spinnaker cloth failure . . . chafe and too much wind.

3. Eye splices NOT USING THIMBLES on spinnaker sheets, guys, etc.(for location see page 129), as acute angle of metal eye pulling on unprotected line after several days of hard racing produced continual chafe at this point with failure, not obvious on round the buoys or overnight racing.

To reduce this kind of failure in eye splices not using thimbles, have <u>leather</u> sewn around loop of eye splice. The leather spreads the contact area, and is tremendously resistant to chafe. Boats using leathered eyes with well trained crews who knew their boat continually checking for chafe, avoided this kind of failure.

Tugboat Hitch

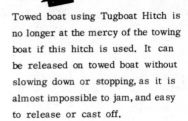

First loop around bitt, cleat, or post, then over, around and back under.

Towed boat using Tugboat Hitch is no longer at the mercy of the towing boat if this hitch is used. It can be released on towed boat without slowing down or stopping, as it is almost impossible to jam, and easy to release or cast off.

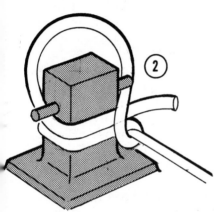

Pull half hitch tight, then add as many extra half hitches as required.

The boat at lower right is aground on a lee shore. A second boat has come to help, but it must stay at least 100' off shore or it will also go aground.

A fishing rod with a two ounce sinker can cast up to 200' to the boat aground, or to a victim in shallow water or heavy surf. A tow line is then secured to the fishing line, then pulled across from either boat.

Leverage is required to work against, in order to pull the boat off the lee shore. One method is to dig in your anchor to pull against, providing your boat can stand the strain.

Another method is to secure an anchor to the tow line, permitting the stranded boat to kedge itself off the lee shore; also see pages 222 and 223.

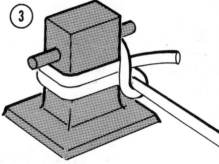

fishing pole

sinker or float

Water is a continually changing dynamic surface....
making weather study much more important on the water
than on land. Storms send advance physical warnings ....
IF a person knows what to look for.Many of the impending
weather changes are written in the beautiful and ever
changing cloud patterns. Latin derivatives are used to
clarify basic cloud terminology.

●

CIRROCUMULUS (ringlet-heap) resembles fish scales
called Mackerel Sky. It has no shadow and indicates a
weather change.CIRROSTRATUS (ringlet-layer) is white,
frozen, cobwebby fog that may mean rain.CIRRUS (ringlet)
is thin,stringy"Mares Tails"that make a beautiful sunrise
and sunset, due to light refraction through ice crystals.

Cirrus and cirrostratus make a HALO (ringlet) around
the sun and moon,that may predict change in day or two.

●

MIDDLE clouds are ALTOCUMULUS (middle−heap),
forming lumpy patterns of flattened globular masses.High
grayish sheet ALTOSTRATUS(middle−flat) may thicken
to nimbostratus,but does NOT have halo around sun & moon.

●

Nothing is more beautiful nor more dangerous than the
CUMULONIMBUS (heap-storm)with high vertical development. Look for anvil top and take no chances as it may
be weak or strong. . . but will soon pass, in most instances
only covering a small area, see pages 206 and 207.

The NIMBOSTRATUS (storm-layer) cloud is flat,uniformly
gray, ragged and wet looking. It often indicates steady
rain over a wide area.

STRATUS (layer) is low and of indefinite shape giving
water a hazy appearance. If on the water surface, it is
called fog, see pages 218 to 221.

CUMULUS (heap) clouds are clean,fluffy,& dome shaped
on the upper surface. If one grows tall enough to reach
elevation where temperature is below freezing,it develops
into the tall, dangerous cumulonimbus (heap−storm).

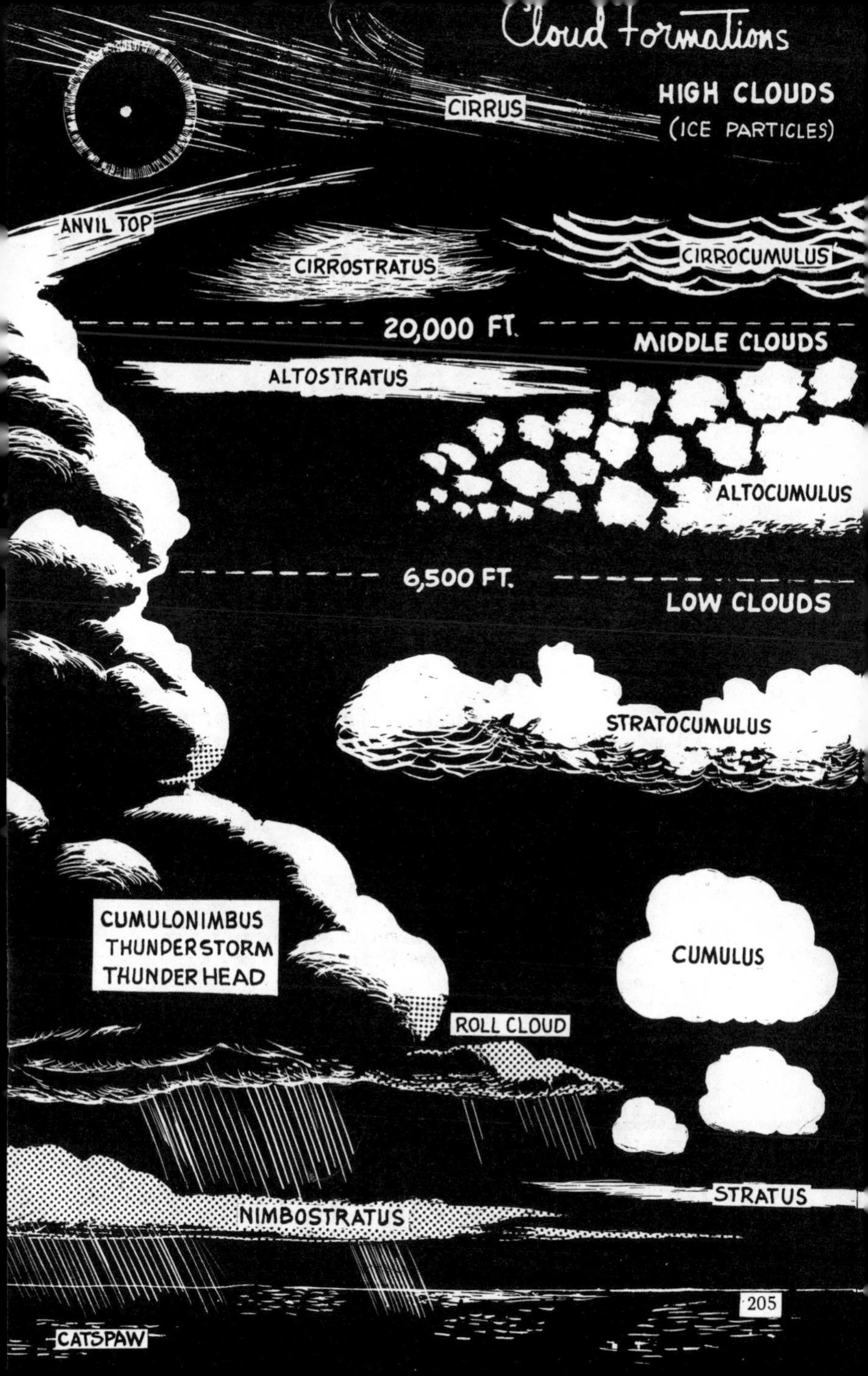

Cloud Formations

CIRRUS

HIGH CLOUDS
(ICE PARTICLES)

ANVIL TOP

CIRROSTRATUS

CIRROCUMULUS

20,000 FT.

MIDDLE CLOUDS

ALTOSTRATUS

ALTOCUMULUS

6,500 FT.

LOW CLOUDS

STRATOCUMULUS

CUMULONIMBUS
THUNDERSTORM
THUNDERHEAD

CUMULUS

ROLL CLOUD

STRATUS

NIMBOSTRATUS

CATSPAW

205

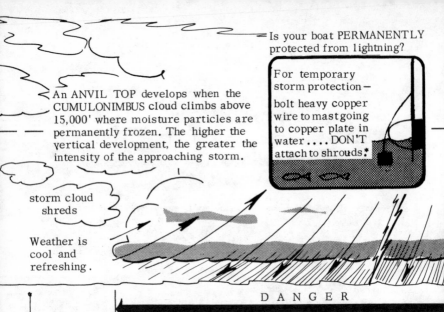

Is your boat PERMANENTLY protected from lightning?

For temporary storm protection —

bolt heavy copper wire to mast going to copper plate in water .... DON'T attach to shrouds.*

An ANVIL TOP develops when the CUMULONIMBUS cloud climbs above 15,000' where moisture particles are permanently frozen. The higher the vertical development, the greater the intensity of the approaching storm.

storm cloud shreds

Weather is cool and refreshing.

D A N G E R

Dangerous strong shifting winds can be found

A simple 24 hour pocket size weather radio should be standard equipment for your car, van, camper, and boat.

STATIC developing on your radio may be first warning of a thunderstorm anywhere from 25 to 100 miles away. It is a good indication that a storm can hit within one to four hours.

First visual signs will appear on horizon from the west, southwest or northwest. It will be a high cloud formation with a DIRTY BOTTOM that has a tall thin and stringy cirrus ANVIL TOP.

The wise boat operator must always expect the worst and prepare accordingly as this type of storm may be light or severe, and more than one storm may be coming through. Scientists have estimated the power of a severe THUNDER-STORM, CUMULONIMBUS, THUNDERHEAD, or SQUALL

The ROLL CLOUD shown is supposed to give 3 to 5 minutes calm before the storm, however the roll could is not as common as many people believe.

*Aluminum has 2/3 the conductivity of copper, the reason the copper plate should be bonded directly to the mast so if your boat is hit by lightning, the surge can be easily dissipated. Stainless shrouds with 1/50th the conductivity of copper may cause too much resistance resulting in confused, dangerous side flashes of lightning.

Sailing   Illustrated

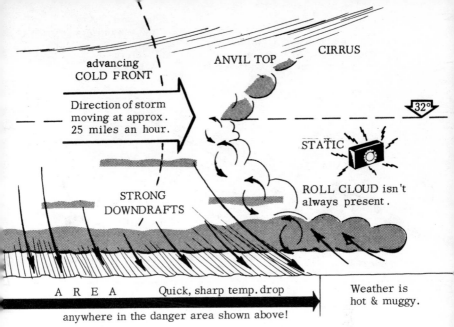

advancing
COLD FRONT

Direction of storm
moving at approx.
25 miles an hour.

ANVIL TOP

CIRRUS

32°

STATIC

**STRONG
DOWNDRAFTS**

ROLL CLOUD isn't
always present.

A R E A   Quick, sharp temp. drop

Weather is
hot & muggy.

anywhere in the danger area shown above!

The thunderstorm usually lasts for a short time and will cover an area less than 200 miles. However a whole series called a SQUALL LINE or LINE SQUALL may be advancing across a large area.

As rank beginners, we admired these beautiful cloud formations from our kayak on the Hudson River on July 4,1948,a day that will long be remembered.What we were watching is exactly what you see above except the anvil top must have gone up over 100,000'.The violence of the 100 mph and over hurricane force winds that hit us in our small kayak will be remembered for a lifetime.

Because one thunderstorm has hit,don't expect that the potential is over. We were hit by three thunderstorms in one afternoon off Staten Island, two were very vicious.

If a storm is on its way don't try to outslug it, head for a protected area with plenty of time. If you are stuck, use a bucket or any kind of a drag attached to the anchor line and sit or lie on the bottom of the boat.

Many people have drowned in storms because they stood up,swung their arms (USCG help wanted signal?) and then hollered for help. After the storm had passed the boat was floating peacefully without occupants ... they had fallen overboard and drowned.

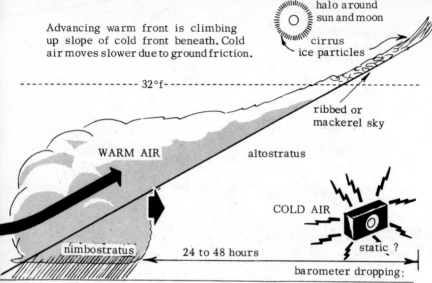

Advancing warm front is climbing up slope of cold front beneath. Cold air moves slower due to ground friction.

halo around sun and moon

cirrus ice particles

32°f

ribbed or mackerel sky

WARM AIR

altostratus

COLD AIR

nimbostratus

24 to 48 hours

static ?

barometer dropping;

Advancing front of STABLE WARM AIR

When weak fronts pass with almost identical humidity and temperature, only a mild wind shift may occur.

A strong advancing warm front usually moves at HALF the speed of the cold front. Another difference, it sends cloud warnings a long way ahead of the front. As it moves in on you, the cloud sequence shown above may be observed.

First notice is the CIRRUS (ringlet) that produces a ring around the sun and moon. As the cirrus thickens, it changes to cirrocumulus or ribbed Mackerel Sky.

The cirrus messenger may be from 24 to 48 HOURS and up to 1000 MILES in advance of the front. After lowering, the ringlet disappears as temp. rises above 32°f. In this middle or alto layer, cloud forms change to altostratus or altocumulus.

When this lowers, precipitation begins with rain pattern depending on intensity of advancing warm front. If the barometer dips little, a nimbostratus bank may follow. If it dips considerably, unstable warm air with a hidden violent cumulonimbus (heap-storm) may follow.

STABLE WARM AIR. With little barometer drop, a high stratus bank may exist to produce heavy rain in the beginning...but it decreases steadily.

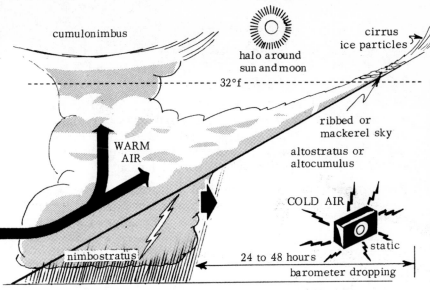

cumulonimbus

halo around
sun and moon

cirrus
ice particles

32°f

WARM
AIR

ribbed or
mackerel sky

altostratus or
altocumulus

COLD AIR

static

nimbostratus

24 to 48 hours

barometer dropping

Advancing front of UNSTABLE WARM AIR

UNSTABLE WARM AIR. With considerable barometer drop, hidden cumulonimbus or series of them may often be concealed behind advancing cloud wall. Thunderstorms and/or lightning may advance before the front. Rain may be variable, alternating between heavy downpours and slow drizzles ... with occasional thunderstorms.

Pattern of strong warm front sequence is first told by physical change in clouds... next by drop in BAROMETER. When front passes, barometer climbs as sky clears.

Greater the barometer drop, the stronger will be the strength of WIND and WAVE conditions as front MOVES THROUGH. After the front has passed, it does not necessarily mean that the wind & wave action will cease.

●

What other physical signs exist of an approaching storm or low pressure? BIRDS for instance find it increasingly difficult to take off and fly. If you see them sitting along the beaches or bluffs looking miserable and sluggish, the chances are that a low pressure area exists or has been moving in. The ART PENS used to illustrate this book start to leak as internal pressure is greater than the surrounding air pressure. When a high pressure area moves in, the ink pressure is less internally so the ink flow is sluggish.

The fore and aft rig was developed to make use of the land and sea breezes prevalent along our seacoasts and on the Great Lakes.

When the land warms up around noon, a SEA BREEZE starts flowing toward the land. It normally increases to midafternoon, disappearing about sundown. The greater the difference between water and land temperature, the stronger the land and sea breezes will result.

From dusk to midnight with land & water surface temp. about the same, a breeze is usually nonexistant. After midnight when land temperature is cooler, the wind starts blowing seaward increasing to about dawn when the temperature differences are equalized and it stops.

The sea breeze is generally steadier, stronger, and more predictable coming across a level surface with relatively constant temperature. The LAND BREEZE is more puffy and changeable due to going over hills, etc.

●

Wind plays many tricks on the sailors. When coming off a high bluff a DOWNDRAFT may occur with sailboats short distance apart going same direction on opposite tacks. When the wind is blowing onto a bluff, it must rise, which often causes a dead air pocket close to the bluff, pg.123.

●

Wind FUNNELS bear close watching. The canyon at right funnels down, increasing the wind velocity. If the canyon makes a slow turn, it may also change direction of wind flow up to 90°. Where two wind funnels converge such as found at Lake Mead(facing page), the overall wind pattern may be 15 mph, but up to 45 miles per hour . . . where the two funnels converge!

Wind funnels also exist when sailing past rows of buildings from which the wind is coming. The greatest velocity may be found flowing down the streets. Downdrafts may also exist when sailing close to buildings.

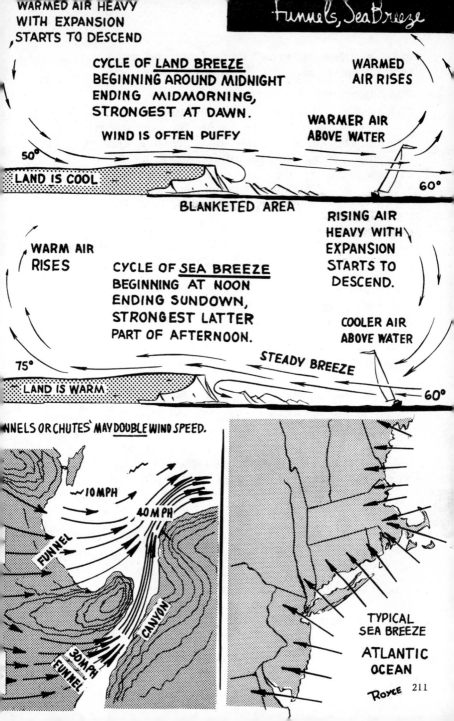

WARMED AIR HEAVY
WITH EXPANSION
STARTS TO DESCEND

Funnels, SeaBreeze

CYCLE OF LAND BREEZE
BEGINNING AROUND MIDNIGHT
ENDING MIDMORNING,
STRONGEST AT DAWN.

WARMED
AIR RISES

WIND IS OFTEN PUFFY

WARMER AIR
ABOVE WATER

50°

LAND IS COOL

60°

BLANKETED AREA

RISING AIR
HEAVY WITH
EXPANSION
STARTS TO
DESCEND.

WARM AIR
RISES

CYCLE OF SEA BREEZE
BEGINNING AT NOON
ENDING SUNDOWN,
STRONGEST LATTER
PART OF AFTERNOON.

COOLER AIR
ABOVE WATER

75°

STEADY BREEZE

LAND IS WARM

60°

NNELS OR CHUTES MAY DOUBLE WIND SPEED.

~10 MPH

40 MPH

FUNNEL

CANYON

30 MPH

FUNNEL

TYPICAL
SEA BREEZE

ATLANTIC
OCEAN

Royce 211

Basic weather patterns result from the sun, rotation of the earth, plus interaction of high & low pressure areas.

Wind direction is in a clockwise direction from a high or hill of air, flowing into the low pressure area in a counterclockwise direction. As the moist warm air reaches the center of the low pressure area, it rises, condenses, beings to precipitate, and a storm is born. So the low pressure area becomes a storm area, with the greater the difference between the low & high pressure areas, the more violent a storm it will produce.

Most U. S. weather or low pressure areas, flow across our continent from west to east, yet direction of the wind will vary according to the location of the high and low pressure areas. The relative pressure of these areas is measured by a BAROMETER as shown at right, then is reported in inches or *millibars. ISOBARS are lines of equal barometric pressure.

Note flow pattern of our weather on upper right of facing page. Westerlies due to earths rotation, generally move these lows about 500 miles every 24 hours during the summer, and about 700 miles, in the winter.

Suppose you do your boating in the New England area. Draw a 500 mile radius from your home, then note how a storm flowing through Illinois or down to the Carolinas, may funnel through your area the following day. New York weather however seldom flows to Chicago. Hurricanes coming from the Caribbean, make a slow turn to north & east, may also flow through the New England area.

Most storm clouds approach from, and may be seen in the SW, W, or NW quadrant anywhere from 15 minutes to several hours away.

Wind direction is reported as that in which the wind comes from. The term hurricane refers to a severe kind of a storm covering a large area. Hurricane strength winds also be found in a thunderstorm, pages 206 and 207.

212   * When buying a barometer, consider one with millibar markings, now the meterologists worldwide standard.

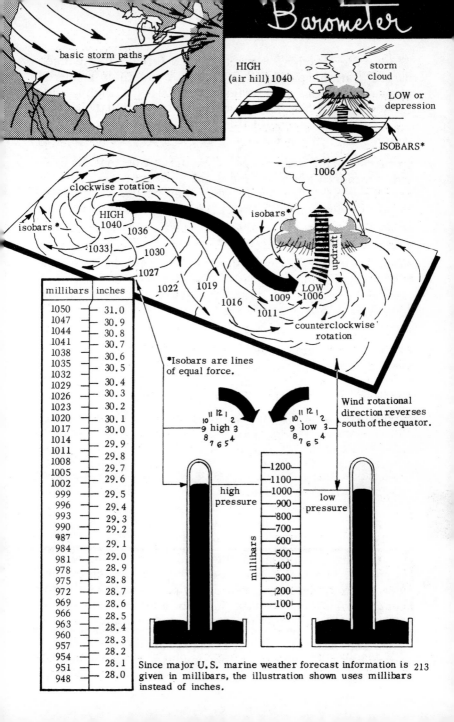

Barometer

basic storm paths

HIGH (air hill) 1040

storm cloud

LOW or depression

ISOBARS*

1006

clockwise rotation

HIGH 1040

isobars *

1036
1033
1030
1027
1022 1019
1016
1011

isobars*

1009 1006 LOW
1006

updraft

counterclockwise rotation

*Isobars are lines of equal force.

Wind rotational direction reverses south of the equator.

millibars	inches
1050	31.0
1047	30.9
1044	30.8
1041	30.7
1038	30.6
1035	30.5
1032	
1029	30.4
1026	30.3
1023	30.2
1020	30.1
1017	30.0
1014	29.9
1011	29.8
1008	29.7
1005	29.6
1002	
999	29.5
996	29.4
993	29.3
990	29.2
987	29.1
984	29.0
981	28.9
978	28.8
975	28.7
972	28.6
969	28.5
966	28.4
963	28.3
960	
957	28.2
954	28.1
951	28.0
948	

high

low

high pressure

low pressure

1200
1100
1000
900
800
700
600
500
400
300
200
100
0

millibars

Since major U.S. marine weather forecast information is given in millibars, the illustration shown uses millibars instead of inches.

213

Tide is the alternate vertical rise & fall of water, caused by gravitational pull of moon & sun. A month is required to go through the four tidal phases. Current is horizontal flow of water. When the tide causes a current that changes direction with change of tide, it is called a tidal current. A river current results only from the force of gravity.

Greatest normal tide range, is a spring tide that occurs twice a month when the sun & moon exert their greatest pull; the neap tides occur, when they nullify each other. Depths shown on our navigation charts are charted as being at Mean Low Tide on east coast, and Mean Lower Low Tide on the west coast.

In addition to these variables, is the elliptical course of the moon around the earth that results in Apogee and Perigee. During a hurricane, much greater highs & lower lows may be expect than found in spring tides, page 167.

The "tsunamis" or tidal wave may pass over the surface of the open ocean at jet plane speeds & be hardly noticed. As they approach the shore, the ocean may go out half a mile, then come in a similar distance above high tide. Shallow water may produce "tsunamis" waves 60-100' high.

Yearly tide & current table predictions are published by the U. S. Coast and Geodetic Survey. For Daylight Saving Time, be sure to ADD an hour.

The moon takes about 24 hours & 50 minutes in order to go around the earth. This corresponds to the two highs & lows in one area as illustrated on facing page showing a complete tidal day. This doesn't always apply near the equator, where tides follow different rhythms.

> Continuous operation on the water provided us with a surprise. Potential collisions on the boat and on the highway seem to increase rapidly at periods of major tide ranges coinciding with the full moon, and reduce rapidly when periods of minimum tide ranges occur.

The "Sea Around Us" by Rachel Carson, is a must for every library, having excellent coverage of tide variables.

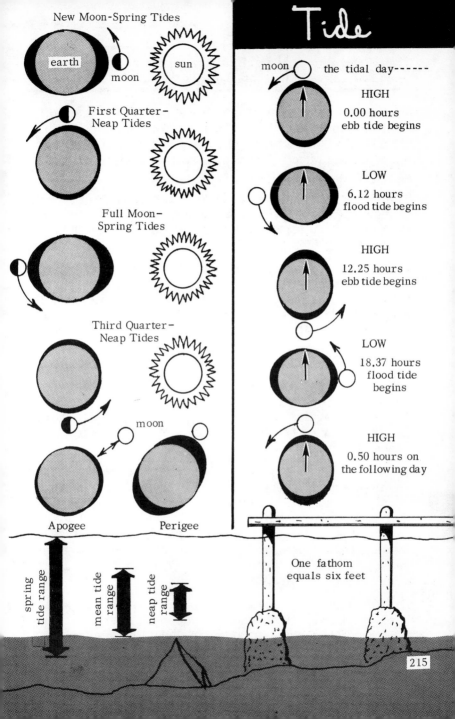

Tide

New Moon-Spring Tides

earth   moon   sun

First Quarter-
Neap Tides

Full Moon-
Spring Tides

Third Quarter-
Neap Tides

moon

Apogee   Perigee

moon   the tidal day------

HIGH
0.00 hours
ebb tide begins

LOW
6.12 hours
flood tide begins

HIGH
12.25 hours
ebb tide begins

LOW
18.37 hours
flood tide
begins

HIGH
0.50 hours on
the following day

One fathom
equals six feet

spring tide range   mean tide range   neap tide range

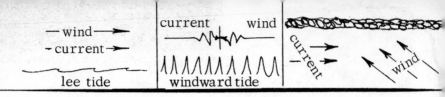

| lee tide | windward tide | |

When wind and current go same direction (1), wave action is minimum. When wind & current go against each other (2), a short stiff wave action develops. Combine strong opposing wind & current acting against seawall or jetty, & a wild stiff vertical chop (3), without pattern develops.

The river current is caused by gravity, a tidal current changes direction with change of tide. Between the two often exists a buffer zone that moves downstream during spring rains, and upstream during August to November.

Spend some time studying effects of current in your area so you can make them work for you. Our first boat was a "Folbot" (18' kayak) in which we spent many wonderful hours analyzing the treacherous New York harbor area tidal currents, afterwards shooting the Housatonic and Platte River rapids. This training proved most valuable for handling sailboats in tidal current areas.

The smoother more predictable current flow as example, is usually found in the middle and deeper part of a stream. For sailing against the current, it is necessary to work the shallower or fringe areas avoiding houses, trees & banks, that may cut off your wind.

Jetties should be given wide berth due to reverse eddies and disturbed current flow on the downstream side. For similar reason, plus the potentials of sudden downdrafts that may cause a sailboat to lose rudder control, avoid sailing close to large bridge supports. Sailing too close to a support of the George Washington Bridge one afternoon, caused a double knockdown from current eddies and from a sudden strong wind downdraft.

Drawbridges may open upon signal in some areas, while opening is only at scheduled times elsewhere. Signal for many drawbridges to open, is three long blasts.

Avoid cutting corners in a river bend as deep water is usually on the outer edge near the steep side of a river bank.

When going downstream past fixed objects, give considerable clearance so current won't set you upon them. Speed and strength of a current may often be judged by the size of eddies and current swirls on downstream side of piling, float, buoy, etc.

Greatest depth is found in center of V pointing downstream. For an upstream V, give it room since this usually indicates an underwater obstruction.

When powerboats meet in a current, the one going downstream has right-of-way (page 235) due to minimum rudder response. Situation with tug and tow is even more critical as discussed on page 240.

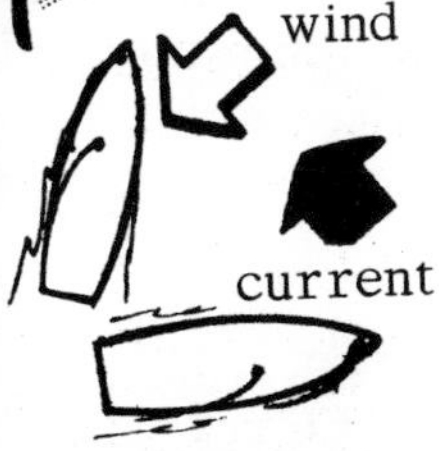

Sailboats generally make better headway toward destination if current can be kept on lee side called "lee bowing". During the spring, a sailor must keep a more critical lookout for floating debris due to spring rains and thaw. During late summer and fall with flow at minimum, more care should be given to shallower water that exposes sand bars, rocks, etc.

The sailor operating in a current situation should always have an anchor ready to go in case of upset. Boat otherwise may turn 180° and be dismasted and/or holed when drifting downstream across bars, etc.

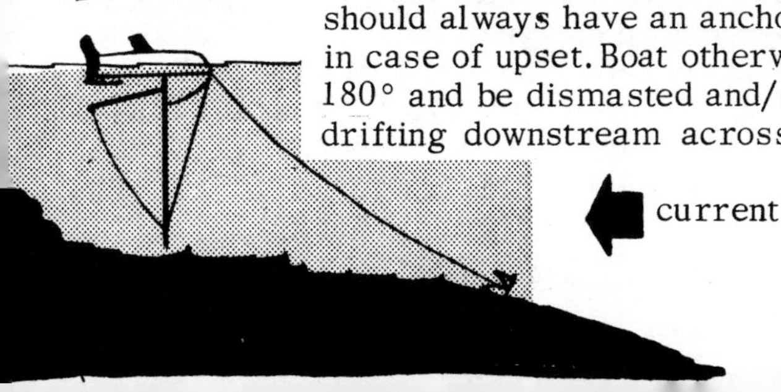

wind

current

217

current

Fog signals must be given, Rule 15 (c). ".. in fog, mist, falling snow, heavy rainstorms, or any other condition similarly restricts visibility, whether by day or night".

Fog signals must be given by all vessels underway, adrift or at anchor, and need to be started before a vessel enters a fog bank, see pages 220 and 221. Speed must be reduced and restricted by vessels ability to stop in half the distance of visibility, Rule 16(a). All vessels must carry a proper lookout with no other duties at the time, Rule & Art. 29. These rules are unfortunately disregarded more times than a newcomer realizes.

Consider air as a large sponge on a warm day, that will soak up a lot of water vapor. On cold days it is a small sponge that can only soak up a small amount of vapor before saturation, dew point, or fog potentials are reached.

Previous editions discussed sling psychrometer to measure amount of moisture in the air. Theoretically it was a good idea yet was seldom used on small boats. We tested a RELATIVE HUMIDITY INDICATOR pg. 63, permanently mounted on the mast, which provided a very practical and liberal education for fog prediction.

We could tell for instance when a fog might be approaching up to five hours in advance...and the type of fog to be expected. A dense fog which still has sufficient visibility for operation, is indicated when relative humidity reaches 88 to 93%.

If the day or night was very clear with a relative humidity 100% or more, it indicated a pea souper moving in. This advance fog warning kept us out of trouble numerous times.

The inexpensive relative humidity indicator fog forecast accuracy has provided continual surprises to us and our students. We highly recommend you buy one such as is shown upper right, permanently mounted on your boat so it is easy to see and is protected from being hit. A word of caution, replace it before the humidity sensor begins to lose accuracy as nature is very hostile to this 218 sensitive instrument. Sailing Illustrated

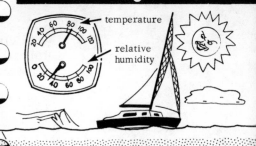

Humidity vs Fog

moisture particles in suspension

Much is written about fogs. What is of major importance is the ability to predict a fog...to keep you out of trouble. We've had much luck with the indicator shown.

Air contains water in gaseous form, invisible below the saturation point, dew point, or maximum humidity that is detailed below.

temperature

relative humidity

heavy falling moisture particles

As humidity increases to 87-93% generally with temperature drop, or inflow of moist air ... often indicated several hours ahead, a light fog moves in. It has sufficient visibility for a boat to keep underway at displacement speed.

During two 14 month tests, the indicator shown was able to predict all fogs encountered.

fog signals are often required

light to medium fog

Displacement speeds for daytime operation, avoid nighttime operation.

visibility 100 yards to a quarter mile

Fog is VISIBLE MOISTURE.

heavy blanket of moisture particles

First evidence of incoming peasoup fog, generally is a clear sky with humidity 100% to 105%. If a light fog exists and humidity climbs to 100% or more, a peasouper may be moving in.

The indicator predicted fogs up to five hours ahead. When the humidity drops during fog conditions, the fog often lifted four to five hours later.

fog signals are mandatory

heavy fog or 'peasouper'

Any boat movement may be hazardous.

DEW POINT is 100% humidity

visibility 100' or less

The temperature and humidity indicator needs to be permanently mounted outside the cabin, since it takes several hours to fully adjust to weather conditions.

Though designed for indoor use, we've had considerable luck with temperature/ humidity indicators made by —

Airguide Instrument Co.
221 Wabansia Ave.
Chicago, Ill 60647

Replace periodically, we replace it yearly!

protective shroud

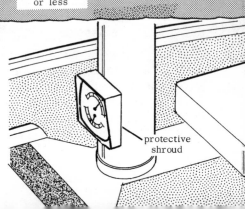

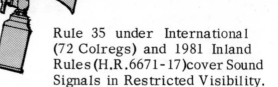

Rule 35 under International (72 Colregs) and 1981 Inland Rules (H.R.6671-17)cover Sound Signals in Restricted Visibility.

A freon horn is the most practical method to use on sailboats and powerboats in a fog as it makes a loud noise for self protection when required. AVOID all mouth operated horns as their signals are very weak ... contributing to a potential collision they are used to prevent.

Int'l/Inland R. 35–In or near an area of restricted visibility- (c)"A vessel not under command;a vessel restricted in her ability to maneuver, whether underway or at anchor; a sailing vessel (Def.Rule 3(c)The term *sailing vessel* means *any vessel under sail* , provided that propelling machinery if fitted, is not being used);------

"a vessel engaged in fishing, whether underway or at anchor; and a vessel engaged in towing or pushing another vessel shall ... sound ... not more than 2 minutes, three blasts in succession .. one prolonged ... followed by two short blasts.

The purpose of *Admiralty Law* is to provide the patterns under which all vessels operate, implemented in the new International and Inland Navigation Rules ... with fog presenting a special set of circumstances.

Responsibility-Int'l and Inland, Rule 2(b).. "due regard shall be had to all dangers .. and to any *special circumstances* .. which may make a departure from the Rules necessary to avoid immediate danger".

The new Int'l/Inland fog rules using one set of signals for SEVEN kinds of operations including sailboats ... add to the confusion and hazard potentials of sailboats operating in fog near commercial vessels.It is difficult to understand the reasoning behind Rule 35(c) if the purpose of Admiralty 220 Law is to prevent collisions and the potential of collisions.

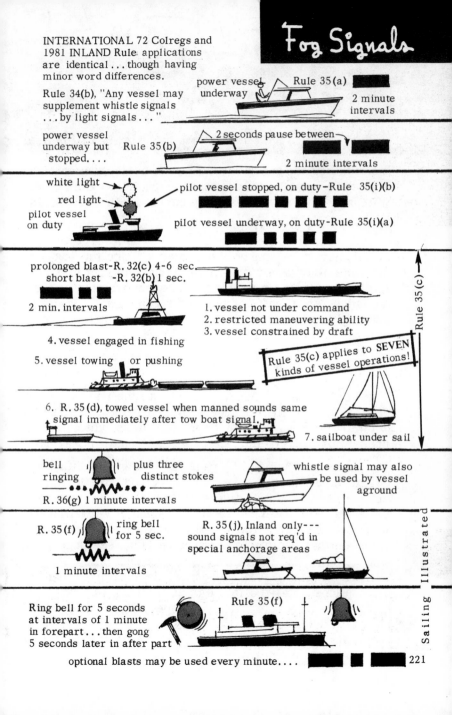

Fog Signals

INTERNATIONAL 72 Colregs and 1981 INLAND Rule applications are identical ... though having minor word differences.

Rule 34(b), "Any vessel may supplement whistle signals ... by light signals ..."

power vessel underway — Rule 35(a)
2 minute intervals

power vessel underway but stopped.... Rule 35(b)
2 seconds pause between
2 minute intervals

white light
red light
pilot vessel on duty

pilot vessel stopped, on duty–Rule 35(i)(b)

pilot vessel underway, on duty–Rule 35(i)(a)

prolonged blast–R. 32(c) 4-6 sec.
short blast –R. 32(b) 1 sec.
2 min. intervals

Rule 35(c)

1. vessel not under command
2. restricted maneuvering ability
3. vessel constrained by draft

4. vessel engaged in fishing

5. vessel towing or pushing

Rule 35(c) applies to SEVEN kinds of vessel operations!

6. R. 35(d), towed vessel when manned sounds same signal immediately after tow boat signal.

7. sailboat under sail

bell ringing plus three distinct stokes
R. 36(g) 1 minute intervals

whistle signal may also be used by vessel aground

R. 35(f) ring bell for 5 sec.
1 minute intervals

R. 35(j), Inland only---
sound signals not req'd in special anchorage areas

Ring bell for 5 seconds at intervals of 1 minute in forepart ... then gong 5 seconds later in after part

Rule 35(f)

optional blasts may be used every minute....

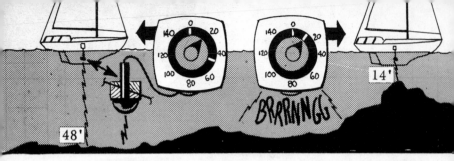

Your author has gone aground... and assisted more boats that have gone aground, than he cares to think about. Virtually all were caused by carelessness, or shoaling.

If you put a boat aground, think twice before asking for or taking assistance. In one grounding on a large boat, an overly eager navy tug wanted to assist. Since the tug crew was mainly trained to handle large vessels instead of yachts... our main problem was to keep the tug at a safe distance. As a puff moved in, the gennie and main were sheeted in hard, while a crew member swung out on the mizzen halyard. The boat heeled sufficiently to break it loose from the sticky mud. The only resulting damage... was to your author's pride.

The Vexilar depth sounder above was the first we know of marketed in our country with an alarm, which is now common to a variety of depth sounders which can be preset for a desired depth to warn of shallow water.

We were reviewing this page for changes when a life-guard supervisor stopped by to report that during the afternoon pea soup fog, five sailboats up to 43' long ended up on the local beach. If each had a sounder with an alarm turned on set for a 100' depth, the owners could have followed that depth to our entrance buoy, see page 245.

NOTE: <u>Maximum tide range</u> periods increase chance of groundings... also <u>affecting</u> the <u>thinking</u> processes and <u>judgment</u> of boat operators, especially in heavy traffic. Worst offenders seem to be powerboats with LEFT hand controls, especially if they are located inside a cabin 222 restricting the operators visibility.

THIS BOAT SHOULD DROP SAILS
AND TRY TO TURN AROUND.

WHAT IS CURRENT, WIND DIRECTION,
IS TIDE EBBING, USE WHICHEVER
WILL BE ADVANTAGEOUS.

IF A KEEL BOAT IS STUCK
WITH AN EBB TIDE, PROP IT UP.
IF THIS ISN'T POSSIBLE LET IT
FALL SO COCKPIT WILL NOT BE
SWAMPED BEFORE RIGHTING,
HAVE ANCHORS OUT.

THIS BOAT MIGHT BE POLED OFF.
HAVE WEIGHT ON OTHER END,
JUMPING MIGHT HELP TO ROCK
THE BOAT LOOSE.

CENTERBOARD BOAT DROPS SAILS
RAISES CENTERBOARD, MAYBE RUDDER,
PADDLES OVER OBSTRUCTION OR
CAN BACK OFF.

ROYCE

IF BOTTOM IS SANDY DON'T USE
ENGINE AS IT MIGHT SUCK IN SAND.
POWERBOAT WAKE MIGHT BREAK
SAILBOAT LOOSE.

IF CENTERBOARD BOAT IS STILL
STUCK, PUSH, POLE OR KEDGE OFF.

THIS BOAT IS
KEDGING OFF AND
WINCHING OUT.

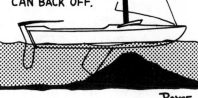

223

We've been outspoken for many years over amateurish "safety" standards faced by those on a vessel in distress, especially facing a long time survival situation. Suddenly we found the answer with a pilot/sailor ... George Sigler.

George

Charlie

George was a navy fighter pilot with many hours combat duty, highly trained in the art of survival. After returning stateside, he and his wife Judy bought a 22' sailboat. He began researching ocean survival methods to find little of practical value.

George sold his sailboat to buy a 15' Mark III Zodiac outfitting it with survival equipment. He was soon joined by Charlie Gore, a navy fighter pilot friend. The inflatable "Courageous" was towed 20 miles out past the Golden Gate Bridge then set adrift July 4, 1974, destination, Hawaii.

2700 miles and 56 days later the navy ordered them picked up, 65 miles from Oahu. The only water consumed came from solar stills changing salt water into fresh water. The food, three pounds of sugar and a few mouthfuls of mahi mahi speared 55 days out. After three days testing by service doctors, they left the hospital in good condition losing around 45 lbs. each in their self-caused ordeal.

A wide variety of items needed for a long time survival situation in which individuals must rely on their own resources, as chances of organized rescue operations have been eliminated, are shown in photo upper right.

All equipment has to be simple AND reuseable. A good example is to eliminate weight and bulk of canned water which is only used once. A sealed solar still in a small container, may be inflated to supply the fresh water needs indefinitely for two adults under survival conditions.

Photo of SIG II Kit shows equipment used by George and Charlie in their 56 day survival trip to Hawaii. It is the basis for increasing numbers of Sigler designed kits for cruising sailboats, powerboats, and fishing boats operating on the ocean and in coastal areas.

George stresses a survival inflatable needs maneuverability. "Courageous" used a small square sail held up by a mop handle, providing maneuvering in a 90° downwind arc ... the difference between sailing one ashore, or drifting past an island, back out to sea.

Many new and practical survival products are coming on the market directly or indirectly because of George Sigler who cared enough to risk his life to test survival products for ocean use .. to help YOU, a field unfortunately dominated for too many years with amateurism.

We've had many long discussions with George to put his highly varied survival information from his experiences into book form ... which is difficult for action oriented Sigler. We hope this book may soon be available at your local book store.

All sailboats and powerboats underway must carry at least one USCG Approved preserver for every person aboard, or the operator is subject to a stiff fine.

USCG Approved preservers were limited before 1970 for recreational use to the cushion which would waste endless energy just hanging onto it if your boat was swamped or sunk . . . plus the illogical AK-1 jacket.

The AK-1 jacket could easily be damaged in boats subject to moisture and spray due to organic cloth material, and metals often corroding easily. Swimming any distance with an AK-1 was almost impossible.

Three major preserver requirements to consider —
- a comfortable swim aid with practical flotation,
- synthetic materials and corrosion resistant metals,
- they can be easily stored yet ready for instant use.

We tested the Stearns vest for almost four years under varied conditions before Approval, wearing two out just due to many hours of actual use.

They protect the body in a sloppy sea, while being warm and comfortable to wear under a jacket in cold sailing conditions. When a storm moved in on a hot day with high humidity, the inner mesh removed condensation making them comfortable to wear . . . plus being excellent swim aids when required.

Other vests without the lining would cause prespiration buildup in cold weather AND warm weather, becoming very uncomfortable to wear in less than a half hour.

When the Stearns vest was Approved, extra flotation was added, plus a strap around the jacket which gave extra protection in sloppy weather if zipper problems developed. We prefer to use the next smaller size as it would fit more comfortably under jackets or windbreakers when used for long periods, especially when sleeping. Our thanks go to Maurice O'Link and his excellent workers producing the outstanding Stearns vest, which finally broke the life preserver Approval stalemate.

226

the Ettinger Approved Flotation Belt

The next excellent preserver with a completely different approach was USCG Approved in early 1978, the product of "Red Dog" Ettinger, inventor of athletic equipment, with an ex-professional football playing background.

Red and his wife enjoyed bass fishing in those hot Tennessee summers. A careening bass boat at top speed hit their anchored boat, sinking it. The wife said that was her last fishing trip unless she had a comfortable preserver to wear in hot, muggy conditions they faced that day.

Red, a gentle genial 6'6" gorilla, decided to make his own preserver design for his wife as bass fishing just wasn't any fun without her.

I met Red at a 1978 USCG/Red Cross seminar when wearing one of his preservers, he walked off the edge of a swimming pool fully clothed, falling into the water. As ALL of the preserver is underwater, the flotation is outstanding.

Red returned in a couple of minutes, repeating the performance wearing a heavy jacket he later took off handing it to me ... weighing over 35 pounds!

The extra dead weight had little effect on his preserver's function with all his flotation material being underwater. I called it a "super-ski belt", he renamed it a flotation belt.

We put his first Approved preservers through the acid test... they were excellent for all-round use. He sent us a new model last fall with improvements especially for flexibility and stowage. We can highly recommend this excellent preserver for all-round sailing use, thanks to the contribution of "Red Dog" Ettinger.

● Stearns Manufacturing Co.
Box 1498
St. Cloud, MN 56301
(415) 252-1642

● Ettinger Enterprises, Inc
5310 Lance Drive
Knoxville, TN 37919
(615) 582-5458

We found the water world beneath our boat fascinating to discover with mask, snorkel, and fins. We found it just part of the story after installing a SEA TEMP* indicator. We can now find warm spots in the ocean for swimming and snorkeling, plus differences in fish activity with a 1° decrease, or 2° increase in water temperature, and when to anticipate hypothermia with water temp. below 70°.

Swimming is an excellent exercise, the perfect way to cool off on a hot day, and after a strenuous sail. But how far can you swim under normal conditions?

It is easy to fall overboard off most sailboats. If it is a nonswimmer, he panics immediately calling for help underwater. This is a hazardous type of rescue which must occur immediately . . . or it will be too late.

Our information indicates <u>3/4 of all drownings occur within 60' of shore</u>. If a person can swim just 100' in case of capsize or falling overboard, he will not usually panic, and be easy to rescue.

If you want to sail, can you swim 100' under normal conditions, and are you comfortable in the water? If not, take swimming lessons, though we wish pool instructors would reconsider the methods they use. We've had to teach a handful of persons they weren't able to teach.

We put flippers and ski belts on them for an hour or two swim a day for ten days or so in our bay. When the ski belt is suddenly removed they usually laugh as they now have honest confidence in their swimming ability which couldn't have been gained without such aids.

The main job is NOT to fall overboard. Have a couple of ski belts easy to reach, to throw to a victim in the water to secure around his waist, giving you ample time to prepare your boat for a pickup. Use a harness, pg. 194, to stay on your boat at night or in rough weather. More details are found pgs. 150-161, in "TrailerBoating Illus."

228 *SEA TEMP Co., 19250 E. Colima Rd., La Puente, CA 91745

If you fall off your boat, can you come back aboard under your own power? We recommend you try to do this under ideal conditions, so you will know enough variables to help a person come aboard under adverse conditions .... or suppose the victim is you.

The bowline stirrup is the best method we've found for a person to come aboard a small sail or power boat by himself. This is an important consideration as an excited crew pulling a victim aboard, might pull him across sharp screw heads, a sharp cleat, or other object, causing unnecessary harm.

Our boat was less than a year old when we added a swim platform as we enjoy swimming and snorkeling, yet it was always ready to use if a student falls overboard, page 63.

"The EVER-READY" BOARDING LADDER* was recently introduced, an excellent boat ladder that fits a wide variety of transoms and boat sizes. It is light, made of stainless, and takes little room. This ladder can be installed with simple tools.

We've checked into a few simple, tragic, man overboard situations, when the victim couldn't climb back aboard, and those on the boat weren't able to help him.

After 15 to 20 minutes, especially in cold water, the victim falls into unconsciousness when the body heat is drained, soon followed by drowning in full sight of friends and loved ones. These drownings could have been avoided IF their owners had taken the time and effort to install a practical rigid boarding ladder. AVOID a rope ladder as it is next to impossible to climb aboard a boat of any size in even good conditions with a flexible ladder.

The sailor who uses reasonable preparation will have his share of excitement, yet the hazards will rank far below those we face daily, the auto and the bathtub.

*Stainless Rails, 46 Center Ave., At. Highlands, NJ 07716   229

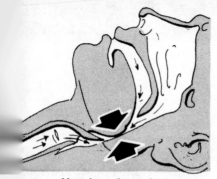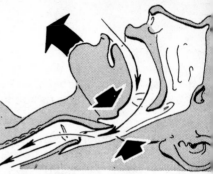

Note how throat becomes a one-way valve while drowning or suffocating with the back of the TONGUE pressing against, and blocking upper air passageway. This must be opened immediately by PULLING or PUSHING jaw into jutting-out position so air can be inhaled into .... and exhaled out from victim's lungs.

Third leading cause of accidental death in our country is drownings ... with approximately 8000 victims a year. What makes it worse, many victims considered beyond help in the past due to long submergence and absence of life signs may have been saved.

It is easy to understand and teach artificial respiration methods. Most people avoid the thought, feeling they will never have any use for it. Then with startling swiftness someone else's life is in your hands ... or the situation reversed and you the victim, with no one in your family capable of administering artificial respiration.

Don't wait to pull drowning victim way up onto the beach, then run to your car looking for a folder to show correct mouth to mouth method as it may be too late. Try mouth to mouth, or mouth to nose method as soon as practical.

━━━━━━━━ BEFORE YOU START ━━━━━━━━

Clear victims mouth and air passages and begin mouth to mouth breathing. Give victim FOUR quick breaths without interruption ... then take a deep breath (twice normal), open your mouth wide, place your mouth over victims mouth and blow.

After artificial respiration method has been started and it is determined the heart has stopped, external heart massage (CPR) should be started combined with artificial respiration.

If your sailboat goes offshore for even short periods ... "Emergency Care" used to teach police, fire, and rescue personnel units should be aboard, published by Robert J. Brady Company, Bowie, MD 20715.

Artificial Respiration

BREAKING AIR BLOCK

TILT HEAD so chin points 45° upward.

PUSH/PULL JAW into jutting-out position to lift tongue from back of throat.

BREATHING METHOD

Open your mouth and place it tightly over the victim's mouth. PINCH NOSE to make a tight seal on adult. BLOW FORCEFULLY to make the victim's chest rise.

Remove your mouth, turn your head to side and listen for OUTWARD RUSH of AIR indicating an air exchange.

For children and infants, cover BOTH mouth & nose with your mouth. Blow gently or use puffs.

BREATHING CYCLE

ADULT-once every 5 seconds (count 1000, 2000, 3000, 4000, 5000) or about 12 per minute. Blow forcefully and vigorously.

CHILD-once every 3 seconds, depending on size.

INFANTS-use short shallow puffs.

if OBSTRUCTION exists

Drowning victims swallow varying quantities of WATER, which with FOOD in stomach, could, if regurgitated obstruct air passage. If vomiting occurs, turn victim on side, wipe out mouth, reposition him and continue breathing.

If NO air EXCHANGE exists, check head & jaw. If still not successful—quickly turn victim on side. Hit several sharp blows between shoulder blades to dislodge obstruction, reposition, and continue breathing.

Occasionally sweep your fingers through victim's mouth to remove foreign matter.

RECOVERY

Continue cycle until victim breathes freely. Keep him quiet as possible until breathing regularly. Have him covered so body temperature doesn't go down. Treat for shock until doctor and/or transportation arrives.

NOTE: many drownings may be caused from
★ HEART ATTACKS. Doctors have been using this type respiration with coronary patients for a long time as emergency measure.

★ also sun strokes

Sailing Illustrated   231

For over 20 years we have been outspoken about the hodgepodge of misguided, redundant, and confusing laws governing sailboat and powerboat operation.

A great step forward has been made in unifying and improving these rules (with a couple of exceptions) with the new International (72 Colregs) coming into force 7/78, followed by the new Inland Rules (H.R. 6671) 12/81. Order your new copy of CG-169 soon as possible to find the location of these rules listed on the following pages.

The two basic rules port tack/starboard tack, and windward/leeward rules now have identical numbers and wording.

The upwind right-of-way over a downwind vessel, the last square rigger heritage, was eliminated Sept '65 in International, eliminated 16 years later under Inland Rules.

Sailboat running light standards are a lot stronger for better visibility under International Rules...excellent insurance to minimize collision potentials by reducing the number of weak, low mounted lights under the old rules. It is not clear at the present time how much International visibility standards may be compromised in Inland Rules.

poor visibility

The tricolor light adds a new idea to night sailing under sail ONLY for sailboats to 39.4' under Int'l...to 65.7' under Inland Rules, using one bulb for red/green/white lenses. If you add the tricolor, consider a combination running, anchor, and strobe installation.

USCG negativism continues toward the strobe. Our only interest, since it is NOT illegal, is that it should be considered a "caution flasher" indicating danger..or an emergency situation is taking place.

good visibility

If jib tack is raised above the deck, visibility underway is greatly improved. In sloppy wave action, waves breaking aboard will drain under the jib without damage to equipment.

International/Inland Rules are covered in Pamphlet CG-169. Buy from Sup't of Documents, U.S. Government Printing Office, Washington, D.C. 20402; or order by phone – (202) 783-3238.

Sailboat International and Inland Right-of-Way Rules are identical.

Rule 12(a). When two sailing vessels are approaching one another, so as to involve risk of collision, one of them shall keep out of the way of the other as follows:

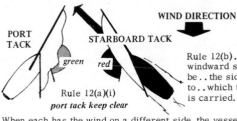

WIND DIRECTION

PORT TACK

STARBOARD TACK

green *red*

Rule 12(a)(i)
port tack keep clear

PORT TACK

STARBOARD TACK

Rule 12(b)... the windward side shall be .. the side opposite to .. which the mainsail is carried.

When each has the wind on a different side, the vessel which has the wind on the port side shall keep out of the way of the other.

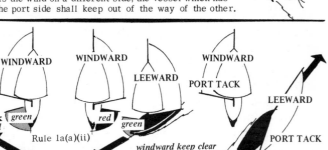

WINDWARD

LEEWARD

WINDWARD

LEEWARD

WINDWARD

PORT TACK

LEEWARD

PORT TACK

green *red* *red* *green*

Rule 1a(a)(ii)

windward keep clear

When both have the wind on the same side, the vessel which is to windward shall keep out of the way of the vessel which is to leeward.

Responsibilities Between Vessels, Rule 18. Except where Rules 9 (Narrow Channels), 10 (Vessel Traffic Services) and 13 (Overtaking)... R. 18(a) A power-driven vessel underway shall keep out of the way of----------------
Rule 18(a)(iv) a sailing vessel.

powerboat keep clear

MEETING

Large Vessels, Narrow Channels, Rule 9(b). A vessel of less than 20 meters in length (65.7 feet) or a sailing vessel shall not impede .. a vessel that can safely navigate only within a narrow channel ...

Overtaking, Rule 13(b). A vessel shall be deemed to be overtaking when coming up .. from a direction more than 22.5° abaft her beam ...

Rule 13(d) .. keeping clear of the overtaken vessel until she is finally past and clear.

sailboat OR powerboat

OVERTAKING

overtaking keep clear

135°

Overtaking, Rule 13(a). Nonwithstanding anything contained in Rules 4 through 18, any vessel overtaking any other shall keep out of the way of the vessel being overtaken.

233

Sailing Illustrated

Sailboats and powerboats must give way to large vessels with highly limited maneuverability - - - - -

● Rule 9(b). A vessel less than 20 meters (65.7') in length or a sailing vessel shall not impede the passage of a vessel that can safely navigate only within a narrow channel or freeway.

● Rule 9(c). A vessel engaged in fishing shall not impede the passage of any other vessel navigating within a narrow channel or fairway.

● Rule 9(c). A vessel shall not cross a narrow channel or fairway if such crossing impedes the passage of a vessel which can safely navigate only within that channel or freeway ...

The powerboat rules are a great improvement as they define the obligations of vessels operating in river and tidal currents missing under previous rules, yet was applied under court decisions little publicized.

A vessel crossing a river shall keep out of the way of a power-driven vessel coming upstream, or downstream.

The vessel coming downstream has the right-of-way, and shall initiate whistle passing signals, over the vessel coming upstream.

Inland Rule 25(e)-a vessel over 12 meters (39.4') operating under sail and power is supposed to display a black cone point down in the rigging, smaller sailboats may exhibit one but aren't required to. We've only seen one tattered cone used in 20 years, nailed to an old motor sailer spreader.

Engine controls should be on the right side of a sailboat cockpit so the operator under power has better visibility of his danger zone to reduce chance of a collision.

Meeting requirements of power boat to power boat at
234 night is simplified with, red−stop. . .green−go.

Powerboat Rules

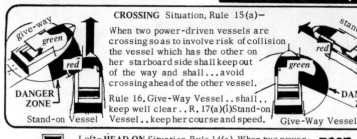

CROSSING Situation, Rule 15(a)—

When two power-driven vessels are crossing so as to involve risk of collision the vessel which has the other on her starboard side shall keep out of the way and shall...avoid crossing ahead of the other vessel.

Rule 16. Give-Way Vessel..shall.. keep well clear.. R. 17(a)(i)Stand-on Vessel.. keep her course and speed.

Stand-on Vessel — Give-Way Vessel

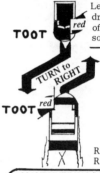

Left— **HEAD-ON** Situation, Rule 14(a). When two power-driven vessels are meeting...so as to involve risk of collision each shall alter her course to starboard so that each shall pass on the port side of the other.

TOOT TOOT

▶ River/Tidal CURRENTS ◀

Exceptions to above rule: Inland Rule 9(a)(ii)... a power-driven vessel ... with a following current shall have the right-of-way over an upbound vessel shall... initiate the.. signals... It is applied under International with Rule 18(a)(ii).

Inland Rule 15(b)...a vessel crossing a river shall keep out of the way of a power-driven vessel ascending or descending the river.

Rule 32(b).. short blast.. about 1 second's duration.
R. 32(c).. prolonged blast.. 4 to 6 second's duration.

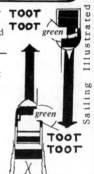

Sailing Illustrated

MANEUVERING/WARNING Signals—

Rule 34(g). When a power-driven vessel is leaving a dock or berth, she shall sound one prolonged blast.

NARROW CHANNEL, Rule 9(a)(i)—

A vessel proceeding along...a narrow channel.. shall keep as near to the outer limit.. as is safe and practicable. Sound Signal-Rule 34(e).

Rule 34(e). A vessel nearing a bend or...a channel or fairway where other vessels may be obscured.. shall sound one prolonged blast.

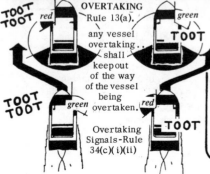

OVERTAKING

Rule 13(a). any vessel overtaking.. shall keep out of the way of the vessel being overtaken.

Overtaking Signals-Rule 34(c)(i)(ii)

Rule 34(a)(i). — three short blasts .. "I am operating astern propulsion".

WARNING Signals, Rule 34(d). When vessels .. in doubt .. to avoid collision, the vessel in doubt.. giving at least five short and rapid blasts on the whistle ... may be supplemented by a light signal of at least five short and rapid flashes. 235

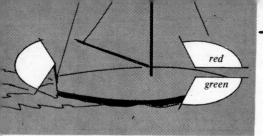

Sailing Vessel Underway

Rule 25(a)..shall exhibit
(1)sidelights;(ii)sternlight.

Def.;Rule 21(b)sidelights..
green light on the starboard
side,and red .. on the port
side showing an unbroken
light... of 112.5° (each).

Int'l/Inland Rule 21(b)continues .. In a vessel of less than 20 meters
(65') the side lights may be combined in one lantern carried *on*
the fore and aft centerline of a vessel .

Inland only Rule 21(b)continues ... a vessel of less than 12 meters
(39.4') ... the sidelights when combined in one lantern shall be placed
as *nearly as practical* to the fore and aft centerline of the vessel.

Int'l/Inland Rule 25(a)(ii) sternlight-Def. Rule 21(c)... a white
light placed as nearly as practical at the stern showing an
unbroken light over an arc ... of 135 degrees ...

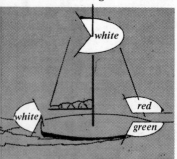

Power Driven Vessel Underway

Int'l/Inland Rule 23(a).. shall exhibit:

(i)a masthead (engine) light forward..
(iii) sidelights; and (iv)a sternlight.

Int'l/Inland Def.; Rule 21(a) "Masthead light" (engine light)..a white
light ... showing ... over an arc ...
of 225 degrees.

Sternlight variables Under Power–

Int'l Rule 21 (c) ... a white light ...
of 135 degrees ...

Inland-Rule 23(c) A power-driven vessel of less than 12 meters
(39.4').. may .. exhibit an all-round 360° white light and sidelights.

Int'l-Rule 23(c) A power-driven vessel of less than 7 meters (23')
.. whose maximum speed does not exceed 7 knots may ... exhibit
an all-round white light... if practical,also exhibit sidelights.

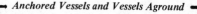
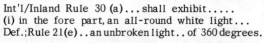

Anchored Vessels and Vessels Aground

Int'l/Inland Rule 30 (a) ... shall exhibit.....
(i) in the fore part, an all-round white light...
Def.;Rule 21(e)..an unbroken light.. of 360 degrees.

Inland (only)Rule 30(g) A vessel of less than
20 meters (65')..when ... in a special anchorage
area .. shall not be required to exhibit anchor lights ...

Inland (only)Rule 30(e)...less than 7 meters (23')
at anchor, not in or near a channel ... where other vessels normally
navigate .. shall not be required to exhibit .. (an all-round white light).

tricolor light   anchor light   strobe light

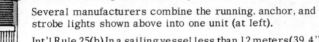

Sailing Vessel Underway-Sail ONLY

Several manufacturers combine the running, anchor, and strobe lights shown above into one unit (at left).

Int'l Rule 25(b) In a sailing vessel less than 12 meters (39,4') (Inland Rule 25(b) is identical, yet for vessel less than 20 meters (65.7').. the lights.. may be combined in one lantern ...near the top of the mast where it can best be seen.

Advantages of tricolor running light... visibility increases with height above water surface...while its visibility cannot be blocked with the jib.

Tricolor running light uses one bulb with less drain than pulpit mounted sidelights/stern light requiring two or three bulbs. A 10 watt bulb may have a mile visibility...while a 25 watt bulb may double its visibility, with an increased battery drain.

If your sailboat has both running light systems, pulpit mounted sidelights and sternlight at eye level are easier to see in close quarter harbor maneuvering situations.

When a sailboat becomes a powerboat, the tricolor MUST be turned off...replaced by the engine light, side lights, and the stern light.

Tricolor light disadvantage.. does your mast have a tabernacle to lower your mast in order to replace a burned out tricolor bulb?

STROBE light (pg. 232) should only be turned on during a dangerous or emergency situation.

Int'l/Inland Rule 25(d)(i) A sailing vessel of less than 7 meters (23').. (if she doesn't show other lights covered).. shall have.. a white light which shall be exhibited in sufficient time to prevent collison (see left).

Light Visibility details Int'l/Inland Rule 22. Due to considerable variables it is not clear at time of detailing how strictly these rules will be enforced- look for USCG, state regulation announcements.

Sailing Illustrated   237

72 Colregs

Rule 25(d)(ii). A vessel under OARS... show white light in... time to prevent collision.

Rule 23(c), POWER-DRIVEN vessel less than 7 meters(23 feet)whose maximum speed(underway) doesn't exceed 7 knots (though it can go faster) may.. exhibit all-round light... if practicable, also exhibit sidelights (shown on vessel under 39.4' long. Outboard powered rowboats and dinghies are included in this rule.)

lengths	
meters	feet
7	23
12	39.4
20	65.7
50	164
100	328
150	492
200	656

Rule 22(b)(c)	less than 12 meters (to 39.4 feet)	12 to 20 meters (to 65.7 feet)	less than 50 meters (to 164 feet)	
R/G 112.5° each	comb. or separate 1 mile vis.	comb. or separate 2 mile vis.	separate 2 mile vis.	Rule 21(b)
masthead 225°	2 mile vis. 3.3' above R/G	3 mile vis. 8.2' above gunwale	5 mile vis. ◄— (Annex 1)	Rule 21(a)
stern light 135°	2 mile vis.	2 mile vis.	2 mile vis.	Rule 21(c)

A POWER-DRIVEN VESSEL THAT EXCEEDS 7 KNOTS—

navigation light definitions Rule 21 (a)(b)(c)
navigation light visibility Rule 22(b) 12 meters to under 50 meters;
(c) vessels less than 12 meters (39.4 feet long)

All powerboat lights are covered in Rule 23(a)----
(i) masthead light (225°)
(iii) sidelights (112.5° each)
(iv) sternlight (135°)

(International Rules require SEPARATE masthead and stern lights... they may NOT be combined as with Inland Rules).

under 39.4 feet long

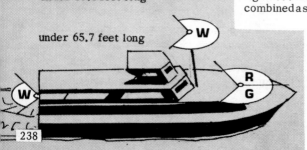

under 65.7 feet long

Int'l/Inland R.21(b) ..a vessel less than 20 meters (65.7 feet) ... sidelights may be combined into one lantern.

Sailing Illustrated

Rule 25(d)(ii). A vessel under OARS may... have ready at hand .. lighted lantern showing a white light... in sufficient time to prevent a collision.

Inland Rules are silent, Int'l Rule 23(c) applies- POWER-DRIVEN vessel less than 7 meters(23') whose maximum speed (underway) doesn't exceed 7 knots (though it can go faster) may... exhibit all-round light... if practicable, also exhibit sidelights (shown on vessel under 39.4' long. Outboard powered rowboats and dinghies are included in this rule.)

Rule 22(b)(c)	less than 12 meters (to 39.4 feet)	12 to 20 meters (to 65.7 feet)	less than 50 meters (to 164 feet)	
R/G 112.5° each	comb. or separate 1 mile vis.	comb. or separate 2 mile vis.	separate 2 mile vis.	Rule 21(b)
masthead 225°	2 mile vis. 3.3' above R/G	3 mile vis. 8.2' above gunwale ←(Annex 1)	5 mile vis.	Rule 21(a)
stern light 135°	2 mile vis.	2 mile vis.	2 mile vis.	Rule 21(c)

Note: crossed out numbers above indicate changes from International to Inland light Rules.

navigation light definitions, Rule 21 (a)(b)(c)
navigation light visibility, R. 22(b) 12, meters to under 50 meters; (c) vessels less than 12 meters (39.4 feet long)

under 39.4 feet long

Rule 38(d)(vi). Vessels under 65.7 feet long "are permanently exempt from" showing separate masthead light (225°) and (135°) sternlight.

under 65.7 feet long

Rule 23(c). Power-driven vessel less than 12 meters (39.4 feet) may ... exhibit an all-round white light...(International Rules require separate stern and masthead lights).

Int'l/Inland R.21(b)...a vessel less than 20 meters (65.7 feet) ...sidelights may be combined into one lantern...

Exemption- Rule 38(d)(vi)... vessels ...under 20 meters (65.7 feet) ... exhibits a white light aft visible all round the horizon.

Sailing
Illustrated   239

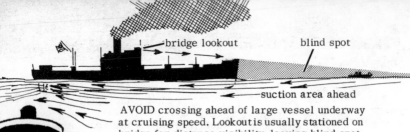

bridge lookout • blind spot

← suction area ahead

suction alongside

AVOID crossing ahead of large vessel underway at cruising speed. Lookout is usually stationed on bridge for distance visibility, leaving blind spot due to overhang of bow which is considerable.

Another reason to keep clear of large vessel at cruising speed is suction area 1/2 to 2 lengths ahead...to fill void developing at stern from propeller suction. Also avoid going close to side of large vessel...especially if ACCELERATING after picking up or dropping off pilot, even more serious and pronounced in shallow water. It may pull your boat against SIDE of large vessel and hold it there.

Tug with tow has limited maneuverability especially going downstream. If your boat suddenly cuts in front of tug, tow-boat operator has two choices...to go through your boat, or hit reverse causing tow to ride up and over tugboat stern.

Another factor to consider is that large vessels MUST maintain steerageway often to 5 knot minimum in narrow channels to respond to rudder. If almost empty and riding high in the water with beam wind, speed may have to be increased to maintain its steerageway and control.

Though a 5 knot speed may leave considerable WAKE, it is nothing compared to that left by destroyers, atomic subs, aircraft carriers operating at full speed. Their wakes may hit like a steep tidal wave if you aren't ready to compensate for the wake keeping damage, upset potentials to minimum.

If large vessel is raising anchor, stand clear as it will have little maneuverability in forward till underway...while its reverse maneuverability is almost negligible.

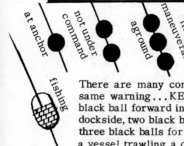

at anchor / fishing / not under command / aground / limited maneuverability / dredging, under-water operation / towing astern / trawling / super tanker

There are many commercial vessel signals carrying the same warning...KEEP CLEAR. The most common is a black ball forward in the rigging for vessels at anchor or dockside, two black balls for a vessel not under command, three black balls for a vessel aground, two cones indicating a vessel trawling, a diamond shape for towing, a cylinder for supertankers operating in channels, restricted by draft, etc.

240   Sailing Illustrated

C3 FREIGHTER 492'loa 69'6"wide
normal cruising speed 16 1/2 knots

T2 TANKER 523'6" loa 68' wide
normal cruising speed 14 1/2 knots

VICTORY SHIP 455'3"loa 62' wide
normal cruising speed 17 knots

It is important for all boat owners to know the handling factors of large vessels before meeting them at cruising speeds.

C3 freighter–1800' would be required to come to stop, 480' to make 90° turn.

T2 tanker–4350' would be required to come to stop, 1880' to make 90° turn.

A 200,000 ton tanker will take around 2.5 miles (10 to 15 ship lengths) and 21 minutes to come to a stop from 15 to 17 knots. A 400,000 ton tanker, larger than the Bantry Bay Class below, at the same speed would take around 30 minutes to come to a crash stop of four to five miles, which during this period of backing full, the ship's master would be unable to steer nor regulate its speed.

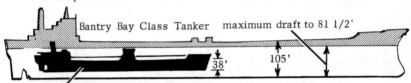

Bantry Bay Class Tanker   maximum draft to 81 1/2'

38'   105'

T2 tanker silhouette is shown for size comparison.

San Pedro, Calif., is one of 20 ports in the world, the only U.S. port able to handle todays "small" super tankers to 50' draft. Silhouette above is Bantry Bay Class, a gargantuan tanker of 326,000 tons, 1135'long, 174'beam, note draft above. Yet it is a flyweight compared to the 2,000' long, 300' beam, with a draft to 100' capable of carrying a million tons of crude oil ... too large to enter any U.S. port.

In 1967 the super tankers were exception coming into San Pedro, yet by 1971 they had become normal operation for the 14 San Pedro Harbor Pilots though handling ability changes radically due to varied designs. Pilots may be taken aboard 10 miles to sea with power applied for first few miles, often drifting the rest of the distance to their dock. To say small boats keep clear, is an understatement.

Crew members use rubber tired bicycles for transportation from one end to the other of these monstrous tankers.

For excellent reference read "Gargantuan Tankers Privileged or Burdened", Captain Edward Oliver USCG, United States Naval Institute Proceedings, September 1970, page 39.

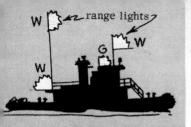

range lights

The 72 COLREGS Navigation Rules went into effect 8/1/78 for International Waters .. while a similar Inland Rules set was adopted for use in our inland waters starting 12/24/81.

You are supposed to display these navigation lights from dusk to dawn while underway indicating your type of vessel and its intended course. Pages 133 and 135 show the differing rules and spec's for identical powerboats. International lights may be used on inland waters, while the inland lights such as the all-round white light, page 135, is illegal for use on international waters.

Power-driven vessels over 50 meters long (164 feet).. "shall exhibit, Rule 23(a)(ii) a second masthead light abaft of and higher than the forward one"...which is called a range light. Tugboat above though under 50 meters long, often carries a range light.

port side   COLLISION COURSE!   starboard side

The two 225° masthead lights called range lights can be seen earlier and farther away than the red and green sidelights.

If the upper range light is directly over the lower one, the large vessel is heading directly towards YOUR boat...you will soon see the second warning, both red and green lights.

If the forward lower range light is either to the left or to the right of the higher range light, collision risk doesn't exist IF your vessel holds its course, and the bearing doesn't change... and the large vessel doesn't change course.

AVOID trying to take the right-of-way from large vessels as they are too big to argue with, their steering ability is limited, and if your engine should quit while passing under their bows it could be the last thing you will remember ... also watch for the huge wake of all large vessels at cruising speed.

Int'l Rule 28 (Inland Rule 28 is silent). Three vertical red lights at night, and a cylinder in the daytime, indicate a deep draft vessel such as a supertanker constrained by draft which cannot leave the channel means KEEP CLEAR.

242   Sailing Illustrated

Large Vessels

Even on the ocean do everything to avoid a collision course with the large and super large vessels since not only are you placing yourself in a difficult position, but you may not be around to argue your case afterwards. While a small 17,000 ton T-2 tanker may stop within a half mile in 5 minutes from cruising speed, 206,000 ton Idemitsu Maru about 2/3 size of Bantry Bay series requires about 21 minutes, 2.5 miles to stop (10-15 ship lengths).

Get out of the way of large vessels in ample time so the harbor pilot and captain don't have to worry about small vessels which might be in their way ... they have many more urgent problems requiring full concentration as only 9% of collisions occur in open waters.

national ensign

pilot aboard
ammunition
explosives or
flammable liquids

vessel underway

It is important for all boat operators to be aware of signs showing whether a large vessel is underway, preparing to get underway, docked, or anchored .. therefore out of control.

Signals shown are rather standard around the world except for Union Jack carried on U.S. military or other vessels under government control docked or at anchor. Any time you see the black anchor ball and Union Jack coming down forward, or national ensign being removed from stern staff, vessel is preparing to get underway ... so keep clear.

national ensign

black anchor ball
in rigging
Union Jack
on bow

docked or <u>at anchor</u>

Our book has considerable complexity requiring the help and advice of several people to prepare this revision----

THANKS!

Optimust-Olaf Harken of Vanguard; Sunfish-owner Bill Earnshaw; Force 5-Jim Ronshagen, AMF Alcort; Catalina 15-Diego Carr, Think Wind; Windsurfer-Matlack Windsurfing; Hobie 14/16-Nick Steele, Hobie Newport; Snipe-Ron Fox, Pheonix Boat Co. Star-Harrison Hine, Seaway Marine; P2/18-builder Owen Minney; Catalina 38-builder Frank Butler.

Rules and Regulations-Stan Holden, USCG; and for proof reading-Benjamin Burns, M.D., who took over at the last moment after our proof reader Douglas Scott lost his life when his plane crashed in a storm of unexpected intensity.

Our 1960"TrailerBoating Illustrated"challenged inventors to produce a better hand propulsion method than oars and paddles, stern mounted, especially for planing hulls. We hoped it would need only one hand, the operator sitting in a comfortable position looking forward.

Several inventors seemed interested, without results, till a local inventor who spent many years in China, not knowing of our challenge, 13 years later produced POWR-OAR. He bought a Sabot after moving to the U.S. Not satisfied with normal operation he produced this new idea requiring a basic patent search almost as far back as Noah's Ark.

He had watched Chinese scull 20' to 30' junks for many years with long sweeps or oars, the start of the idea. It was combined with a fishes tail, providing much better underwater propulsion shape than the end of an oar.

Major sculling oar power loss motion occurs as the oar reaches end of arc. It must stop, be rotated, then reverse direction. A swivel motion was added to the blade so at the end of the arc it made efficient change of water pressure, instead of fighting itself and wasting power as with the sculling oar. The blade displaces water at stern pushing your boat forward, similar to the tail of a fish.

Still not being satisfied, it was also redesigned to work as a dinghy rudder for steering. A lanyard was released when it was changed to propulsion, the lanyard pulled in to again become a rudder...race committees, beware!

Dinghy space is at a premium. When disassembled it has short sections needing minimum stowage area, weight around 3 pounds. If parts fall overboard during a capsize, they will float. As the size of dinghy or rowboat increases, so must the size of the propulsion blade become larger. POWR-OAR seems to have an excellent future.

244 Moderncraft, 1306 W. Glenoaks Blvd., Glendale, Calif. 91201

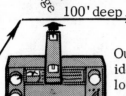

335°M

to wedge

100' deep

weak   strong   overpowered

Our Newport jetty radiobeacon at left was ideal for new boat operator practice. Being low power it could be picked up about six miles out with the rdf set shown.

Steering on NULL, impulses began to show on sensitivity needle above. About 300 yards out with batteries in good condition, it would be overpowered on null. Fathometer meanwhile has been picking up the bottom, shallowing **BRRWNGG** rapidly till preset alarm sounds at 100'.

A sharp right turn following 100' contour would take boat to entrance buoy. Hard left turn following compass course would take boat between jetties into harbor. A week before this page was written, we took our boat into the harbor with students aboard, in a pea soup fog. Accuracy was so good using this method, we almost hit the entrance buoy.

USCG insists rdf beacons only be used for cross bearings instead of homing. While ideal for freighter or 50' craft with more expensive equipment ... it is impractical for majority of smaller craft in pitching, rolling sea. For these, homing is ideal, yet practice is required in good weather to know capabilities & limitations of equipment.

After continuous practice with rdf through past years ... we feel many rdf limitation theories, seem based more on "Witch Doctor Tales", than actual use. Practice with your rdf, and make up your own mind as to its practical usage.

In late '64 USCG moved beacon 600 yards inshore of this position to wedge area known for spectacular body surfing wave action, a left turn putting boat on beach, a right turn into a rock jetty. It was an outstanding case of bad judgment till returned to original position in '74, ten years later.

The U. S. Buoyage System is numbered proceeding from the sea. Two ways to remember correct side to pass buoys: (RRR)Red Right Returning, (BPOE)Black Port On Entering.

When buoys can be passed on either side with one being preferred, it is indicated by color of topmost band. The red & black combination buoys are also used for junctions & obstruction buoys. Mid channel vertically banded black and white buoys may be passed on either side.

Black and white horizontally banded buoys indicate fish traps;quarantine –yellow buoys; anchorage –white;dredging –white with green top;special purpose-orange & white bands. It is your **author's** feeling that another buoy just used for obstructions, is needed for our present system.

We have two traps that exist for the person entering new waters without advantage of a chart. In one is a conflict of parallel buoyage systems with underwater obstruction between;the other,when two systems meet and terminate together, such as found off City Island in the Long Island Sound. Many owners have tried to take a boat between the two, hitting a submerged rock called "Big Tom".

After a storm, it is a good idea to bear close watch on floating buoys in exposed positions, that may have drifted off position, or the light is out. If such be the case, notify the closest USCG unit immediately.

Water depths on east coast are charted from Mean Low Water, west coast charts at Mean Lower Low Water. The latest correction date will be stamped on bottom of chart.

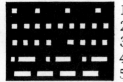

1 Buoy lights shown are;1.flashing, 2. quick
2 flashing,3. interrupted quick flashing, 4.
3 short long flashing, 5.occulting.2 indicates
4 important turns,wrecks,etc.,where special
5 caution is required; 3 indicates junction
lights or buoys and 4, mid channel buoys. As 5 requires shore current, its use is generally limited.

Sailing   Illustrated

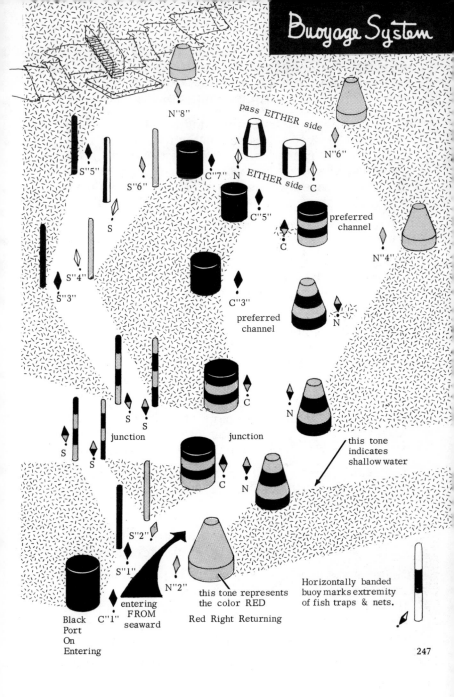

Buoyage System

N"8"

pass EITHER side

N"6"

C"7" N EITHER side C

S"5"

S"6"

S

C"5"

preferred channel

N"4"

S"4"

S"3"

C"3"

preferred channel

N

S

S

junction

junction

C

N

this tone indicates shallow water

S

S

C

N

S"2"

this tone represents the color RED

Red Right Returning

Horizontally banded buoy marks extremity of fish traps & nets.

S"1"

N"2"

entering FROM seaward

Black Port On Entering

C"1"

247

The best first boat to buy is in a class that is popular in your area, with sufficient basic controls to learn primary functions. Later you may want new ideas to improve your racing potentials . . . or step up to a more complex class.

FINN is a highly competitive single hander, International Olympic Class, though small in number. "Wild Turkey", page 249, took second in the 1970 Finn Worlds, probably the worst dinghy for a new sailor to choose. This Finn is still supposedly competitive if the wooden mast is replaced with an aluminum NEEDLESPAR mast.

Some ideas have applications to other classes such as a preventer for shroudless dinghies, halyard ball lock, etc.

INT'L 14 is a custom built, development class with a history going back to the turn of the century. Chances are no two will be rigged exactly alike, and you may find a variety of different hulls competing for the hardware.

"Daring" is as unusual a dinghy as you may find, pages 250-1, detailed when a few months old, shortly after winning the Yachting's One-Of-A-Kind Series with a 1-1-1-1-1 record . . . the mast, a converted TV antenna.

Turnbuckles are eliminated with tension adjusted by using a jack under the mast. Jumpers are continuous, coming down the mast to cockpit, then aft to end of cb trunk, to pull the upper part of the mast forward sailing downwind.

The centerboard is a jibing board using a small wedge in the aft end of the centerboard trunk, to force the board to point a degree or so higher into the wind, to increase pointing ability. The wedge is removed when changing tack, then wedged into the other aft side of the cb trunk. The jibing board is finding use in other classes such as Lido 14.

Centerboard uses a saddle arrangement to reduce helm pressure by pulling the board forward or aft for sailing closehauled to minimize leeway without raising the board, also used in FD class. These are just a few ideas to start analyzing. You might just be that person to make a new contribution . . . so start thinking!

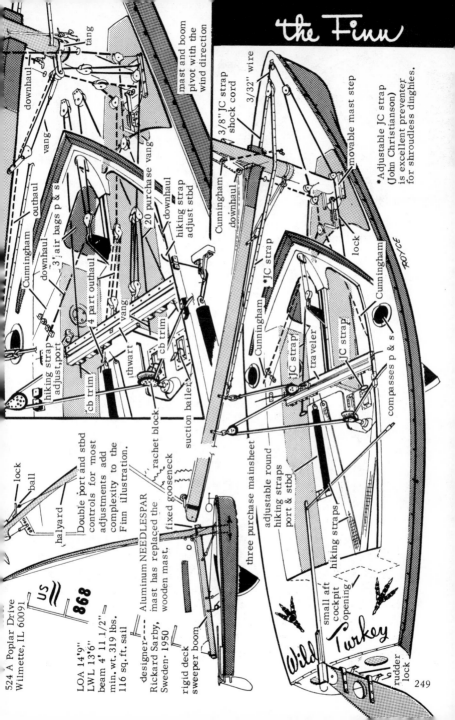

the Finu

tang

downhaul

vang

mast and boom pivot with the wind direction

3/8" JC strap shock cord

3/32" wire

movable mast step

*Adjustable JC strap (John Christianson) is excellent preventer for shroudless dinghies.

Cunningham outhaul

downhaul

3' air bags p & s

20 purchase vang

4 part outhaul

downhaul

hiking strap adjust stbd

Cunningham downhaul

lock

Cunningham

ROYCE

hiking strap adjust, port

vang

cb trim

thwart

cb trim

rachet block

Cunningham *JC strap

Cunningham *JC strap

JC strap

traveler

JC strap

compasses p & s

cb trim

suction bailer

lock

ball

halyard

Double port and stbd controls for most adjustments add complexity to the Finn illustration.

three purchase mainsheet

adjustable round hiking straps port & stbd

hiking straps

small aft cockpit opening

rudder lock

524 A Poplar Drive
Wilmette, IL 60091

US
868

LOA 14'9"
LWL 13'6"
beam 4' 11 1/2"
min. wt. 319 lbs.
116 sq. ft. sail

designer----
Rickard Sarby,
Sweden · 1950

Aluminum NEEDLESPAR mast has replaced the wooden mast.

fixed gooseneck

rigid deck sweeper boom

Wild Turkey

249

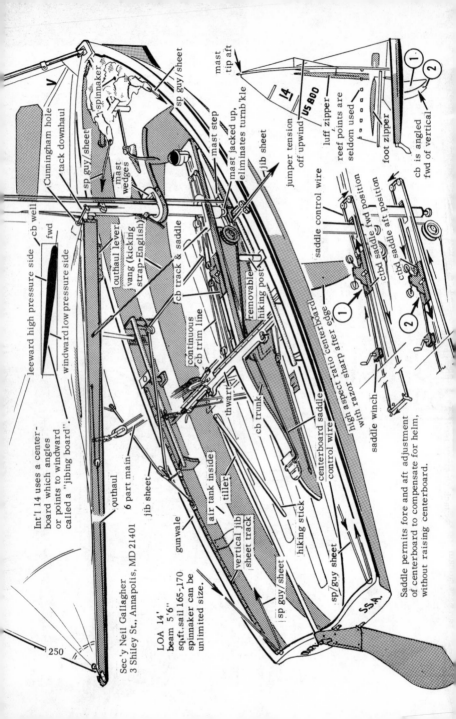

Int'l 14 uses a centerboard which angles or points to windward called a "jibing board".

Sec'y Neil Gallagher
3 Shiley St., Annapolis, MD 21401

LOA 14'
beam 5'6"
sqft.sail 165-170
spinnaker can be
unlimited size.

Saddle permits fore and aft adjustment of centerboard to compensate for helm, without raising centerboard.

250

leeward high pressure side
windward low pressure side
cb well
fwd

Cunningham hole
tack downhaul
sp guy/sheet
spinnaker
mast wedges
outhaul lever
vang (kicking strap-English)
cb track & saddle
continuous cb trim line
removable hiking post

sp guy/sheet
mast tip aft
mast step
mast jacked up, eliminates turnb'kle
jib sheet

jumper tension off upwind
luff zipper
reef points are seldom used
foot zipper
cb is angled fwd of vertical
US 800
14

outhaul
6 part main
jib sheet
gunwale
air tank inside
tiller
vertical jib sheet track
hiking stick
thwart
cb trunk
centerboard saddle control wire
centerboard control wire
saddle control wire
high aspect ratio centerboard with razor sharp after edge

ctbd saddle fwd position
ctbd saddle aft position
saddle winch

sp/guy sheet
sp/guy sheet
S.S.A.

The Int'l 14 is a development or open design class raced worldwide, with a history of over 70 years.

International 14

jumper tension on

mast tip fwd

jumper tension off upwind, and on downwind. Tension increases as wind eases.

jumper lead

high aspect ratio rudder(vs. catboat barn-door rudder, see page 5)

triple block

swivel cam cleat

car

traveler adjust for reaching

6 part main

double ended 4 part traveler

thwart

traveler adjust end for beating

jumper tension cleat

sp guy

knee

sp sheet fairlead

vertical jib sheet track

inwale

gunwale

mast jumper tension cleat

reel

sp pole

fixed guy

jib roller reef

jib sheet

shock cord pole lift

sp stowage strut

roller reef trim line

mast partner

mast step

sp sheet

wire downhaul

tack tension cleat

sp halyard

jumper lead

sp sheet

two part outhaul with lever control

tack tension eased

outhaul eased

fixed gooseneck

Lee shroud has semi-automatic release lever used for sailing off the wind.

inwale

traveler track

thwart

vang

vang drum

sp downhaul cleat

vang cleat

self bailer

tension on

tension off

jumper end

stbd jumper lead

port jumper lead

sp sheet

ROYCE

Jumper tension method was later changed to Hyfield Lever on forward side of mast.

251

United States Coast Guard ensign is flown from USCG vessels in commission. It has vertical orange and white stripes, with blue eagle and stars on a white background.

The United States Power Squadron ensign is flown from a members boat. It has blue and white vertical stripes, with white stars and anchor on red square background.

Coast Guard Auxiliary flag is flown from members boat after passing inspection. Color is dark blue with white diagonal stripe.

Red flag with white diagonal stripe indicates diver below, ir swimming to or from diving area. Flag may be on boat, float, or both.

For several years we've recommended a pennant be flown from bow of boat racing after five minute signal is given. It would be advantageous for jockeying in tight quarters with numerous classes in large regatta, also to avoid collisions with boats not racing.

racing pennant

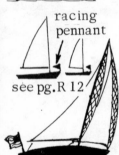

see pg. R 12

English and Canadians fly their ensigns from stern staff under sail, power, and at anchor, while traditional U.S. protocol is to fly it from leach of mainsail under sail.

Since the leach mounted ensign tangles with backstay when tacking or jibing, and hardly helps mainsail shape ... our U.S. sailing public is fortunately finding it more practical to carry it on the stern staff also under sail in increasing numbers each year finally adopted nationwide by U.S. in 1971.

Union Jack was crew flag for centuries indicating limited authority of professional crew at anchor or when docked. It is flown on anchored or docked military craft today; for reference see 'The Bluejackets' Manual'.

252

Flag Etiquette originated from Navy usage. The New York Yacht Club then through precedent, established proper usage for the public, followed by NAYRU, CCA, etc.

An exception to this is the Ensign, which was formerly flown from a flag halyard going from outer end of boom to outer end of gaff, see below. Flag halyard was eliminated on marconi main having a large roach, with Ensign next sewn to leach or peak of main or mizzen.

Those in charge of U.S. sail etiquette finally realized impracticality and minimum use of roach mounted Ensign in 1971, agreeing to its stern mounted use under sail, power, and at anchor.

National Ensign, the Yacht Ensign, USPS Ensign, CGA flag

owner absent flag (blue), meal flag (white), guest flag (blue, white stripes)

honoring a foreign ensign when in another country

yacht club burgee

officers flag or the owners private signal

Note: on a sloop the yacht club burgee is often given preference, instead of the officers flag or private signal from the masthead.

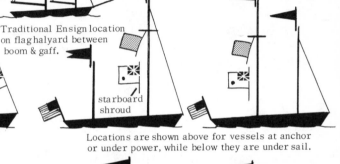

masthead
flag halyard
sail doesn't have roach
starboard spreader
starboard signal halyard

Traditional Ensign location on flag halyard between boom & gaff.

starboard shroud

Locations are shown above for vessels at anchor or under power, while below they are under sail.

black anchor ball
Union Jack

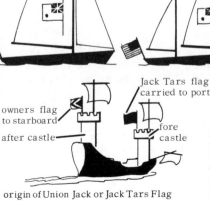

Jack Tars flag carried to port
owners flag to starboard
after castle
fore castle

origin of Union Jack or Jack Tars Flag

When sailing near moored or anchored U.S. Navy or Coast Guard craft, watch the black anchor ball and Union Jack. If both are being lowered, keep clear as the vessel is raising anchor or leaving a dock, and needs room.

Commercial vessels usually follow the same procedure, without flying the Union Jack.

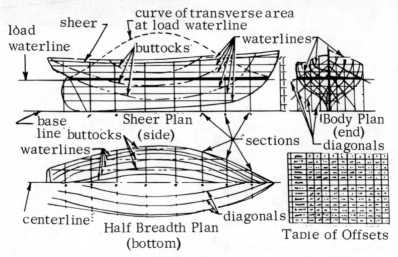

Shown above are drafting methods and terms used by naval architects to develop the lines of a boat, and to show hull form.

To understand these lines, it is necessary to know the sections, waterlines, buttocks, and diagonals shown in flat plan view above, and in perspective on the following pages.

Lines of a boat are shown with a side view called the SHEER PLAN, plus an end view or BODY PLAN comprised of a half view looking forward, & another half view looking aft. The HALF BREADTH PLAN or bottom view shows buttocks with waterlines on one side of the centerline & diagonals on the other. As the lines are symmetrical for port and starboard, it is only necessary to show one side.

These measurements are then enlarged to full size in the mold loft, using measurements given on the table of offsets. The sections or STATIONS shown in black on facing page, are the forms to which planking & bulkheads will fit, conform, or be shaped.

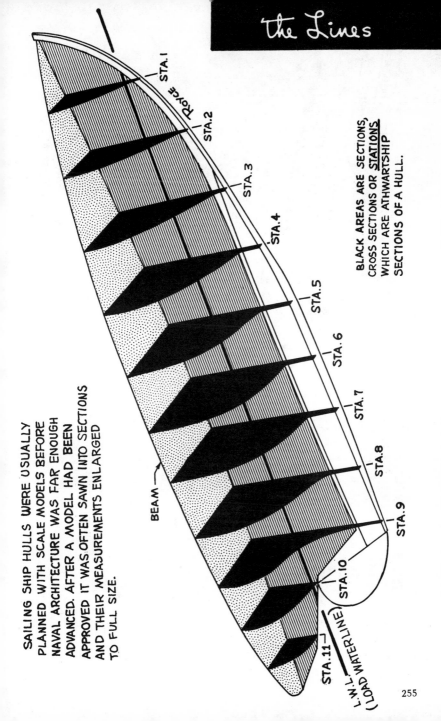

the Lines

SAILING SHIP HULLS WERE USUALLY
PLANNED WITH SCALE MODELS BEFORE
NAVAL ARCHITECTURE WAS FAR ENOUGH
ADVANCED. AFTER A MODEL HAD BEEN
APPROVED IT WAS OFTEN SAWN INTO SECTIONS
AND THEIR MEASUREMENTS ENLARGED
TO FULL SIZE.

BLACK AREAS ARE SECTIONS,
CROSS SECTIONS OR STATIONS
WHICH ARE ATHWARTSHIP
SECTIONS OF A HULL.

STA. 1
STA. 2
STA. 3
STA. 4
STA. 5
STA. 6
STA. 7
STA. 8
STA. 9
STA. 10
STA. 11

BEAM

L.W.L.
(LOAD WATERLINE)

255

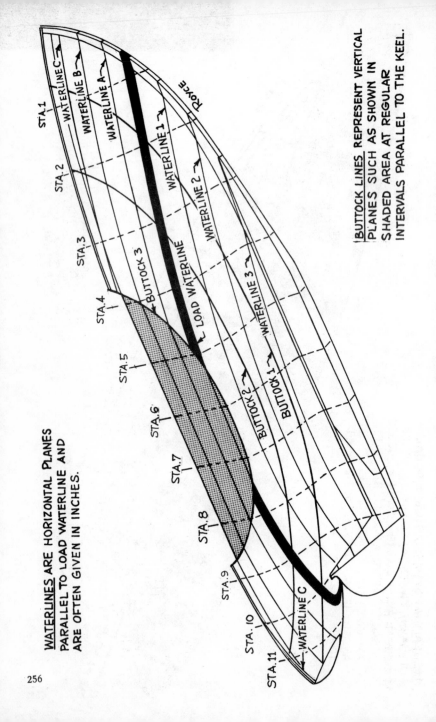

WATERLINES ARE HORIZONTAL PLANES PARALLEL TO LOAD WATERLINE AND ARE OFTEN GIVEN IN INCHES.

BUTTOCK LINES REPRESENT VERTICAL PLANES SUCH AS SHOWN IN SHADED AREA AT REGULAR INTERVALS PARALLEL TO THE KEEL.

STA.1
STA.2
STA.3
STA.4
STA.5
STA.6
STA.7
STA.8
STA.9
STA.10
STA.11

WATERLINE C
WATERLINE B
WATERLINE A
WATERLINE 1
WATERLINE 2
WATERLINE 3
WATERLINE C

LOAD WATERLINE

BUTTOCK 3
BUTTOCK 2
BUTTOCK 1

ROYCE

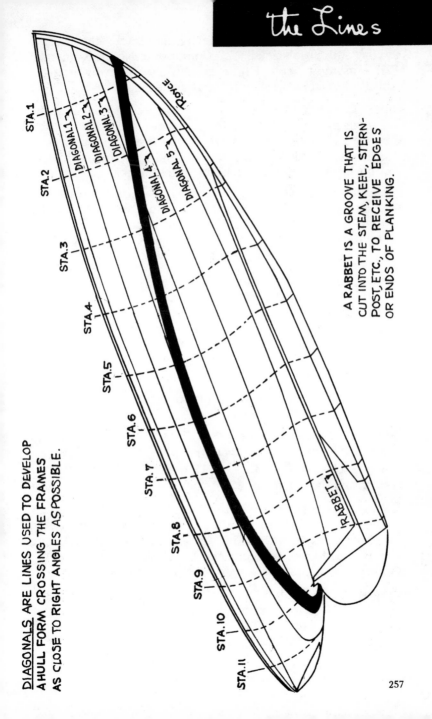

DIAGONALS ARE LINES USED TO DEVELOP A HULL FORM CROSSING THE FRAMES AS CLOSE TO RIGHT ANGLES AS POSSIBLE.

STA.1
STA.2
STA.3
STA.4
STA.5
STA.6
STA.7
STA.8
STA.9
STA.10
STA.11

DIAGONAL 1
DIAGONAL 2
DIAGONAL 3
DIAGONAL 4
DIAGONAL 5

RABBET

A RABBET IS A GROOVE THAT IS CUT INTO THE STEM, KEEL, STERN-POST, ETC., TO RECEIVE EDGES OR ENDS OF PLANKING.

One-design classes may race against each other using
"Portsmouth Yardstick Book".Contact Mr.Nolan Richards,
117 Kingswood Drive, Florence, AL 35630; or by using
Yachting's One-of-a-Kind Regatta method.

All factors equal in olden times, the longer sailboat usually
won most races due to the longer waterline speed factor,
page 140.A handicapping method was needed so a variety
of sailboats could race on an equal basis, all theoretically
coming in at the same moment mathematically.

It started with the 1790's Custom House Rule, updated
1883 to 1900 under the Seawanhaka Rule, followed by the
Universal, then the International Rules. In the 1930's the
Royal Ocean Racing Club(RORC) and Cruising Club of
America Rules (CCA) were introduced.

The Ocean Racing Rating(ORR-boat only)developed from
the CCA formula with many calculations having plus and
minus values formulated into a FEET rating including
weight, displacement, length, sail area, mast height, boom.
length, beam, freeboard, heeling moment, etc. The boat
must be remeasured any time hull or rigging changes
have been made.

The foot rating is converted into SECONDS per MILE
listed in the USYRU Handbook----

boats	sec.per mile	miles	seconds	corrected time
A (20'ORR)	306.6	x 10 =	(3060 sec.)	or 51 min. 0.0 sec.
B (30'ORR)	218.0	x 10 =	(2180 sec.)	or 36 min. 20.0 sec.
subtract the difference			880 sec.	14 min. 40.0 sec.

Sailboat B finished the 10 mile race in 2 hours, the shorter
sailboat A finished 13 minutes and 40.0 seconds later..
the shorter sailboat winning the race by a minute. Longer
hull B would have to cross the finish line at least 14 min.
and 40.0 seconds earlier to save her time and win.

Midget Ocean Racing Club (MORC) began with sailboats
having a 25' LOA to improve trailerable sailboats, now
covering boats to 30'. The MORC formula is comparable to
258 the CCA Rating Rule.

12 meter ← ← 6 meter

Meter boats are designed to a flexible formula providing when all factors are finalized, they will fall into a certain meter rating.The cubes above,for example, have measured capacities... which maybe long and squat, or tall and slim,yet have the same cubic capacity, the reason 12 meter sailboats range fron 64' to 70' long. Meter and ton boats are individually designed under their formulas to be as competitive as possible.

The International Ocean Rule (IOR) became popular in the U.S. around 1970, also called "ton racing", "level racing",or "level class rating".The IOR developed a new breed of racing sailboats,with tall rigs,short booms,and pinched sterns such as the Catalina 38 pages 76-81.

1/4 ton-19' to 28'(length approximate) with 18.0 IOR rating; two berths, lockers, 3-4 crew maximum.

1/2 ton-26'to 31'loa with 21.7 IOR rating; 3 berths, galley, lockers, hanging locker, 4-5 crew maximum.

3/4 ton-27' to 35' loa, 24.5 IOR rating;four berths, galley, lockers, head, bulkheads, 5 to 6 crew maximum.

One ton-32' to 39' loa, with 27.5 IOR rating. It has same accommodations as a 3/4 tonner, 6 to 7 crew maximum.

IOR designs are built to a rating formula in feet similar to the flexible cube theory above,the main elements being length, beam, bulk, and sail area. For more details write USYRU Offshore Office, Box 209, Newport, RI 02840.

Each new rule going back to 1790 is introduced with good logic for its time to eliminate previous inadequacies with strong supporters...and outspoken critics.

Yet the following day a new army of sharpshooters begin to develop new rule beating designs...as the perpetual rating gamesmanship continues.

The term SLOOP originated from the Dutch "sloep", the French "chaloup", and the English "shallop". In the beginning it was generally thought of as a large rowboat having a mast and sails that could be raised and used basically for harbor work.

The Dutch introduced the "sloep" to New York. In time a broad, shoal draft craft evolved using inboard ballast, being full in the bows, and carrying a tall mast. Later on it grew in size for commercial use up to 80' in the North River Sloop. Other uses of the term was a square-rigged Sloop of War (pg. 289), and today an English Navy gunboat.

Up to the turn of the century most large sailboats carried a bowsprit. They were called SLOOPS, while smaller ones without bowsprits were called KNOCKABOUTS. When better metals and improved engineering came along to make the taller masts practical, the term knockabout disappeared. The bowsprit is now limited to character boats, and to keep the anchor chain away from cruising hulls at anchor.

The MASTHEAD SLOOP rig has its jibstay going to the masthead. It is preferred for much of todays' ocean sailing boats from 24' where the wind is on the surface. Rigging is simple for cruising craft with a mast not designed for bending. All other factors equal, a masthead sloop will have a shorter mast than the standard sloop, making it able to carry a larger gennie to windward.

The STANDARD or FRACTIONAL sloop rig has jibstay or headstay going 3/4, 5/6, 7/8 or so, not all the way up to masthead. It is preferred for smaller one-design classes racing in protected areas where the wind may be several feet above the surface of the water.

The FRACTIONAL rig is preferred for all sizes of racing craft with mast bending being used to provide better sail trim starting with Snipe, Lightning, and Flying Dutchman ...all the way up to the highly complex 50' offshore racing dinghies. Many changes have taken place since 1956 when we were the first to question calling a sloop without a

260 bowsprit...a sloop.   Sailing Illustrated

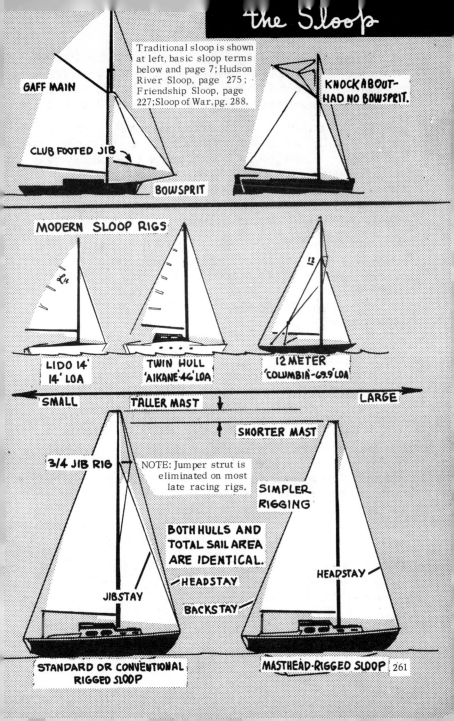

the Sloop

GAFF MAIN

CLUB FOOTED JIB

BOWSPRIT

Traditional sloop is shown at left, basic sloop terms below and page 7; Hudson River Sloop, page 275; Friendship Sloop, page 227; Sloop of War, pg. 288.

KNOCKABOUT— HAD NO BOWSPRIT.

MODERN SLOOP RIGS

LIDO 14' 14' LOA

TWIN HULL 'AIKANE' 46' LOA

12 METER 'COLUMBIA' 69.9' LOA

SMALL

TALLER MAST

LARGE

SHORTER MAST

3/4 JIB RIG

NOTE: Jumper strut is eliminated on most late racing rigs.

SIMPLER RIGGING

BOTH HULLS AND TOTAL SAIL AREA ARE IDENTICAL.

HEADSTAY

JIBSTAY

HEADSTAY

BACKSTAY

STANDARD OR CONVENTIONAL RIGGED SLOOP

MASTHEAD-RIGGED SLOOP

261

The sloop is permanently rigged for one headsail or jib, while the CUTTER is generally rigged to carry two. Since it requires more space forward for headsails, the mast is usually stepped further aft, carrying a smaller mainsail.

Another definition . . . the cutter has its mast stepped 2/5 or more of the waterline length aft. In some cases two headsails are used, while others under this rule such as the Calkins 50, only have provisions to carry one jib. Others under this rule such as the Owens Cutter may sail as a masthead sloop (cutter ?), or under the basic cutter definition with double headsails.

Americans tend toward light displacement, light weight, easy turning sloops for weekend racing and cruising. Reduce the amount of material required and the resulting boats weight, and it makes a price savings to the buyer. Because of this, long distance cruising merits of this type fiberglass hull are still not clear.

The cutter was developed for extended use in pilot boats off the English coast requiring the advantages of a sloop, yet being able to ride it out in rough weather under inner jib or forestaysail, when the sloop would have to run for cover under storm jib, or is down to bare poles.

Two decades ago many cruising sailboats carried two masts. A slow but steady change began to favor the heavy, long-keeled cutter up to 36' to about 1970. Blue-water cruising sailors then began choosing larger cutters up to 50' as self-tailing winches and improved reefing hardware began to appear. The cutter could usually point higher than ketches and schooners, had better storm riding ability, with less rigging.

Eric Hiscock is one of our favorite cruising authors. He has probably seen more miles cruising the world under cutter rig than any other cruising sailor. He catalogs his excellent experiences in books such as "Cruising Under Sail", "Beyond the West Horizon", "Around the World in Wanderer III", etc. They are very informative for the 262 future generation of blue-water cruising sailors.

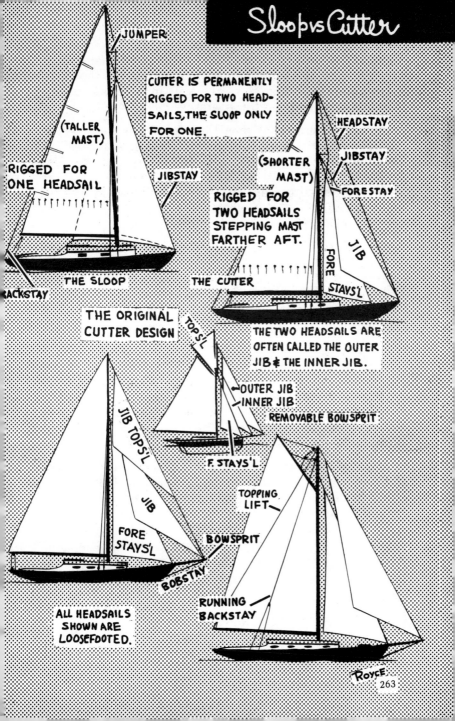

Sloop vs Cutter

JUMPER

CUTTER IS PERMANENTLY RIGGED FOR TWO HEAD-SAILS, THE SLOOP ONLY FOR ONE.

(TALLER MAST)

RIGGED FOR ONE HEADSAIL

JIBSTAY

THE SLOOP

BACKSTAY

HEADSTAY

JIBSTAY

(SHORTER MAST)

FORESTAY

RIGGED FOR TWO HEADSAILS STEPPING MAST FARTHER AFT.

JIB

FORE

THE CUTTER

STAYS'L

THE ORIGINAL CUTTER DESIGN

TOPS'L

THE TWO HEADSAILS ARE OFTEN CALLED THE OUTER JIB & THE INNER JIB.

OUTER JIB
INNER JIB

REMOVABLE BOWSPRIT

JIB TOPS'L

JIB

FORE STAYS'L

F. STAYS'L

TOPPING LIFT

BOWSPRIT

BOBSTAY

RUNNING BACKSTAY

ALL HEADSAILS SHOWN ARE LOOSEFOOTED.

Royce

Some larger sloops were yawl rigged and changed at a later date to sloop rig...and visa versa.This shows that many owners and designers are still in doubt as to which is the better sail rig for boats over 30'.

Some feel Carleton Mitchell has amply proved yawl rig superiority with his "Finisterre" detailed pages 67-69. Others feel prime factor in its outstanding racing record isn't the boat...but Mitchell. In recent years it has become much better known for its participation in books and magazine articles written by Carleton Mitchell for the National Geographic Society.

You may usually identify a yawl from a distance by size DIFFERENCE between the main and jigger. When it is closer you will be able to see the rudder post and tiller or wheel located BETWEEN the masts. While mizzen mast of ketch is located over engine or propeller shaft, jigger on a yawl is usually stepped aft of waterline, and often to either side on smaller yachts not to interfere with tiller.

In a light breeze while beating, the yawl will be carrying the gennie, main, and jigger. As the wind increases, the jigger acting as a steering trim tab will be eased, and finally dropped to minimize weather helm, page 135.Under storm conditions the yawl can reduce sail for balance similar to sloop and cutter methods.

A mizzen staysail, or a larger mizzen spinnaker may be carried while reaching or running downwind, for which the sloop has no provisions. For long distance cruising the jigger has another advantage distasteful to some sailors as it may be used as an outrigger for trolling. This may help to provide a continuous supply of fresh fish which reduces amount of canned goods otherwise carried aboard.

A single masted boat is usually preferred in the U.S. to boats with two masts under 30', as it will otherwise end up with too much rigging and not enough sail area. An exception to this occurs in the Hawaiian Islands where a common occurrence seems to be too much wind.

YAWL WITH A FULL COMPLEMENT OF SAILS

SPINNAKER WITH A HALF BRAU

TILLER

JIBBOOM

BOOMKIN

THROAT

LAZY JACKS

JACKSTRUT (MUST ABSORB TREMENDOUS THRUST)

JACKSTAY

TOPS'L

CLUB FOOTED JIB

CAT YAWL *Royce*

EARLY YAWL, USUALLY SQUARE RIGGED 265

The ketch design under square sail dates to Colonial times. Coastwise commerce was their specialty later taken over by schooners. The extra speed of our early schooners more than made up for the larger crews that were required to operate them.

At the turn of the century, the ketch's popularity was revived for cruising boats with smaller crews and ease of handling, for owners not desiring extra speed of schooner.

The ketch has a larger combination of smaller sail areas that may be used without reefing, than the yawl. This is especially important in larger vessels as mainsail area is easier to reef, than on yawl of equal length.

It is difficult to generalize about todays ketch rig, without including hull form and sail design. Some have good pointing ability for weekend racing and cruising... while the poor design is limited to downwind racing, and a lot more of its hours spent under power with wind above the beam.

The MAIN TRYSAIL or WISHBONE RIG is classed as a ketch. The wishbone rig is raised and lowered with the sail. Advantages claimed are ease of handling, and no need to reef as sails are divided into many areas, any of which may be used for the desired combination.

The BACK STAYSAIL eliminates extra rigging normally required for second mast, with a permanent backstay going to stump mast. Resulting sail, is said to have a depressing effect on stern for downwind sailing. Most of these craft have been rerigged to other standards.

We treasure our autographed copy of "Sea Quest" given to us by author Charles A. Borden, who passed away just a couple of days later (Ballentine Books, Inc.).

Endless books and articles have tried to record experiences and philosophies of this blue water cruising field, yet it required Charles to provide the multi-faceted classic of this field. If you want a stimulating 'mental vacation' away from smog, politics, ecologists, and endless other 266 artifical pressures of everyday life ... try "Sea Quest".

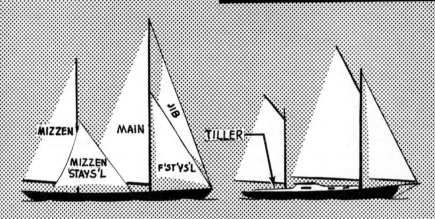

MIZZEN — MAIN — JIB — MIZZEN STAYS'L — F'ST'YS'L — TILLER

SPRING STAY — MIZZEN MAST — MAIN MAST

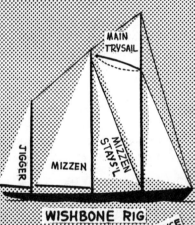

MAIN TRYSAIL — JIGGER — MIZZEN — MIZZEN STAYS'L — **WISHBONE RIG**

Royce!

EARLY KETCH

BACK STAYSAIL — **BACK STAYSAIL RIG**

267

Is this the future of commercial ocean transportation???

During the latter 1700's schooners began taking the coastal trade away from square riggers as they could sail higher to windward, and the smaller crews reduced cost. Along the coast a schooner could generally depend on a land/sea breeze for a steady beam reach.

The schooner started as a two-masted sloop. It kept growing in size until 1902 when the seven masted "Thomas W. Lawson" was launched. Americans simplified the sail names finally, each after a day in the week. The Lawson was 385 feet long, 50 feet beam, oversparred and under-canvassed, using a crew of 16. English sailors scorned our "day" sail terms, sticking to traditional terms shown.

Schooner racing has long been a U.S. tradition. It began formally when the "America" proved victorious over her English competitors in 1851.

Fishing schooners for many years raced back from the Grand Banks . . . and to the winner went the highest price for its fish. Fishing eventually became of second importance with racing and betting taking the lead. The day of the schooner was then in its prime producing huge racing machines flying acres of canvas.

Suppose a person has a conventional schooner rig that he wants to use for a long distance downwind cruise. If it was rigged with square sails on the forward mast it became a TOPSAIL SCHOONER. If it started as a STAYSAIL SCHOONER, then rigged with square sails on the forward mast, it could then become a half and half or HERMAPHRODITE BRIG, see page 282.

BLOCK ISLAND schooner was developed by Block Island fishermen to be launched from their beaches. Boulders were used for ballast on the way out, with rocks dumped overboard, using fish for ballast on the return trip.

The first schooner to sail around the world required 3 years, was the 68' "Shearwater" owned by Ernest and Carrie Minney, returning to Newport Beach in 1979.

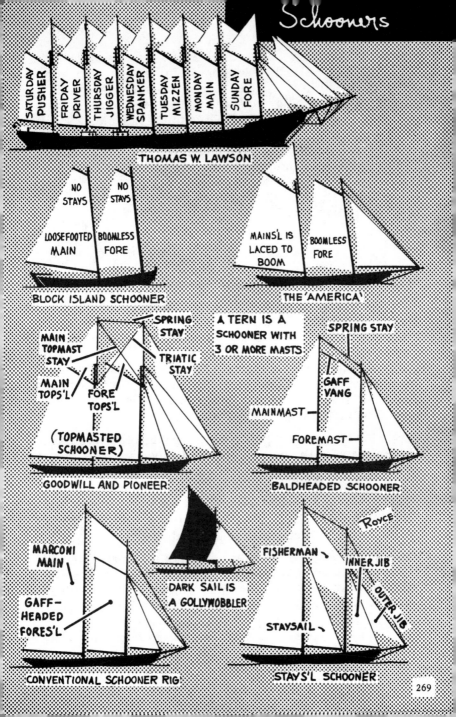

Schooners

SATURDAY PUSHER — FRIDAY DRIVER — THURSDAY JIGGER — WEDNESDAY SPANKER — TUESDAY MIZZEN — MONDAY MAIN — SUNDAY FORE

THOMAS W. LAWSON

NO STAYS — NO STAYS
LOOSE FOOTED MAIN — BOOMLESS FORE

BLOCK ISLAND SCHOONER

MAINS'L IS LACED TO BOOM — BOOMLESS FORE

THE 'AMERICA'

SPRING STAY
MAIN TOPMAST STAY
TRIATIC STAY
MAIN TOPS'L
FORE TOPS'L

(TOPMASTED SCHOONER)

GOODWILL AND PIONEER

A TERN IS A SCHOONER WITH 3 OR MORE MASTS

SPRING STAY
GAFF VANG
MAINMAST —
FOREMAST —

BALDHEADED SCHOONER

MARCONI MAIN
GAFF-HEADED FORES'L

DARK SAIL IS A GOLLYWOBBLER

CONVENTIONAL SCHOONER RIG

ROYCE
FISHERMAN —
INNER JIB
OUTER JIB
STAYSAIL —

STAYS'L SCHOONER

269

The MOTOR SAILER is a compromise boat having a 50-50%, 40-60%, 30-70%, etc., ratio between sail and power. While some are questionable, there are many very able cruising boats in the motor sailer class. For the calms or narrow channels, the engine is used, if the wind comes up the sails are used. In some situations both engine and wind power are used. A good 85-15% compromise is the 40' Newporter.

On my first visit to the Puget Sound, many motorboats had small STEADYING SAILS shown. In a stiff wind the side to side roll of motorboats, combined with the fore and aft pitching can be most uncomfortable. If steadying sail is used for all courses except a following wind and sea, roll is minimized producing easier ride.

The LJUNGSTROM is one of the few original types of sailboats, as almost all others were outgrowths of a previous type. Mast has no stays and the sail is reefed or furled around a revolving mast. When sailing before the wind the sail area is doubled, vaguely resembling a spinnaker. The Ljungstrom is one of the very few fore and aft rigged boats without booms that doesn't have to worry about accidental jibe damage.

The CANEYE is a Chesapeake Bay rig resulting from combination of the bugeye and log canoe.

The SPRITSAIL was quite popular with the early Dutch when they first settled in New Amsterdam, or New York. This type rig is found today in a few sailboats all the way from the small OPTIMIST PRAM, to some of the THAMES BARGES to 70' long, still using wind propulsion.

The SLIDING GUNTHER is an adaptation of the gaff rig, with gaff locked into vertical position. It is the English version to have all spars and sails to fit inside a dinghy. The American version, is to have a two piece mast with upper half fitting into a sleeve secured to the bottom half of the mast, also providing stowage in dinghy.

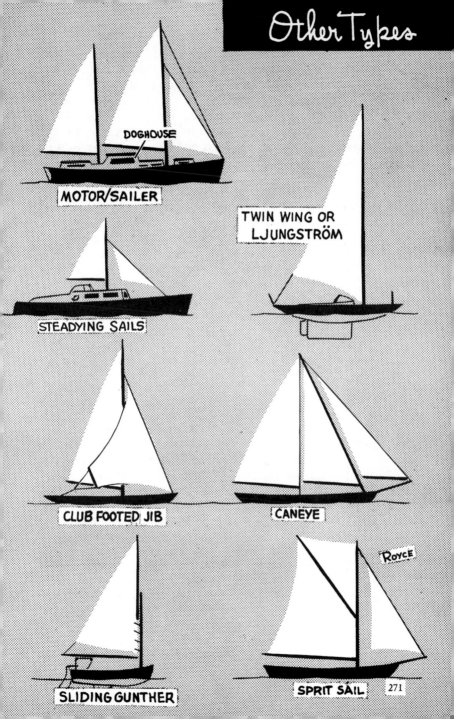

Other Tykes

DOGHOUSE

MOTOR/SAILER

TWIN WING OR LJUNGSTRÖM

STEADYING SAILS

CLUB FOOTED JIB

CANEYE

SLIDING GUNTHER

ROYCE

SPRIT SAIL 271

SHARPIES were numerous in the seventies and eighties, developing into a very popular sailboat on the eastern end of the Long Island Sound.It was an inexpensive,easy to build flat bottomed boat, some of which were up to sixty feet long. This peculiar rig sometimes carried a centerboard forward, and another aft. Sharpies were probably developed by oystermen that had previously used dugout canoes.

The SKIPJACK has a semi-V bottom with hard chines, straight frames, and is simple to build. The skipjack is sloop, yawl, or schooner rigged. The FLATTIE is an early sharpie with a mast having a small amount of rake aft.

The GLOUCESTER, ESSEX, or FRIENDSHIP SLOOP was developed by fishermen as an all-weather offshore boat. MUSCONGUS BAY SLOOPS were similar in appearance above the waterline but had a shallower draft. These were all New England built boats that were named after the fishing towns in which they were built, and from which they sailed.

The Chesapeake has its LOG CANOES to which early colonists added sails. It is hard to call the modern 30' to 40' sailboat that may carry up to eight sails with acres of sail a log canoe, but the name remains. As these shallow draft boats are very tender, it is common when beating to windward in a race, to have a crew member riding way out on the boomkin to raise the bow... and out on HIKING PLANKS that extend several feet over the weather side of boat. In the traditional design the masts aren't stayed.

Do you enjoy the beauty and action of sailing in large size photos with words trimmed to a minimum ... order SAILING (16 1/2" x 11"), 125 East Main Street, Port Washington, Wisconsin 53074, a monthly publication the whole family enjoys.

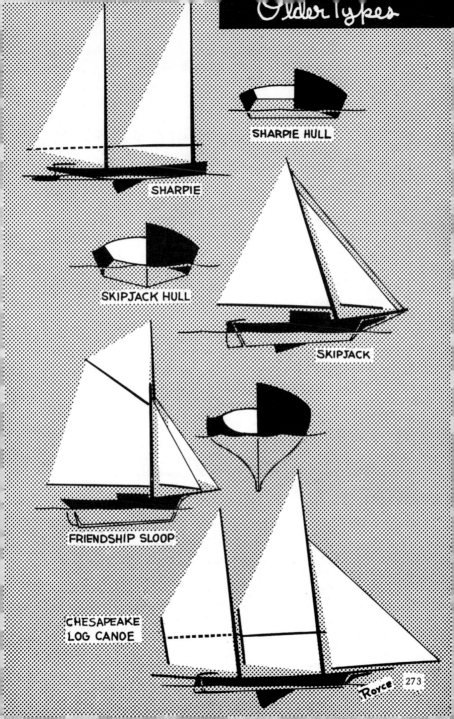

Older Types

SHARPIE HULL

SHARPIE

SKIPJACK HULL

SKIPJACK

FRIENDSHIP SLOOP

CHESAPEAKE
LOG CANOE

Royce 273

It is believed our present day marconi or jib-headed rig was developed in Bermuda, and named by the British as the BERMUDIAN RIG.

Whether it started by the adaptation of a lateen sail to a mast instead of to a yard, or by eliminating the gaff on a gaff headed mainsail, is an unrecorded page of history. A BERMUDIAN SCHOONER of the 1830's is shown with an overlapping boomless foresail and a similar main. The mizzen was loosefooted yet bent to a boom.

The HUDSON or NORTH RIVER SLOOP was developed for shallow protected waters from New York to Albany. This type sailboat sometimes had to jibe all standing on the upper reaches of the Hudson, hence the origin of the HUDSON or NORTH RIVER JIBE. This type vessel carried a huge spread of canvas, and due to the area had to be close winded.

The inspiration for the CHESAPEAKE BUGEYE with two raking masts & a pointed stern is believed to come from the Bermudas, as it resembles the early Bermuda rig. The extreme rake of the mainmast is useful for loading & unloading cargo as the main halyard block is directly over the cargo hatch.

The SHARPSHOOTER is a Bermudian catboat with a loosefooted mainsail. This was developed by a yankee that combined the New England Cat with the early Bermudian rig. The boat is reputed to be difficult to handle if it is caught in irons.

A sailboat with a high pointed stern to lessen chance of its being pooped is called a PINK. As the name refers to the hull form instead of to the rig, it may be found in any type vessel from lateener, to sloop, to schooner.

Laugh and cry with Farley Mowat, articulate author of "The Boat Who Wouldn't Float", Little, Brown, & Co. Your sailboat problems will seem minor afterwards!

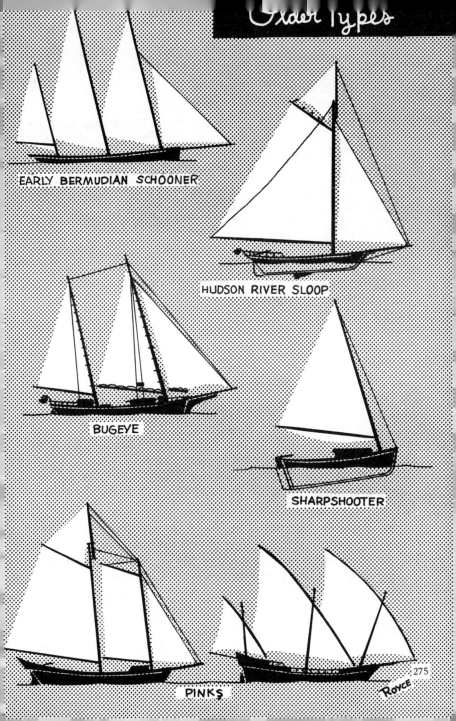

EARLY BERMUDIAN *SCHOONER*

HUDSON RIVER SLOOP

BUGEYE

SHARPSHOOTER

PINKS

275

Royce

sambuk (dhow)

the lateener family

felucca

baggala (dhow)

xebec

The beginning of sail has not been recorded. It may have started with a square sail. Sailors eventually found if the yard was tilted at an angle, the craft could sail higher into the wind, producing the lugger, page 281. Merchants on the Nile could float their cargo downstream to market, yet didn't like to row home upstream. They increased the length of the lugger yard, to produce the lateeners above to catch winds coming over high nearby hills.

Lateeners changed little through the centuries from the early Phoenicians to recent Arab merchants following the yearly monsoon winds, until OPEC money changed their life style. If you only buy five sailing books, one of them should be "Sons of Sinbad" by Alan Villiers, Charles Scribners Sons, of his year (1934) sailing dhows. This is the only book we've found covering their sailing methods from a culture and philosophy foreign to westerners.

Lateen yards were 80' to 150' long, with several tree trunks lashed together. The crews scrambled up the yard or yards maintaining a precarious foothold without rat lines or foot ropes. The back of the crews ankles were sometimes lashed together for a better foothold.

The Dutch used lateen sails to outsail Spanish vessels blockading their ports. The British Navy adopted the lateen rig until their defeat of the Spanish Armada, changing to the square rig around 1700 A.D. The lateen mizzen was 276 retained, later replaced by a gaff-rigged spanker.

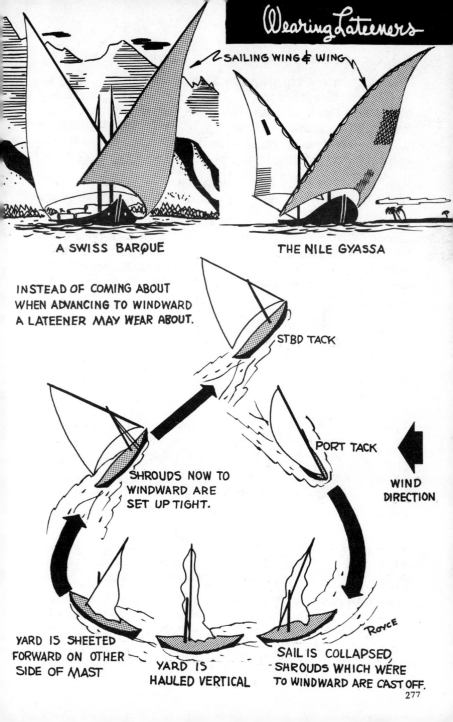

Wearing Lateeners

SAILING WING & WING

A SWISS BARQUE

THE NILE GYASSA

INSTEAD OF COMING ABOUT
WHEN ADVANCING TO WINDWARD
A LATEENER MAY WEAR ABOUT.

STBD TACK

PORT TACK

WIND DIRECTION

SHROUDS NOW TO
WINDWARD ARE
SET UP TIGHT.

YARD IS SHEETED
FORWARD ON OTHER
SIDE OF MAST

YARD IS
HAULED VERTICAL

SAIL IS COLLAPSED,
SHROUDS WHICH WERE
TO WINDWARD ARE CAST OFF.

Royce

277

Will the lug rig power the cruise ship of the future????

The modern lug rig with the best of ancient ideas, plus the latest of engineering and materials, was introduced by Blondie Hasler. It was installed on his "Jester" a few months before the first single-handed OSTAR race in 1960. His wooden mast without stays nor shrouds was stepped on the keel, designed to bend like a tree under load.

The North American 29 is detailed, with "Pake" #1, built in 1979, which is docked a short distance from our slip.

The junk rig key is full-length battens dividing sails into panels, with the yard or top batten heavier as it has to take the full weight of the sail. Since sail weight is taken care of by lazy jacks, the boom or bottom batten doesn't have to be much stronger than the other battens.

The head is secured to the yard, the yard to the mast, then the yard, panels, and battens are raised by a halyard. Rope parrels secure the sail to the mast, run loosely around the mast at each batten. The balanced lugsail stays on one side of the mast, held out by parrels on one tack, with chafing strips shown to protect the battens and the sails when pressed against the mast on the other tack.

The battens have a series of sheetlets which can flatten or increase the leach sail twist, with a single sheet trim line leading to the inside steering station.

This lug rig can be reefed in seconds, dropping as many panels into the lazy jack cradle as desired, with all control lines handled from the inside steering station.

We enjoyed several hours with Webb Chiles before he left San Diego 11/13/78 in "The Chidiock Tichborne" for a five year sail around the world, the first stop was the Marquesas 2800 miles away. His last letter, 1/2/82, to us states .. "we've survived two 50-60 knot storms, a swamping and 14 days adrift in the Pacific, and she has no engine, so we've sailed every inch of the way".

"The Ocean waits to measure or to slay me.. the Ocean
278 waits and I will sail".   S a i l i n g   I l l u s t r a t e d

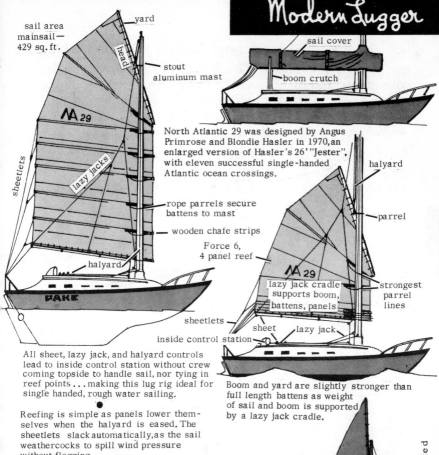

Modern Lugger

sail area
mainsail—
429 sq. ft.

yard

head

stout
aluminum mast

sail cover

boom crutch

ΛΛ 29

sheetlets

lazy jacks

North Atlantic 29 was designed by Angus
Primrose and Blondie Hasler in 1970, an
enlarged version of Hasler's 26' "Jester",
with eleven successful single-handed
Atlantic ocean crossings.

halyard

rope parrels secure
battens to mast

wooden chafe strips

Force 6,
4 panel reef

parrel

ΛΛ 29

lazy jack cradle
supports boom,
battens, panels

strongest
parrel
lines

halyard

DAKE

sheetlets

sheet   lazy jack

inside control station

All sheet, lazy jack, and halyard controls
lead to inside control station without crew
coming topside to handle sail, nor tying in
reef points ... making this lug rig ideal for
single handed, rough water sailing.

Boom and yard are slightly stronger than
full length battens as weight
of sail and boom is supported
by a lazy jack cradle.

Reefing is simple as panels lower themselves when the halyard is eased. The
sheetlets slack automatically, as the sail
weathercocks to spill wind pressure
without flogging.

The battens and panels fall down into the
lazy jacks on both sides of the boom to
form a cradle. The batten/lazy jack method
prevents the lug sail reefed area from
filling accidentally.

After sufficient panels are reefed, the sheet
and remaining sheetlets are hardened, then
the panels fill and the lugger is underway.

Halyard is released in a sudden squall, the
sail furling itself in less than 10 seconds.

Have the boom cradle in position for
docking and anchoring. Release sheet
and halyard. When sail is down release
lazy jack control so sail assembly
falls into boom crutch for furling,
then add sail cover.

Sailing Illustrated

CHIDIOCK TICHBORNE

Webb Chiles open 18'9" "Chidiock Tichborne"
lugger had sailed to Singapore at time of
sketch above after its San Diego launching.

279

● EASTERN LUG RIGS. The Chinese have made practical use of their lug-rigged JUNKS for several centuries, using pole masts and bamboo sails. They developed the single stern-mounted rudder before the Europeans. Sometimes we feel a considerable share of the imported Chinese junks are seconds ... sold to unsuspecting dreamers.

The high stern becomes troublesome running before a rough sea, yet the big rudder and high stern helps the bow to weather cock into the wind, so Chinese luggers ride easily at anchor. Modern Chinese lugger concept was introduced to us by Hasler, pages 278-9.

● WESTERN LUG RIGS. Some luggers were used for harbor work, yet most of their fame came as the "hot rods" of the time for slavers, pirates, and smugglers. Their main ability was to point higher in light winds than square riggers in hot pursuit, see lugger beginning, page 276.

Most western and European luggers were rather small, with some in the Mediterranean, up to 80 feet long. The luggers had a rather vicious reputation if caught in irons, requiring a good helmsman and skilled crews.

Clumsy, plunder-laden Spanish sailing vessels on their way back to home port, were often ambushed by pirates as they drifted between Caribbean islands in light winds.

The luggers, hidden ashore when not in use, were their successful attack boats for the light winds. They were loaded to the gunwales with pirates who boarded and took over many of these vessels. After the valuables were removed, the Spanish vessels were scuttled to destroy the remaining evidence.

Captured crew members were often eager to join the pirates ... as the alternative was rather discouraging.

"Posted Missing" by Alan Villiers, pub. by Scribners, is a fascinating educational book analyzing why many varied vessels have disappeared ... including a battleship ... no kidding!

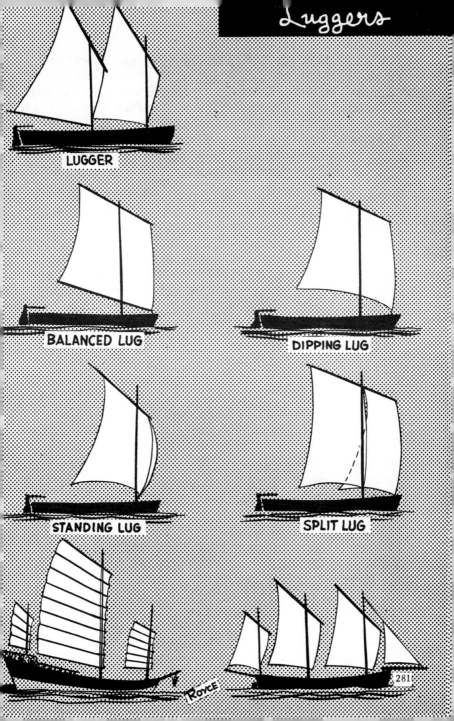

LUGGER

BALANCED LUG

DIPPING LUG

STANDING LUG

SPLIT LUG

Royce

281

A vessel had to have three or more masts all carrying square sails to be SHIP RIGGED. The CLIPPERS could be square rigged or schooner rigged as term referred to narrow beam hulls with fine lines ... rather than rigging. Previous hulls often seemed based on theory .. a CODFISH HEAD (wide blunt bows at waterline) and MACKEREL TAIL (slim stern at waterline). This theory was popular for several hundred years till advent of faster clipper hull.[*]

Square riggers were designed to sail BEFORE the wind, following the prevailing winds and currents around the world. When they neared a coastline, square riggers often had to fight adverse headwinds ... or anchor to wait a wind shift, as they couldn't normally sail higher than 6 points of the wind, or 65-70° from eye of wind, if bottom was clean. Windward ability was decreased as bottom growth began to develop.

A compromise then began between them and the fore & aft rigged vessel which could point higher, and required half to third of crew on a similar size square rigger.

The HERMAPHRODITE BRIG is a half and half vessel while a BARKENTINE was more for coastal work, having two masts, fore and aft rigged. The BARK had three or more masts with only one being fore and aft rigged. A bark was made more for extended cruising than speed, an ideal combination for WHALERS.

BRIG & BRIGANTINE were two masted square riggers. If no provisions had been made to hang a mainsail, it was a brigantine. The SNOW had a close resemblence to the brigantine, except it had a third or trysail mast about a foot abaft the main or second mast.

For readers wanting to learn in depth the peak and decline of commercial square rig ships from 1890, we highly recommend "The Way of a Ship" by Alan Villers, Charles Scribner's Sons. It is THE classic of this much spoken of yet little understood era of square riggers.

[*]Alexander Laing "Clipper Ships & Their Makers", G.P. Putnam

Square Riggers

FULL RIGGED SHIP, CLIPPER HULL

BRIG

HERMAPHRODITE BRIG

BRIGANTINE

BARKENTINE

BARK

BARK

Royce

283

Square rigger language is complex...as over 280,000 sailing vessels have been registered, each conforming to the owner,captain,or mates wishes. The only element remaining standard was location of lines coming to the same belaying pins on deck, whether American, Dutch, English, or Finnish square rigged vessels.

If we go to the 16-17th centuries we see bulky hulls, high poops, blunt bows, & oversized sails. As masts were taller on later ships it was necessary to divide some of the sails into two areas...upper & lower tops'ls,upper & lower "tugalants", as examples. This added to amount of lines, but simplified reefing in a storm when even small sails were dangerous and backbreaking to take in.

On facing page the upper & lower "tugalants" have been combined to show "moons'ls" that were quite small & only found on a few large sailing ships.

Again let us say sailing is a spoken instead of a written language so we find topgallant called"tugalant"; foresails, fors'ls;skysails,skys'ls;studding sails,stuns'ls;crossjack, crojik; etc. The slang usage simplified the pronounciation.

As square riggers grew in size the pole mast began to disappear, the trees no longer being tall enough. Trees had to be cut into sections & joined together between the HOUNDS & MAST CAP. Overlapping parts of these were called DOUBLINGS. The masts were solid & not long by themselves. Add three or four on top of one another, and it made a sizeable mast.

Deck terminology should be self explanatory except for the POOP DECK, which was sometimes a complete deck of its own. Other times it was the area directly behind the helmsman, though a part of the quarter deck. Note illustration of quarter deck on following page.

Want to know sailing in the 1819 "state of the art" as learned by seamen then? Their text"Lever's Young Sea Officer's Sheet Anchor", has been republished exactly as it was in 1819, by the Edward Sweetman Co. It is a 284 MUST for a knowledgeable sailor's library (pg. 184)!

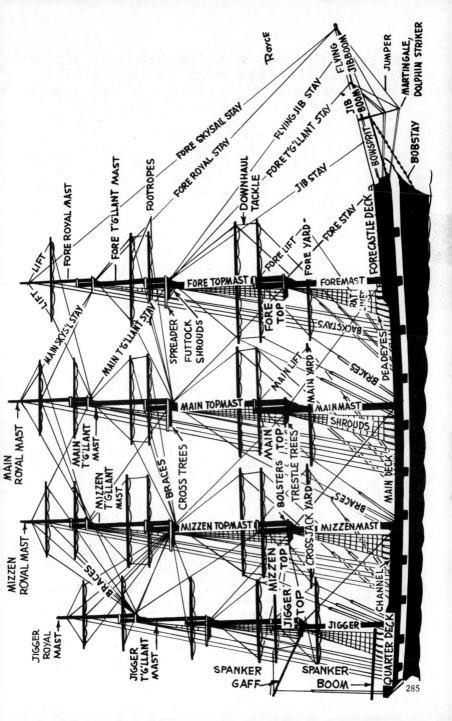

Where is the CROW'S NEST? That was usually highest vantage point on a square rigger. On the whaler it was quite obvious, as there was a platform to stand on, plus two waist high iron hoops to encircle the lookouts.

The forward supports to the masts were STAYS; the aft, BACKSTAYS; while SHROUDS support mast on either side. BRACES control horizontal movement of yards that lead aft, except on after mast of a ship with three or more masts. In this case they lead forward on the mast that is the furthest aft.

The YARDS are hoisted by HALYARDS, and supported by LIFTS that lead thru blocks at masthead or fairleads, & then to the top, or below to the deck.

The CLEWS of squaresails are secured to yard beneath them, except for the foresail, mainsail, crojik, and jigger, that have SHEETS going aft, and TACKS going forward to hold the corners down.

Clewlines and buntlines are used for taking in or hauling up a sail. The BUNTLINE is on the forward side of sail, the CLEWLINE on the after side of sail.

REEF TACKLES go to leaches of squaresails. In reefing they are used to haul the leach up and out, giving slack for passing the earing & rousing cringle up into place.

BOWLINES lead forward from the BOWLINE BRIDLE. They were used on lowers and topsails to hold the leach well forward when sailing close hauled. Bowlines were supposed to be obsolete by the time of the clippers.

DOWNHAUL TACKLES are used to haul tops'l yards to just above the lower tops'l yards. The downhaul tackles also support the lower tops'l yard that usually had no lifts.

Present day USCG square rigger training ship "Eagle" is covered in "Eagle Seamanship", published by M. Evans and Company, Inc., 216 E. 49th St., New York, NY 10017.

Sailing Illustrated

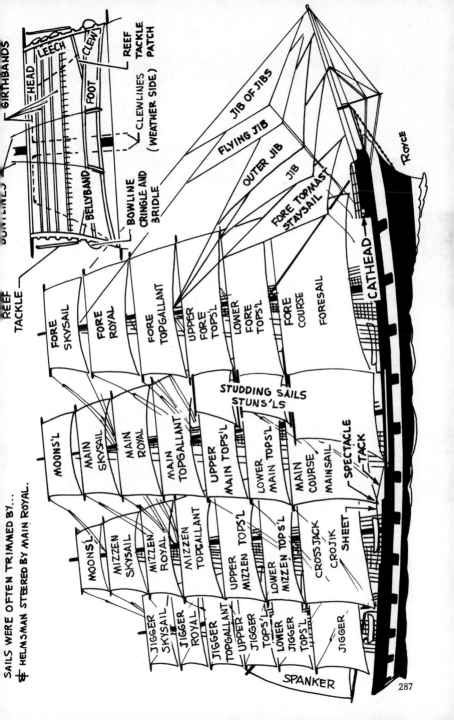

GIRTHBANDS

HEAD

LEECH

CLEW

REEF
TACKLE
PATCH

FOOT

CLEWLINES
(WEATHER SIDE)

BELLYBAND

BOWLINE
CRINGLE AND BRIDLE

BUNTLINES

REEF
TACKLE

JIB OF JIBS

FLYING JIB

OUTER JIB

JIB

FORE TOPMAST
STAYSAIL

FORE SKYSAIL

FORE ROYAL

FORE TOPGALLANT

UPPER
FORE TOPS'L

LOWER
FORE TOPS'L

FORE COURSE

FORESAIL

CATHEAD

Royce

MOONS'L

MAIN
SKYSAIL

MAIN ROYAL

MAIN
TOPGALLANT

UPPER
MAIN TOPS'L

STUDDING SAILS
STUNS'LS

LOWER
MAIN TOPS'L

MAIN TOPS'L

MAIN
COURSE

MAINSAIL

SPECTACLE

TACK

SHEET

MOONS'L

MIZZEN
SKYSAIL

MIZZEN
ROYAL

MIZZEN
TOPGALLANT

UPPER
MIZZEN TOPS'L

LOWER
MIZZEN TOPS'L

CROSS JACK

CROJIK

JIGGER
SKYSAIL

JIGGER
ROYAL

JIGGER
TOPGALLANT

UPPER
JIGGER
TOPS'L

LOWER
JIGGER
TOPS'L

JIGGER

SPANKER

SAILS WERE OFTEN TRIMMED BY....

⚓ HELMSMAN STEERED BY MAIN ROYAL.

287

Early vessels and todays' junks have high sterns to help weather-cock bow into wind, so they will ride easier when at anchor.

Naval vessels have terms which usually apply to their armament rather than rigging; a FIRST RATER carried 100 or more guns; a SECOND RATER, 90-99 guns; while a THIRD RATER carried 76-89 guns; a FOURTH RATER 54-75 guns. First and second rates had three gun decks while third and fourth rates had two.

FRIGATES were ship rigged with the main batteries in a single row. They usually carried 38 guns even though they could have anywhere from 24 to 50 guns. Frigates were made for speed and could prey on merchant ships, or act as scouts for the lumbering raters.

The size below a Frigate is the French CORVETTE or SLOOP OF WAR as it was called in the American and English Navies.

The 14 gun English REVENUE CUTTER of the early 1800's was used in the English Channel to prevent smuggling. In war time it was used as a dispatch boat, being the fastest type of vessel in the fleet.

These terms were more or less standard from defeat of the Spanish Armada up to the advent of steam. During a battle the smaller and faster ships ranged the flanks, while LINE-OF-BATTLE SHIPS or SHIPS-OF-THE-LINE (1st, 2nd, and 3rd raters) went into action in the main line of the fleet.

It is interesting to find that most of the present day terms have been carried over from canvas powered days of the navies. As an example the term BATTLESHIP came from the name LINE-OF-BATTLE SHIPS.

Term SLOOP for instance is used in the British Navy as a patrol boat for colonial areas. In size and type of use it will correspond to a U.S. gunboat.

Also read "The Ship" by Bjorn Landstrom; "Book of Old Ships" by Gordon Grant; the Hornblower series by C.S. Forester.

REVENUE CUTTER
OF 1815

SLOOP OF WAR
OR CORVETTE

A FRIGATE
OF 1820

SQUARE
SPRITS'L

A FIRST RATER
OF 1750

HEAD

289

Royce

Our GLOSSARY is a dictionary of technical, obscure, and obsolete words. In it we provide coverage of tradition sailing terms in recent use, as well as obsolete sailing terms of the past frequently found in sea stories such as the Hornblower series ... your authors and many of our readers favorite type of relaxation.

●

ABACK-set of ship's sails with wind on leeward side, in square rigger the sails would be pressed toward mast tending to force vessel astern, page 151.
ABAFT-comparison term of one object on shipboard being further aft than another; ABAFT the BEAM for example, is aft of the beam.
ABAFT the BEAM-bearing of object seen between beam and stern.
ABANDON-time to leave a sinking ship.
ABEAM-right angle from fore and aft centerline of boat, off the beam or on the side of a vessel, page 83.
ABLOCK-tackle taken in until both blocks come together.
ABOARD-in or on board a vessel.
ABOUT or ABOUT SHIP-to change tack, when bow of ship goes thru eye of wind, and pays off on other tack till sails again fill with wind, pages 108, 109.
ABOVE or ABOVEBOARD-above decks, straight forward or honest.
ABOX-square rigger maintaining position as waiting for pilot by bracing head and after yards on opposite sides or tacks, page 151.
ABREAST-side by side, alongside or abeam.
ABURTON-method of stowing casks athwartship and end to end.
ACCOMMODATION LADDER-ladder or portable steps to climb aboard ship.
A-COCK-BILL-position of anchor hanging from cathead;see 285 for location of cathead. Position of yards on square rigger topped up at angle with deck.
ACCOUNT, TO GO ON THE-a sailor turned pilot.
ADMIRALTY KNOT-6080 feet (Int'l Nautical Mile is 6076. 10').
ADRIFT-broken from the moorings or drifting.
ADVANCE-distance boat moves in original course after rudder is put over.
AFLOAT-boat or other buoyant object resting on surface of water.
AFORE-forward, opposite of abaft.
AFOUL-entangled or fouled in any way.
AFT-at, near, or toward the stern, page 82.
AFTER BODY-stern section of boat.
AFTER BOW SPRING-bow spring leading aft for docking, page 174.
AFTER BROW-an aft portable gangplank.
AFTER QUARTER SPRING-spring leading aft from boats bow, page 174.
AFTER WAIST SPRING-spring coming from amidship and going aft.
AFTER YARDS-yards abaft the foremast, page 285.
AFTER SAILS-sails bent to masts abaft the foremast.
AGROUND-keel or hull of boat resting on bottom, stranded, pages 222-225.
AHEAD-toward the bow or in front of, page 83.
AHOY-a greeting used in hailing a vessel or boat.
A-HULL-vessel hove to under bare poles, with helm alee.
AIR or FLOTATION TANK-sealed tank for buoyancy in capsize, pages 29, 31.
ALBATROSS-largest sea bird with wing span to 13', in Southern Hemisphere.
ALEE-to leeward side;helm away from wind, page 108.
ALIVE-wide awake.
G1

al ALL ABACK-when all sails are aback, see ABACK.

ALL-A-TAUNT-O-ship shape or all gear hauled in tight.

ALL HANDS-the entire crew.

ALL in the WIND-pointing too high, all sails shaking, pages 98, 104.

ALL NIGHT IN-maintaining no night watches.

ALL STANDING-'brought up standing' is be quickly brought to a stop;also, to turn in fully clothed, or be fully equipped.

ALOFT-up above;up the mast or in the rigging.

ALONGSIDE-side by side, by the side of a vessel or pier.

ALOW-below deck, or low in the rigging near the deck.

ALOW and ALOFT-all sails including studding sails are set, page 287.

ALTAR-steps of a drydock.　　　　　　AMAIN-on the run, all at once.

AMBERGRIS-intestinal secretion of sperm whale used for blending ability in manufacture of perfume.

ANCHOR-device which digs into bottom preventing a boat from drifting, pg. 159.

ANCHORAGE-suitable place for anchoring.

ANCHOR AWEIGH-anchor broken out of bottom, or coming to surface.

ANCHOR HOY-lighter with derrick for handling heavy anchors.

ANCHOR LIGHTS-anchor riding lights carried on anchored vessels.

ANCHOR WATCH-deck detail to watch vessel anchored at night.

ANEMOMETER-wind velocity measuring instrument.

ANEROID BAROMETER-mechanical barometer without liquid.

ANGLE BAR-used to form inboard side of a waterway.

ANTI-CYCLONE-spiral eddy of wind that is flowing out.

ANVIL TOP-cirrus peak of thunderhead, pages 204-209.

APEAK-cable in vertical line with vessel over anchor. Also position of yards or oars when vertical or nearly so.

APORT-to the left or port side of a vessel when looking forward.

APPARENT WIND-wind direction felt on boat underway, pages 100, 102,131.

APRON-timber behind lower part of stem above fore end of keel.

ARC BOTTOM-see page 17.

ARDENT-sailing craft with excessive weather helm.

ARM-lower part of yachtsman and old fashioned anchor.

ARMING-cavity at bottom of lead line with tallow to bring up a bottom sample.

ARTIFICIAL RESPIRATION-see method on pages 230-231.

ASH BREEZE-calm requiring sailboat to use oars...or iron spinnaker.

ASHORE-the same as aground.

ASTERN-in direction of stern;object bearing outside & behind vessel, pg. 83.

ATHWARTSHIP-across the keel of a vessel, page 82.

ATOLL-small circular coral island enclosing a lagoon.

ATRIP-position of anchor as it is raised above bottom.

A-TRY-vessel in gale without any sails set.

AUTO PILOT-mechanical helmsman set to compass heading.

AUXILIARY-engine used as secondary propulsion in sailboat.

AWEATHER-to windward, towards the weather side, 110.

AWEIGH-the same as ATRIP.

AWNING-tarp covering boat or deck for protection from sun or rain.

AYE-yes;reply than an officers orders are understood.

b BACK-to back sail is throw it ABACK;to BACK JIB is to hold it while coming about till wind catches its leeward side, pages 95, 108, 173.

BACKBOARD-vertical board rest used for helmsmans back.

BACKSTAY-mast support leading aft to deck or another mast, 35, 51-3,63,67,79,81.

RUNNING BACKSTAYS are temporary or shifting backstays, pages 68,70,109.

BACK STAYSAIL RIG-see page 267.

BACK WASH-churning water thrown aft by propeller.

BACKWATER-stop rowboat progress by reversing direction of the oars.

BACK WIND-sail back winds another by throwing wind on leeward side, 108,147.
BAG-a sail bags when leach is taut yet center of sail is slack.
BAGGY-WRINKLE-chafing gear made from old rope, 75.
BALANCING RING-ring fitted at balance point on shank for fishing older anchors.
BALANCED RUDDER-part of area is forward of rotation axis for powerboats.
BALDHEADED SCHOONER-schooner without topsails, page 268.
BALE-outer end of stock on old-fashioned anchor.
BALLAST-heavy material on bottom of sailboat to provide stability (in hold).
BALLAST TANKS-double bottom water tanks pumped out or flooded at will.
BALLOON STAYSAIL-used under spinnaker, pg. 69.
BANK-side of a river or shoal, page 216.
BAR-shoal or bank; CAPSTAN-BARS are heavy timbers that work the capstan.
BARE POLES-sailboat in gale with no sails set, page 137, 138.
BARE, SAILING-sailing with sheets too far in, page 104.
BARGE-ship's boat used by flag officers;THAMES BARGE is a flat bottomed
roomy boat for carrying cargo on the Thames River in England.
BARK (barque)-3 masted sailing vessel square rigged on fore & main, with the
mizzen fore and aft rigged, page 283.
BAR KEEL-a heavy steel or iron external keel.
BARKENTINE (barquentine)-3 masted sailing vessel square rigged on fore,
yet main and mizzen are fore and aft rigged, page 283.
BARNACLE-small shell fish that enjoys the bottom of your boat.
BARNEY POST-short post in cockpit with jam cleat for main sheet.
BAROMETER-instrument for registering atmosphere's pressure, page 212.
BARRATRY-shipmasters dishonest action such as unauthorized sale of ship.
BARRIER REEF-above-water reefs along a coast.
BATTEN-thin rigid strip fitted to pocked on after edge of sail to keep its shape,
page 91 ;metal strips fitted over hatch coamings to secure tarp.
BEACHCOMBER-unemployed derelict seaman found on waterfront.
BEACON-danger or recognition navigation mark placed on or near object.
BEAM-the greatest width of a vessel, pages 82, 83.
BEAM-ENDS-vessel listing or hove over till beam is almost vertical. Method
was used to scrape and repair boat bottoms before use of drydock.
BEAM SEA-wind at right angle to keel, BEAM REACH, BEAM WIND, page 99.
BEAR-object bears so & so when in direction a person is looking.
BEAR DOWN-to approach vessel from windward.
BEAR IN- to approach an object or shore.
BEARING-direction of object as to vessels heading or compass course, pg. 83.
BEAR OFF-steer away from wind, shore or object.
BEAR UP-steer up towards eye of wind, shore or object.
BEAT-advancing to windward on alternate tacks, pages 100, 101.
BECALMED-vessels sails hang limp & lifeless when becalmed.
BECKET-eye or loop made with fiber or wire rope.
BEE-BLOCK-chock taking standing part of reef pendant near aft end of boom.
BEES-pieces bolted to outer bowsprit end to reeve foretopmast stays thru.
BELAY- change order;make fast or secure rope to cleat or pin.
BELAYING PIN-iron or wooden pin fitted into railing to secure lines, page 73.
BELL BUOY-buoy with bell actuated by sea, page 247.
BELLY-fullness of sail when swelled out by wind.
BELLY STRAP-rope beneath boat for carrying out a kedge anchor.
BELOW-beneath or under the deck (seldom called 'downstairs').
BENCH HOOK-hook with swivel in cloth counteracting pull of sailors needle.
BEND-a knot by which one rope is made fast to another, page 189.
BEND a SAIL-make sail fast to spar or stay, 88-97. BEND a CABLE is make it
fast to anchor.BENDING SHACKLE connects chain cable to ring of anchor.
BENEAPED or NEAPED-boat aground at high tide, following tides cannot float,223.
BERMUDIAN RACING DINGHY-see page 44.
G3

be BERMUDIAN SAIL-British term for marconi or jib-headed sail, pages 7, 274.
BERTH-dock or anchorage for boat, or place a person sleeps on board.
BERTH DECK-lower complete deck used for berthing near waterline.
BETWEEN DECKS-space between decks.
BIBBS-trestle-tree timber supports bolted to hounds of the mast.
BIGHT-bend in shore making cove, bay or inlet;bend in rope.
BILGE-curve of hull between gunwhale & keel, 16 ;largest dia. of cask.
BILGE BLOCKS-blocks in dry dock upon which ships bilge rests.
BILGED-when bilge is broken.
BILGE KEEL-keel at turn of bilge to reduce rolling of vessel·
BILGE STRINGERS- see STRINGERS, page 73.
BILGE WATER-water settled to bilge of boat, page 73.
BILGE WAYS-timbers bolted together & propped under keel for launching.
BILL-point at end of fluke on anchor.
BILL-BOARD-bed or plates for anchor to rest without marring deck.
BILL of HEALTH-port health certificate obtained as vessel clears port.
BILL of LADING-receipt from a vessel for cargo received.
BINNACLE-compass stand containing compensating magnets, 67, 75, 77.
BITE-to take hold.
BITTER END-last inboard link of an anchor chain or anchor line, 163, 186.
BITT-take turn around bitts with cable so it can be veered or held tight.
BITTS-posts in deck to secure mooring or towing lines, pages 63, 73, 190.
BLACK GANG-engineering force when coal was principle fuel,
BLADE-back of anchor palm, flat part of oar or propeller.
BLANKET-leeward sailboat has wind taken out of sails by one to windward. A
bridge, headland or building can also blanket sails.
BLOCK (pulley)-wood or metal container with pulley.
BLUFF-steep shore or full-bowed ship.
BOARD-tack or leg to windward when beating or closehauled, page 101.
BOAT BOOM-swings from boats side when at anchor to secure dinghy.
BOAT COVER-tarp or cover that protects a boat.   BOAT-see SHIP.
BOAT HOOK-pole with hook to pick up mooring buoy or ring.
BOS'N'S CHAIR-canvas or wood seat to raise man working aloft.
BOATSWAIN'S CHEST-deck chest for bos'n's gear.
BOATSWAIN, PETTY-officer in charge of rigging & calling crew to duty.
BOBSTAY-rod, chain or wire from stem to cutwater securing bowsprit, 71,285.
BOLLARD-vertical post on dock to which hawsers may be secured.
BOLSTERS-canvas covered wood for rigging eyes to rest on at trestle-trees.
BOLT-rolls of canvas.
BOLTS-round iron bars for securing;early bolts without threads were peened
over to prevent their working loose.
BOLT ROPE-to which material is sewn going around sail, page 89.
BONE-spray at stem of vessel underway.
BONNET-extra canvas piece secured to foot of jib by lacings.
BOOBY HATCH-a small raised hatch.
BOOM-spar for extending foot of fore & aft or studding sail.
BOOM CRADLE (boom crutch)-support for boom when sail is furled, page 89.
BOOM HORSE-boom band metal fitting used as traveller for sheet block.
BOOM IRONS-rings on yards for studdingsail booms to be rigged out.
BOOMKIN-spar projecting from stern to secure backstay, page 71.
BOOT TOP-different color strip of paint at waterline, page 71.
BOTTOMRY-marine law term for mortgaging ships.
BOUND, WIND-adverse headwind keeping sailboat in port.
BOW-forward part of a hull-pages 82-3.
BOW BREAST-forward mooring line used in docking.
BOW BREAST MOORING-chain offshore permanent mooring using breast line.
BOWER-main anchor.   BEST BOWER-largest anchor.

BOW LINE-docking or moorling line led forward thru bow chock, pages 173-4.
BOW MOORING-same as BOW BREAST MOORING.
BOW PAINTER-line leading from boat to buoy or other boat, pages 95, 167.
BOWSE-to haul in and down on a tackle.
BOWSPRIT-spar extending forward from bow to secure headstays, pages 70-5, 285.
BOWSPRITTING-sentence of sailor roped to bowsprit. He had choice of starving
to death as food & water allowance was small, or cutting the ropes & drowning.
BOX-HAULING-wearing a square rigger by backing the head sails.
BOXING OFF-boats head is paid off after missing stays.
BOXING the COMPASS-calling names of 32 compass points in order.
BRACE-line controlling horizontal movement of square sail yard, pages 285-6.
BRACKISH-mixture of fresh and salt water.
BRAIL-lines used to furl fore & aft sails vertically against the mast.
BREAKER-waves broken by shoals or ledges, small fresh water cask.
BREAK GROUND-to break loose anchor from bottom.
BREAK OFF-to stop.   BREAK OUT-to unstow.
BREAKS-a wave breaks when it curls forward into the surf.
BREAK SHEAR-vessel that is restless at anchor, see BULL ROPE.
BREAKWATER (splash board)-low bulkhead forward to prevent waves and spray
from coming into cockpit;a sea wall to break force of waves.
BREAST-meet the sea;docking line leading at right angles to vessels centerline.
BREAST BAND (breast rope)-canvas band across leadsmans chest lashed to chains.
BREAST FAST-line securing vessel broadside to wharf or other vessel.
BREAST HOOKS-knees in forward part of vessel, page 73.
BREAST OFF-shove out from dock or another vessel.
BRIDLE-rope span with ends secured for sheet block to ride on, pages 33, 35.
Boat moored to a bridle or span between two anchors.
BRIDLE-PORT-foremost port used for stowing anchors.
BRIG-ships jail;two masted square rigger, page 283.
BRIGANTINE-2 masted square rigger, square rigged on fore, fore & aft on the
main. The 'Yankee' was tops'l schooner by previous def.; now called brigantine.
BRIGHTWORK-varnished woodwork or polished brass that is not painted.
BRING -TO-stop sailing vessel by bring head to wind.
BROACH-TO-bow of vessel running before wind digs in & boat jibes.
BROADSIDE-side of vessel;firing salvo of all guns on one side of ship.
BROKEN BACK (hogged)vessel that droops at either end.
BROW-portable gang plank.
BROW LANDING-platform extending over ship's side to support gang plank.
BUCKLERS-plugs fitting into hawse pipe holes when at sea.
BUCKLING-bending or working.   BUGEYE-see page 275.
BUILDING SLIP-location of building ways.
BULB KEEL-racing keel with cigar shaped weight at bottom, page 21.
BULKHEAD-below deck partition separting one part of vessel from another.
BULL-sailors term for small one or two gallon keg.
BULL ROPE-shock cord leading from bowsprit end to mooring buoy to keep
buoy from bumping boat when wind & tide are opposed, page 174.
BULL the BUOY-a vessel that bumps a buoy with its side.
BULLSEYE-round wooden thimble used for changing lead of rope.
BULWARKS-railing around deck to prevent men & gear from going overboard.
BUMBOAT-boat alongside vessel in port with articles for sale.
BUMKIN (boomkin)-permanent stern spar providing backstay support, page 70.
BUMPKIN-support for main braceblocks from both quarters;timbers projecting
from vessel to secure the fore tack.
BUMPKIN SHROUDS-iron ropes securing bumpkin vertically to vessel's side.
BUNK-sleeping berth.
BUNT-middle of sail; loop of line or bagging portion of loosely hanging sail.
BUNTING-thin flag material or flags.

Bo

bu BUNTLINES-lines used to haul up body of square sail, pages 286-287.
BURGEE-pointed or swallowtail flag indicating club boats owner belongs to, 253.
BURTON-special tackle often used to hoist heavy anchor aboard.
BUOY-floating marker for piloting, pg. 248; marker for permanent mooring,167.
BUOYANCY TANKS-airtight tanks for buoyancy in upset boat, page 32.
BUTT-where two planks or other members touch end to end. SCUTTLE BUTT
is gossip while drinking from water cask for crew kept on deck.
BUTTOCK-part of vessel between quarter & stern post, pages 254-256.
BY THE BOARD-overboard.   BY THE HEAD-bow lower than stern.
BY THE LEE-running with wind on same side as boom, page 123.
BY THE RUN-let go altogether.   BY THE STERN-stern lower than bow.
BY THE WIND-closehauled, page 99.

C CABIN-enclosed space of decked over boat, pages 52-4,63,67-75,79-81.
CABLE-large dia. rope, pg. 129; 200 yards or 1/10 nautical mile.
CABLE LENGTH-600 feet or 100 fathoms.
CABOOSE-deckhouse for cooking, usually called a galley in smaller boats.
CALL-bos'n's pipe.   CALM-wind under one knot, page 137.
CAMBER-athwartship curve of deck and cabin,page 73.
CAMEL-wooden float acting between dock and boat.
CAN BUOY-cylindrical black odd numbered buoy to port entering from seaward.
CANEYE-combination of Chesapeake log canoe and bugeye, page 271.
CANT-to turn a vessels head.   CANTED-inclined.
CAP-wooden block for holding spars.   CAPSIZE-to upset, page 145.
CAPSTAN-mechanical device for hoisting or heaving.
CAPSTAN-BAR-wooden or metal bar for heaving capstan around by hand.
CARDINAL POINTS-four main points of a compass.
CARLINE-timbers used as support for cabin or hatch, page 73.
CARRICK BEND-page 189.
CARRY AWAY-to part a rope, break a spar, to break or tear loose.
CARRY ON-carry all sails possible.
CARVEL-opposite of lapstrake, smooth planked.
CAST OFF-let go, pages 95, 172.
CAST, TO-sailboat bow pays off on tack it will use underway; to throw.
CAT-tackle used to heave anchor to cathead.
CATAMARAN-twin-hulled craft, pages 17, 18, 47-49, 83.
CATBOAT, CAT RIG-boat with one sail stepped well forward pages 5, 23-29.
CATCH-ALL-see SAVE ALL.
CAT-HARPIN-iron leg to confine upper rigging to mast.
CATHEAD-timbers projecting from bow to secure anchor, page 287.
CATENARY(Br.)-sag or curve of anchor cable between boat & anchor, pg. 161.
CATSPAW-ruffled patch of water due to stronger wind puff at that spot, pg. 205.
CAT the ANCHOR-secure anchor for sea.
CAULK-fill boats seams with oakum or cotton to make them tight.
CAULKING OFF-sleeping.
CENTERBOARD-hinged plate lowered to reduce leeway sailing to windward,19.
CENTERBOARD TRUNK-watertight housing for centerboard, page 19.
CENTER of EFFORT-center of sail area, page 133.
CENTER of LATERAL RESISTANCE-center of underwater profile, pages 133-5.
CHAFE-to damage by rubbing, anything used to prevent it is called CHAFING
GEAR. A CHAFING MAT is woven from rope strands.
CHAIN LOCKER-compartment for storing chain.
CHAIN PLATES-straps bolted to vessels side to secure shrouds, page 69.
CHAINS-station for leadsman under bowsprit.
CHAIN STOPPER-short length of chain for quick release of anchor for anchoring.
CHANNEL BUOY-buoy marker showing extreme limits of channel, page 249.
CHARLEY NOBLE-galley smokestack named after meticulous Br. Admiral, 75.

CHANNELS-ledges bolted lengthwise & built out to increase spread of shroud, 285.
CHECK-ease off gradually to ease cable from parting.
CHEEKS-side of block;projections trestle trees rest on each side of mast.
CHINE-intersection of boats side and bottom, page 17.
CHINES-drive oakum into seams of boat.
CHIP LOG-early device to measure boat speed, see Laing's 'Clipper Ship Men'.
CHIPS-ships carpenter.
CHOCK-wedges a dinghy is secure to when hoisted aboard ship.
CHOCK-A-BLOCK(two blocked)-upper & lower blocks of tackle run together.
CHRONOMETER-accurate clock used for navigation.
CHOW-food.   CIRRUS-high frozen clouds, 205-9.
CLAMP DOWN-swab down a deck.
CLAMPS-thick planks supporting end of beams on inside of a vessel.
CLAP ON-add more sail or haul away on a rope.
CLAPPER-moveable wooden piece to prevent jaws of gaff from jamming.
CLAW OFF-trying to clear a lee shore sailing closehauled.
CLEAN-boat with smooth lines.
CLEAR-work clear of bar or shoal;untangle lines, gear, or rigging;land is
cleared as vessel sails away;leaving port with all formalities transacted.
CLEAR for RUNNING-ready to run without fouling.
CLEARING PAPERS-they indicate all regulations met & approved by the port
authorities before leaving.
CLEAT varied fittings to secure rope without making a hitch, pages 22-81, 144,190.
CLEW-lower aft corner of fore & aft sail, pg. 5, 7, 33, 89; for spinnaker, the side
to which sheet is secured, pages 126-9;for square sail see page 287.
CLEWLINE-hauls up clew of square sail, page 287.
CLINCH-half-hitch which is stopped to its own part.
CLINKER (clinker built)-overlapping planks, opp. of smooth planking, page 16.
CLINOMETER-instrument measuring heel or degree of roll, page 134, 145.
CLIPPER BOW (schooner bow)-stem with forward curve and flaring sides.
CLOSE-HAULED-sailing close to wind as efficiency permits, pages 99, 104.
CLOSING-a vessel closes with the shore or another vessel.
CLOUD FORMATIONS-see pages 205-209.
CLOVE-HITCH-two half hitches around rope or spar, page 191.
CLUB-spar on bottom of staysail or topsail, page 71.
CLUBBING-using anchor to use current going downstream or around a point.
CLUB TOPSAIL-topsail with foot laced to club, luff laced to a sprit.
CLUMP BLOCK-small oval block with rounded shell.
COAMING-railing around cockpit, hatches, etc., page 72.
COCKBILL-see A-COCK-BILL.
COCKPIT-opening aft for feet or passengers.
CODLINE-eighteen thread line.
COFFERDAM-partitions separating tanks in the hull of a ship.
COIL-to lay a rope in a circle.
COIR-weak buoyant rope made from coconut fibers, often found on lateeners.
COLD WALL-current flowing southward of cold water, inside Gulf Stream.
COLLAR-eye to go over masthead, found on end of shroud or stay.
COLLIER-a ship that carries coal.
COME HOME-anchor broken loose and being pulled in.
COME UP-slack away so gear may be belayed after hauling.
COMING ABOUT-changing course so bow swings thru eye of wind to pay off on
other tack, pages 101, 109.
COMMISSIONING PENNANT-ship of war pennant flown at the main truck.
COMPANION-wooden covering over staircase to a cabin.
COMPANIONWAY-staircase to cabin or below, page 67.
COMPASS (mariner's, magnetic)-magnetized needles floating on compass card,
that tends to point to the magnetic north and south poles, pg. 244-245.
G7

CO COMPASS CARD-calibrated card having points of the compass.

  COMPASS POINT -11 1/4° or 1/32 part of a full circle.

  COMPASS ROSE-graduated circle printed on chart with points of the compass.

  COMPENSATE-correcting compass from local attractions on boat.

  COMPOSITE, COMPOSITE BUILT-vessel with wooden skin & metal frame.

  CONE-signal displayed on sailboat under power & sail, page 236;racing,page R2.

  CONNING-direction helmsman is steering a vessel.

  CONTROLLING DEPTH-minimum depth of anchorage or channel.

  CORDAGE-term for all kinds of rope.

  CORINTHIAN-:-amateur interested in a sport without thought of compensation.

  CORVETTE-page 289.

  COSTON SIGNALS-colored fireworks sometimes used for signalling.

  COUNTER-the side of a vessels quarter.

  COURSE-angle sailboat is sailing into or away from the wind, page 99; it can also be the compass heading of a boat, 244-247.

  COURSES-sails set to lower yards-fore course & main course, page 287.

  COW HITCH-page 191.

  COWL-vent opening, often bell shaped, page 73.

  COW'S TAIL (fag, irish pennant)-untidy frayed end of rope.

  COXSWAIN-person in charge of steering a boat.

  CRADLE-frame vessel rests on when hauled out of the water.

  CRAFT-general term for small vessels.

  CRANK(cranky, tender)-top heavy sailing vessel that heels too easily.

  CRANSE IRON-metal cap or ring at end of bowsprit to secure stays.

  CREEPER-metal device with claws for dragging bottoms.

  CRINGLE-rope eye formed around metal thimble, spliced into the bolt rope of a sail, pages 5, 287.   CROJIK-same as cross jack, page 287.

  CROJIK YARD (cross-jack yard)-lower yard on mizzen mast, page 287.

  CROSS PAWL-timbers bracing boat frames during construction.

  CROSS PIECE-timber connecting two bitts.

  CROSS SPALES-timbers securing frames together until knees are bolted.

  CROSS TREES-cross pieces near top of mast, spreading shrouds so they can make a greater angle to the mast, page 285.

  CROWD ON-use all sail possible.

  CROWFOOT-several small ropes used to suspend an awning.

  CROWN-camber of deck, page 73;for anchor, see page 158.

  CROW'S NEST-lookout platform or area up mast, see page 286.

  CRUTCH-support for boom when sails are furled, page 89.

  CUDDY-small shelter cabin.

  CUT OF THE JIB-general appearance of a vessel or a person.

  CUTTER-single masted sailboat with mast stepped 2/5 or more of the waterline length from the bow, pages 9, 263.

  CUTWATER-foremost part of bow or stem, page 73.

  CYCLONE-circular wind storm of strong intensity.

d DAGGERBOARD-plate raised/lowered vertically to reduce leeway, 18, 23-27, 51, 83.

  DAN BUOY-used to mark fishing nets, or navy buoy markers in foreign waters.

  DANFORTH ANCHOR-see pages 158, 159, 162.

  DANGER BUOY-buoy marking danger spot or area.

  DASH-long period of sound or light in Morse Code.

  DASHER BLOCK -small signal halyard secured to end of spanker gaff.

  DAVIT-pair of posts with curved arms for raising & lowering a dinghy. Spar with sheave at its end for fishing an anchor is called a FISH DAVIT.

  DAVY JONES-spirit of the sea.   DAVY JONES LOCKER-bottom of sea.

  DAY'S DUTY-24 hour tour of duty aboard ship.

  DAY'S WORK-noon to noon navigation work to determine a ship's position.

  DEAD AHEAD-directly ahead of vessels course, page 83.

  DEADEYE-wooden block thru which lanyards are rove to set up rigging.   G8

DEAD LIGHT-ports placed in cabin windows.
DEAD MEN(Irish pennants, cow's tail)sloppy loose end of a rope.
DEAD RECKONING-time & distance record of a vessels course.
DEADRISE-vertical distance between turn of bilge and keel.
DEAD-RISING(rising-line)-where floor timbers terminate on lower futtock.
DEAD ROPE-line not led thru a block or sheave.
DEAD WATER-water pulled along with a vessel underway.
DEADWOOD-strengthening members securing keel to stern and stem, pg. 72.
DECK-planked floor of a ship or boat, page 72.
DECK BEAM-athwartship support for deck, page 73.
DECK CHEST-chest for deck gear secured topsides.
DECKHEAD-under surface of the deck.
DECK HORSE-athwartship rod for sheet block traveller.
DECK LIGHT-piece of glass fitted flush to deck.
DECK STOPPER-stopper with lanyard for lashing cable,fitted with stopper knot.
DECK TACKLE-heavy double purchase used above deck.
DECLINATION-angle measured from earths center thru a celestial body.
DEEPS-fathom of a lead line which is not marked.
DEEP SEA LEAD-50 lb. lead used in 120 fathoms or more.
DEEP SIX-throw it overboard.
DEGREE-1/360 th part of a circumference.
DEPARTURE-bearing of coast object from which vessel commences dead rec'ning.
DERELICT-abandoned ship at sea.
DEVIATION-compass error due to objects on boat that varies with heading, 245.
DEW POINT-air saturation point, page 219.
DHOW-general term for lateeners, page 279.
DIAGONAL-see pages 254, 257.   DIAMOND KNOT-ornamental knot.
DINGHY- open boat,or partially decked over without cabin, pgs.23-49. 23,32,41.
DIP-dipping an ensign, is to lower & rehoist it as a salute, 253.
DISMANTLE-strip a vessel of spars, masts, and rigging.
DISMAST-carry away the masts of a vessel.
DISPLACEMENT-weight of water displaced by a vessel.
DOG-metal fitting used to close hatches, covers, etc.
DOG'S EAR-small bight of sails leach when reefed.
DOGHOUSE-enclosure or shelter built over companionway, page 75.
DOG VANE-small wind vane usually made of bunting.
DOG WATCH-half watches from 4 to 6 and 6 to 8 p.m.
DOLDRUMS-belts of little wind on either sides of Equator.
DOLPHIN-spar mooring buoy;strap around mast secures puddening at slings
of lower yard.
DOLPHIN-STRIKER(martingale boom)-spar projecting below bowsprit to
counteract strain of head stays, page 285.
DORY-flat-bottomed boat with narrow stern and flaring sides.
DOT-short period of sound or light in the Morse Code.
DOUBLE BLOCK-block with two sheaves.
DOUBLE ENDER-boat with pointed bow and stern.
DOUBLE SHEET BEND-page 189.
DOUBLING-sailing around point of land;overlapping parts of two masts, pg. 284.
DOUSE(dowse)-lower & take in sail;put out light; cover with water.
DOWNDRAFT- wind flow with vertical angle, page 123, 206-207.
DOWNHAUL-line used to pull down tack of sail, pages 88-91, 119, 121.
DOWNHAUL TACKLE-page 286.
DOWN HELM-bring boat up into wind.   DOWN THE MAST-no wind.
DRAFT-water depth required to float a vessel, page 222;sail airfoil 10, 102-5.
DRAG-anchor failing to hold vessel;storm anchor used to keep vessels head or
stern to wind in heavy weather, pages 156-7;machine for dragging bottom;area
of turbulence behind or to leeward of sail, page 103.

dr DRAW-sail filled with wind (draft); a boat draws enough water to float it.
DREDGE-vessel used for digging out a channel.
DRIFT-vessels leeway, pages 106-7; amount of current; distance between the blocks of a tackle, or spare end of a rope.
DRIFT LEAD-lead weight over anchored vessels side indicates dragging anchor.
DRIFT, TO-to move with the tide or current.
DRIVE-drifting in a current or scudding before a gale.
DRIVER-6th mast of 7 masted schooner. DROGUE-storm anchor, page 157.
DROP-distance from head to foot of a square sail.
DRUM-HEAD-top of the capstan.
DRY SAILING-boat kept on trailer when not being used.
DUB-reduce end of a timber.   DUCK-light canvas.
DRY BULB THERMOMETER-measures air temperature.
DRY DOCK-basin for repairing vessels that can be pumped dry.
DUFF-flour and water.   DUMB COMPASS-pelorus.
DUNNAGE-sailors personal effects; loose material stowed in boat.
DUTCH COURAGE-artificial courage caused by drinking.

e EARING (earring)-short lines securing reefed sail to boom, page 149.
EASE-to slacken; put helm alee and luff sailboat head to wind.
EASE IN-to slowly work up to a dock, mooring or slip.
EASE OFF-to slack off.   EASE OUT-to slack out.
EASING-OUT LINE-line for easing out. EASE RUDDER-bring it more amidship.
EASE UP-to slowly let up or work out.   EASY-slowly, carefully.
EBB TIDE-tide passing from high to low point, with tidal current ebbing out to sea, pages 214, 216.
EDDY-circular or confused air or water currents, page 217.
EDGE AWAY-slowly pay off from course, dock, or berth.
ELBOW-2 crosses in a hawse.   EMBARK-go on board or to begin.
END LINK-open link next abaft end shackle.   END ON-head on, 235.
END SEIZING-round seizing at the two ends of a rope.
END TO END-reversing position of object such as rope.
ENLARGED LINK-wider link connecting common link to swivel or short or a long-end link.
ENSIGN-national or organizational flag carried aboard a vessel 252, 253; a navy officer equivalent to a army second lieutenant.
ENTRANCE-a vessels bow just above the waterline.
EQUINOX-date that the sun crosses the equator during spring and fall.
EUPHROE (euvrou)-wooden piece helping to extend an awning.
EVEN KEEL-floating level.
EYE-closed loop of rope.
EYE BOLT-bolt or iron bar to secure a tackle.
EYELET HOLES-holes in a sail for reef points or cringle.
EYE of the WIND-into center of the wind, pages 98-104.
EYE SPLICE-spliced loop in end of rope, page 196-201.
EYES of a VESSEL-forward portion of weather deck or ships bow.

f FAG (fagged)-untwisted or frayed end of rope; Irish pennant or cow's tail.
FAIRBODY-line formed by outside bottom edge of plank touching keel; rabbet,
FAIRLEADS (fair leader)-fitting to change direction of rope lead, 7,12,31-5,43,47.
FAIR TIDE-current running with vessel. FAIRWAY-a navigation channel, pg.249.
FAIR WIND-favorable wind.   FAKE-single turn of rope in a coil.
FAKE (flake)DOWN-each coil of rope overlaps the one inside of it.
FALL-hauling part of rope, also part of tackle which force is applied.
FALLING GLASS-lowering barometer pressure, page 212.
FALLING HOME (tumble home)-side of boat inclining inboard above waterline.
FALL OFF (falling off)-paying off to leeward or from the wind.
FALSE KEEL-protective wood strip bolted outside main keel, page 72.

FANCY LINE-downhaul for gaff;line used to cross haul lee topping-lift.
FANNING-sailboat with little headway in light airs.
FASHION BOARD-panel to prevent water entering companionway.
FAST-to make fast is to secure, also docking lines.
FATHOM-one fathom equals six feet, a depth measurement of water, 215.
FATHOMETER-electronic instrument for sounding water depth, page 222,243.
FAVOR-reduce load as in a weak spar or old sail.
FEATHER-sailboat class;turning oar blade at end of stroke to reduce splashing.
FELUCCA-lateener that can also be rowed, page 279.
FENDER-cushions to prevent chafing on a boats side.
FENDERBOARD-board used with two or more fenders to give hull protection.
FENDER SPAR-floating spar fender secured alongside a boat.
TO FETCH-sailboat able to make windward mark without changing tack, 106.
FIBERGLASS HULL-boat hulls made of fiberglass cloth & resin.
FIBER ROPE-rope made of organic instead of synthetic or metal materials.
FID-pointed pin or stick for working rope, page 202. Short bar passing thru
hole in heel of bowsprit or topmast resting on trestle-trees,
FIDDLE-bar with sheaves for leads with light running gear.
FIDDLE HEAD-ornamental timber substitute for figure head.
FIDDLES-strips around tables to prevent dishes from sliding off.
FIDDLEY-framework of deck hatch around a ladder going below.
FIELD DAY-one for general ship cleaning.
FIFE-RAIL (pin-rail)-wooden railing around mast for belaying pins, pg. 73.
FIGURE EIGHT KNOT-page 184.
FIGUREHEAD-ornamental head, bust, or figure carried under bowsprit.
FILL AWAY-sails filling & boat gathering headway after changing tack, pg.109.
FIN KEEL-straight or bulb section on bottom of keel, page 20.
FISH-strengthen spar with lashing or splints;heaving anchor flukes on gunwale.
FISH BLOCK (fish-davit, fish-hook, fish-davit)- parts used for fishing an anchor.
FISHERMANS KNOT-page 189.
FIT OUT-overhauling period before trip, or before boat goes into the water.
FIX-finding vessels position by land or celestial observations.
FLAKE-see FAKE DOWN.
FLARE-upward outward curve of bow or side, opposite of tumble home.
FLARE-UP-a signal light designed to flare up.
FLAT-a sail empty without wind pressure.
FLAT ABACK-wind on wrong side of sails of a square rigger.
FLAT BOTTOM-page 17.   FLAT CALM-no wind pressure.
FLAT SPINNAKER-page 125.   FLATTEN IN-haul in on sheets.
FLAW (catspaw)-a gust of wind, 205.
FLEET-haul blocks of purchase apart;shifting position of fall or block.
FLEMISH DOWN-coil rope flat on deck with each roll outside of another.
FLEMISH HORSE-additional foot rope at ends of topsail yards.
FLOAT-raft moored alongside or pier making access to a boat easier, pg. 169.
FLOOD-incoming tidal current, page 215.
FLOOR-bottom of boat on each side of keelson, page 72.
FLOTATION TANK-air tank to prevent swamped boat from sinking, 26-31.
FLOTSAM-floating wreckage, driftwood, etc.
FLOW-spilling the wind by easing the sheets also called luffing.
FLOWING SHEETS-sailboat running before the wind with sheets eased.
FLUKE-wind irregularities;digging ends of an anchor.
FLY-horizontal length of a flag.
FLYING MOOR-sailboat dropping anchor underway, then sails, and finally a
second anchor. Vessel then drops to midway point between the anchors.
FOGHORN-pages 220-221.   FOOT -lower edge of sail, 5,7,89,287.
FOOT ROPE-support under bowsprit for reefing or lowering sail.
FORE-opposite to aft, forward part of a boat.

fo FORE AND AFT-lengthwise, parallel to the keel, pages 6, 84.
FO 'Ç 'SLE (forecastle)-square rigger crews quarter forward, pages 253, 285.
FOREFOOT-timber between keel and stem, page 73.
FORE MAST-foremost mast of schooner or square rigger, pages 269, 282-289.
FORE PEAK-extreme bow space foreward, page 63.
FORE REACH-movement of sailboat passing through eye of wind.
FORESAIL (fore staysail)-pages 269, 287. FORE TOPMAST STAYSAIL-pg. 287.
FORGE AHEAD-shoot ahead when going in stays or coming to anchor.
FORWARD-in front of, page 84.
FORWARD PLATFORM-mounted forward of foremast in eyes of a boat.
FOTHER (fodder)-draw a sail under vessels bottom filled with oakum to stop leaks.
FOUL-jammed, stuck, not clean.
FOULED ANCHOR-caught or twisted up in its own anchor line, page 161.
FOUL HAWSE-twisted or crossed anchor lines.   FOUND-equipped.
FOUNDER-a boat filled with water and sinking.
FRAME-ribs of a boat, page 73.
FRAP-pass ropes around sail or awning to keep it from blowing loose.
FREE-sailing with wind aft, pg. 99.; after water is pumped out of boat.
FREEBOARD-vertical distance of boat above waters surface.
FRIENDSHIP SLOOP-page 272.   FRESH BREEZE(fresh gale)-pg. 137.
FRESHEN-an increasing wind.
FRESHEN THE NIP-shift a stay or portion of anchor line to reduce chafe, 156.
FRIGATE-page 289.
FULL AND BY (full and bye)-close hauled square rigger term, page 99.
FULL SPREAD-all sails set.
FURL-to roll sail snugly on top of boom, 86, 87, or under a yard.
FUTTOCK PLATES-corresponds to platform of a top.
FUTTOCK STAFF-short spar serving as topmast rigging shear-pole.
FUTTOCK TIMBERS-part of a frame.

g GADGET-term used only by a landlubber.
GAFF-spar for head of a gaff sail, pages 5, 260-269; scandalizing, page 148.
GAFF JAWS-inboard end fitting of gaff around a mast, page 5.
GAFF SAIL-quadrilateral sail fitted with gaff, page 5.
GAFF TOPSAIL-sail above & with foot spread by gaff, pages 70, 265.
GAFF VANG-line going to gaff peak used to steady the gaff, page 269.
GAGE-position of vessel in regards to wind, sun, or another vessel.
GAIN the WIND-to work to windward of another sailboat.
GALE-force 7-10, page 137, 139.   GALLEY-floating kitchen, page 74.
GALLOWS-permanent frame to rest end of boom after sail is lowered.
GALLOWS-BITTS-strong frame amidships for spare spars, etc.
GAMMONING-fastenings of bowsprit on vertical stem.
GANG PLANK-board used as walkway from ship to dock.
GANGWAY-step aside, get out of the way; ladder or passageway aboard a ship.
GANTLINE (girthline)-line secured aloft & rove through a single block.
GARBOARD STRAKE-planks on both sides of keel, page 73.
GARLAND-strap or rope lashed to spar when hoisting it aboard.
GARNET-purchase for hoisting on the mainstay.
GASKET-canvas strip for furling a sail, pages 86, 87.
GATHER WAY-pick up momentum.   GEAR-general term for rigging.
GENOA JIB (gennie)-largest size jib, pages 12-15.
GHOSTING-sailboat making little way in light breeze.
GIMBALS-bearing rings & pivots to keep compass card level on boat.
GIMLET-turn anything around on its end, turning anchor around by its stock.
GINGERLY-with caution.
GIRT-boat with tight mooring line that does not swing to tide or wind.
GIRTHLINE-see gantline.   GIRTHBAND-page 287.

GIRT the SAIL-line leading across lee side of sail making a hard ridge.
GLASS-trad. barometer term, pg. 212.   GLORY HOLE-lazarette.
GOB-LINE (gaub-line)-a martingale support or guy.
GO ABOUT-change tack over bow, 99; 109. GO ADRIFT-break loose.
GO FREE-running, page 99.   GO LARGE-same as running.
GOLLYWOBBLER-large sail peculiar to schooner, pages 15, 269.
GOOD FULL-course between close reach & close hauled.
GOOSENECK-fitting that secures boom to mast, pages 23,27,35,46,59,89.
GOOSE WING-same as sailing wing and wing, pages 99, 105, 111, 123, 277.
GOOSE WING JIBE-only bottom part of sail jibes, page 123.
GORES-sail cloths cut at angle to give sail desired shape.
GORING CLOTHS-sail material cut obliquely adding to depth of sail.
GRAFTING-weaving yarns together to cover a rope.
GRAPNEL (grappling iron)-small anchor with several claws, page 159.
GRATING-framework made of wood or metal to let in air or light.
GREAVE-cleaning ships bottom by burning.   GREAT GUNS-a violent wind.
GREEN SEA-large amount of water taken aboard that isn't foamy.
GRIP-an anchor when it bites and holds, page 160-162.
GRIPES-sailboat with excessive weather helm, page
GROMMET-rope ring, an eye sewn on edge of sail (cringle), page 5.
GROUNDING-running ashore, page 223.
GROUND SWELL-large wave or waves crossing shoal or bar.
GROUND TACKLE-general term for anchor & anchor gear, pages 158-163.
GUDGEON-eye supports for rudder pintles, sample page 31.
GUNKHOLING-shallow water sailing.
GUN-TACK PURCHASE-purchase made with two single blocks.
GUNTER (sliding gunther)-a vertical gaff in small dinghy, so mast, boom, and
gaff can be stored in boat when not in use, page 271.
GUNWALE-boat or cockpit railing, 23.   GUSSET-a brace.
GUST-sudden wind puff.   GUY-steadying line, pages 125-130.
GYASSA-pages 276-277.   GYBE-British for jibe.

HAIL-call to men in different part of ship or another vessel.
HALF MAST-a flag hoisted half way.
HALF RATER-small sailboat with jib & main, no bowsprit, see knockabout.
HALF SEAS OVER-quite drunk.
HALYARD   (halliard, haliard)-lines used to raise sails, flags, gaffs, 5, 7, 88-96.
HAND-crew member.   HANDICAP RATING-pages 2, 258-259.
HAND, TO-to furl a sail or haul in a patent log.
HAND LEAD-small sounding lead.   HAND RAIL-steadying rail on ladder.
HANDSOMELY-opposite of hasty; smoothly, moderately.
HANDSPIKE-wooden bar used for heaving at a windlass.
HAND TIGHT-tight as can usually be pulled by hand.
HANDY BILLY-see watch tackle.
HANKED ON-sail secured to stay by hanks, page 93.
HANKS-hooks or rings which secure jibs or staysails to their stays.
HARD-A-LEE-command to come about, page 109.
HARD-A-WEATHER -put helm up to sail further away from the wind. 111.
HARD DOWN (hard-a-lee)-shove tiller far to leeward as possible.
HARDEN IN-haul in on a sheet to flatten a sail.
HARD OVER -same has hard down or hard-a-lee, also helms alee.
HARD UP-order to shove tiller rapidly to eye of wind.
HATCH-opening in a deck with a cover, pages 51-3, 63, 67, 75, 77.
HAUL YOUR WIND-sail closer to wind; HAUL is a clockwise wind shift.
HAULING LINE-line from aloft used to haul up gear.
HAULING PART-part of tackle upon which power is applied.
HAUL TO WINDWARD (hauling her wind)-change from run to reach.
G13

ha HAWSE-space forward from vessel to directly over anchor.
HAWSE BLOCK-wooden plug fitting into hawse hole in vessel at sea.
HAWSER-heavy line used for warping, springs, etc.
HAWSER-LAID ROPE-3 strand left-handed lay rope.
HEAD-toilet compartment aboard a vessel;originally small lower deck forward
with most privacy, well defined on vessels such as Santa Maria, Mayflower, etc.
In later days it was the forward part of a vessel on schooners, etc.,pg. 63, 139,289.
HEADBOARD-page 7.
HEAD of SAIL-upper corner of a sail, pages 7, 287.
HEADSAILS-originally, all staysails set forward of foremast, pages 12-15.
HEAD SHEETS-sheets secured to headsails or staysails.
HEAD STAY-forward stay, pages 28, 70.
HEAD to WIND-position of sailboat in eye of the wind, pages 98, 108.
HEADS UP-warning to watch out or look up.
HEADWAY-moving ahead.
HEAVE AWAY, order to heave around a capstan or to haul away.
HEAVE DOWN-to pull vessel over to repair or inspect bottom when dry docks
and ordinary docking facilities are absent.
HEAVE IN-to haul in.
HEAVER-short wooden bar used as purchase and tapering at either end.
HEAVE SHORT-to heave in till boat is riding almost over its anchor.
HEAVE-TAUT-to haul in till a line has a strain upon it.
HEAVE TO-bring boats head to wind by sail or engine and holding it there,151.
HEAVE, TO-to haul, to throw;a boat rising and falling in a seaway.
HEAVING LINE-small line used for heaving, pg. 194;ANCHOR heaving, pg. 162.
HEEL-lower end of spar or after end of keel.
HEELING(heel, to heel)-to list or lay over, pages 100, 132-134.
HELM-tiller or wheel,22-81, 108-110.   HERMAPHRODITE BRIG—page 283.
HIGH and DRY-boat aground above high water mark, page 223.
HIKE-climbing to windward to prevent excessive heeling.
HIKING STICK- pages 23-63.   HITCH-page 191.
HELM DOWN(helms alee) -tiller pushed away from wind, page 109 to come
about;opposite of HELM AWEATHER for jibing, page 111.
HOGGED(hog backed)-vessel drooping at either end due to shrouds turned
down too tight(reverse sheer pg. 62, is designed with ends lower than midship).
HOGGING MOMENT-position of vessel with wave under middle.
HOIST-vertical edge of a sail or flag.   HOIST, TO-to haul aloft.
HOLD-below decks space for cargo, stores or ballast.
HOLD, TO-anchor digging in so that it will not drag.
HOLYSTONE-large porous flat stone used to clean & whiten deck or woodwork.
HOME-sheets slacked far as possible;anchor broken out of bottom.
HORNS-jaws of gaff or boom;arms of cleat.   HORN TIMBERS-page 72.
HORSE, DECK HORSE(traveller)-athwartship rail or bar for sheet block.
HOUNDS-wood shoulders bolted to mast to support trestle-trees, page 284.
HOUSE-to secure or stow in a safe place.
HOUSE FLAG-special flag on mainmast of merchant ship denoting company.
HOUSING-inboard part of bowsprit;part of mast below upper deck.
HOVE DOWN-sailboat heeling excessively or to have bottom scraped.
HOVE TO(heave to)-page 151.   HUDSON RIVER SLOOP-page 274.
HUG-to keep close.   HULK-stripped & worn out vessel.
HULL-body of vessel without mast or gear.
HULL DOWN-sailing vessel with only spars visible due to distance.
HULL SPEED-speed limit of displacement vessel, pages 140-143.
HURRICANE-wind force above 65 knots, 137-9. Named after Caribbean
natives with similar name that originally called it a 'big wind'.

●

i IN-a person is said to be in a vessel, not on her.
INBOARD-towards fore and aft centerline of vessel.
IN BOWS-order to boat oars & stand by with boat hooks for landing.
INHAUL-opposite of outhaul.
IN IRONS-sailing vessel head to wind, bow won't pay off on either tack, 99, 104.
INITIAL STABILITY-resistance of sailing vessel to heel, page 17.
INNER JIB-headsail forward of fore staysail on vessel with two or more headsails.
INNER KEEL-the keelson.   IN SAIL-order to take in sail.
INSHORE-in the direction of the shore.
IN STAYS (in irons)-head to wind, all sails shaking, pages 99, 104.
IN the WIND-pointing too high or pinching, page 104.
INWALE-strip of wood at sheer line, page 251.

j JETTY-dike at mouth of a river, pier or wharf, page 217.
JEWEL BLOCKS-single leads for stuns'l halyards at the yardarms.
JEW'S HARP-shackle connecting cable to anchor.
JIB-modern usage is sails secured to stay or stays forward of mast. Also called headsails and staysails, pages 7,13,15,29-83,93.
JIB BOOM-spar extension beyond bowsprit for add'l headsails, page 285.
JIBE (B r.—gybe)-changing wind or tack over stern of sailboat, page 111.
JIB HEADED-same as marconi and bermudian, first called leg-of-mutton, pg. 3.
JIB TOPSAIL-headsail forward of mast tacked higher than jib, page 70, 263.
JIB-purchase which is on a halyards bight.
JIGGER (mizzen) -aft sail on yawl or ketch, pg. 265; after mast of a four masted ship carrying spanker, page 285 ; handy small tackle for general use aloft.
JIMMY LEGS-master at arms.
JIMMY SQUAREFOOT (Davy Jones)-mythical ocean bottom character.
JOE DECOSTE-sail piece acting as lee for lookout in the weather rigging.
JOGGLE-SHACKLE-long jawed shackle used for cable work.
JOLLY BOAT-work boat or dink carried on stern of coastal sailing vessel.
JOLLY ROGER-pirate flag displaying skull and crossbones.
JUMBO-fore staysail on fore and aft rigged sailing vessel, page 14.
JUMP-a short, quick, choppy sea.
JUMPER-stay on outer end of whiskers to martingale preventing spar from jumping up, page 285 ; chain stays from outer end of jib-boom to lower end of martingale boom or dolphine striker.
JUMPER STAY-extra stay going from rail to masthead, 7,113-4,119,121,261
JUMP SHIP-leaving without authorized permission.
JUNK-lateen or lug rigged Chinese or Japanese sailing vessel with sails of woven matting, pages 278-281; term for old rope.
JURY-makeshift or temporary rig to take damaged vessel back to port.
JUTE ROPE-rope that comes from fiber of jute plant.

K KAPOK-buoyant vegetable fiber used in cushions, jackets, etc.
KECKLING-chafing stuff made of old rope that is wound around cables.
KEDGE-small anchor for warping a ship ahead, or kedging off bar.
KEDGING (to kedge)-move vessel by hauling on kedge anchor. Drifting with anchor just touching bottom is called DREDGING or CLUBBING.
KEEL-fore and aft backbone of ship, pages 20-21, 72.
KEEL BLOCK-line of blocks to take a vessels keel in a dry dock.
KEELEK-small kedge anchor.
KEEL HAUL-ancient sailors punishment where main is hauled under keel of ship and up other side by ropes or whips from yardarms.
KEELSON-timber connecting floors to keel that are running fore and aft.
KEEP AWAY-change course from wind, or far enough to avoid danger.
KEEP HER FULL-order to keep the sails filled.
KEEP HER OFF-order to keep sailing vessel further from the wind.
KEEP HER SO-an order of steady on her course.

ke KEEP YOUR LUFF-sail close hauled without flutter in sails luff.
KELLET or SENTINEL-page 161.   KELP-seaweed.
KENTLEDGE-shaped pieces of pig iron ballast.
KETCH-two masted sailboat having after mast forward of rudder post, 266-7.
KETTLE-BOTTOMED-vessel with a flat bottom.
KEVEL(cavil)-variation of cleat.
KICK-distance vessels stern is thrown away from direction of turn.
KILLOCK(killick)-page 159.   KINK-twist in a rope.
KING PLANK-main deck plank which others feed into, page 73.
KING POST-short mast to support a boom such as loading cargo, pg. 240.
KING SPOKE-marked upper spoke of wheel when rudder is amidships.
KNEE-timber with two arms connecting vessels beams to frames, page 73.
KNIGHTHEADS-vertical timbers on either side of bowsprit.
KNOCKABOUT-obsolete term of sloop without a bowsprit, page 260.
KNOCKED DOWN-sailboat heeled so far it doesn't recover, page 144.
KNOT-one nautical mile per hour, or 6076 to 6080', one min. of latitude.

l LABOR-a vessel labors when it rolls or pitches heavily in a seaway.
LACING-lines used to secure sail to spar or mast, page 5.
LAID UP-dry docked, such as a boat thru the winter months.
LAND BREEZE-night breeze from land to sea, page 211.
LAND FALL-when land is first sighted.A good landfall is the intended one.
LAND HO!-the hail when land has first been sighted.
LANDLOCKED-entirely surrounded by land.
LANDLUBBER-sailors term for person that doesn't go to sea.
LANDMARK-a distinct object on shore.
LANDS-overlapping part of plank in clinker built boat.
LANYARD-a lashing;ropes for setting up rigging, rove thru deadeyes.
LARBOARD-term formerly used for port or left side of vessel, page 82.
LARGE-see page 99.   LASH-secure or bind with rope.
LATCHINGS-loops on head rope of bonnet by which it is laced to foot of sail.
LATEEN-triangular fore & aft rigged sails secured to long yard and hoisted
obliquely to mast, page 26, 44, 279.
LATITUDE-distance north or south of equator measured in degrees.
LAUNCH-the long boat.   LAUNCH, TO-to set afloat.
LAY(laid)-direction strands of rope or hawser are twisted, page 184;to come
or go such as LAY FORWARD, LAY AFT, LAY ALOFT.
LAY OFF-to rule off a course.
LAY, TO-same as fetch;sailboat lays mark if it doesn't have to change tack.
LAYUP-hauling out a boat for the winter season.
LAZARETTE-below deck space aft where provisions, parts,etc., are kept.
LAZY GUY(preventer)-rigging to steady boom to prevent jibe in rough sea.
LAZYJACKS(jacks)-lines used to gather sail for raising or lowering, 5,279.
LAZYLIFTS-lazyjacks which also combine use of topping lift.
LEACH(leech)-after edge of fore & aft rigged sail, 5,7, 11;square sail, 287.
LEACH LINE-line in leach used to tighten leach of a sail.
LEAD-shaped piece of lead with line secured to upper end, and hole on bottom
to get sample of bottom formation;obsoleted by fathometer to record depth.
LEADEN-when skies are a dull leaden hue.
LEADER-line with eye in upper end free to slide on topmast, used to keep a
topsails luff close to the mast.
LEADING EDGE-forward part of a sail.
LEADING WIND-a beam or quarter wind.
LEAD LINE-line secured to lead, marked at regular intervals to test depth.
LEADSMAN-sailor detailed to chains under bowsprit for heaving the lead.
LEAGUE-distance memasurement of three nautical miles.
LEAK-accidental crack or opening allowing water to enter boat.

LEAVE-permission granting leave period from station or ship.
LEE-wind blows onto lee shore, wind flows from the windward to the leeward side of a vessel, and from windward rigging to rigging on leeward side.
LEEBOARD-pivoted board secured to side of sailboat, pages 18, 29.
LEECH-see leach.
LEE HELM-sailboat out of balance that will turn to beam reach if rudder is suddenly released, pages 132-5.
LEE HELMSMAN-assistant helmsman on lee side of steering wheel.
BY THE LEE (running on the lee)-running with wind on same side, page 123.
LEE-OH!-helm has been put down for sailboat to come about.
LEE TIDE-tidal current running with the wind, page 216.
LEE, UNDER THE-object or another boat between you and the wind.
LEEWARD-direction which is away from the wind.
LEG-length of tack or board, page 101; brace to keep stranded boat upright, 223.
LEG of MUTTON-original term for marconi, bermudian & jib headed sail.
LET DRAW-fill sail on desired tack.   LET FLY-drop the sheets.
LET HER OFF-order to head farther from the wind.
LET HER RIDE-sailboat is on course.
LET HER UP-order to head up or point higher into the wind.
LET GO-drop an anchor.
LIE TO-square rigger slowing down by reducing sail to make little or no progress, or by counter bracing yards; also heave to, page 151.
LIFEBOAT-ships boat for emergency use.
LIFE BUOY-ring buoy for life saving.
LIFELINE-stout line around deck to prevent crew being washed overboard. A sailor can also have lifeline secured to his waist, pages 194, 228.
LIFE PRESERVER-buoyant aid to keep a person afloat, pages 226-9.
LIFE RAFT-float made of cork, canvas, or rubber.
LIFT-line such as topping lift to take weight of a spar, pages 75, 96. On square riggers it could be tackle going from yardarms to masthead, purpose being to support & move yard, 285; clearing in fog; wind may lift or raise sail slightly.
LIGHT-lift along; to light out is move out; lighten up is to slack away.
LIGHT AIRS-page 137.   LIGHT BREEZE-page 137.
LIGHTER-harbor craft for loading & unloading ships, or to carry merchandise.
LIGHTNING-sailboat class, pgs. 34-7; damage prevention, page 206.
LIGNUM VITAE-hard wood with own lubricant, used for blocks (pulleys).
LIMBERHOLE (limbers)-drain holes cut into frames next to keel, page 73.
LINE-rope becomes line when used in operation of a vessel, see rope definition.
LINES-drawings of a hulls contours, page 254.
LINES, HEAVING-light line with weight on end for heaving, pg. 194.
LIPPER-small sea coming over the rail.
LIST-vessel inclination due to excess weight on side or either end.
LIZARD-line leader for running rigging fitted with a thimble or thimbles.
LJUNGSTROM-sailboat eliminating danger of accidental jibe, pages 270-271.
L. O. A. (length over all)-extreme length of a hull, page 254.
LOCK-canal compartment used to bring vessel to different water level.
LOCKER-chest, box, or clothes wardrobe to stow items away.
BOATSWAIN'S LOCKER-where rigging & small stuff are stowed.
CHAIN LOCKER-compartment where chain cables are kept.
LOFTY-high, towering, such as masts or clouds.
LOG-device to estimate vessels speed, see CHIP LOG.
LOG BOOK-boats diary containing daily record of course, distance, weather, ships activities and other items of importance.
LOG CANOE, CHESAPEAKE-page 273.   LOG LINE-line secured to log.
LOG SHIP-marked line & float used to determine a vessels speed.
LONG BOARD-long tack, page 101.   LONG BOAT-largest ships boat.

lo LONG in the JAW-a rope that has stretched.

LONGITUDE-distance in degrees east or west of Greenwich, England, meridian.

LONGITUDINAL-fore and aft strengthening member of vessels structure.

LONG LEGGED-deep draft vessel.

LONGSHOREMAN-laborer who loads and unloads cargo.

LONG SPLICE-joining two ropes so dia. is not increased at splice.

LOOF-part of vessel where planks begin to bend as they approach stern.

LOOKOUT-observer on vessel to report objects seen, pages 154, 240.

LOOK UP-order to point closer due to favorable wind shift.

LOOM-illusion at sea; part of an oar.   LOOSE-to unfurl a sail.

LOOSE-FOOTED-fore and aft sail not secured along full length of boom, 23-25.

LOUVRE-wire mesh cap covering end of a ventilator pipe.

LOW-area of low pressure, pg. 212.   LUBBER-a beginner.

LOWER AWAY-order to lower down object such as a lifeboat, or sail.

LUBBER LINE (lubbers point)-mark on compass stand indicating it is on the fore and aft centerline of a vessel, or one that is parallel.

LUFF-bring sailboat higher into wind, or without changing course to slack off on the sheet, both procedures being to break sails airfoil, pgs. 104, 168; the luff is the forward edge of fore and aft sails, pgs. 5, 7.

LUFF EARING-short line to secure luff reef cringle to boom while reefing, 149.

LUFF HER-order to bring sailboat into wind to break sail airfoil.

LUG (lugger)-pages 280-1.   LULL-period of calm.

LURCH-sudden rolling of a vessel to one side.

L. W. L. (load waterline)-waterline reached with boat trimmed to float to the designers specifications, pages 254.

m MACKEREL SKY-page 204.   MADE-put together, not one piece.

MAGAZINE-space provided in a ship to store explosives.

MAIN DECK-highest full length deck of a ship, page 285.

MAINMAST-the taller of the masts on ketches, yawls, and two masted schooners; usually second mast from bow on square riggers, pages 264-285.

MAINSAIL-fore & aft sail set to after side of mainmast, pages 7, 11, 26-91, 264-284   ; it is hung from main yard on a square rigger, page 287.

MAKE SAIL-to set sail.   MAKE FAST-secure or belay a rope.

MAKE STERNBOARD-caught in irons & going astern under sail.

MAKE WATER-to leak.   MALLET-serving or caulking mallet.

MAKE LAND-a landfall.   MANILA-see page 185.

MANGER-space aft of hawse pipes in square rigger having low coaming to keep out water.

MAN ROPE-steadying ropes used in going up & down vessels side or ladder.

MAN the BOAT-order to climb into a rowboat.

MARCONI RIG-triangular sail with luff secured to vertical or nearly so mast. Other names are jib-headed and Bermudian, pages 6, 275.

MARES TAILS-pages 205-209.   MARITIME-pertaining to the sea.

MARINA-facility offering docking & other facilities to boat owners.

MARK-lead line markings to record water depth visually or by feel.

MARL-take frequent turns, each being half hitched, at frequent intervals on line.

MARLINE-small two stranded twine used for marling.

MARLINESPIKE (marlinspike, marlingspike)-pointed wood or steel wedge used to open strands of rope and wire for splicing, 202.

MAROON-abandon a person by putting him ashore.

MARRY-sewing rope ends together to thread one thru block; joining ropes by worming over both in order to haul equally on both.

MARTINGALE (dolphin striker)-short perpendicular spar extending from bow-sprit, used for counteracting pull of headstays, page 285.

MAST-vertical spar to support rigging, yards and sails, pages 5, 7.

MAST CAP, page 284.   MASTER-captain of a vessel.

MASTHEAD LIGHT-white running light carried fwd by power vessel underway pages 236-241;light carried by anchored vessels in undesignated anchorages.
MASTHEAD SPINNAKER-pages 124-5.   MAST HEEL(step)-pgs. 23,73, 28, 41.
MAST HOLE-deck opening for mast.
MAST HOOP-wooden mast hoops found on traditional gaff rig, pages 5, 71.
MAST STEP-frame or slot to secure lower end of mast, pages 23, 73.
MAT-used to prevent chafing, made of old rope strands.
MATE-officer ranking next to the captain ... or his wife.
MATTHEW WALKER-stopper knot used on standing end of lanyard.
MEAL PENNANT-white rectangular flag flown on pleasure craft, page 253.
MEND-refurl improperly furled sail;rebend sail to boom.
MERIDIAN-true north and south line.
MESSENGER-light line used to haul over heavier line or cable,172, 194, 203.
METEOROLOGICAL-pertaining to the weather.
MID-CHANNEL BUOY-buoy to be passed on either side, page 249.
MIDSHIPMAN-usually naval cadet.
MIDSHIPS, AMIDSHIPS-widest part of vessel;order to center rudder.
MILDEW-fungus activity on organic product, see 'TrailerBoating Illustrated'.
MILE-nautical mile is 6080'(Int' Naut. Mile,6076.10'), one min. of latitude.
MIRAGE-seeing an object not there.
MISS STAYS, TO-sailboat failing to change tack, page 99.
MITCHBOARD-boom crutch on rail to support boom when sail is lowered.
MITER(Br. -mitre)-type of sail cut, pages 11, 13.
MIZZENMAST-after mast in 2 & 3 masted sailing vessels, 264-269, 284.
MIZZENSAIL -sail set from mizzenmast.
MIZZEN STAYSAIL-staysail set from mizzen masthead, pages 69, 124, 266.
MODERATE BREEZE-page 137.   MODERATE GALE-page 137.
MOLE-breakwater used for loading pier.
MONKEY FIST- knot worked in end of heaving line.
MONKEY BLOCK-small single block which swivels.
MONKEY GAFF-small gaff on after masthead to display colors underway.
MONSOON-wind periodically blowing one direction for several months, then the other direction for the rest of year.
MOONSAIL-rare small sail above skysail carried in light winds, page 287.
MOORING-permanent anchorage or dock space for a boat, pages 165-7, 175.
MOTHER CAREY'S CHICKEN-the stormy petrel.
MOTORBOAT ACT-regulations are given in CG-169, pages 232-235.
MOULD LOFT-large room for preparing full size boatbuilding templates.
MOULDS-patterns of which frames of a boat are worked out.
MOTOR SAILER-vessel combining features of sail & power boat, 270-271.
MOUSE-turn small stuff around hook to prevent jerking out of its hold.
MUFFLE-oars muffled by canvas around looms in the rowlocks.
MULE-questionable sail, page 14.
MUSHROOM-heavy permanent mooring anchor, pages 159, 167.

n NAUTICAL-pertaining to ships, navigation or seamen.
NAVEL PIPE-pipe thru which anchor chain passes to chain locker(Br. term).
NAVIGABLE-sufficient water depth to permit passage of vessels.
NAVIGATION-skill of conducting vessel from port to port.
NEAPED-boat gone ashore at height of spring tide and following tides fail to float her. NEAP TIDE occurs between full & new moon, having a smaller range than a spring tide, page 215.
NEAR-close to wind.   NEPTUNE-mythical god of sea.
NESTING-stowing one boat inside of another, or mooring several together.
NETTING-rope net work   NIGGER HEAD-drum or winch head.
NIMBUS-storm clouds, page 204.
NIP- twist in line passing through fairlead;part of anchor line in chock.
G19

no NOCK -upper forward end of sail without a boom.
NO HIGHER-order for sailboat to point no higher into wind.
NORMAN-pin to prevent hawsers from slipping off a bollard.
NORTH RIVER SLOOP-page 275.   NOSE-cutwater of vessel.
NOTHING OFF-order for sailboat not to pay of further from the wind.
NOT UNDER CONTROL (or command)-disabled vessel out of control.
NUN BUOY-red navigation buoy tapered at top found on starboard side of a
channel when entering from seaward, page 247.
NUT-projections to secure anchor stock located on anchors shank.

O OAKUM-yarn strands of old rope used for caulking, etc.
OAR-wooden pole with blade on one end used for rowing.
OARLOCK-guide fitted to boat acting as pivot for oars.
OFF AND ON-stand toward land & off again on different tacks.
OFFING-to seaward but a safe distance from shore.
OFFSHORE WIND-wind blowing from the shore, page 211.
OFFSETS-naval architect measurements used to lay out boats lines, page 254.
OFF the WIND-sailing downwind in fore and after, page 99;all courses but the
beam reach and closehauled for a square rigger.
OIL BAG-oil filled bag container used to calm rough seas, page 157, 163.
OILSKINS-waterproof clothing.
OLD FASHIONED ANCHOR-similar to yachtsman, with permanent stock, 159.
OLD MAN-the captain.   ON-wind blowing on the lee shore.
ON A WIND-close hauled, page 99.   ON THE BEAM-abeam, 82-3, 99.
ON THE BOW-object bearing from forward to abeam, page 82.
ON THE QUARTER-object bearing between beam and stern.
ON THE WIND (on a wind)-racing sailors term for closehauled.
ONE DESIGN-sailboats built to same specifications. See page 2.
OPEN-unprotected anchorage, away from shelter, a boat without decking.
OPEN HAWSE-riding to two anchors without swivel or crossing each other.
OPEN UP-boat leaking as seams start to open up, or planks shrink.
ORLOP DECK-lower partial deck on old sailing vessels, on or above the
protective deck and below the berth deck.
OUTBOARD-beyond a vessels side;portable propulsion unit-page 181.
OUT FOOT-one vessel sailing faster than another.
OUTHAUL-line use to haul OUT the clew, pages 7,23- 83, 89.
OUTLYING-objects at a distance from shore.
OUT OF TRIM-improperly ballasted, page 115.
OUT POINT-sail closer to wind than another sailboat. page 98.
OUT RIGGER-spar spreading standing or running rigging;spar extending from
side of canoe to prevent upset, pages 17, 49, 81.
OUTSAIL-sailboat that can sail faster and outpoint another.
OVER ALL (L. O. A.)-extreme fore & aft vessel measurement, page 254.
OVERBOARD-over the side,   OVERCAST-cloud covered sky.
OVERFALL-tide rip, shoal, seas breaking due to currents over a shallow area.
OVERHAND KNOT and LOOP-page 184.
OVERHANG-part of vessel extending beyond waterline at bow & stern, page 152.
OVERHATTED-sailing vessel which is oversparred.
OVERHAUL, TO-gain on another boat;slacken rope;examine rigging & make
ready;lengthen fall by separating blocks of a tackle.
OVERLAP-in racing a sailboat within 2 overall lengths of boat to windward.
OVER RIGGED-heavier sailing gear than necessary.
OVER SPARRED-vessel with heavier spars than necessary.
OVERTAKEN-sailboat being overtaken by another, pages 233, 235.
OWNERS FLAG-private signal carrying boatowners own design, page 253.

●

PACKET-mail boat with a regular schedule.
PAD-metal eye permanently secured to deck or bulkhead.
PAINTER-short piece of rope secured to bow of boat, pages 95.167.
PALM-leather fitting over hand to thust needle through sailcloth.
the flat part of an anchors fluke or blade on old fashioned anchors.
PARA-ANCHOR-parachute surface anchor for deep water, page 155-6,161.
PARACHUTE SPINNAKER- pages 124-5.
PARBUCKLE-raising cylindrical object upwards or over side by bight of two ropes, hauling in on one rope while making the other fast.
PARCEL, TO-wrap canvas strips tightly around a rope with its lay.
PARREL- rollers to slide gaff jaws up & down a mast.
PART-to break;hauling, standing or running part of a rope.
PARTNERS-framework where mast goes thru the deck, pages 23,28,29, 32,41,73.
PASS, TO-take securing turns with a lashing or rope.
PASSAGE SAILS & PASSAGE WINDS-downwind sails used to follow the steady trade wind routes of square riggers, page 131.
PASS A LINE-reeve & secure a line.   PASS A STOPPER-reeve & secure stopper.
PATENT ANCHOR-originally Navy anchor or stockless, term now obsolete.
PATENT LOG-distance recording device on vessel, see CHIP LOG.
PATENT BLOCK or SHEAVE-sheave with roller bearings.
PAUNCH MAT-thick mat often placed at slings of a yard.
PAWLS-short iron bars to prevent capstan barrel from turning backwards.
PAY, TO-to fill a boats seams after it has been caulked.
PAY OFF-turn bow of sailboat away from the wind.
PAY OUT-to slacken out on a cable, rope, or line.
PAZAREE-line used for guying clews out when running before wind. Line is attached to clew of fores'l, rove thru block on a swinging boom(also passaree).
PEA-point of hook or anchor.
PEA COAT-sailors dark blue winter jacket.
PEAK-upper after corner of a gaff sail-pages 5.148.
PEAK HALYARD-hoists peak of gaff sail, pages 5,70, 148.
PELORUS-sighting vane over compass card to take bearings and azimuths.
PENDANT-wire or rope attachment between parts for mooring, jib luff, etc.
PENGUIN-sailboat class, page 28.
PENNANT-long narrow three cornered flag, page 253; bunting streamer for commission, homeward bound, etc.;often substituted for pendant, page 63.
PENNANT, REEF-line to secure clew earing of reefed sail to boom, page 149.
PERMANENT BACKSTAY-one that clears boom, 35,37,43,51-3,63,67,75,79, 81,83.
PIER-HEADED LEAP-wild jump deserter makes as ship approaches the dock.
PIG-cast piece of metal ballast.
PILE-spar projecting above water with lower end driven firmly into bottom.
FENDER PILES are those at the corner of a dock.
PILLOW-block supporting inner end of a bowsprit.
PILOT BOAT-stationed at harbor entrance carrying pilots that are transferred to large vessels coming into a harbor.
PILOT'S LUFF-making a weather mark by pinching a boat.
PILOT RULES-see CG-169, page 233.
PIN-axle of sheave in block;short wood or iron rod for belaying ropes.
PINCH(pinch her)-pointing too high to windward, page 104.
PINK STERN-sailboat with high, narrow, pointed stern, page 275.
PINRAIL-railing with holes for belaying pins, page 73.
PINNACE-loosely, a boat or vessel that can be sailed or rowed.
PINTLE-metal pin used as swinging support for rudder, sample pg. 31.
PITCH-fore & aft plunging & rising of vessel, 152, 270−271 ;pine tree product used to fill seams of a wooden vessel.
PITCH POLE- boat or catamaran turning end over end(cartwheeling).
PIVOTING POINT-point in a vessel about which it turns, CLR, pg. 133.

pl PLAIN SAIL-regular working sails, page 9.

PLAT-braiding, used only with small stuff.

PLATFORM DECK-partial deck below lowest complete deck.

PLIMSOLL MARK-marking of allowed loading depths on merchant ship side.

PLOW-English anchor resembling a plow, page 159.

PLUG-drain plug in a boat.

POINT-11 1/4° or 1/32 part of circumference;work end of rope with knittles.

POINTING-sailing closehauled. One sailboat may point higher than another.

POINTS, CARDINAL-North, South, East, West.

POINTS, REEF-cords going thru reinforcements on sails foot while it is being reefed, pages 5, 7, 149.

POLE MAST-one piece mast;highest mast on ship such as sky-sail pole.

POOP-partial deck aft above main deck. If wheel is on main deck, it is the deck portion aft of the helmsman, page 284. A sailboat is POOPED when running before the wind, a heavy sea breaks aboard over stern;a worn out feeling.

POPPETS-timbers on fore & aft part of bilgeways when launching.

PORCUPINE-fraying of wire rope.

PORT, PORTHOLE-opening on vessels side, page 72.

PORT CAPTAIN-official in charge of harbor berthing, activities, etc.

PORT (also see larboard)-left side of boat when looking forward, pages 82, 83.

PORT TACK-wind coming over port bow, beam, or stern, pages 98, 101, 111, 233.

PORTOISE-gunwale of a boat.

PORTUGUESE MAN OF WAR-jellyfish with vertical sail like fin.

POUNDING-flat hull surface rising, falling & hitting the waters surface hard.

PRAM-rectangular dinghy. . Optimist Dink, pg. 23, Sabot, 29.

PRATIQUE-limited quarantine;permit stating vessel free of contagious diseases.

PRAYER BOOK-small flat holystone.

PREFORMED ROPE-wire rope resisting being unlaid.

PRESS OF SAIL-all sail a vessel can carry.

PREVENTER-line running forward from boom to prevent a jibe, pages 120-3.

PRICKER-small marlinspike.

PRIDE OF THE MORNING-early morning mist before a lovely day.

PRIVILEGED VESSEL-it has right-of-way & must maintain course, 232-235.

PROFILE-side view silhouette of a vessel.

PROLONGED BLAST-one of 4 to 6 seconds duration, page 235.

PROW-part of bow above water.

PUCKER STRING (leach line)-line used to tighten leach of a sail.

PUDDEN (puddin)-fender to protect vessels side.

PUDDENING-oakum, matting, or yarns used to prevent chafing.

PUNT-rectangular flat bottom boat or dinghy.

PURCHASE-rope & block arrangements to increase hauling power.

PUT TO SEA-to leave port.

•

q QUADRANT-navigation instrument;metal fitting on rudder to secure steering ropes.

QUADRILATERAL SPINNAKER-obscure European spinnaker, see shadow.

QUANT-(Br.)-long punting pole.

QUARANTINE-period of time before a ship is cleared by port doctor as having no evidence of contagious diseases.

QUARANTINE BUOY-yellow buoy quarantine anchorage, page 248.

QUARTER-vessels side aft of beam & forward of stern, pages 83, 98.

QUARTER DECK-part of upper deck abaft mainmast, officers territory, 285.

QUARTER MASTER-petty officer attending to helm, binnacle, signals, etc.

QUARTERING SEA-wind & waves on a ships quarter, page 99.

QUAY-wharf used to discharge cargo.

QUICK WORK-part of ship's side above gunwales and decks.

QUILTING-woven rope covering on outside of container.

QUOIN-wood wedge which the breach of a gun rests on.

•

RABBET-groove cut in keel, sternpost, stem, etc., for end or edge of plank, pg. 257.
RACE-water disturbed due to confusing currents.
RACK-seizing two ropes together with cross turns of spun yarn.
RACK BLOCK-set of blocks for fairlead made from single piece of wood.
RAFFEE-triangular sail set above square sail, page 131.
RAIL-top of bulwarks on edge of a deck, page 73.
RAISE-bringing an object on the horizon into view.
RAKE-inclination of mast from the vertical, pages 26-7, 33-39, 114-121.
RANGE-difference between fall & rise of tide, page 215; two objects in line used as aid to steer a course.
RANGE ALONGSIDE-come close abeam of another boat.
RANGE LIGHTS-vertical white lights indicating vessels direction, page 238.
RANGE OF CABLE-lay qunatity of cable on deck ready to use.
RAPT FULL-all sails full.   RATER-Naval term, pages 288, 289.
RATLINE-horizontal rope ladders up the shrouds to go aloft, pages 75, 285.
RAT TAIL-bolt rope worked down to a small point,
RATTLING DOWN-rigging ratlines.
RAZEE-vessel of war with one deck cut down.
REACH-all courses between running free and close hauled, page 99.
REACHING JIB-page 13.
READY ABOUT-preparatory order to coming about, page 109.
REEF-to shorten sail, pages 133, 146-149.
REEF BAND-reenforcing band on sail with reef points & earrings, 5, 287.
REEF, SPANISH-tie a knot in the material of a headsail.
REEF CRINGLE (reef earing)-metal eye in sail for reefing, page 149.
REEF POINTS-short lengths of rope through reefband to secure foot of sail when it is reefed, pages 5, 7, 149.
REEF TACKLE-tackle used to haul out foot of sail; in a square sail, to haul in the middle of each leach for reefing, page 70.
REEVE, TO-to pass end of rope thru a lead, hole, or block.
REGISTRY-ships certificate showing nationality and ownership.
RELIEVING TACKLE-emergency tackle.
RENDER-rope slides or runs freely through a block.
RHUMB LINE-a straight line is the shortest distance between two points.
RIB-frame of vessel, pages 72-73.   RIDE-to lie at anchor. pg. 288.
RIDE OUT-weather a storm safely underway or at anchor.
RIDERS-upper layer of barrels stowed in a hold.
RIDING CHOCKS-deck chock thru which anchor line rides.
RIDING DOWN the RIGGING-sliding down rigging in a boatswains chair.
RIDING LIGHT-white anchor light displayed in fore part of anchored vessel.
RIG-arrangement of a boats sails, masts, and rigging.
RIGGING-standing rigging is permanent including shrouds and stays, while running rigging consists of halyards, braces and sheets which raise, trim and control the sails, page 67.
RIGHT-sailboat returning to upright position after heeling.
RIGHT-HANDED-rope is usually twisted from right to left, page 184.
RIGHT THE HELM-put it amidships.
RING-ring at upper end of anchor to which cable is bent, page 159.
RINGBOLT-eyebolt used for leading running rigging.
RINGBUOY-circular preserver.
RINGTAIL-small sail set abaft spanker in light winds, see page 44.
RIP, TIDE-water disturbance caused by confliciting currents or winds.
RISING (riser)-fore & aft stringers to support thwarts on a small boat.
RISING GLASS-rising barometer.
ROACH-outward upward curve of leach, pages 5, 7.
ROADSTEAD (road)-open anchorage at a distance from shore.
ROCKER-upward curve of boats bottom, see 'TrailerBoating Illustrated'.

ro RODE-small boats anchor line.
ROGUE'S YARN-colored yarn in center of rope for identification.
ROLL-side to side motion of a vessel, see pg. 162.
ROLL CLOUD-pages 205-207.
ROLLER REEFING-sail is rolled around revolving boom for reefing, 149.
ROLLING TACKLE-used to steady square rigger yards in heavy seas.
ROPE- strands of fiber or wire braided or twisted together, pages 184, 185.
Ropes used in operation of a sailboat became lines. Ropes which remained
ropes on square riggers were;foot ropes, yard ropes, bell ropes, bucket ropes,
bolt ropes, back ropes, top ropes & man ropes.
ROUND TREE-unfinished spar.   ROUND BOTTOM-page 16.
ROUND DOWN-overhauling tackle so lower block will come down.
ROUND IN-haul in.   ROUNDLY-quickly, steadily.
ROUNDS-Jacob's ladder rungs.
ROUND TO(round up)-change course heading from run to reach, pg. 108.
ROUND TURN- a full turn around any object.
ROUSE IN-to haul in by manpower.
ROWLOCK (oarlock)-pivoting point on boats side for oars.
BOWSER CHOCK-chock which is closed.
ROYAL-sail above topgallant in a square rigger, pages 285-287.
ROYAL YARD-yard to which the royal sail is set, pages 285-287.
RUBBING STRAKE-additional planking outside & below gunwale to reduce
damage of chafe to a vessels side.
RUDDER-flat plate hinged to stern used to steer a vessel,pages 5-7, 23-53.
RUFFLE-drum roll used when rendering honors.
RULES OF THE ROAD-found in CG-169, pages 232- 241.
RUN-after underwater narrowing part of a vessel.
RUNNING(to run)-sailing before the wind, pages 99, 105, 111, 120-123, 131.
RUN AWAY-desert;seize a line and to haul it on the run.
RUN DOWN-sail along a coast;overtake & collide with another vessel;run
down the trades;sail north or south at a given parallel of latitude.
RUNG HEADS-upper ends of floor timbers.
RUNNER-purchase used for tightening a backstay, pages 43,70-71, 109.
RUNNING BACKSTAYS-a temporary backstay set up to windward as a boat
comes about, and the leeward one slacked off, pages 43, 70, 71, 109.
RUNNING BY THE LEE-sailing with wind over same quarter as boom, pg.123.
RUNNING LARGE-page 99.
RUNNING LIGHTS-carried by vessels underway from dusk to dawn, 236-239.
RUNNING RIGGING-see rigging;used to raise, set, trim sails, pg. 67.
RUN OUT-to send out such as to run out a towing hawser.

S SADDLES-wood brackets secured to lower part of mast for boom to rest on.
SAG-drift to leeward;waist of ship settling below level of bow & stern.
SAIL BAG-pages 86-96.   SAIL COVER-protects furled sails.
SAILING FREE (running)-sailing with the wind aft, page 98.
SAIL HO! cry used when a sail was sighted at sea.
SAILING THWART-midship plank to support mast on boat that can be rowed.
SAILING TRIM-most efficient trim of sails, pages 104-105, 114-135.
SAILS-flexible vertical airfoils using wind pressure to propel a sailboat.
SALTINGS (marshes)-flat land flooded at high tide.
SALVAGE-pay for saving cargo or ship from danger.
SAMPSON POST(samson post)-strong post in bow or stern to secure dock
lines, anchor lines, or tow lines, pgs. 63 and 73, also called mooring bitt.
SAND BAGGERS-see page 44.
SAVE ALL(catch all) small sail set under foot of lower sails.
SCALE-to climb up;rust formation on metal plating.
SCANDALIZING-dropping peak halyard on a gaff rigger, page 148.

SCANTLINGS-standardized part dimensions used in ship building.
SCARF (scarphing)-join timber ends by tapering and overlapping them.
SCEND-boat lifting to a swell or seaway.
SCHOOL-large body of fish.
SCHOONER-see pages 5, 268, 269.   SCHOONER BOW-fiddle or clipper bow.
SCOPE-length of mooring or anchor line let out, page 161.
SCORF-groove in dead eye or block to take wire or rope strap.
SCOTCHMAN-grommet at luff of tops'l, at end of mitre gore for purchase;to
secure pole or haul leading edge of sail towards mast and down, page 70.
SCOW-rectangular sailboat hull, pg 45;barge for hauling sand, gravel, refuse,etc.
SCRAPER-small hand tool used for scraping sides, decks, masts, etc.
SCREEN-sidelight boards limiting horizontal arc of red & green sidelights,236-9.
SCREENED LIGHT-box limiting arc of light in horizontal arc, pages 236-239.
SCREW STOPPER-chain stopper fitted with turnbuckle.
SCROWL-timber substitute for a figurehead.
SCUD-low lying mist clouds usually moving quite fast.
SCUDDING-driving before a gale with steadying sails or no sails.
SCULL-short oar;to propel small boat with single oar by working it from side
to side over the stern, action resembles movement of a fishes tail.
SCULLERY-compartment used for stowing and washing dishes.
SCUPPERS-overboard drainholes on deck, page 69, 72.
SCUPPER LIP-protrusion to prevent water coming aboard thru scuppers.
SCUTTLE-deliberately sink a vessel;small hatch or trunk for air & light.
SCUTTLE BUTT-crews fresh water drinking cask;crew meeting place also.
SEA-waves or swells.
SEA ANCHOR—anchor getting purchase from waters surface.STORM ANCHORS
pg.157, only become effective in strong winds.The PARA-ANCHOR pgs. 155, 156,
161, gives maximum purchase in light and strong winds.
SEA BOAT-seaworthy vessel with ability to weather storms, page 154.
SEA BREEZE-cooling breeze blowing from large body of water, page 211.
SEA BUOY(farewell buoy)-last large buoy of channel to seaward.
SEA CHEST-intake between sea valve & ships side; sailors trunk.
SEACOCK-a drain;vessel may be flooded if seacocks are opened, page 154.
SEA DOG-an old seasoned sailor.
SEA GOING-a vessel capable of going to sea.
SEA KINDLY-vessel riding comfortably in rough weather, page 152.
SEA LADDER-portable ladder to climb up or down side of a ship.
SEA LAWYER-belligerant seaman enjoying arguments against authority.
SEAM-space between planks;stitching holding two cloths together.
SEA ROOM-enough distance from land permitting unrestricted maneuvers.
SEAWAY-area with rough or moderate sea running.
SEAWORTHY-vessel able to meet usual sea conditions, page 154.
SECOND DECK-first complete deck below main deck.
SECTION-vessel shape at right angle to keel, pages 254-255.
SECURE-to make fast.
SECURE FOR SEA-order for extra lashings on all movable objects.
SEIZE-binding together ropes with small stuff.
SEIZINGS-small stuff for binding.   SELVAGE-yarn marled together.
SENNIT (sinnit)-braided breeze yarn.   SENTINEL (kellet)-page 161.
SERVE (serving)-bindings against rope lay to prevent chafing.
SERVING BOARD-small flat board with handle used for serving small rope.
SERVING MALLET-mallet having groove cut lengthwise in head to serve rope.
SET-direction of tide, current, or leeway course of a sailboat.
SET A COURSE-to steer.
SET FLYING-sail filling before it is in place, see spinnaker, page 126, 127.
SET TAUT-preparatory order to heave in, to take in slack.
SETTLE-ship slowly sinking, lower a sail slowly.
G25

REVISED EDITION

ROYCE'S *TrailerBoating Illustrated*

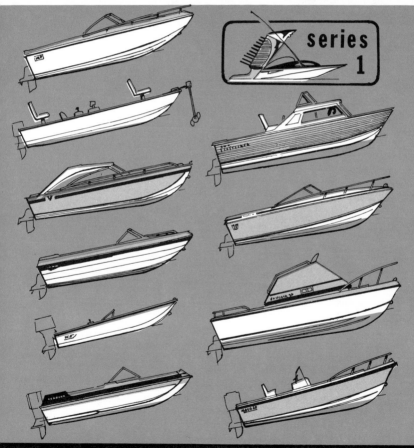

series 1

planing hulls · trailers · seamanship

ROYCE'S
SAILING ILLUSTRATED

Follow the present and future trends of sailing with the "Sailor's Bible" first published in 1956 now celebrating its 26th year in print!

This book started with wooden hulls, canvas sails, and manila rope. The new 8th revised edition includes every new development in the world of sail along with the new Unified Rules of the Road and lighting requirements.

Chances are you will find at least one well thumbed copy handy when sailors gather at an inland yacht club, a clambake, or when deep water sailors meet in a foreign port to splice the main brace while trying to justify their "almost true" sea stories.

26 YEARS
IN PRINT

352 pages
Several hundred illustrations
$8.95

- *MARINER'S CATALOG (Int'l Marine Pub. Co.)* — *"our favorite how-to-sail manual: Royce understands beginners. He knows what they are up against and makes every effort — without an ounce of patronization — to make things clear, simple, and concise."*

- *WEBB CHILES* — *author of "Storm Passage" sailed around the world in 279 days . . . "This book is by far the best of its kind" . . .*

- *NEXT WHOLE EARTH CATALOG* — *" . . . Probably Royce has taught more people to sail than any other book, and its jam-packed paperback fit-in-the-hand format, just begging to be taken and kept aboard, shows why. It has a quick reference thumb index that works, and the emphasis is on showing the procedures rather than talking about them. Good keepaboard fare."*

- *LATITUDE 38* — *"There's one book that's awfully good if sailing is completely new to you, and that would be Patrick Royce's SAILING ILLUSTRATED . . . It's got the basics of everything, presented in a very entertaining fashion. We recommend it highly."*

- *SAILING ILLUSTRATED has had worldwide acceptance with orders coming direct from the North Pole, South Pole, and Timbuktu (Russia excepted). Many sailors buy three copies, one for their boat, the second for the home library, and a third for a special friend.*

WHAT THE EXPERTS SAY ABOUT
THE TRAILERBOATING CLASSIC...

TRAILERBOATING ILLUSTRATED

SEA — *"Seldom is a boating book offered in this price range which contains so much information about so many things . . . The author draws from many years of practical experience and does not hesitate to recommend or turn thumbs down on equipment or seamanship techniques. A book that should be in every boating enthusiast's library."* Dix Brow.

TRAILER BOATS — *"If you study this book before buying a boat, it may save you a lot of money. If you have a new boat read every page before launch time for that memorable (or catastrophic) event."* Norm Phillips.

CASTOFF — *"The smaller the boat and higher its performance, the more fun it is when things are going right. When it is out of tune, things start to go wrong very fast. By exposure to these ideas we hope to keep the reader out of trouble."*

ARIZONA WATERWAYS — *"The book covers about just everything a person needs to know to efficiently operate and enjoy a trailerable powerboat . . . The book is written in easy to understand language and illustrated with hundreds of illustrations . . . it's convenient to thumb through and take aboard your boat."*
Nancy Wolff.

YACHTING NEWS — *"This book has distilled the basics of boating, and sifted them into their sequence so you can grasp a good foundation of boats, trailers, props, rope handling, and seamanship, by an author/pioneer who helped this diverse and challenging boating field grow from a struggling dream to reality."*

"If your boat is new, five, ten or twenty years old, you will find this book applicable since it sticks to the hard to find basics without getting lost in endless details."

FIELD & STREAM — *"I first saw a copy of Patrick Royce's "TrailerBoating Illustrated" in 1962 about two years after it had been published. I've found it a constant source of reference and intriguing reading ever since. I'm pleased to report current publication of a revised edition.*

"This is a unique 191 page handbook, lavishly illustrated with line sketches. Royce is a commercial artist as well as a lifelong boater, and a man of extraordinary humor that surfaces in his sketches and words.

"Unlike most trailerboating manuals, Royce's handbook covers survival at sea". . . . F.M. Paulson

TRAILERBOATING ILLUSTRATED. Revised edition. 6"x9". Paperback.
192 pages/$8.95

introduction

displacement
hull

planing
hull

planing
problems

propellers

rope/
anchors

trailers

weather
buoyage

seamanship

right-of-way

accident
prevention

survival
swimming

fire
fighting

Courageous

outboard motor
overboard

Order Form

Please rush copies as noted below:
How Many?

• 1983 PACIFIC BOATING ALMANACS
* _____ Southern California, Arizona, Baja edition / 8.95
* _____ Northern California & Nevada edition / 8.95
* _____ Pacific Northwest edition / 8.95

• ROYCE PUBLICATIONS
* _____ Sailing Illustrated / 8.95
  _____ Trailerboating Illustrated-1: Planing Hulls-
        Trailers-Seamanship / 8.95

• CLYMER BOATING MAINTENANCE HANDBOOKS
  _____ Sailboat Maintenance / 9.95
  _____ Powerboat Maintenance / 9.95
  _____ British Seagull Outboards / 8.95
  _____ Chrysler Outboards (3.5 to 20 HP) / 8.95
  _____ Chrysler Outboards (25 to 140 HP) / 8.95
  _____ Evinrude Outboards (1.5 to 35 HP) / 8.95
  _____ Evinrude Outboards (40 to 140 HP) / 8.95
  _____ Johnson Outboards (1.5 to 35 HP) / 8.95
  _____ Johnson Outboards (40 to 140 HP) / 8.95
  _____ Mercury Outboards (4 to 40 HP) / 8.95
  _____ Mercury Outboards (50 to 200 HP) / 8.95
  _____ Stern Drive Service / 9.95

• OTHER SELECT MARINE BOOKS
  _____ Complete Book of Inflatable Boats / 7.95
  _____ Cruising Guide to Channel Islands / 16.95
* _____ Cruising Ports: Calif. to Florida / 17.95
* _____ Dix Brow's Sea of Cortez Guide / 19.95
  _____ Exploring the Coast by Boat - B.C. & Wash. / 9.95
  _____ Exploring the Seashore - B.C., Wash. & Oregon / 11.95
* _____ Marine Animals of Baja Calif. / 17.95
  _____ Pac. Coast Inshore Fishes / 12.95
  _____ Landfalls of Paradise - Guide to Pac. Islands / 29.95
  _____ Sail Before Sunset / 12.95
  _____ 141 Dives in Protected Waters of Wash. & B.C. / 11.95
  _____ Pac. Coast Nudibranchs / 14.95
  _____ Pac. Coast Subtidal Marine Invertebrates / 12.95
  _____ VHF Radio Procedures Guide / 3.95

• TIDAL CURRENT CHARTS
  _____ Puget Sound, Southern Part / 6.95
  _____ Puget Sound, Northern Part / 6.95
  _____ San Francisco Bay / 6.95   *New

Send order to your neighborhood bookstore, marine store, or
Western Marine Enterprises, Inc., Box Q, Ventura, CA 93002

☐ Rush the books checked above.
  Check or money order is enclosed.

_____ Sub total

_____ California Residents add 6% sales tax

  $1.25 _____ Shipping charge per order

_____ TOTAL ENCLOSED
Ship to: (Name and complete address)

_____

_____

_____ Zip _____

• **Money Back Guarantee**
If not completely satisfied, return your order within 10 days for a full refund.

Note: Prices listed here are in effect June 1983 and are subject to change without notice. In Canada, order from Gordon Soules, 525-355 Burrard St., Vancouver, B.C. V6C 2G8.
Prices in Canada are generally higher than U.S. prices.

se SET the COURSE-give helmsman course to be steered.

SET the WATCH-dividing ships crew into watches.

SETTEE-long, sharp bowed lateen rigged sailing ship.

SET UP, TO-to tighten rigging or to flatten the sails.

SEXTANT-navigation instrument that determines altitude of sun and stars.

SHACKLE-shaped metal fitting with pin or bolt; 15 fathoms of chain.

SHADOW-obsolete quadrilateral spinnaker with short gaff.

SHAKE-sails shake when boat is pointing too high or sail is luffing, page 99.

SHAKEDOWN CRUISE-first cruise of newly commissioned vessel.

SHAKE OUT-let out a reef;hoist the sails.

SHAKINGS-rope,waste canvas,small stuff.   SHANK-arm of anchor,page 158.

SHANK PAINTER-line securing fluke of anchor to billboard.

SHAPE-cone or ball used in distance signals.

SHAPE a COURSE-plot proper course to reach specific port or point.

SHARK'S MOUTH-opening thru awning around a mast.

SHARPIE-page 273.   SHARPSHOOTER-page 275.

SHARP UP-yards braced as near fore and aft as possible.

SHEARS-two or more spars raised at angles & lashed together for hoisting or lowering heavy objects.

SHEAR HULK-old vessel used to put in or take out spars on other sailing vessels.

SHEATHING (sheathed)-copper plates covering ships bottoms.

SHEAVE-wheel of a block.

SHEEPSHANK-bend or hitch temporarily used to shorten a rope.

SHEER-sudden course change; side view of boat, page 8; sheer plan, page 254.

SHEER ABOUT-boat that is restless on mooring or when anchored.

SHEER OFF-bear away.   SHEER PLAN-side view, page 254.

SHEERPOLE-rod across foot of shrouds for spreader to prevent untwisting.

SHEER STRAKE-topmost plank in ships side, page 73.

SHEER, TO-to move across.

SHEET-trimming line secured to sails boom or clew, pages 5-95.

SHEET ANCHOR-loosely used term for various kinds of anchors.

SHEET BEND-page 189.   SHELL-outer casing of a block.

SHIFT-change sails clothes, etc.

SHIFTING BACKSTAY-another term for running backstay, page 70-71, 109.

SHIP-(trad.) sailing vessel square rigged on 3 or more masts,page 282. Today it usually refers to a power driven vessel over 75' long, that is capable of taking passengers and/or cargo for long seagoing voyages.

SHIP, TO-a boat is shipping water when water comes aboard.

SHIPPING ARTICLES-agreement between Navy & recruit, or ships officers and crew with agents or owners.

SHIPSHAPE-everything in place.

SHIPS PAPERS-documents carried on ship required by various authorities.

SHIVER (shake)-sail airfoil broken by pointing too high into wind, pages 99, 104.

SHOAL-shallow.

SHOD-anchor won't bite as it is caked with mud or clay.

SHOE-false keel to give vessel more draft;lower rudder support, see skeg, 72.

SHOOT-momentum or distance a sailboat will keep going when pointing head to wind, for going through a crowded mooring area, page 165.

SHORE (shore up)-to prop up or buttress an object.

SHORT BOARD-short tack;LONG BOARD is a long tack, page 101.

SHORT HANDED-not enough crew members.

SHORTEN-reducing sail area by reefing or dropping sail, page 146-149.

SHORT STAY-scope of anchor line almost vertical.

SHOT-15 fathoms of chain.

SHOULDER of MUTTON-quad. sail with short gaff or club, often boomless, pg. 3.

SHOVE OFF-push bow of boat away from dock while getting underway.

SHOW A LEG-make haste.

SHROUD LAID-four strand right handed rope.
SHROUDS-a mast is secured fore and aft by stays, and shrouds going to either side, also called sidestays, pages 28, 31-83.
SIDE BOYS-crew manning side of ship in honor of visiting officers or officials.
SIDE LIGHTS-red & green running lights, see pages 236-239.
SIGHT the ANCHOR-raise anchor to see if it is clear, and let it go again.
SILL-horizontal timbers between frames to form and secure openings.
SILT-sediment, mud.   SINGLE STICKER-one masted vessel.
SING OUT-call out.   SISTER SHIPS-built to same design.
SKEG-after keel timbers or extension supporting a rudder, pages 28, 29, 37, 72.
SKIFF-small light pulling boat.
SKIN-outer surface of furled sail;outer planking of a vessel.
SKIPJACK-page 273.   SKIPPER-the captain.
SKYSAIL (skysail yard)-next above royal, page 287.
SKY SCRAPER-triangular skysail.   SKY PILOT-chaplain.
SKYLIGHT-hatch covering admitting air and light.
SLABLINE-small line used to haul up foot of course, page 287.
SLACK-ease off, part of sail or rope that hangs limp.
SLACK CLOTHS-baggy sail.
SLACK IN STAYS-sailboat that has long keel changes tack slowly.
SLACK WATER-period of tide change when there is no current.
SLANT OF WIND-favorable wind change.
SLEEPER-partially submerged log;knees connecting aft timbers to transom.
SLEW (slough) - swampy river inlet area where fresh & salt water mingle.
SLICK-smooth water on lee side of drifting vessel; an oil slick, page 157.
SLIDING GUNTHER-small sailboat with sliding topmast or vertical gaff.
Purpose is to permit all spars capable of being stowed in dinghy, page 271.
SLING-a tackle to hoist or lower.
SLINGS-ropes securing center of yard to mast.
SLIP-dock or pole mooring area.   SLIPPERY HITCH-page 191.
SLIP THE MOORING-cast off from the mooring, page 95.
SLOOP-one masted sailboat. Traditional term now obsolete required sailboat to have a bowsprit. SLOOP vs CUTTER difference was considerable during last century, pages 262-3.
SLOOP OF WAR-vessel mounting 18-32 guns, no particular rig, page 289.
SLUSH-grease used for making a mast slippery.
SMACK-small sloop or cutter rigged fishing boat.
SMALL STUFF-smallest rope, marline, or yarn.
SMART-seamanlike, snappy, an efficient ship.
SMITING LINE-used to break light sail sent up in stops.
SNAKE-wrapping rope with small stuff, similar to worming.
SNIED-crooked.   SNIPE-page 33.
SNORTER (snotter)-rope sending down royal & topgallant yards, etc.
SNUB-check a rope suddenly.
SNUG DOWN-reduce sail, close hatches, secure loose objects before a blow.
SNUGGED DOWN-under small but comfortable sail area.
SNY-small toggle on a flag.
SNYING-curved plank used to work in vessels bow.
SO-order to stop hauling as object is now in correct position.
SOFT EYE-eye at end of rope that does not contain a metal thimble.
SOLDIERS WIND-fair wind.
SOLE-(Br.) cabin or saloon floor;timber extension on bottom of rudder.
SOUND-measuring depth of water.   SOUNDINGS-charted depths.
SOU'WESTER-oilskin hat having a broad rear brim.
SPAN-rope or chain with both ends made fast to same object so purchase can be hooked into its bight for lifting.
SPANKER-aft mast & sail of full rigged ship or bark, pages 283-287.

sp SPANKING BREEZE-good wind coming over stern or quarter.
SPAR-general term for yards, booms, gaffs, masts, etc.
SPAR BUOY-pole spar for piloting used in buoyage system, page 249.
SPEAK-communicating with vessel in sight. SPECTACLE-page 287.
SPELL-interval or period of time given to any job.
SPELL, TO-to relieve another.
SPENCER-small boomless sail set from gaff and hoisted from a small 'spencer' mast that is abaft the fore and main masts.
SPIDER HOOP (or band)-metal band around mast to contain belaying pins.
SPILE-pile.   SPILL-to empty wind out of sail.
SPILLING LINE-used in bad weather to spill wind out of a sail.
SPINNAKER-large triangular racing sail fitted to mast & boom, 124-130.
SPITFIRE JIB-small heavy weather jib, page 14. The spinnaker staysail or ballooner has been recently nicknamed spitfire, pages 68, 69.
SPLICE-weaving strands of two ropes together-pages 195-201.
SPLICE THE MAIN BRACE-have a drink.
SPLINE-thin wooden strip fitted to seam instead of stopping.
SPOKE-handle of a steering wheel.
SPONSOR-person christening a ship when it is launched.
SPOON DRIFT-spray swept from top of wave in bad weather covering area.
SPRAY-particles of water blown from top of waves, page 137.
SPREADER-horizontal strut used to support the mast to spread shrouds, 7, 68.
SPRING-pivot line used for docking, undocking, or preventing boat from moving ahead or astern while at dock, pages 174, 175.
SPRING STAY-horizontal stay between lower mastheads.
SPRING TIDE-occurs at maximum range between new & full moon, that takes place twice monthly instead of during the spring, page 215.
SPRIT (sprit sail)-quadrilateral sail with peak extended by spar called sprit that goes from peak to tack, page 271, later version. The original had the sprits'l yard with quadilateral square sail under bowsprit shown on page 289, common from Columbus' Santa Maria'to the 1800's.
SPRUNG-mast, spar, or hull that is warped or strained.
SPUDS-vertical timbers used in holding a dredge in place.
SPUN YARN-rough stuff used for seizings, etc.
SPURLING LINE-wire or chain between telltail and tiller.
SPURS-half beams to support deck where full length beams cannot be used. Timbers bolted to vessels side above water fixed to bilgeways.
SPURSHORE-spar used to hold a vessel clear of a dock.
SPY GLASS-small hand telescope.
SQUALL-sudden violent gust of wind;a local storm, page 206-7.
SQUARE A YARD-bring it square with the braces.
SQUARED-yards squared by lifts on horizontal plane, and at right angles to the keel by braces.
SQUARESAIL-quad. sail set from yard on square riggers that is most efficient for sailing downwind or following trade winds around the world, 131, 282-289.
STAFF-a mast or pole used to hoist flags upon.
STABILITY-vessel steady, firm and stable.
STAYSAIL SCHOONER-page 269.   STAR-page 21, 42-3.
SQUARE MARK-running rigging marked to indicate correct setting.
STAGGER-overcanvassed vessel that does not ride well.
STANCHIONS-upright support posts-page 66-81.
STAND-period when tide is rising or falling that has intervals between, without apparent vertical motion.
STAND BY-preparatory order.   STANDING LUG-page 281.
STANDING OFF & ON-sail towards and away while waiting instead of anchoring.
STAND ON-maintain ones course and speed.
STANDING PART-part of line or fall made fast & not hauled upon. pg. 184.

STANDING RIGGING-permanently secured rigging, see page 67.
STARBOARD-right side of vessel looking forward, pages 82, 83.
STARBOARD TACK-sailing with wind over st'b'd bow, beam or stern, 98, 233.
START, TO-to slack off, to loosen.
STATION BILL-posted list with crews instructions.
STAUNCH-able, stiff, steady, seaworthy. STAVE IN-to crush in.
STAY-support for mast, pages 28, 31-83.
STAYS, IN- caught in irons, page 99.
STAYSAIL-fore & aft triangular sail set upon a stay, pgs. 13-15; schooner, 269.
STAY TACKLE-used to hoist cargo, made fast to stay.
STEADY-order to maintain present course.
STEADYING LINE-one used for steadying purposes.
STEERAGE-portion of vessel occupied by passengers paying lowest fare.
STEEVE-bowsprit's angle with the horizon.
STEM-forward vertical timber of keel supporting the bow planks, page 73.
STEM THE TIDE-sailing against current yet still making some headway.
STEP-block for stepping mast, pages 28, 32, 73.
STERN-after end of a boat or ship, page 82.
STERNBOARD-sailboat in irons going backwards.
STERN LIGHT-12 pt. white stern light on vessel, pages 236-239.
STERNPOST-after end of a vessel.
STERNSHEETS-part of open boat abaft rowers for passengers.
STEVEDORE-worker loading & unloading cargo.
STIFF-sailboat with minimum heel, opposite of crank.
STIRRUPS-rope supports for yard footropes. BOWLINE or FABRIC STIRRUP is
used as foot pivot to take person aboard boat, page 192.
STOCK-crosspiece on anchor, page 158. STOCKS-frame for building a ship.
STOOLS-short channels for the backstay deadeyes.
STOPPER-short stout rope used for various purposes.
STOPPER KNOT-terminal knot on rope to stop it running thru block, etc.
STOPS-weak yarns to temporarily secure spinnaker or balloon jib, pg. 127.
STOPWATER-small wooden plug driven into hole bored across a joint, that
can hardly be caulked to prevent leakage, page 72 ;also called treenail.
STORM SAILS-small heavy weather sails pg. 15 ;steadying sails, 150, 271.
STORM WARNINGS -pages 136-139.
STOVE IN-broken in. STOW-to place.
STOWAWAY-person illegally aboard. STRAKE-a side plank, page 73.
STRAND-number of yarns woven together, page 184.
STRANDED-vessel driven ashore, 223. STRAP-binding around a block.
STRATOCUMULUS-page 205. STRATUS-flat cloud, page 205.
STREAM ANCHOR-medium sized anchor.
STREAM, TO- let out a sea anchor or log.
STRETCHER-oarsman footbrace. STRIKE-to lower.
STRINGER-fore & aft strip on inner side of timbers or frames, page 73.
STROP-rope or metal band.
STUDS-metal fittings across chain links to prevent kinking.
STUDDINGSAILS (stuns'ls)-sails extending beyond square sail yards, pg. 287.
SUN OVER THE FOREYARD-first drink time expression.
SUPERSTRUCTURE DECK-partial deck above f'c'sle, upper, main or poop deck
which does not extend full width of vessel.
SUPPORTERS-knee timbers under the catheads.
SURF-swell of a wave as it breaks as it goes into the shore.
SURGE-effect of large wave on boat; to slack suddenly.
SWAB-rope mop. SWALLOW-groove in block for sheave.
SWAMP-boat full of water in sinking condition.
SWAY (sway aloft)-to hoist aloft. SWEDISH JIB-original genoa jib, pg. 125.
SWEEP-long oars. SWELL-long easy waves not breaking.

SW SWIFT (swifter in)-bring stays or shrouds together by turns of rope.
SWIFTER-foremost shrouds;ropes confining capstan bars.
SWIG, TO (swig off)-hauling on rope & taking in slack.
SWING SHIP, TO-swinging ship thru all points of compass to record deviation.
SWING, TO-wind or tide changes anchored/moored vessels heading.
SWIVEL-two fitted links turning upon an axis between, rather than than kinking.
SYPHERING-overlapping plank edges for a bulkhead.

t TABERNACLE (Eng.)-housing that permits sailboat mast to be lowered and raised again after vessel has gone under a bridge, or for trailering,51-54,56-57.
TABLING-broad hem sewn around a sail, page 11.
TACK-sailing course,page 98;sails forward lower corner, pages 5, 7, 126-130.
TACK, CHANGE-change wind or boom to other side of boat, pages 109, 111.
TACKLE-combination of blocks to form a purchase.
TACKLINE-signal halyards;line to haul down tack of gaff topsail.
TAFFRAIL-railing around or across the stern, pg. 75.
TAFFRAIL LOG-device to determine vessels speed.
TAIL-short rope spliced to block so it can be secured to an object.
TAIL ON-pull on a rope.   TAKE IN-lower or stow a sail.
TAKE OFF-remove sail;decreasing tide velocity & range,changing to neap tide.
TAKE UP-tighten or shorten rigging;planks swelling & no longer leaking.
TANG-fitting on spar or mast to secure rigging to.
TAN, TO-treat organic material sails to prevent mildew.
TAR-sailor; preservative for standing rigging.
TARP (tarpaulin)-heavy canvas covering.   TAUNT-tall sparred vessel.
TAUT-stretched tight, snug.   TEETH-into the wind.
TELL-TAIL (or tale)-flexible wind indicator,7, 12, 13, 29, 100, 101, 119.
TEND-taking care of anchored boat especially at tide change.
TENDER-dinghy; sailboat with insufficient stability or too much sail area.
TENON-mast heel fitted to go into a step.
TEREDO-sea worm that eats into unprotected wood surfaces.
THAT'S HIGH-order to stop hoisting.   THIMBLE-metal ring.
THOLE PINS-rowlock pins.   THREE SHEETS in the WIND-very drunk.
THROAT-forward upper corner of gaff or spritsail,and the end of a boom or gaff nearest the mast, pgs. 5,23.
THRUM-yarn made for chafing gear or a collision mat.
THRUST-page 107.   THUMB CLEATS-jam cleats.
THWART—athwart seats on a small vessel, pages 28, 29.
TIDE-alternate rise and fall of ocean water, page 215.
TIDE RACE (tide rip)-tidal current eddies caused by uneven bottom shoal waters.
TIDE RODE-moored boat riding to tide & not wind;opp. of WIND RODE.
TIDEWAY-part of channel where current is strongest.
TIE ROD-page 72.
TIER-stow cable in chain locker;short rope or strip of canvas to secure a sail.
TIER, CABLE-between decks area or hold where cable is stowed.
TIGHT-a boat that does not leak.
TILLER-steering handle fitted to head of rudder, pages 23-53.
TIMBER-large pieces of wood used in boat building often bent to shape.
TIMBERHEADS-frames coming thru deck for belaying ropes or hawser.
TOGGLE-pin thru eye or bight of rope used as a quick release.
TO LEEWARD-away from the wind, page 110.
TOMPION (pron. tompkin)-plug in cannon to keep out dampness.
TONGUE-wooden block between gaff jaws which travels on a mast.
TONNAGE-vessel cargo capacity measured in tons.
TOP-mast platforms used to spread rigging above, page 285.
TOP A YARD-raise up one end of a boom or yard.
TOPGALLANT (pron. tu-gallant)-3 rd mast and sail above the deck, page 285.

TOP HAMPER-rigging and spars above deck.

TOP HEAVY-vessel too heavy aloft.   TOP LIGHT-signal light carried to top.

TOP LINING-lining to prevent chafe against top rim on after part of sail.

TOPMAST-second mast above deck, page 285.

TOPPING LIFT-line taking booms weight while sail is being raised, 63, 67, 75, 96.

TOPPING LIFT BRIDLE-bridle thru which topping lift is rove.

TOP ROPE-used for raising and lowering topmasts.

TOPSAIL-triangular sail set above a gaff, page 269.

TOPSAIL SCHOONER-schooner square rigged on her foremast, page 269.

TOPSIDES-above deck.

TOUCH-luffing a sailboat until the leach is also luffing.

TOW-pulling a vessel thru the water.   TOWING LIGHT-see page 238.

TRACK-course of a vessel.

TRADES-steady tropic winds blowing NE or SE near equator, page 131.

TRAIN TACKLE-used to run guns in and out.

TRANSOM-stern planking of a square sterned boat, pages 23-81.

TRAVELLER-track with slide or car to adjust mainsheet. ROD with ring or roller slide is also used, 23-63,116-121BRIDLE is a flexible traveller, 23-51,116.

TREENAILS (trunnels)-wooden pegs before metal nails. Their history and use is very interestingly described in 'Clipper Ship Men' by Laing, pg. 286.

TREND—basically the general direction.

TRESTLE TREES-timbers supporting cross trees & heel of mast above, 285.

TRIATIC STAY-stay connecting mainmast and foremast, pg. 269.

TRICE-haul up.   TRICK-time period at wheel.

TRIM-fore & aft balance of vessel;trim sails more efficiently.

TRIPPING LINE-used to capsize sea and storm anchor, pages 156, 161, 152.

TROUGH-hollow between the crests of two waves.

TROCHOIDAL WAVE-made by wind in deep water, the stronger the wind the greater the distance will be between wave crests, page 140.

TRUCK-wooden cap at masthead;wheels of a gun carriage.

TRUE WIND-direction it blows on dock differing from apparent wind underway.

TRUNK-vertical shaft;centerboard trunk,   17-19   ;rudder trunk, page 72.

TRUNNION-cannon axis on which it rests, is elevated and depressed.

TRUSS-line keeping center of yard in towards the mast.

TRYSAIL-loosefooted storm sail, page 15.

TUCK, TO-splice or weave rope.

TUMBLE HOME (falling home)-inward curve of vessels side above waterline, common on vessels to 1800's making it difficult for pirate ships to board.

TURKS HEAD-ornamental knot.   TURN-loop in a rope.

TURNBUCKLE-threaded link to pull two eyes together for setting up standing rigging, pages 69, 112.   TURN IN-go to sleep.

TURNING BUOY-marks channel turn.   TURN TURTLE-upset.

TO TURN-tack to windward steering a zigzag course, page 101.

TURN, TAKE A-pass a rope once or twice around an object.

TURN UP, TO-make fast or belay a rope on a pin or cleat.

TYE-rope or chain connected to bunt of square yard, on which tackle is attached for hoisting.

TYPHOON-hurricane in the Eastern seas often occurring at change of the monsoon, a seasonal wind.   TWIN SPINNAKERS-page 131.

U UNA RIG-English catboat named after 'Una', first U.S. catboat sent to England.

UNBEND-to cast off;undo;remove sails from spars.

UNDER BARE POLES-vessel with no sails set in storm, page 137.

UNBITT-cast turn of a cable off the bitts.

UNDER FOOT-anchor directly under hawse hole.

UNDER HACK-confinement as punishment for an officer.

UNDER MANNED-short handed, not enough crew members.

un UNDER the LEE-to leeward of a sailboat, building, or headland.
UNDERTOW-off shore current noticeable in the surf.
UNDERWAY-vessel not aground, at anchor, made fast to shore or dock.
UNFURL-unfold a sail.
UNION-upper inner corner of a flag, the rest is called the fly.
UNION JACK-crews flag with 50 (?) stars flown from f'c'stle on docked or
moored vessel, indicating crews limited authority, page 252.
UNMOOR-leave one anchor down and heave up on the other.
UNREEVE, TO-hauling a line out of a block.
UNSHIP, TO-to remove or take apart.   UP ANCHOR-order to weigh anchor.
UP and DOWN-anchor cable vertical, further hauling will break anchor out.
UPPER DECK-partial deck over main deck amidships.
UPPER TOPSAIL-page 287.   UPPER WORKS-above main deck.
USCG-United States Coast Guard.   USPS-United States Power Squadrons.
USEFUL LOAD-the vessels dead weight tonnage.

V BOTTOM-hull form with bottom V section, page 17.
VANE-a mast head wind vane.
VANG, BOOM-purchase to flatten sail with boom, 23-75, 118-121.
VANGS-gaff steadying line leading from gaff peak, page 269.
VAST-order to cease or stop.
VEER-wind direction change;slack sheets and allow to run off.
VEER and HAUL-to alternately slack up and haul away.
VEIL-thin cloud formation.
VELOCITY of TRANSLATION-speed of a storm center.
VERY SIGNAL-red, white & green star signals fired by a pistol, page 225.
VIOL-larger messenger often used in breaking out anchor by capstan.
VIOL BLOCK-similar to snatch block but minus a hinge.
VISIBLE-capable of being seen with clear atmosphere on a dark night.

w WAIST-portion of upper deck between f'c'sle and quarter deck.
WAISTERS-elder seaman or green hands used in an old fighting ship.
WAKE-disturbed water foamy path behind a moving vessel, pages 140-141.
WALES-strengthening timbers running fore & aft in a vessels sides.
WALE SHORES-timbers holding vessel upright in drydock.
WALL-a knot on the end of a rope.   WALL SIDED-vessel with vertical sides.
WARDROOM-commissioned officers quarters in a warship.
WARE-same as WEAR or to WEAR SHIP, pages 101, 111.
WARP-move vessel by hauling in on lines going to dock or anchor.
WARPING CHOCK-on dock used for hauling or warping along a vessel.
WASH-waves made by a boat moving thru the water.
WASHBOARD (washstrake)-thin planking above railing on a small boat to
increase the height of the side, especially for heeling.
WATCH-working shifts aboard ship.   WATCH, ANCHOR-small port watch.
WATCH AND WATCH-shifts in which watches alternate every four hours.
WATCH CAP-canvas covering a funnel not being used;wool sailors cap.
WATCH HO!WATCH-warning cry of sailor heaving a deep-sea lead.
WATCH TACKLE-one made of a single and double block.
WATER BORN (water borne)-not touching bottom.
WATER BREAKER-small drinking water cask.
WATERLINE-painted on vessels side to indicate proper trim, 254-257.
WATERLOGGED-swamped but afloat.
WATER MONKEY-clay jar used to keep drinking water cool.
WATERS EDGE-inshore waters such as next to a beach.
WATERWAY-navigable channel;gutter drain on deck leading to scuppers.
WAY-movement thru water;HEADWAY-going forward; STERNWAY-a boat
going backwards;a vessel is underway when drifting.
WAYS-framework in shipyard on which a vessel is built.

WEAR -on square rigger it meant changing tack by changing the wind over the stern to advance to windward instead of coming about, page 101.Fore and after sailing downwind changes tack by changing the wind over the bow instead of over the stern to prevent an accidental jibe, also called wearing, page 111.The lateener wears ship by changing tack with wind over stern, page 277.

WEATHER-windward side, shroud, bow, etc. of vessel, pages 98, 113.

WEATHER, TO-safely pass to windward of object without changing tack.

WEATHER BOUND-sailboat staying in port due to storm or wind direction.

WEATHER EYE OPEN-be on the alert.

WEATHER GAGE (or gauge)-the vessel which is to windward of another.

WEATHER HELM-heeling sailboat wanting to come head to wind, pgs. 132-135.

WEATHERLY SHIP-one making little leeway working to windward.

WEATHERLY ROLL-ship rolling going to windward.

WEATHER SHORE-wind coming off the shore.

WEATHER TIDE-current and wind going opposing directions.

WEDGE-used to steady a mast in many older classes, page 26.

WEIGH, TO-raise anchor.

WELL-order meaning sufficient;cockpit for legs, 33;cb & db wells, pgs. 18,19.

WELL DECK-portion of main deck having poop and raised f'c'sle.

WELL FOUND-well equipped vessel with all gear in good condition.

WESTING-position of sun between noon and sunset.

WESTERLIES-prevailing winds in temperate zone coming from NW & SW.

WET BULB THERMOMETER-device to measure humidity.

WHALE BACK (turtle back)-sailboat with high crown so person always walks on a horizontal part of the deck when boat is heeling.

WHALEBOAT-double ended navy lifeboat and utility boat 24-30' long.

WHEEL-steering wheel used instead of tiller or lever, pgs. 67, 69, 108, 110.

WHERRY-light rowboat belonging to the navy.

WHIP-rope rove   block;whipping a ropes ends to stop them
from fraying, page 200.   WHIP upon WHIP-one added to another.

It was difficult to find adequate glossaries of sailing terms in the initial preparation of our book from 1950-1956 ... the reason for so many terms in our glossary.

The picture has changed considerably in recent years due to worldwide sailing interest beginning with, "Lever's Young Sea Officer's Sheet Anchor", pg. 184, which is an exact reprint of an 1819 sailing text for professionals.

We had the pleasure to meet Karl Freudenstein of Bonn, Germany, pg. 82, in 1974, after he wrote to us, questioning derivation of port and starboard. We were soon to find he and his wife Ingrid linguists mastering a combination of six languages, their hobby translating sailing terms when not traveling on official business.

Karl recommended the Country Life Book of, "Nautical Terms Under Sail", the world of square riggers, iron men, and wooden ships, distributed by Hamlyn Pub. Group, London, NY, Sydney, and Toronto ... ISBN 0 600 36586 7.

Sailing Illustrated

WHISKER POLE-spar used to hold out clew of jib while running, pg. 121.
WHISKERS-crosstrees at bow to spread bowsprit shrouds, page 73.
WHISTLE BUOY-one having a whistle actuated by water movement, page 249.
WHITE CAP (white horses)-breaking crest of a wave, page 137.
WHITE SQUALL-sudden furious storm. WHOLE GALE-page 137.
WIDE BERTH-to give room.
WINCH-mechanical device to increase hauling power, page 108.
WIND BOUND-adverse winds trapping sailboat in port or channel.
WIND FUNNEL-narrowing hill or canyon condition that compresses and
accelerates the speed of the wind, page 211.
WINDLASS-winch for hauling in cable.
WINDJAMMER-square rigged sailing vessel;a windy person.

■WIND FORCE SCALE (BEAUFORT SCALE)-page 137.

WIND RODE-anchored boat swings to wind rather than to the current.
WINDSAIL-canvas air scoop funneling air into a vessel.
WINDWARD-toward the wind, weather side of a boat, pages 98, 99, 123.
WING and WING-running before wind with sails on opposite sides, pages
WITHE, WYTHE-metal band on end of mast or boom, with eye or ring thru
which another mast or boom or rigging is made fast.
WISHBONE-ketch, page 266.   WISHBONE ANCHOR-page 158.
WITH THE SUN-clockwise or right handed.
WOOLD-to wind rope around a spar.
WORK (working to windward, on the wind)-sailing closehauled-pages 100-101.
WORKING GEAR-general term for gear.
WORKING SAILS-used for ordinary weather & conditions, page 9.
WORK UP-advance to windward, pages 100, 101.

WORMING-filling in the lay of a rope with small stuff to make a smoother
surface for parcelling and serving.
WRECK BUOY (English)-red and white horizontally striped buoy marking a
wreck. A similar type buoy doesn't exist in the U. S. buoyage system.
WRING-strain, bend or twist mast out of shape by setting rigging too tight.
WRING-BOLTS-bolts which secure planks to the timbers.
WRING-STAVES-strong planks used with wring-bolts.

X XEBEC-lateener often three masted with long overhanging bow & stern, 279.

y YACHT-vessel designed for pleasure or state, this can include the presidents
yacht or the neighbors dink (rowboat is not included).
YANKEE-large triangular headsail, also called raffee, pg. 131.
YARD-spar from which square sails, lateen sails and lugger sails are bent.
YARDARM-outer tapered extremity of a yard.
YARDARM to YARDARM-square riggers alongside with yardarms touching.
YARD SLINGS-chain suspension of square rig yard.
YARN-fibers twisted into strands for rope, page 184.
YARNS-tall tales.   YARE-prepared, prompt, eager, lively.
YAWL-two masted sailboat, after mast stepped abaft rudder post,66-71, 265.
YAW, TO-sailboat having hard time holding steady course as when a rough
sea is on either quarter or the stern, page 152.
YELLOW FLAG-signifies ship is in quarantine.
YEOMAN-sailor in charge of a store room.
YOKE-athwartship plate attached to rudder head to control rudder.
YOKE LINES-rope leading from either end of rudder yoke to turn rudder.
YOUNG FLOOD-beginning of flood or incoming tide or current.

Z ZAROOK (zaruk)-lateener little changed since the original 12th century
Venetian design.
ZULU-Scotch lug-rigged fishing vessel.

AUTHORS NOTE: Key USYRU Racing Rules are shown, a few due to space are left out. Purpose is to provide visual presentation of the rules plus pictorial understanding of intent, as well as varied rules involved in a situation out of context with rule numbering. Such familiarization will reduce study time and help locate surrounding rules involved in a protest.

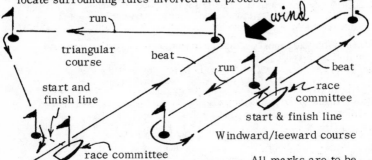

When displayed on a committee boat—
RED flag–"Leave all marks to port".
GREEN flag–"Leave all marks to stbd".

All marks are to be passed to port on both courses shown above.

BLUE flag or shape- Finishing Signal-"When displayed by committee boat means "The committee boat is on station at the finish line".

Sailing the Course, 51-1(a) A yacht shall START and FINISH only as prescribed in the starting and finishing definitions.
51.2 A yacht shall sail the course so as to round or pass each MARK on the required side in correct sequence, and so that a string representing her wake from the time she STARTS until she FINISHES would, when drawn taut, lie on the required side of each MARK.

4.4(a) Unless otherwise prescribed. . .signals for starting a race shall be made at five-minute intervals exactly, and shall be either–

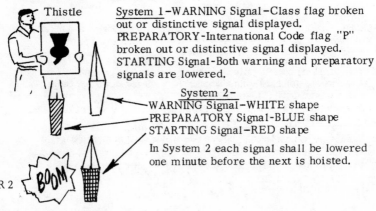

System 1 –WARNING Signal–Class flag broken out or distinctive signal displayed.
PREPARATORY-International Code flag "P" broken out or distinctive signal displayed.
STARTING Signal-Both warning and preparatory signals are lowered.

System 2–
WARNING Signal–WHITE shape
PREPARATORY Signal-BLUE shape
STARTING Signal–RED shape

In System 2 each signal shall be lowered one minute before the next is hoisted.

4-International Flag Code Signals

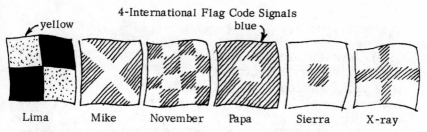

Lima	Mike	November	Papa	Sierra	X-ray

L-When displayed ashore, "A notice to competitors has been posted on the notice board".
When displayed afloat, "Come within hail", or "Follow me".

M-Mark Signal-When displayed on a buoy, vessel, or other object means-"Round or pass the object displaying this signal instead of the MARK which it replaces".

N-Abandonment Signal:-"All races are ABANDONED".

N over X-Abandonment and Re-sail Signal:- All races are ABANDONED and more will shortly be re-sailed".

N over First Substitute:- "All races are CANCELLED".

X-Individual Recall:-Broken out immediately after the starting signal is made, accompanied by one long sound signal, means:- "One or more yachts have started prematurely or have infringed the Round the Ends Starting Rule 51.1(c)".

P-Preparatory Signal:-"The class designated by the warning signal will START in five minutes exactly".

First Substitute-GENERAL RECALL signal means:-
"The class is recalled for a new start as provided in the sailing instructions".

Unless the sailing instructions prescribe some other signal, the warning signal will be made one minute after this signal is lowered.

S-SHORTEN COURSE Signal means:-

(a) at or near the starting line, "Sail the shortened course prescribed in the sailing instructions".

(b) at or near the finishing line "FINISH the race either:
    (i) at the prescribed finishing line at the end of the round still to be completed by the leading yacht or
    (ii) in any other manner prescribed in the sailing instructions under rule 3.2(a) (vii)".

Y-Life Jacket Signal Means... "shall be worn while RACING by all helmsmen and crews, unless specifically excepted in the sailing instructions"... A wet suit is not adequate personal buoyancy.

R 3

44 — Yachts Returning to Start

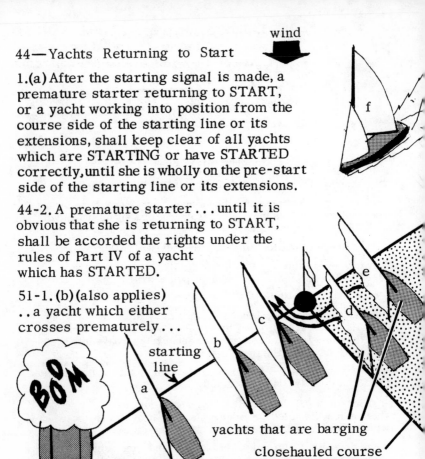

wind

1.(a) After the starting signal is made, a premature starter returning to START, or a yacht working into position from the course side of the starting line or its extensions, shall keep clear of all yachts which are STARTING or have STARTED correctly, until she is wholly on the pre-start side of the starting line or its extensions.

44-2. A premature starter ... until it is obvious that she is returning to START, shall be accorded the rights under the rules of Part IV of a yacht which has STARTED.

51-1.(b) (also applies) .. a yacht which either crosses prematurely ...

f

e

d

c

b

a

starting line

yachts that are barging

closehauled course

42-4. (Anti-Barging Rule). When approaching starting line to START, a LEEWARD YACHT shall be under no obligation to give any WINDWARD YACHT room to pass to leeward of a starting MARK surrounded by navigable water;but,after the starting signal,a LEEWARD YACHT shall not deprive a WINDWARD YACHT of room at such MARK by-

sailing either above the compass bearing of the course to the first MARK or above CLOSE-HAULED.

R 4

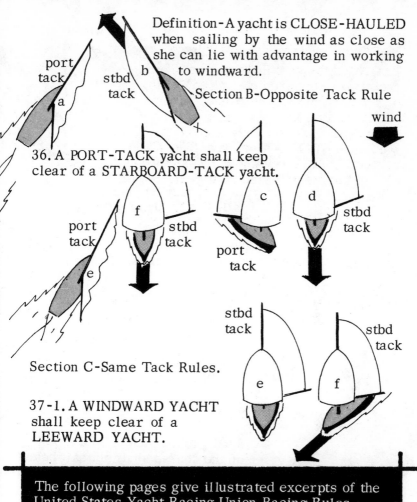

Definition - A yacht is CLOSE-HAULED when sailing by the wind as close as she can lie with advantage in working to windward.

Section B - Opposite Tack Rule

36. A PORT-TACK yacht shall keep clear of a STARBOARD-TACK yacht.

Section C - Same Tack Rules.

37-1. A WINDWARD YACHT shall keep clear of a LEEWARD YACHT.

The following pages give illustrated excerpts of the United States Yacht Racing Union Racing Rules. These have been reprinted in part by permission of the USYRU and illustrated by the author.

Copies of the complete official racing rules may be obtained from USYRU headquarters, P.O. Box 209, Newport, Rhode Island 02840.

These regulations are very complex — know them thoroughly before racing. Otherwise a person may be disqualified, ending with expensive damage claims.

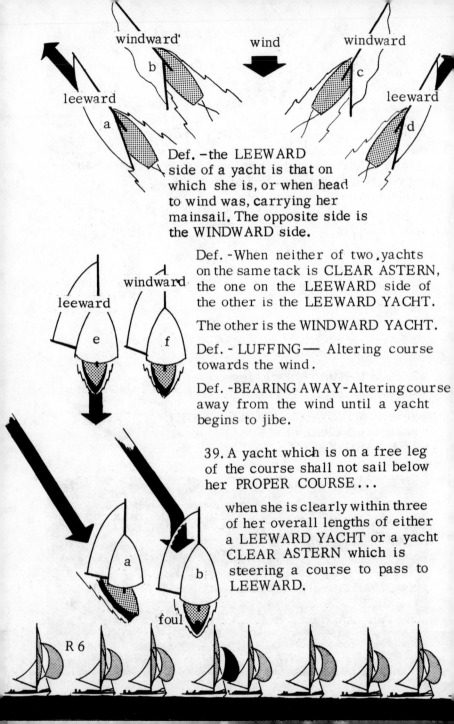

windward'

wind

windward

b

c

leewawrd

leeward

a

d

Def. – the LEEWARD side of a yacht is that on which she is, or when head to wind was, carrying her mainsail. The opposite side is the WINDWARD side.

leeward

windward

e

f

Def. – When neither of two yachts on the same tack is CLEAR ASTERN, the one on the LEEWARD side of the other is the LEEWARD YACHT.

The other is the WINDWARD YACHT.

Def. – LUFFING— Altering course towards the wind.

Def. – BEARING AWAY – Altering course away from the wind until a yacht begins to jibe.

39. A yacht which is on a free leg of the course shall not sail below her PROPER COURSE...

when she is clearly within three of her overall lengths of either a LEEWARD YACHT or a yacht CLEAR ASTERN which is steering a course to pass to LEEWARD.

a

b

foul

R 6

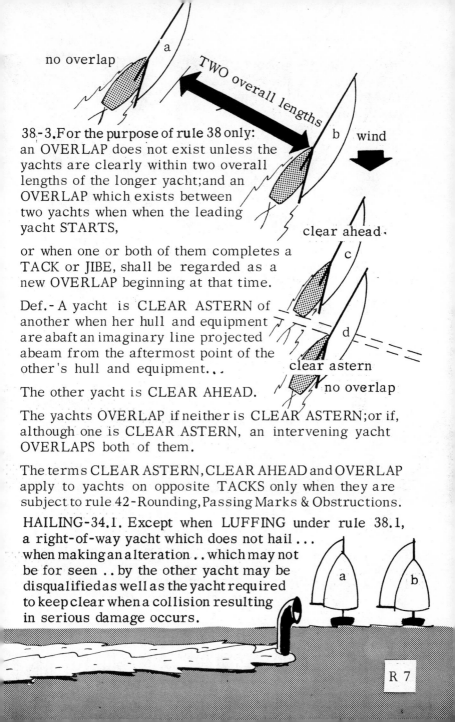

no overlap

a

TWO overall lengths

38.-3. For the purpose of rule 38 only: an OVERLAP does not exist unless the yachts are clearly within two overall lengths of the longer yacht; and an OVERLAP which exists between two yachts when when the leading yacht STARTS,

b wind

clear ahead

or when one or both of them completes a TACK or JIBE, shall be regarded as a new OVERLAP beginning at that time.

c

Def.- A yacht is CLEAR ASTERN of another when her hull and equipment are abaft an imaginary line projected abeam from the aftermost point of the other's hull and equipment...

d

clear astern

The other yacht is CLEAR AHEAD.

no overlap

The yachts OVERLAP if neither is CLEAR ASTERN; or if, although one is CLEAR ASTERN, an intervening yacht OVERLAPS both of them.

The terms CLEAR ASTERN, CLEAR AHEAD and OVERLAP apply to yachts on opposite TACKS only when they are subject to rule 42-Rounding, Passing Marks & Obstructions.

HAILING-34.1. Except when LUFFING under rule 38.1, a right-of-way yacht which does not hail ... when making an alteration .. which may not be for seen .. by the other yacht may be disqualified as well as the yacht required to keep clear when a collision resulting in serious damage occurs.

a   b

R 7

38-6. A yacht shall not LUFF unless she has the right to LUFF all yachts which would be affected by her LUFF, in which case they shall all respond even when an intervening yacht or yachts would not otherwise have the right to LUFF.

38-5. A WINDWARD YACHT shall not cause a LUFF to be curtailed because of her proximity to the LEEWARD YACHT-

unless an OBSTRUCTION, a third yacht or other object restricts her ability to respond.

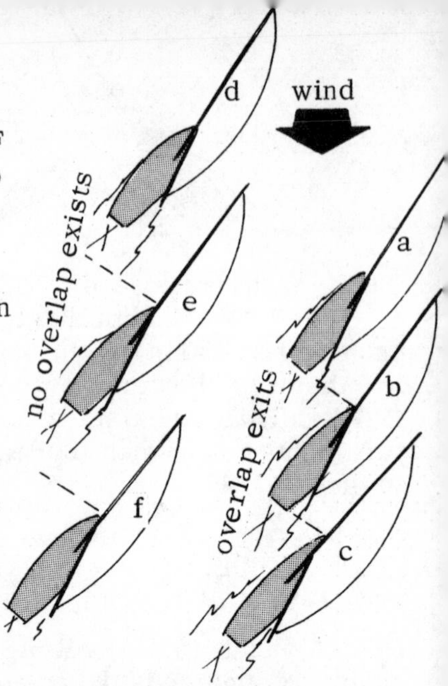

d wind

no overlap exists

overlap exits

e

a

b

f

c

luffing h (2.)

windward h

g

(1.) leeward

g

Definition .. The yachts OVERLAP when neither is CLEAR ASTERN; or when, although one is CLEAR ASTERN, an intervening yacht OVERLAPS both of them.

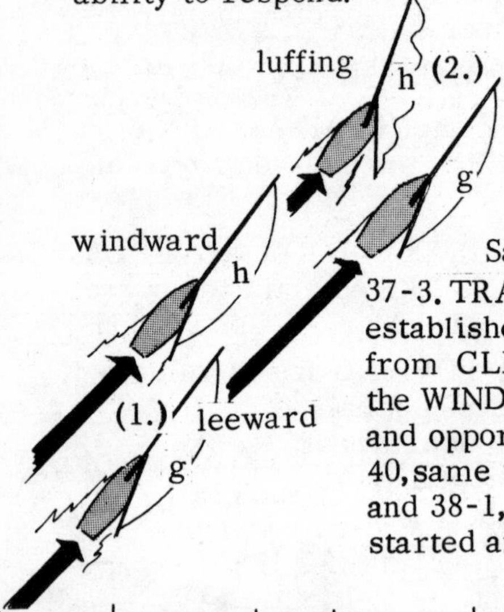

Same TACK-Basic Rule
37-3. TRANSITIONAL-a yacht which establishes an OVERLAP to LEEWARD from CLEAR ASTERN shall allow the WINDWARD YACHT ample room and opportunity to keep clear. (also-40, same tack-luffing before starting; and 38-1, luffing rights after she has started and cleared the starting line.)

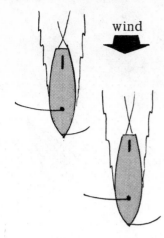

wind

overlap started

Same Tack-Luffing and Sailing above a proper course after starting.
Same Tack-LUFFING and sailing above a PROPER COURSE after STARTING.

38-1. After she has STARTED and cleared the starting line, a yacht CLEAR AHEAD or a LEEWARD YACHT may LUFF as she pleases, subject to the PROPER COURSE limitations of this rule.

38-2. A LEEWARD YACHT shall not sail above her PROPER COURSE while an OVERLAP exists, if when the overlap began or ...

at any time during its existence, the helmsman of the WINDWARD YACHT (when sighting abeam from his normal station and sailing no higher than the LEEWARD YACHT) has been abreast or forward of the mainmast of the LEEWARD YACHT.

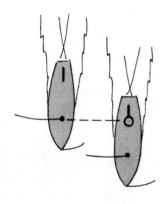

overlap completed

38-4. When there is doubt, the LEEWARD YACHT may assume that she has the right to LUFF unless the helmsman of the WINDWARD YACHT has hailed "Mast Abeam", or words to that effect.

The LEEWARD YACHT shall be governed by such hail, and when she deems it improper, her only remedy is to protest.

R 9

38-5. Curtailing a Luff — a WINDWARD YACHT shall not cause a LUFF to be curtailed because of her proximity to ..
... unless an OBSTRUCTION, a third yacht or other object restricts her ability to respond.

wind

Definition — An OBSTRUCTION is any object, including a vessel under way, large enough to require a yacht if not less than one overall length away from it to make a substantial alteration of course to pass on one side or the other, or any object which can be passed on one side only, including a buoy when the yacht in question cannot safely pass between it and the shoal or object which it marks.

Rule 64—Aground or Foul of an Obstruction

A yacht after grounding or fouling another vessel or other object... in getting clear, use her own anchors, boats, ropes, spars, and other gear... but may receive outside assistance only from the crew of the vessel fouled. A yacht shall recover all her own gear used in getting clear before continuing in the race.

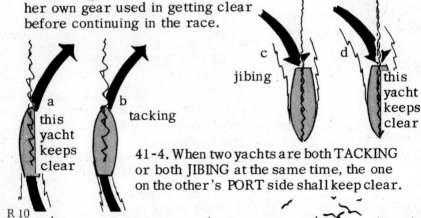

a this yacht keeps clear

b tacking

c jibing

d this yacht keeps clear

41-4. When two yachts are both TACKING or both JIBING at the same time, the one on the other's PORT side shall keep clear.

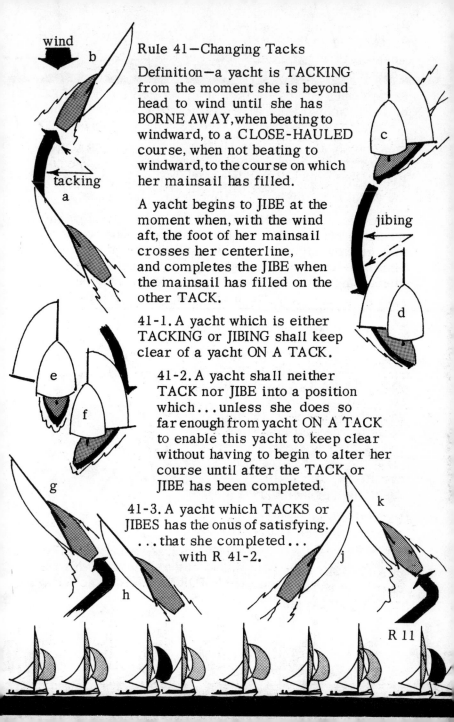

wind

Rule 41—Changing Tacks

Definition—a yacht is TACKING from the moment she is beyond head to wind until she has BORNE AWAY, when beating to windward, to a CLOSE-HAULED course, when not beating to windward, to the course on which her mainsail has filled.

A yacht begins to JIBE at the moment when, with the wind aft, the foot of her mainsail crosses her centerline, and completes the JIBE when the mainsail has filled on the other TACK.

41-1. A yacht which is either TACKING or JIBING shall keep clear of a yacht ON A TACK.

41-2. A yacht shall neither TACK nor JIBE into a position which...unless she does so far enough from yacht ON A TACK to enable this yacht to keep clear without having to begin to alter her course until after the TACK or JIBE has been completed.

41-3. A yacht which TACKS or JIBES has the onus of satisfying. ...that she completed... with R 41-2.

tacking

a

b

c

jibing

d

e

f

g

h

j

k

R 11

Except when race area is officially patrolled by the CG or CGA, yachts racing have no special rights over yachts not racing. Standard rules page 232, apply meanwhile.

Since 1960 we have recommended a special RACING PENNANT be flown from bow of sailboat the moment five minute signal is given for that class (above) until the yacht has finished or dropped out of the race.

If practiced, especially in areas having considerable pleasure boat traffic, sailboat and powerboat owners may give racing sailboats more advantage of existing situation. We see no reason why this racing pennant also acting as a dinghy telltale, can do anything but help racing sailors. Why doesn't USYRU promote this idea?

35. Limitations on Altering Course

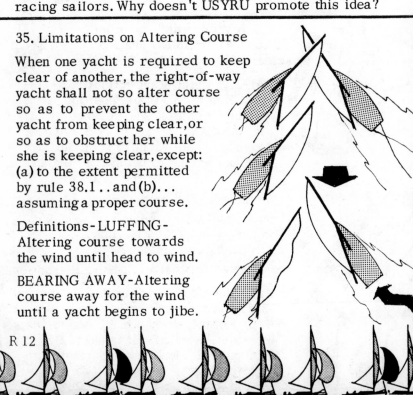

When one yacht is required to keep clear of another, the right-of-way yacht shall not so alter course so as to prevent the other yacht from keeping clear, or so as to obstruct her while she is keeping clear, except: (a) to the extent permitted by rule 38.1.. and (b)... assuming a proper course.

Definitions - LUFFING - Altering course towards the wind until head to wind.

BEARING AWAY - Altering course away for the wind until a yacht begins to jibe.

43-1. Hailing. When two CLOSE-HAULED yachts are on the same TACK and safe pilotage requires... to make a substantial alteration .. to clear an OBSTRUCTION... but cannot TACK .. she shall hail .. for room to TACK...

wind

"Sea Room"

(1)

(2)

(3)

43-2. The hailed yacht .. shall either: –
(a) TACK, in which case, the hailing yacht shall begin to TACK either: –
(i) before the hailed yacht has completed her TACK,
(ii) when she cannot then TACK without colliding with the hailed yacht....

(b) reply "You TACK", or words to that effect, when in her opinion she can keep clear without TACKING or after postponing her TACK. In this case: –

(i) the hailing yacht shall immediately TACK and
(ii) the hailed yacht shall keep clear.
(iii) the onus ... shall lie on the hailed yacht which replied "You TACK".

43-3 (a). When ... an OBSTRUCTION ... is also a MARK, the hailing yacht shall not be entitled for room to TACK and clear the hailed yacht and the hailed yacht shall immediately so inform the hailed yacht.

(b) If, thereafter, the hailing yacht again hails for room to TACK ... she shall after receiving room ... retire immediately or exonerate herself by accepting an alternative penalty ... in the instructions.

(c) When, after having refused to respond to a hail under rule 43.3(a), the hailed yacht fails to fetch, she shall retire immediately, or exonerate herself by accepting an alternative penalty ... in the instructions.

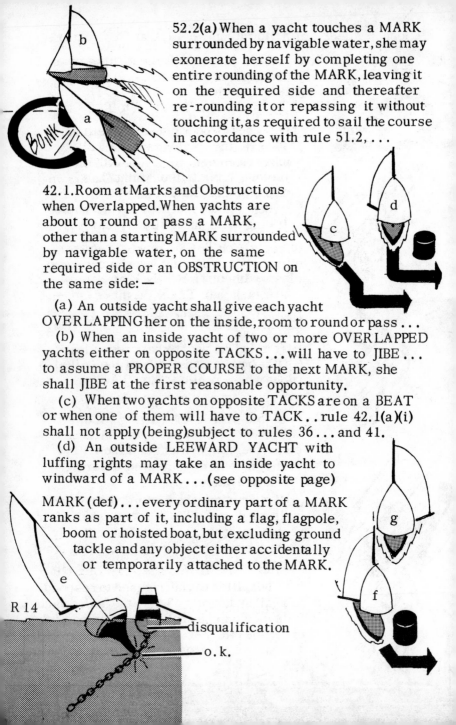

52.2(a) When a yacht touches a MARK surrounded by navigable water, she may exonerate herself by completing one entire rounding of the MARK, leaving it on the required side and thereafter re-rounding it or repassing it without touching it, as required to sail the course in accordance with rule 51.2, . . .

42.1. Room at Marks and Obstructions when Overlapped. When yachts are about to round or pass a MARK, other than a starting MARK surrounded by navigable water, on the same required side or an OBSTRUCTION on the same side: —

(a) An outside yacht shall give each yacht OVERLAPPING her on the inside, room to round or pass . . .

(b) When an inside yacht of two or more OVERLAPPED yachts either on opposite TACKS . . . will have to JIBE . . . to assume a PROPER COURSE to the next MARK, she shall JIBE at the first reasonable opportunity.

(c) When two yachts on opposite TACKS are on a BEAT or when one of them will have to TACK . . rule 42.1(a)(i) shall not apply (being) subject to rules 36 . . . and 41.

(d) An outside LEEWARD YACHT with luffing rights may take an inside yacht to windward of a MARK . . . (see opposite page)

MARK (def) . . . every ordinary part of a MARK ranks as part of it, including a flag, flagpole, boom or hoisted boat, but excluding ground tackle and any object either accidentally or temporarily attached to the MARK.

R 14

disqualification

o.k.

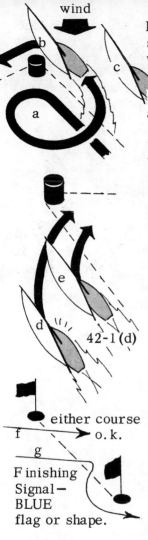

wind

Definition – a MARK is any object specified in the sailing instructions which a yacht must round or pass on a required side.

51-2. A yacht shall sail the course so as to round or pass each MARK on the required side in correct sequence, & so that a string representing her wake from the time she STARTS until she FINISHES would, when drawn taut, lie on the required side of each MARK.

51-3. A MARK has a required side for a yacht as long as she is on a leg which it begins, bounds, or ends. A starting MARK begins to have a required side for a yacht when she STARTS. A finishing MARK .. ceases to have a required side for a yacht as soon as she FINISHES.

51.4. A yacht which rounds or passes a MARK on the wrong side may exonerate herself by making her course conform to the requirements of rule 51.2 (which is listed above).

42-1 (d). An outside LEEWARD YACHT with luffing rights may take an inside yacht to windward of a MARK provided she hails ... provided she also passes to windward of it.

51-5. It is not necessary for a yacht to cross finishing line completely. After FINISHING she may clear it either direction.

42-1 (d)

either course o.k.

f

g

Finishing Signal – BLUE flag or shape.

P.S. How about thanking the race committee for their help?

R 15

Launching between five rainstorms that day in May, 1950 - Adams Boat Yard, Jamaica Bay, NY. Our "Lady Hilda" was a twenty footer, V-bottom centerboarder. Does any reader know where our old friend is . . . hopefully still afloat.

The lovely Hudson, summer of 1951. Oooooops ... who forgot the outhaul adjust AND the battens?????

MODERN SAILING TERMS

● **the MAINSAIL**
aspect ratio – 8, 9
boom thrust adjuster – 119
deck sweeper boom – 119, 249
draft, drive area – 9, 10
foot reef, cunningham reef,
hooligan reef – 11, 117
gaskets – 63, 86, 87
gooseneck – 23-67, 87, 89
Hyfield lever – 251
leachline – 28, 116-119
luff downhaul, cunningham
hole or cringle hook – 24-77
prevang – 63, 120-121
roach line – (leachline)
rod (horse) with ring or
rollerslide – 75
slugs, stops – 87
tack pennant – 63, 65, 232
Twistfoot main has "shelf"
or full radius foot – 43, 77
tube halyard lock – 249
vang (Br.-kicking strap) – 7,
23-48, 63, 116-121, 143, 149
traveler, track with car –
43-49, 63, 77, 250
wind funnel – 13, 36, 104, 119
window – 7, 24, 27, 28, 31-47
zipper foot & luff – 116, 250

● **the JIB**
Barber hauler – 34-37, 43, 49,
118, 119
bridle, jibstay – 47, 48, 83
fairlead – 7, 12, 31-53
furling line, lanyard – 13, 49
jib telltale – 7, 12, 13, 118, 119
windowshade reefing jib,
roller reefing jib – 13, 39,
49, 250
reaching hook – 33
reaching track – 83
cloth downhaul, adjustable
luff jib, variluff, strechy
luff jib – 13, 33, 35, 43
Swedish hook, snap hook with
"panic" button – 92
Swedish jib, genoa jib – 125
tack downhaul – used on a
stretch luff jib (above)
tunnel, jib luff – 13
wind funnel, slot effect –
34, 104-105, 119

● **the SPINNAKER**
dip pole jibe, lazy guy rig – 130
fixed guy – 128
guy downpull, curley-cew,
pigtail – obsolete terms
mizzen staysail, also called
mizzen spinnaker – 69
running guy – 37, 39, 45, 128
running guy downhaul or
downpull, tweaker – 37
reaching strut – 125
retriever – 39
spinnaker launcher – 39
tang holder for sp. sheet,
guy, halyard assy. – 35
trapeze ring – 38
tunnel, launching tube – 39
turtle, spinnaker bag with
metal ring – 126
twinger – 37, 128, 130
tri-radial spinnaker – 125

Sailing Illustrated

● the MAST

arc bend-33, 35, 41, 43, 91
Bendy (flexible) mast, floppy
  rig, flexible rig, automatic
  mainsail flattener, wet
  noodle rig-33, 39, 43, 91, 117
breadboard-on older Lightning
Hyfield lever-251
jumper tension adjust-251
limited swing spreaders-33,
  39, 43
mast jack-250
mast partner-23, 28, 29, 32
mast puller-33, 43
mast wedges-250
movable mast step-249
rake-116-121
self-swiveling mast-27, 28,
  29, 47, 48, 49
shroud release-32, 121, 251
sidestay (shroud)
stubby mast (outrigger)-44
tang, bow (Lightning)-35
tang fittings-68, 69

● STEERING

barndoor rudder-5
high aspect rudder-41, 80
keel mounted rudder-20
keel trim tab-12 meters
  use small keel trim tab
  to reduce weather helm,
  steering with aft rudder
rudder lock-31
spade rudder-20, 74
tradewind steering-131
wind vane gear-131

● EQUIPMENT

flopper stoppers-63, 162
Para-Anchor-63, 155, 160, 161

● BOARDS and KEELS

bilgeboards, twin bilgeboards,
  twin boards-44, 45
bilgeboard adjust-45
bilge keels-21
bulb keels-21, 43
fin keel-20
jibing board-250
keel window-43
retractable keel-51, 52, 53
saddle-38, 39, 119, 350
stub (bilge) keels-21

● HULL terms

"Ama" float-44
Barney post-mid cockpit
  post for mainsheet cleat
bitt, mooring bitt-59, 190, 191
bridge deck-83
catamaran-17, 46-49, 83
console-used on older Stars
crossbar, strut-38, 49, 83
Displacement, def.-20, 141
hiking post, "ladies aid"-250
hiking straps-23-25, 28-43
"Iako" arm-44
inspection port-38, 39, 41-43
monkey bar-44
outrigger-17, 44
raised deck-62
scow-44, 45
self bailer-28, 33, 49
smoke head-67, 75
strut, crossbar-38, 47-49, 83
thwart-23, 28, 29, 32, 39
trailboard-70, 75
transom flap drain-32-38
trimaran-17
tunnel, scow-45

Sailing   Illustrated

Contents

SAIL, HULL BASICS

sail types 3
gaff rig . . . , ... 5
marconi rig 7
kinds of sailboats 9
the mainsail 11
staysail, jib 13
other sails 15
weight stability 16
leverage stability . . . 17
dagger, lee boards . . . 18
centerboards 19
keel variables 21

SAILBOAT DETAILS

Optimus Dinghy 23
Force 5, Laser . . 24 — 25
Sunfish/Windsurf . 26 — 27
Penguin/Sabot . . . 28 — 29
Lido 14 31
Thistle/Snipe . . . . 32 — 33
Lightning . . . . . . 34 — 37
Flying Dutchman . . 38 — 39
C 15 41
Star . . . . 42 — 43
Outrigger/Scow . . 44 — 45
Pacific Cat . . . . . 46 — 47
Hobie 14 & 16 . . . 48 — 49
Catalina/Balboa . . . 50 — 53
balance/tb mast . . 54 — 57
cockpit controls . . 58 — 59
"Pink Cloud" . . . . 62 — 63
ideas . . . . 64 — 65
"Finisterre" . . . . 66 — 69
older yawl . . . . . . 70 — 71
structure terms . . 72 — 73
Newporter . . . . . . 74 — 75
Catalina 38 . . . . . . 76 — 81
"Patty Cat II" . . . . 82 — 83

bearings 85

SAIL HANDLING

sail storage 87
bending a main 89
flexible mast 91
bending a jib 93
leave mooring 95
sail sequence 97

SAILING METHODS

courses and tacks . . . 99
windward terms 101
windward theory 103
sail theory 105
drive forces 107
coming about 109
jibing, wearing 111
rigging tension 113
aluminum mast 114
hull trim 115
airfoil controls 117
upwind adjustments . . 119
sail twist 121
downwind methods . . . 123

SPINNAKERS

kinds 125
operation 127
jibing 129-130

BALANCE

trade wind rigs 131
steering balance . . . 133
hull/sail trim 135

HEAVY WIND-
WIND FORCE SCALE . 137

storm warnings 139
hull speed factors . . 141
planing methods 143
the upset 145

reefing #1 147
reefing #2 149
heave to 151
the broach 153
beat or run? 155

ANCHORING, DOCKING
surface anchors 157
bottom anchors 159
anchoring 161
anchoring methods . . 163
crowded moorings . . 165
permanent mooring . .167
docking 169
approach lee dock . . . 171
leave lee dock 173
docking variables . . . 175

ENGINE OPERATION
single screw action . . 177
inboard operation . . .179
outboard operation . . 181

FUNDAMENTALS 183
rope basics 185
rope size, kinds 187
joining rope 189
hitches 191
bowline, square 192
coiling 193
heaving line,
    waist lifeline . 194
braided eyesplice 195-199
whipping 200
eye splice 201
short splice 202
tugboat tow 203

WEATHER/TIDE/CURRENT
cloud formations . . . 205
thunderstorm 207
advancing fronts 209
funnels, sea breeze . . 211

barometer 213
tide variables 215
currents 217
humidity vs fog 219
fog signals 221

EMERGENCY PROCEDURES
aground 223
George Sigler · · · · · .225
preservers 227
overboard 229

**ARTIFICAL
    RESPIRATION** 231

REGULATIONS
sail right-of-way . . . 233
power right-of-way . .235
running lights . . .236-241
day signals 242
large vessels 243
rdf 245
buoyage system 247

COMPLEX DINGHIES
Finn 249
International 14 251
flag etiquette 253

SAILBOAT KINDS
the lines 254-257
handicap rating 259
the sloop 261
the cutter 263
yawls 265
ketches 267
schooners 269
older types 272-275
lateeners 276-277
luggers 278-281
square riggers . .282-287
naval terms 289

GLOSSARY . . . . G 1-G 35
RACING RULES . R 1-R 15

Day Sailer

Skimmer, Moth

Butterfly

Cottontail

Javelin

Five-O-Five

Y Flyer
or Yankee

Jet 14

Cal Series

Holiday Series

Flying Scott

Arrow

Columbia Series

Islander Series

Luder 16

Renegade 27

Loa 17

Pearson Series

K38·K50

Kettenburg Series

Vaurien

Twin Keel
Imperial

Twin Keel
Alacrity

Polar Bear
'Tail to Wind'

Mobjack

Pilot

Tartan 27

Commander

Morgan Series

Mustang

Kestrel

Rawson Series

Hinkley Series

Lapworth 36	Nipper	Catfish	Westphal
Starfish (sailboard)	Starfish (dinghy)	Sea Scouter	Widgeon
Constellation	Flying Saucer	Pintail	Scorpion
Osprey, Gannet	Vineyard Haven	Redhead	Town Class
Tempest (cabin)	Vivacity	Whistler	Buckeye
Outlaw	Lehman Interclub	Teal	Quad Trainer
Pacific Class	Corsair	Flying Kitten	Wanderer
Tech Dinghy	Narrasketuck	Elvestrom Junior	Indian

470	**&**	**⚡**	
Four Seventy	Four Twenty	Electra	Folkboat, Firefly

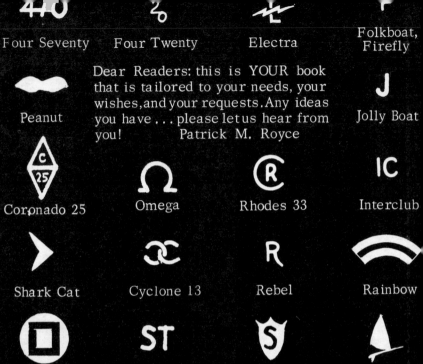

Dear Readers: this is YOUR book that is tailored to your needs, your wishes, and your requests. Any ideas you have . . . please let us hear from you! Patrick M. Royce

Peanut			Jolly Boat
Coronado 25	Omega	Rhodes 33	Interclub
Shark Cat	Cyclone 13	Rebel	Rainbow
Twin Keel Signet	12'6" Signet	Shields	Windsurfer
Dolphin	Enterprise	Snowbird, Squall, S Class, Spencer	Malibu Outrigger
Kings Cruiser	Cascade	Victory	Wildcat
Swiftsure	Ghost	Fish	Lion